BEYOND
COMMUNICATION

BEYOND COMMUNICATION

Reading Comprehension and Criticism

edited by
Deanne Bogdan
Ontario Institute for Studies in Education
and
Stanley B. Straw
University of Manitoba

Boynton / Cook Publishers
Heinemann
Portsmouth, NH

Boynton/Cook Publishers
A Division of
Heinemann Educational Books
70 Court Street   Portsmouth, NH 03801
Offices and agents throughout the world

The following have generously given permission to use quotations from copyrighted works:

Pages 43–44: "The Interactive Reading Process: A Model" from *Theoretical Models and the Process of Reading*, 3rd edition, edited by H. Singer and R. B. Ruddell. Reprinted by permission.

Pages 148–149: From *The Painted Door* by Sinclair Ross. Used by permission of the Canadian Publishers, McClelland and Stewart, Toronto.

Page 203: "The House Was Quiet and the World Was Calm" from *The Collected Poems of Wallace Stevens*. Copyright 1947 by Wallace Stevens. Reprinted by permission of Alfred A. Knopf, Inc.

Versions of some of the essays have been published previously:

Chapters 5–7:
Excerpts from "Feminist Criticism and Total Form in Literary Experience," by Deanne Bogdan. *Resources for Feminist Research/Documentation sur la Recherche Feministe 16* (3): 20–23 (September 1987). Reprinted by permission of the publisher.

Excerpts from "A Taxonomy of Responses and Respondents to Literature," by Deanne Bogdan. *Paideusis: Journal of the Canadian Philosophy of Education Society 1* (1): 13–22 (Fall 1987). Reprinted by permission of the publisher.

Excerpts from "Is It Relevant and Does It Work? Reconsidering Literature Taught as Rhetoric," by Deanne Bogdan. *The Journal of Aesthetic Education, 16*(4): 28–39 (Winter 1982). Copyright © 1982 by the Board of Trustees of the University of Illinois. Reprinted by permission of the University of Illinois Press.

Excerpts from "Virtual and Actual Forms of Literary Response," by Deanne Bogdan. *The Journal of Aesthetic Education 20* (2): 51–57 (Summer 1986). Copyright © 1986 by the Board of Trustees of the University of Illinois. Reprinted by permission of the University of Illinois Press.

Chapter 13:
"Ways of Teaching Literature," by James Moffett, first appeared in *Coming on Center: Essays in English Education*, 2nd edition. Copyright © 1988 by Boynton/Cook Publishers, Inc.

Library of Congress Cataloging-in-Publication Data

Beyond communication : reading comprehension and criticism / edited by Deanne Bogdan and Stanley B. Straw.
   p. cm.
   Includes bibliographical references.
   ISBN 0-86709-250-5
   1. Reading comprehension.   2.   Books and reading.   3.   Criticism.
I. Bogdan, Deanne. II.   Straw, Stanley B.
   LB1050.45.B49 1990
   428.4'3—dc20

89–36994
CIP

Designed by Hunter Graphics
Printed in the United States of America
90 91 92 93 94 9 8 7 6 5 4 3 2 1

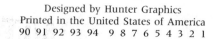

CONTENTS

ACKNOWLEDGMENTS

This book is an attempt to point out the convergences of two seemingly divergent fields — reading comprehension theory and literary critical theory. In conceptualizing and subsequently editing the book, we have become acutely aware of how the authors represented here — although from different backgrounds and interests — are members of a single interpretive community, a community whose goal is to probe language and literature as it reaches *beyond communication*. These authors employ different interpretive strategies indicative of different backgrounds and interests, which are reflected in their individual chapters. Yet together they make up a community of scholars, researchers, and teachers who wish to challenge traditional conceptions of literary reading. Because so many of our authors have drawn from the same sources as foundations for their work, we have pulled those sources into a single "Works Cited" list at the end of the book. When appropriate, we have also cross-referenced chapters within the book to alert the reader to their intertextuality. None of the individual authors (except ourselves as editors) has read all of the chapters in the book; however, many of the authors are intimately acquainted with the work of the others. In fact, as we travel to conferences and professional meetings, and as we talk to one another, we increasingly find this group of people gathered together — sometimes by phone, sometimes in meetings, sometimes with drinks — to discuss, probe, and analyze reading, literature, criticism, and instruction. Already the dialogue has begun. *We invite you to join us.*

We would like to thank the many people who have helped us bring this project from a glint in our eyes back in 1986 to conception and to delivery (the birth metaphor being one we have been using for some time now). First of all, we would like to acknowledge our contributors. Their writing, thinking, and reflection have helped us grow in our own understandings of the field. We are convinced they will do the same for you. Second, we would like to acknowledge the outstanding work of the people at Heinemann-Boynton/Cook, especially Bob Boynton and Dawne Boyer, for believing in this project and putting that belief into action; their encouragement, response, and unfailing good humor have made it possible for us to continue in the midst of the "morning sickness." We would also like to thank our individual institutions, the Ontario Institute for Studies in Education and the Faculty of Education at the University of Manitoba; our directors and department heads, especially Dwight Boyd of OISE and John Seymour and David Jenkinson of the University of Manitoba, have been both gracious and supportive, and have found various resources, both personally and financially, for completing the book. We would also like to thank Northrop Frye for his interest and response. Our appreciation is extended to the Social Science and Humanities Research Council of Canada for partial funding for the development of the research that led to the development of this project. Other individuals who have helped by either reading or preparing the manuscript include Pat Sadowy and Louise Sabourin of the University of Manitoba, Ria Bleumer, Margaret Brennan, Jill Given-King, Hilary Davis, Maureen Ford, Alice Pitt, Dale Campbell, and Beulah Worrell of the Ontario Institute for Studies in Education. Finally, we would like to express our deep appreciation to our families and friends who have had to live through our prenatal classes and intense mood swings: Joseph, Elisabeth, and Stasia Bogdan, Marita Watson, and Raymond Lavery.

NOTES ON THE CONTRIBUTORS

Richard Beach is Professor of English Education at the University of Minnesota, Minneapolis. He is coauthor of *Literature and the Reader, Research on Response to Literature, An Annotated Bibliography,* and *Teaching Literature in the Secondary School* (forthcoming). He is coeditor of *Perspectives on Literacy, New Directions in Composition Research,* and *Becoming Readers and Writers during Adolescence and Adulthood* (forthcoming). He has published articles on theory and research related to response to literature, the revision process, developmental differences in literary response and writing, writing of autobiography, and discourse pragmatics. He is treasurer of the National Conference on Research in English and a trustee of the Research Foundation of the National Council of Teachers of English.

Deanne Bogdan is Assistant Professor in the Department of History and Philosophy at the Ontario Institute for Studies in Education, University of Toronto. She holds degrees in music, English literature, and the philosophy of education. After several years teaching secondary school English, she pursed doctoral studies, with a dissertation on Northrop Frye's literary theory and its educational implications. Since then, she has taught at the Ontario Institute for Studies in Education in the areas of philosophy of literature, literature education, aesthetics, women's literature, and feminist criticism. Her articles have appeared in *English Journal, English Education, Educational Theory, Journal of Aesthetic Education, Journal of Education,* and *English Quarterly.* She is currently working on a book forthcoming from Boynton/Cook-Heinemann entitled *The Re-Educated Imagination: Issues in the Defense and Censorship of Literature.*

Patrick Dias is Professor of Education at McGill University, Montreal where he directs the Centre for the Study and Teaching of Writing. He has written and lectured mainly on response to literature, the development of writing abilities, and teacher education. He is the author of two books: *Making Sense of Poetry: Patterns in Response* (Ottawa:

Canadian Council of Teachers of English) and *Developing Response to Poetry* (with M. Hayhoe, Milton Keynes, England: Open University Press). He is currently directing an international study of resonse to poetry in Australia, Britain, Canada, and the United States.

Michael Gee is a doctoral student in the Language, Literature and Reading program at the Ohio State University. He has taught in elementary classrooms in Indiana and Ohio for fifteen years. His interests include the reading/writing relationship, the uses of reading and writing as tools for thinking, and the construction of classroom discourse.

Evelyn Hannsen is a former junior high school English teacher. She did her graduate work in language education at Indiana University and is currently teaching in the School of Education at the University of San Diego.

Jerome C. Harste's writings range widely. To first graders in Columbia, Missouri, he is known as "Our Favorite Author," the writer of children's books such as *It Didn't Frighten Me* and *My Icky Picky Sister* (Willowisp Press); to professionals he is known as a whole-language advocate and a strong supporter of teachers. "Curriculum," he maintains, "has fallen through the cracks. Curriculum is much too important to be left in the hands of those who rarely come in contact with kids. Children — not tests and materials — must be our curricular informants. Teachers must retake control of their classrooms." Harste's research has focused on what young children know prior to coming to school. With Carolyn Burke and Virginia Woodward, he wrote *Language Stories & Literacy Lessons* (Heinemann), which received the David H. Russell Award for Distinguished Research in the Teaching of English by the National Council of Teachers of English in 1987.

Russell Hunt teaches literary theory, eighteenth-century literature, and other courses in English at St. Thomas University, Fredericton, New Brunswick. He has been a visiting research associate at Indiana University and the Center for Studies in Literary Education at Deakin University, Australia, and a visiting professor at the Institute for the Empirical Study of Literature at Siegen University, West Germany. He is currently engaged with Douglas Vipond in a long-term study of the social nature of "literary" and other kinds of engaged reading, and is preparing a book on collaborative investigation as a learning and teaching strategy.

Susan Hynds is Associate Professor in the Reading and Language

Arts Center at Syracuse University, where she serves as program director of English Education and director of the Writing Consultation Center. In 1984 her dissertation study was named a finalist for the NCTE Promising Researcher competition. She is current vice-chair of the NCTE Assembly on Research. She has taught English, speech, and drama on levels from six to twelve for nine years. Her research explores the relationships between social understanding and response to literature, as well as the interpersonal dimensions of collaborative writing. Articles have appeared or are forthcoming in *Research in the Teaching of English, The Journal of Teaching Writing, The Reading Teacher, Contemporary Psychology,* and *The Review of Education.* She is editor of two forthcoming books, *Developing Discourse Practices in Adolescence and Adulthood* (with R. Beach) and *Perspectives on Talk and Learning* (with D. Rubin). Other publications have appeared or are forthcoming in *The Second Handbook of Reading Research.*

James Moffett is an author and consultant in education. He has been on the faculties of Harvard, the University of California at Berkeley, San Diego State University, the Bread Loaf School of English (Middlebury College), and Phillips Exeter Academy. He is author of *Teaching the Universe of Discourse, Active Voice: A Writing Program across the Curriculum, Coming on Center: Essays in English Education, Storm in the Mountains: A Case Study of Censorship, Conflict, and Consciousness,* and *Student-centered Language Arts and Reading.* He is editor of *Points of Departure: An Anthology of Nonfiction* and senior coeditor of *Points of View: An Anthology of Fiction* and a series of student writing, *Active Voices I–IV.*

Robert Morgan currently works within the Cultural Studies Department at Trent University, Peterborough, Ontario, where he teaches courses entitled "Media" as well as "Language and Society." At the graduate level, he is a faculty member of Trent's "Methodologies Program for the Study of Western History and Culture." He has taught high school English for many years in Toronto; this experience led to his doctoral research on the historical origins of secondary English programs within the province and their affiliations with other social technologies. He holds a Ph.D. in Education from the Ontario Institute for Studies in Education and has published work on concepts of language and the history of education.

Pat Sadowy is a graduate student at the University of Manitoba in the Faculty of Education, Winnipeg, Manitoba. She has taught elementary school for more than ten years in Manitoba and has served as a resource teacher in gifted education. She has completed research on models of reading and reading education, the role of the basal reader in teaching reading at the elementary level, and is presently completing research on the ways in which composition is taught in Candian language arts programs. She has taught courses at the University of Manitoba in elementary language arts and the writing process. Her publications include work in language education, art education, and her own poetry.

Kathy G. Short teaches children's literature at the University of Arizona, where she is an assistant professor in Language, Reading, and Culture. She has worked extensively with teachers in their efforts to develop curricula that actively involve students in reading and writing. Teachers especially know her for her love of literature and her ideas for integrating children's literature into the curriculum. She is coauthor of *Creating Classrooms for Authors* (Heinemann, 1988) with Jerome Harste and Carolyn Burke.

Stan Straw is Professor of Education at the University of Manitoba in Winnipeg. He holds his Ph.D. from the reading/language arts program at the University of Minnesota. He has published research studies on the relationship between sentence-combining instruction and comprehension, on procedures in teaching reading and literature, and on the effect of collaborative learning on growth in reading and response. He has coedited a previous book with Victor Froese entitled *Research in the Language Arts: Language and Schooling* published by University Park Press. For the past five years, he has been editor of *English Quarterly*, the theory, scholarship, and research journal of the Canadian Council of Teachers of English.

Robert J. Tierney is on the faculty at the Ohio State University where he teaches graduate courses in reading and writing. Tierney is interested in the relationship between literacy and thought processes, especially those involving a sense of projection or visual images. He is a native of Australia and has taught at various grade levels in Australia and the United States.

INTRODUCTION

Stanley B. Straw & Deanne Bogdan

In the past decade or so, there has been a growing perception that reading comprehension theory is experiencing significant rethinking about the nature of reading and reading comprehension.[1] In the decade prior to that, a parallel shift was taking place in literary theory and criticism. A number of theorists have posited a continuing movement from more traditional conceptualizations of reading, literary and nonliterary, to more "transactional" ones, and further to more socially based ones. Although many have seen it as a major rethinking about reading, and some have suggested that a shift in thinking is taking place, they have not presented it in a larger historical perspective (see, for example, Fish, 1980; Harste, Woodward, & Burke, 1984; Holub, 1984; Hynds, in this volume, Chapter 10; Kamil, 1984; Smith, 1985).

A mere movement or change of focus from the status quo to a more liberal position in any field of study does not, in itself, constitute a major rethinking of the underlying assumptions of that field; the underlying assumptions associated with the conservative position in the field may be so entrenched that they appear "normal" (in Holub, 1984, p. 5). Holub (1984) maintains that literary theory has hardly espoused any underlying assumptions—that the research has been so diverse and idiosyncratic that a basic set of "normal" tenets accepted generally would be difficult to describe. We would like to make the case here, however, that both reading-comprehension theory (and practice) and literary theory (and practice) have had basic assumptions

1

that have not been seriously questioned within the past 200 years (at least), and, more importantly, that that position is now being questioned. In many ways, we have crossed a threshold toward a radical future in how reading comprehension and literary reading will be thought about. Because we are in the midst of the shifting thinking in both reading-comprehension theory and literary critical theory, with nearly as many scholars on the "conservative" side of this revolution (essentially those who support a status quo position) as there are on the "revolutionary" side (those who subscribe to a dramatic change in our thinking about our own field), the shift is not self-evident.

Many researchers and scholars do not believe that we are experiencing this kind of dramatic or lasting rethinking; they would suggest that we are merely extending the boundaries of our present knowledge. In reading-comprehension theory, for example, Samuels and Kamil (1984) do not discuss a current rethinking in their review of models of reading, although earlier in the same volume, Kamil (1984) suggested that reading research had been undergoing a major shift. By the same token, Singer and Ruddell (1985), in the third edition of their seminal volume of important research and writing in reading theory, do not identify a radical rethinking in their documentation of the important events in reading.

Major reconceptualizations are often difficult to recognize from the inside—that is, from either the inside of the field in which they are happening or from inside a particular shift while it is taking place. We feel that the advantage of a book such as this one—one that examines the parallels between two fields—is that it can help us to gain perspective on our own assumptions and development in light of the assumptions and developments in correlative fields. Many of us are hypothesizing a reconceptualization of reading but are having some difficulty in denying the work of the past or in identifying the precise nature of the thinking of the future, one that could change the landscape of comprehension research and literary criticism.

A word now about the terminology we will be using in the discussions that follow, both in this introduction and in the chapters later in this volume. In speaking of the theories and practices of reading, responding to, interpreting, criticizing, evaluating, and understanding literature specifically, we will use the terms "literary theory," "literary criticism," and "literary critical theory" more or less interchangeably. In speaking of the theories and practices that underlie the analysis of the reading process and the comprehension of written language, regardless of the "literariness" of the text, we will use the term "reading-comprehension theory." For the two fields combined, in discussing them as a single area of study, we will use the term "reading."

Although we are not suggesting that our vision is somehow clearer or sharper than that of our colleagues, we will hypothesize about the basic premise of the shift that is leading to what we see as a revolution in reading—a revolution evident in both literary critical theory and reading-comprehension theory. Later in this volume, we and our contributing authors will discuss the historical contexts out of which this shift is growing, assess the implications of the movement in conceptualizations of reading and in reading practice, and speculate about directions for the future.

A NEW CONTRACT

Prior to the past twenty years, nearly all the purposes for reading could loosely be grouped under a basic notion of *communication*. In the past few years, with the advent of the importance of the reader in the act of reading, many authors are no longer suggesting that the primary purposes of reading are for communication. These more recent ideas have taken on a number of different names, for example, "transactional views of reading" (Goodman, 1985; Harste, Woodward, & Burke, 1984; Rosenblatt, 1978), "constructionist views," "unity in reading" (Goodman, 1985), "audience-oriented criticism" (Suleiman & Crosman, 1980), "reader-response criticism" (Tompkins, 1980), and "reception theory" (Holub, 1984). What they all have in common is a notion that the *central* purpose for reading is not communication, though one of its purposes *may be* communicative (i.e., a communication from author to reader); the central purposes of reading are *internal to* and *generated by* the reader. We have chosen to group these under the rubric of *actualization models* (after Maslow, 1954) because the purposes of readers in these conceptualizations are to realize their own potential and meaning within their own unique circumstances. These purposes may be, at any time, communicative, but only in that communication fulfills some more important purposes generated from the reader's need to receive communication.

We might have chosen to call these "realization" models or "constructive" models, but we feel the term "actualization" captures the spirit of what the emerging theories are attempting to address: that the purpose of reading is to realize the meanings hypothesized by the reader and to fulfill a set of needs and wants generated wholly within the reader, regardless of the motivations and intent of the author, regardless of the assumptions about the meaning of text, regardless of the meanings that other readers may ascribe to any particular text. One person, for example, may read history to learn, another may read it for enjoyment, a third may read it to reinforce some political motivation. All these readers will be reading with different purposes and conceptions of what the act of reading can offer them; they will go away from the reading with very different meanings — meanings that in some way fulfill their own particular and unique wants and needs — they will go away "actualized" — their own meanings will be realized in some peculiar way uniquely their own. By the same token, any single reader may read the same text at different times for different purposes — at one time for pleasure, at another time for information, at another for memorization. Again, what drives each of these readings is a need in the reader to fulfill or actualize his or her own purposes.

This we see as the essence of the rethinking about reading — a movement from communication to actualization as reading's central purpose. This shift has dramatic and revolutionary implications for how the reading process is described, both by psychologists and by literary critics, and how we, as readers and scholars, work out the particulars of reading — in and out of literature — on the one hand, and how we instruct students in learning to read, including instruction in the interpretation and evaluation of literary texts, on the other.

This shift can be characterized as a change in the underlying contract of language. Umberto Eco (1979) suggests that the "standard communication model proposed by information theorists" (p. 5) is made up of three elements: the Sender (the *author*), the Message (the *text*) and the Addressee (the *reader*). These are the "players" in the traditional communication contract of language. The operation of this contract is that meaning is somehow generated by the author, then is encoded in text where it resides (either as an artifact itself or as a reflection of authorial intention) until it is decoded or apprehended by the reader. Smith (1985) has described this operation as a "shunting" metaphor (p. 195), in which the information is transferred unchanged from author to reader via the text. The assumed contract, then, is between the author and the reader, in which the author's responsibility is to encode intent in text, and the reader's responsibility is to extract approximately the same meaning from the text. The communication contract allows for some reader input, perhaps, but not so much or of the kind that it undermines the message of the author as it is realized in the text. The communication contract further assumes that "reading" begins when the text is introduced or encountered by the reader, and that reading ends when the reader has successfully apprehended the "message." What happens after the meaning is apprehended is something else besides reading (e.g., response, reaction, evaluation). This is the traditionally accepted paradigm in reading, both in reading-comprehension theory and in literary critical theory. Historically, this has been the principal driving notion of reading: the continuity of point of view that is shared by such divergent stances as biographical criticism and information-processing theory, as New Criticism and interactive comprehension models, so that they are really reflections of a similar point of view.

The shift that has been taking place over the past twenty or so years in both reading-comprehension theory and literary critical theory undermines that basic premise of the communication contract. It replaces it with an actualization contract, which is in reality a contract that readers have with themselves. This new contract implies that readers will search out or find meaningful texts that will help them understand the meaningful events in their lives. Reading begins long before any particular text is encountered, by virtue of a reader's knowledge of the world in general and of language and other texts in particular. Reading continues long after the contact with text in that the text becomes part of a person's repertoire of experience to be remembered, reflected upon, and recomprehended. Any particular act of reading becomes, then, part of the lifelong experience of coming to know and reflecting upon the experience of coming to know. In reading, readers only apprehend the author's meaning of a text as it meets their own needs and theories of the world. As readers, we will create (or "apprehend") some other meaning than the "intended" meaning if the authorial intent does not both meet our needs and fit into our theories of the world. In fact, if we need to create the author's intent, we will. If we do not, we will create some other "more useful" meaning — or create no meaning at all (i.e., the text will carry no meaning for us at the time we read it).

Take, for example, the differences among the readings of the book of Revelations by a Moslem, a Christian, and an atheist. The Christian may well see it as a description of the coming Apocalypse; the Moslem may see it as a metaphor for the Islamic fundamentalist struggle; and the atheist may see it as either literary artifact, on the one hand, or gibberish, on the other. Who is to say any of these meanings is wrong? In fact, there is reason to believe that none of them is wrong — they are all correct in that they lead to an actualization of the reader.

One of the reasons we have some assurance that this revolution is taking place is our observation of similar revolutions in a number of different, but related, fields: in literary theory and criticism (in many ways versions of the shift have already happened and could be a signal for the changes in reading theory), in composition (with notions of writing to learn and discovery writing), in general instructional theory, in linguistics and language—acquisition theory, and in literacy education. The movement in literary theory is discussed in the three chapters immediately following this in conjunction with the work in reading comprehension theory and in Bogdan's chapters, and some of the work in composition is discussed later in this volume. The work in general instructional theory as it relates to reading literature has been discussed elsewhere (see Straw in Hynds & Rubin's forthcoming monograph on talk and learning, as well as Dias's and Morgan's chapters in this volume, Chapters 12 and 14, respectively), and in other chapters in this book (e.g., Hunt's and Hynds's, Chapters 4 and 10, respectively). The work in language acquisition is described by Bohannon and Warren-Leubecker (in Gleason, 1985).

The exact nature of the rethinking in reading-comprehension theory as it intersects with literary critical theory, even among those in the field who believe we are in the midst of a major reconceptualization, has not been adequately catalogued or described. We hope that this volume will contribute to the task of documenting the ways in which thinkers and practitioners in reading are integrating the insights and research that come out of their awareness of the rich interdependencies between comprehension and literary critical theory. As contributing authors ourselves, we each have individual angles of vision on both the correlations and disjunctions that constitute how these two fields are coming together. These viewpoints are, of course, expressed in our own chapters. It has been exciting for us as authors and editors to observe just how our own conceptualizations interrelate with those of our contributing authors, each of whom has a unique perspective of and emphasis on the intersection between comprehension and literary theory. Taken together, the stances articulated by our authors are far too fluid for any mapping of a single or joint point of view.

THE CHAPTERS IN FOCUS

All our authors deal in some way with what we aver is the major shift from a communication model of reading literature to an actualization model. This shift entails a conceptualization of reading within an educational context whose main purpose is the realization of personal and social goals for the reader rather than the perception or reception of some "message" from author or text. Each writer talks about this reconceptualization under different rubrics. Hunt and Hynds discuss socialization; Hunt adopts a historical literary critical perspective, Hynds, a motivational one. Hanssen, Harste, and Short talk about transactions and dialogue; Dias and Beach about personal response; Moffett about inductive pedagogical methods; Tierney and Gee about response as conversation; and Morgan about reading as a socially constructed technology. Straw gives a historical overview of reading-comprehension theory and literary criticism, and Bogdan discusses the influence of worldview on the dialectic between aesthetic and political factors in deploying interpretive strategies.

All our authors, as well, draw parallels, whether implicitly or explicitly, between the speculative and the observational, between the hypotheses of literary theory and the empirical research in reading comprehension. Though they may identify the genesis of interpretive strategies differently—from the personal experience of the reader, from the interaction between reading and text, from the social communities to which the reader belongs—they all envision a genesis from outside the traditionally held belief of the locus of meaning—the text or the author.

Two other foci in the chapters that make up this volume are related to the movement from a communication to an actualization contract. They are the role of the text in the process of actualization and the dynamic between engagement and detachment in reading.

What the precise role of the text is in shaping meaning for the reader has been one of the major debates for years in literary theory and, to a lesser extent, in reading comprehension. Within an actualization contract, many theorists suggest that the text provides constraints on meaning; that is, text can provide parameters within which readers make their own meaning and can still reconcile that generated meaning to the printed text. Reading-comprehension theorists in the past have assumed that text provides narrow constraints as is evidenced by such practices as the administration of reading-comprehension tests. Literary theorists, on the other hand, have often dealt with more implicit texts and have often viewed text as much as a guide to meaning as a formula for meaning. Whatever the point of view, however, how theorists view the role of text and the constraints that text places on the act of reading significantly affects how they describe reading and actualization. The authors represented here view the constraints of text in a variety of ways in an attempt to explain how reading has moved beyond communication.

The second focus in the book is related to the assumptions associated with the dynamic between engagement and detachment. Some authors view the goal of reading and literary study to be one of producing an engaged reader, a reader who becomes immersed in the aesthetics of text and the experience of reading. Other authors suggest that a full reading must include a detached assessment of the text and the reading experience. Still others suggest that engagement and detachment are terms relating to the oscillating dynamics of reading, that reading involves both being carried away by the transactions of reading (engagement) as well as being acutely aware of how the reader is being engaged (detachment). The chapters of the book present a variety of discussions around engagement and detachment, particularly as they relate to the phenomenology of reading and to reading pedagogy.

Given the possibilities for divergence in the field, we are in many respects surprised by the points of convergence in the various chapters of this book—an occurrence that reinforces our conviction that the shift is in fact taking place in both reading-comprehension theory and literary theory from author- or text-based assumptions about reading to more sociocognitive, reader-based assumptions about reading. We also see our authors drawing similar conclusions about literature and reading education in arguing for techniques that reject the hegemonies of the past and the autocracies of author and text. In one way or another, each chapter celebrates the reader's emergence from the ethos that prescribed very narrow parameters for reading and interpreting literature to one that is emancipatory in its emphasis on empowerment and choice. This new vision we see being expressed in terms of the kinds of constraints on the possibilities of meaning—be they experiential, textual, social, aesthetic, political, pedagogical—that readers work through in owning and negotiating meaning in the act of reading.

The book is organized under three main categories: historical, phenomenological, and pedagogical accounts of the act of reading. Some of the chapters are intended to be read in concert with each other, while other chapters exist as discrete reflections of their authors' formulations of the ways in which literary theory and reading comprehension have moved "beyond communication." The chapters by Straw and his colleagues (including this introduction) are intended to be viewed as a whole in that they trace the parallel developments of reading-comprehension theory and literary critical theory. Bogdan's chapters present an extended argument about the relationship between ideology and reading and are also intended to be read as one piece, since the middle and last chapters double back on the assumptions of the communication model. Although both of these sets of chapters could be read within the context of the larger arguments they make, they are presented as separate chapters because each makes a unique argument and contribution to the whole.

In the first three chapters of the book, Straw and Straw and Sadowy trace the development of notions about reading and how they have affected practice in both reading comprehension and literary theory. In the first chapter, "Dynamics of Communication: Transmission, Translation, and Interaction in Reading Comprehension," Straw and Sadowy trace the historical developments of conceptualizations of reading as viewed from a reading-comprehension theory perspective; they employ the historical periods presented in detail later in this introduction as their framework for discussing the development of reading-comprehension theory and research. In the second chapter, "Conceptualizations of Communication in the History of Literary Theory: Readers Apprehending Texts and Authors," Straw uses the same framework in discussing the development of conceptualization about literary critical theory in North America from 1850 to the rise of poststructuralism. In both chapters, the authors describe the kinds of constraints that each era tended to place conceptually on reading: authorial constraints during the nineteenth century, textual constraints during the period of transmission, structural constraints during the period of interaction. They also discuss how these three periods had two important aspects in common, first, an underlying notion about the communicative nature of reading, and, second, a conception of the detachment of the reader from the act of reading.

In the final chapter in this series of historical accounts, "Challenging Communication: Readers Reading for Actualization," Straw describes the movement away from a communication model of reading to a conceptualization of reading as actualization—reading to realize readers' own purposes for reader/text interactions. Straw describes transactional theories of reading and response, and then suggests that they are steps to a more constructive notion of reading, a notion that would unite reading, literary response, and composing as a single process. He shifts the discussion about engagement and detachment away from a traditional experience/spectator argument to suggest that engagement and detachment are necessary ingredients in the act of composing text as a reader—but that though both are necessary, neither is sufficient. He also discusses the kinds of constraints that operate in a compositional model of reading and how a reader can employ those constraints in creating text. He ends his chapter by suggesting the direction that he feels reading and response theory will be taking in the near future.

In Hunt's chapter, "The Parallel Socialization of Reading Research and Literary Theory," the author traces the analogous progression in reading-comprehension research and literary criticism from positivistic, behaviorist principles and methods typified by early reading models and inherent in the interpretive assumptions of New Criticism, to the "cognitivist revolution" heralded by Noam Chomsky in reading and the structuralist revolution initiated by Northrop Frye in literary theory, through to the significance of the larger social matrix to both reading theory and literary criticism currently in the ascendant. For Hunt, the importance of this social dimension is a transactional one, and he sees its greatest potential for advances in reading comprehension related to the constraints of aesthetic experience afforded by readerly engagement with rich and complex literary texts.

Deanne Bogdan is also concerned with textual engagement and

aesthetic experience, but whereas Hunt accepts them as "givens" of reading life, Bogdan problematizes them as part of a humanist ideology with social and political implications. Beginning in her first chapter, "In and Out of Love With Literature: Response and the Aesthetics of Total Form," with a taxonomy of literary responses based on a neo-Aristotelean structuralist theory of response to literature, she walks the reader through a description of types of responses considered in terms of what she calls the "aesthetics of total form." Within this purview, engagement with the text and detachment from it are regarded as alternative states in a dialectical process struggling to integrate literary experience and the awareness of that experience. In her subsequent chapters, "From Meditation to Mediation: Breaking Out of Total Form," and "Reading and 'The Fate of Beauty': Reclaiming Total Form," Bogdan dismantles and reassembles her own taxonomy in the light of poststructuralist literary theories—feminist criticism, deconstruction, Marxism, and psychoanalytic criticism—and the possibilities they hold for a redefined conception of engagement and detachment described as "the feminization of total form." For Bogdan, the constraints on reading are seen within the context of human desire, the search for truth, and the potential for social change that the transformation of consciousness through reading affords. In her formulation, reading goes "beyond communication" to an inquiry into the metaphysics and epistemology of literary response, to a concern for the grounds and conditions of reader response.

In their chapter, "Reading Comprehension: Readers, Authors, and the World of the Text," Robert Tierney and Michael Gee realize from the vantage point of reading comprehension a synthesis between engagement and detachment similar to Bogdan's notion of dialectical literary critical reading going "beyond communication" to any ongoing dialogue between reading and author in the reader's negotiations of meaning. For these authors, constraints on the reading act are envisaged in terms of the similarities between reading and the composing process, in which readers play various roles such as "planner," "editor," and "monitor" in constructing a meaning consonant with their own prior knowledge and experiences, on the one hand, and their own goals and expectations for the reading itself, on the other. Tierney and Gee's conception of engagement is less one of emotional absorption than of an active reflection on the reading experience as it is created by the reader. That techniques for this kind of integrated meaning making through reading can effectively be modeled and demonstrated to students is a conviction of these authors. At first glance this appears to be a modified version of the communication model, but in fact, their constructionist view of text and reading continually evolving through the reader's own agency comprises one of the closest analogies in reading-comprehension research to poststructuralist literary theory.

Richard Beach's chapter, "The Creative Development of Meaning: Using Autobiographical Experiences to Interpret Literature," is yet another example of the successful integration of the cognitive with the affective in readers' uses of reading for self-actualization. Like Hunt, before, and Hynds, later, Beach is an example of the reading researcher-cum-literary critic conducting empirical studies within the purview of literary theory. Proceeding from a definition of "analytic conceptualization" taken from VanDeWeghe, Beach develops an exploratory model of how the evocation of past personal experience as a form of narrative builds bridges between texts and readers such that readers do not simply receive or apprehend the text, but utilize both previous personal experience and text in the formation of new knowledge.

Like Tierney and Gee, Beach regards the reader's beliefs and experiences as interactive with, and productive of, textual significance. Both chapters stress the importance of personal constructs in interpretation and the formation of new knowledge, but Beach is singular in the emphasis on the restructuring of the reader's self-concept. Prominent in both chapters is the use of small-group activity to enhance the pedagogical efficacy of their respective conceptualizations.

Susan Hynds' chapter, "Reading as a Social Event: Comprehension and Response in the Text, Classroom, and World," has affinities with both Beach's and Hunt's. Like Beach, Hynds adapts the insights of literary criticism to stress the importance of personal constructs in making reading "real" for the student. Like Hunt, she offers an instructive overview of literary theory, viz. reader-response criticism, moving, as Hunt does, from the communication model (which she describes as a "conduit metaphor") to one informed by the principles of social pragmatics. Both Beach and Hynds echo Bogdan's concern for the influences of worldview on the reading act. Hynds' mastery of the history and philosophy of reading-comprehension theory and reader response theory, and her integration of that mastery with her empirical achievements vis-à-vis students' handling of the theoretical and practical implications of constraints—aesthetic, social, cognitive, psychological—as well as the predispositions, values, beliefs, textual features, and pedagogical environments—is one of the most comprehensive articulations of the constitutive elements of reading. Her focus on volition as a major factor in reading and the importance of providing "space" wherein students can express strong identifications with textual material resembles Dias's insistence on freeing up the classroom to afford students greater control in pursuit of their ownership of literary meaning.

"In Conversation: Theory and Instruction," by Hanssen, Harste, and Short, applies four main tenets of contemporary literary theory to the movement from communication to actualization in reading theory and practice. Proceeding from a conception of reading as "a way of outgrowing ourselves," the authors describe Bakhtin's notion of dialogue as the internalizing of thought-through-interaction, of storying as knowing, and of intertextuality as the retelling of stories and show how readers make connections and disjunctions through personal experience, and make interpretive communities as the creators of social contexts that mold the possibilities of thought. They demonstrate how these ideas from literary critical theory can be applied to instruction by their working through, in three different "stories" of classroom practice, integrations of theory and practice. Their approach to the intersection of reading-comprehension research and literary criticism recapitulates the interests of the other writers in applying the insights of literary critical speculations about the reading act as going "beyond communication." They take literary critical constructs across levels, from primary to secondary to college, in a persuasive account of the creative and critical at work as a simultaneous process of engagement and detachment.

Of all the contributors, Dias believes most strongly in "direct and unmediated" encounters with "natural" texts as the key to producing "readers for life," as he expresses in his chapter, "A Literary Response Perspective on Teaching Reading Comprehension." His privileging of engagement in the aesthetic reading of literary texts aligns him with Hunt, in contrast to Bogdan and her reservations about engagement. Like Hynds, Dias deplores the artificiality of the school reading situations and the rigidity of competency-based reading models, which he asserts are incompatible with the goals and processes of literary reading. For Dias, the goal of the reading teacher is to empower students as "autonomous" readers. This means subverting the authority of teacher-imposed interpretations and even less overtly prescriptive "guides" to good reading, which, in his view, are counterproductive to the student in forging the path toward reading independence. Implicit in Dias's conceptualization of response to literature is his conviction that going "beyond communication" in all forms of reading entails the literary text as an archetype of all texts inasmuch as the potential for self-actualization is greatest in the literary text because of dynamism inherent in literary reading. In literary reading, he sees the potential for readers to break free of the constraints imposed by traditional communication models attendant upon it. Dias's enthusiasm for collaborative learning is shared with Beach; Tierney and Gee; Hanssen, Harste, and Short; and Moffett.

James Moffett's "Ways of Teaching Literature," the most directly pedagogical of all the chapters, underlines the importance of inductive pedagogical reading methods. Contrasting sharply with Bogdan and Morgan in their advocating that student readers be made self-consciously aware of the presuppositions of literary critical approaches to text, Moffett cautions against the authoritarian implications of direct analysis, relying on sound instructional techniques that allow students to discover for themselves the playing out of the multifarious constraints on the reading process. At the same time, embedded in his discussion are some of the salient theoretical problems educators themselves ask about the teaching of literature. Like Dias, Moffett believes that entering a work directly with as few outside constraints as possible is the best route toward good reading and reading instruction. Like Dias and Hunt, he regards the literary/aesthetic as the prototype for developing communication; like Bogdan and Tierney and Gee, he is interested in the development of critical judgment as well as renewed visions of the self. For Moffett, perhaps more so than any of our authors, reading theory is a praxis: pedagogy is not an "application" or "outgrowth" of theory, but rather the enactment of theory. Moffett's conviction that the subversive element inherent in all strivings for literacy — the transformation of consciousness — surfaces best when "connections" — what Hanssen, Harste, and Short would call "intertextual tying" — are allowed to "thicken," by the structuring of tasks. These may look simple but, in fact, they are powerful in that they are intended to equip students to think for themselves about the implications of the "basic communication triangle" (text, author, and reader). Seeing a tacit consonance between literary theories and the ways students can learn to think about literature, Moffett suggests that his ten-things-to-do-on-Monday-morning in the end provide the foundations for making the student the best possible "comprehender." These methods are formal in that they are structured activities, but they are informal insofar as they are premised upon the interdependence of the students' own learning processes and discourse itself.

Just as Moffett suggests a "technology of reading" that allows for the development of personal response, Robert Morgan attempts to demystify reading practices by examining the technologies that have been accepted practice over the last century. In his chapter, "Beyond Reader-Response Theory: The History and Politics of Reading," Morgan builds a bridge between the historical and phenomenological, and between the phenomenological and pedagogical. In many ways, his chapter cuts across the basic assumptions held by the other authors in this volume. He challenges underlying conceptualizations of the reading act and how reading pedagogy can be and is political. In doing so, he asks the reader of this volume to reconceptualize all three earlier sections of the book; he also cuts across the other authors' discussions of engagement and detachment by pointing out that both these points of view have been politically motivated in the past and have been used in similar ways to manipulate and control reading, both in schools and beyond. In terms of the constraints on reading, Morgan situates all the other authors in the book within the constraints of their own technologies: Bogdan's dialectical technology; Dias's engagement technology; Hynds' volitional technology; Hunt's social pragmatic technology. In many ways, Morgan transcends the discussions of engagement and detachment, constraints of reading, and even our own conceptualization of communication and actualization by identifying the need for metainstruction in reading. He identifies the historical foundations of conceptualizations of reading and questions the pedagogical parameters that have constricted continuing conceptualizations of the purposes and modes of reading, and in reading literature in particular. In many ways, he makes us aware that we have been politically naive in the way we think about reading and stresses the need to become aware of the politics of reading in order to take control of our own conceptualizations and, more importantly, to allow students to take control of their own reading.

THE HISTORICAL CONTEXT

One of the ways of characterizing the shift in thinking from a communication contract to an actualization contract is through a history of theories of reading. Harry Singer in 1985 suggested that prior to the appearance of Holmes' 1953 theory of reading comprehension, "All the previous research in reading had been atheoretical" (p. 630). Although the work done in reading and reading instruction prior to the midtwentieth century may not have been driven by fully articulated theories of the reading process, they were informed by a set of basic assumptions about the act of reading, the reading process, and the underlying psychological processes involved in reading.

By the same token, although literary "theory" prior to the 1960s was more a description of practice—how a person might come to know and interpret a particular piece of literature—than a theory of reading, this practice was also informed by a set of basic assumptions about the locus of meaning, the meaning of art, the knowledge needed for effective interpretation, and the purpose of reading and critical activities.

We will briefly trace the development of those assumptions and conceptualizations of reading, particularly in North America, during the past century or so, and, in particular, the assumptions about the locus of meaning—that is, the place where it was assumed that meaning resided. The discussion will attempt to characterize what we see as the large movements in reading, both in reading-comprehension theory and literary critical theory rather than to account for all of the work carried out in either of those highly productive fields of scholarship. In developing these characterizations, we have found some notable exceptions to the general thrust during each of the major periods we identify; sometimes these exceptions are the most memorable researchers and scholars, memorable primarily because they were exceptions. We have not attempted, therefore, to account for every thinker, writer, and scholar over this period; the persons who may appear to be excluded may not be mentioned primarily because they were "prophets in the wilderness" at the time they were writing, and were, in some ways, at odds with the prevailing thinking of their own time. We do not intend, then, to catalogue all the thinking and theory development in the next few pages, but rather to identify the conventional wisdom of each period and to characterize the primary assumptions underlying the general concepts about reading in any particular era. Further, we intend to identify some general patterns of development in the theory and practice of reading both as they have been realized in descriptions of the reading-comprehension process and as they have been realized in critical literary writings. Sometimes the theory and practice are most evident in teaching practices; at times they are most evident in research work; at other times, they are most evident in the influential writings of the period.

Over the past two or three hundred years, there has been a general change in assumptions about the locus of meaning — or at least the place where meaning was assumed to be located by the scholars and researchers of the time — a change that has been identified by others in historical descriptions of literary history (e.g., Eagleton, 1983; Jefferson & Robey, 1982). Prior to and during the nineteenth century, until the advent of empirical research in reading in the 1880s and, later, the advent of formalism and New Criticism in literary theory, meaning was generally assumed to reside with the author; that is, text was a representation of what the author meant, and the author was the ultimate arbiter of meaning. Because of this assumption about the residence of meaning, the process of reading was assumed to be an act of *transmission*, and text was merely viewed as a vehicle for the author's meaning. Text was seen to carry no meaning except that which was prescribed by the author. Because of the importance of the author here, the primary knowledge needed by a reader in order to read, understand, and interpret text was perceived to be knowledge about the author, his or her life, his or her historical context, and his or her moral/philosophical stance.

Toward the end of the nineteenth century in reading-comprehension theory, and after the First World War in literary critical theory, there was a significant change in the thinking about the locus of meaning. Rather than meaning being placed with the author, text gained importance beyond merely being a vehicle for the meaning ascribed to it by the author. Text became reified, highly visible. During this period, the author increasingly faded in importance, and meaning was ascribed to text. The act of reading, instead of being a "reading of the author" became a "reading of the text," and the purpose of learning to read was to learn the code in which meaning resided. The practices of this period can be characterized as *translation*; readers became puzzle solvers, translating the meaning of the text through their own "skill," either as readers or interpreters. In this view, knowledge about the author and history of a text was anathematized. The *procedures* of reading seemed most important: in reading comprehension, these were the basic underlying skills such as decoding skill, word knowledge, and structural-analysis ability; in literary criticism, this was the skill of "close reading" and the explication of text. This point of view was prevalent through the first six or seven decades of this century, with some of the most influential work in *translation* being done near the end of the era. Though this point of view was more resilient to change in reading-comprehension theory than it was in literary critical theory, the shift to *interaction* models can roughly be dated, according to Hunt (in this volume, Chapter 4), as beginning in the late 1950s with the publication of Chomsky's *Syntactic Structures* (1957) and Frye's *Anatomy of Criticism* (1957). The *translation* notion, however, flourished in both fields until well into the 1970s and is still widely practiced, particularly in public schools and universities (e.g., Just & Carpenter, 1980/1985; Hirsch, 1987).

With the reemergence of cognitive psychology, with the emergence of transformational-generative linguistics and the subsequent application of psycholinguistics to reading comprehension during the 1960s, and with the application of structural linguistics to literary criticism about the same time, another major shift in thinking and theorizing about reading and literary criticism took place. In this movement, the result was an emphasis on more *interactive* theories in reading comprehension and structuralism (and all of it variants) in literary criticism; the text again became less visible and the author again gained some prominence in the act of reading. Along with the author, however, the reader gained importance as well, so that reading became characterized as a problem-solving (rather than a puzzle-solving) activity in which the author and reader shared both world knowledge and linguistic knowledge via the text. The reader becomes important in this activity in that what the reader *knows*, rather than what the reader can *do*, became a critical element in the act of reading. In the interaction formulation, we see the increased importance of knowledge about the "sign" system. The text was important only in that it encodes a set of structures and meaning (ascribed to it by the author) and perceived by the reader (who has ascribed a similar meaning to the text as the author through the reader's knowledge of the sign system). Certainly this is the beginning of the rise of the reader in the act of reading, a trend that is continuing today as is the genesis of the major rethinking in reading that we are hypothesizing.

The next major movement in reading grew out of a variety of research and scholarship efforts about reading and epistemology, a direct development from the interactive theories. This movement can be identified within the past ten years in reading-comprehension theory, within the past twenty in literary critical theory. These theories, *transactional* ones, further enhance the importance of the reader in the act of reading, and, in many ways, decrease the importance placed on either the author or the text. In transactional theories, the act of reading is no longer seen as merely a communication act, but rather as an act of actualization on the part of the reader during the act of reading. Here we have the important change in thinking from the communication contract to the actualization contract: meaning in these theories grows out of the encounter of reader with text. In transactional models, the reader takes a very active role in the (re)construction of text and the creation of meaning in the presence of text. (The "re" in reconstruction in the previous sentence is written that way because of a continuing disagreement among scholars about whether meaning is wholly constructed by the reader—a somewhat radical position—or whether it is reconstructed by the reader—a somewhat conservative position). At the present time, there has been a general shift from interactive models of reading and interpretation to transactional models of comprehension and criticism.

However, other changes have taken place that lead us to believe that transactional models are merely a step to more *constructive* models of reading, interpretation, and criticism—models in which reading will be viewed as a subset of composition—or rather, that both composition and reading will be viewed as subsets of a *single literacy process*, a single process that will simultaneously account for both reading and writing activities. These models, only just now being created, we are calling *constructionist* in that both the author and the text again become invisible during the act of reading. Meaning resides exclusively, or almost exclusively, with the reader. In constructionist models of reading, the reader becomes the author in the sense that the meaning of any text is seen as a total creation of the reader within the particular social milieu of the text, the reader, and the act of reading. Because the reader will need to have as much skill as—or perhaps more than—the author, all reader knowledge becomes critical to reading. Not only will readers need to have large bodies of knowledge about content and possible meanings, but they will also need to have a myriad of procedures through which to access and employ those bodies of knowledge.

In this introduction, we have attempted to lay out the major issues addressed by the authors in this volume as well as a historical context out of which the present research and theoretical activity in reading is taking place. We offer these readings here, not because they necessarily provide any answers, but because they probe the issues in reading that lead beyond communication.

NOTE

1. The ideas presented in this introduction, in particular the concept of changing contract, were generated and refined through many hours of often intense discussion and reflection. The dynamics of engagement and detachment were primarily worked out by Bogdan as part of her hypotheses about the nature of literary response (Bogdan, 1986a, 1986b) and are explicated later in this book in her chapters on the aesthetics of response. The work on the historical context was generated by Straw based on his hypotheses about the history of models of instruction (Straw, 1989); each of the periods identified in this introduction is further explicated in his chapters in this book.

HISTORICAL
CONCEPTUALIZATIONS

CHAPTER 1

DYNAMICS OF COMMUNICATION
Transmission, Translation, and Interaction in Reading Comprehension

Stanley B. Straw & Pat Sadowy

Until recently, reading comprehension theory and research has had few documentations of its own history. Consequently, there have been few theoretical frameworks, in terms of historical development, guiding conceptualizations about the field and, in particular, giving researchers a sense of the historical contexts out of which the work presently being done has developed. In the past few years, however, we have seen a small number of historical reviews or retrospectives published (Gray, 1984; Venezky, 1984), but these reviews have not focused on the development of a framework of how either researchers or practitioners have conceptualized the nature of the act of reading in the past or the concomitant consequences of those conceptualizations. Our purpose in this chapter is to trace how researchers and teachers have thought about reading during different historical periods and how those conceptualizations have changed over the years from the advent of the public school system in North America. The review presented here attempts to trace the dominant conceptualizations of reading from the late eighteenth century through the development of interactive models of reading in the late 1970s and early 1980s. From our review, we have come to believe that past notions about the

21

nature of reading have one central concept in common—a belief that the primary purpose behind the act of reading is a need and desire to communicate—what we call the *communication contract* (after Eco, 1984, and Moffett, 1968). We believe that a primary tenet of how people have thought about reading for the past 200 years (at least) has been centered around the communicative purposes of reading. Reading has been conceptualized primarily as an act of communication as realized in the transference of messages from an author to a reader as evidenced in text.

We believe that a number of changes have taken place over the past 200 years in the ways that people think about—in the ways they conceptualize—reading. We do not believe that the *nature* of reading has changed over this time period; however, the ways in which researchers, teachers, and the general public have *thought about* reading have changed. We have hypothesized three major movements within the history of conceptualizations of reading—from a *transmission* notion of reading (roughly, from 1800 to 1890), to a *translation* notion of reading (roughly, 1890 to the late 1970s), to an *interactive* notion of reading (a notion predominant now within the reading establishment). We are also hypothesizing a significant change in the past few years in the interactive notion; these, which we call *transactional* and *constructionist* notions of reading, are discussed in Chapter 3. Our purpose in this chapter is not to be definitional; it is to aid the reader in thinking about the reading process, how general conceptualizations about reading have changed over time, and how those developments reflect the theory, research, and pedagogy of reading.

EARLY CONCEPTUALIZATIONS OF READING: THE EPISTEMOLOGY OF TRANSMISSION

The most conservative and historically resilient conceptualizations of reading have been those we are calling *transmission*. In transmission, the predominant metaphor has been a conduit metaphor—that is, a conceptualization of reading as information, knowledge, or meaning shunted from the author to the reader via the vehicle of the text (Hynds, in this volume, Chapter 10; Mosenthal, 1987a, 1987b; Smith, 1985). This conceptualization has been reinforced, furthermore, by conceptualizations of education—in particular, reading education—that are articulated as the movement of information or meaning from a source (the teacher), unchanged, to a passive learner (the student). (See Straw, 1990, for a more complete discussion of transmission models of teaching.) In the traditional transmission conceptualization, the author was valorized as the source and locus of meaning. Underlying this notion was the *communication contract*—that reading was part of a dynamic of moving knowledge from author to reader.

In the purest interpretations of the transmission model, the power of the author was absolute: all meaning and authority resided with the author; the reader's task was to accept meaning from a written text as the author intended—unchanged. This was a passive task, the reader's role essentially being one of recipient rather than reasoner (as was true with later conceptualizations of reading). In this purest interpretation of the model, the most "successful" understanding of an author's message was probably indicated by the ability of a reader to memorize an author's work and recite it from memory. Text was equated with authorial intent and was seen as the vehicle or container through which that intent was moved from author to reader, from meaning maker (the author) to meaning apprehender (the passive recipient).

Insofar as the reader was perceived to be a passive recipient of the author's meaning, the text was perceived to be transparent because it was merely the vehicle of the movement of meaning. This communication/transmission notion of language is classical (e.g., Greek and Roman) in that both Plato and Aristotle saw language as mimetic (it reflected the world), and the power of communication lay in the power of the rhetoric—that is, the ability of the sender (author) to shape the message (the text) so that it persuaded and moved the audience (the reader). These classical notions were dominant in North America prior to the onset of experimental, psychological research in reading and reading comprehension.

The importance ascribed to author in the transmission theories was also reflected in the notions of what it meant to be a good reader. The good reader was the reader who could recognize or apprehend the author's intent in a text. It was important, therefore, for the reader to be aware of historical and biographical, and especially moral and philosophical, information about the author. The *procedures* of reading and interpreting were not important; what was important was the *knowledge* that one had about the authorial context in order to "find out" what the author was intending—declarative knowledge over procedural knowledge. The process of reading was defined by one's knowledge of the author and his or her most probable intents. In addition, the quality of writing was often judged by the moral "uprightness" of the author: authors who were morally sound were thought to be worth reading, regardless of either the content or themes of the texts they wrote, or the quality of the writing.

Perhaps the most obvious examples of transmission notions of reading have their roots in religious study. In the book of Exodus (Chapters 20, 24, and 34), the story is told of Moses receiving the Ten

Commandments, messages written by God, which were literally etched in stone so that all who saw them would share the same message. This valorization (in fact, deification) of author is still evident in university classrooms in which professors distribute lecture notes and handouts to their students, the implication being: "Here is the material that you need to know; read these and you will know what I know in the same way that I know it."

Reading as transmission prevailed in Colonial America. The Bible, "God's book" (Westerhoff, 1978, p. 76), was the most important book both in the home and in the school. Elson (1964) suggested that moral and religious material, either taken directly from the Bible or based heavily on biblical stories and themes, were the predominant material in school texts, accounting for a majority of the reading material until at least 1870. Whenever meaning was unclear, the reader was at fault; the text was infallible because its "author" was infallible.

These beliefs about God as author were transferable to other authors as well. The literature of Colonial America comprised almost entirely religious writings, writings that were inspired by God, whose authors wished their listeners/readers to accept the word of God through their words. It is important here to note the word "accept" rather than "understand," "comprehend," or "interpret." If interpretation took place, it was carried out by those trained to interpret in a particular way (i.e., to read with a special understanding) — priests, ministers, and the like — those people who knew the author best. They would then pass the meaning along complete to the receiver (the conduit metaphor). There was, consequently, a heavy duty placed on an author to transmit the message clearly, resulting in an emphasis on the eloquence and rhetorical ability of an author. An example taken from Michael Wigglesworth is illustrative of this:

> How sweetly doth eloquence even enforce truth upon the under-standing, and subtly convey knowledge into the mind, be it never so dull of conceiving, and sluggish in yielding its assent. So let a good orator [or author] put forth the utmost of his skill, and you shall hear him so lay open and unfold, so evidence and demonstrate from point to point what he hath in hand, that he will make a very block understand his discourse. Let him be to give a description of something absent or unknown; how strangely doth he realize and make it present to his hearers' [readers'] apprehensions, framing in their minds as exact an idea of that which they never saw, as they can possibly have anything that they have been longest and best acquainted with (in Nye & Grabo, 1965, pp. 335–336).

This was, essentially, a Lockean epistemological concept in which the student, reader, listener, or receiver of information was a *tabula rasa*, a blank slate, upon which the teacher, author, speaker, or sender of information would "write" knowledge in complete form.

From a transmission point of view, authors were perceived as specially talented people whose mission was to spread messages, generally messages about God, via print. Only secondarily was reading seen as an activity for pleasure. The major purpose of text was to send the authors' messages. Readers were asked to believe that those messages came to them directly from the authors, unmediated. Context or environment, whether economic, social, or political, was not considered important because context was either seen as the same for both reader and author, or the reader was expected to adopt the context of the author for the purpose of receiving the message. Often, in fact, authors wrote for audiences of other authors whom they knew to be very much like themselves (e.g., the "coffeehouse" groups in London during the seventeenth and eighteenth centuries, and the "Concord writers" in New England in the mid-nineteenth century).

One's literacy was defined not in terms of any particular works (since the text itself was, for all real purposes, invisible, being merely the vehicle of the message), but rather in terms of the authors with whom one was familiar. To be literate, one would, for example, have had to have read the Bible, biblical essays, the classics (preferably in the original language), and authors such as Shakespeare, Chaucer, Milton, Johnson, and Pope.

Reading comprehension during the nineteenth century was based on a number of assumptions:

1. The purpose of reading in general and in reading literature specifically was to communicate a message from the author to a reader.

2. Meaning resided wholly with the author of a text. In order to tease out that meaning, the reader was obliged to examine and understand the history of the period in which the text was written, the biographical information surrounding the author, and, in particular, the philosophical or moral stance out of which the author was writing. In this way, the intention of the author of any particular text could be understood.

3. The single correct meaning of any piece of literature lay with the intention of the author. If readers could deduce the intent of an author, then they had arrived at the correct meaning.

4. Text, for all practical purposes, was invisible, in that it was merely the messenger, but not to be confused with the message itself.

The advent of increased literacy, the appearance of texts with more "implicit meanings," and the interest of psychologists in reading

however, led to a movement from *transmission* to *translation* near the
end of the nineteenth century.

THE TRANSITION FROM
TRANSMISSION TO TRANSLATION

The industrial revolution changed life-styles tremendously. Much of
this was attributable to a population shift from rural to urban living as
thousands of people moved from farms to work in city factories
(Hoffman, 1987). Concomitantly, people's attitudes toward education
shifted: literacy and general education became less exclusive and
increasingly valued (Gere, 1987). Part of the consequence of this shift
in terms of reading was that people either needed to read for their
jobs (as they had not needed to in the past) or wanted to read for
pleasure during their increased leisure time. University attendance was
increasing, and the nature of the programs of studies was changing.
In the first half of the nineteenth century, the study of the classics
prevailed at the university level. Around 1850, English studies began
to emerge as a credible discipline. As it emerged, a division developed
between the teaching of reading and the teaching of literature — that
is, between reading as a discipline, either housed in psychology or
education departments, and literature study and criticism as a discipline,
housed in English and rhetoric departments. Along with this division
between reading and literature, the teaching of reading was delegated
to the public school and the teaching of literature to the university.
(See Gere, 1987.)

In addition, and perhaps most importantly, with the appearance
of an interest of psychologists in reading and in the skills that people
brought to the act of reading, gradually people's conceptualizations of
reading changed: authorial dominance was overshadowed by a new
phenomenon, text dominance, and reading was conceptualized as
translation rather than *transmission*.

TRANSLATION IN READING
COMPREHENSION

According to William S. Gray in his 1941 reading monograph (reprinted
in 1984), around 1885, a new movement evolved in reading. Its chief
aim was to broaden the cultural life of the nation and to promote
interest in the "better types" of literature. It found expression in
society at large in the development of libraries and in the increase in
the number of magazines published.

The purpose of the literature advocated for children was not unlike the purpose of previous reading material: through literature, children would learn about their civic responsibilities and their cultural heritage, a point of view still largely evident in Britain when reported at the 1966 Dartmouth Conference (Dixon, 1967) and a view that has been expressed by advocates of the recent "cultural literacy" movement (e.g., Hirsch, 1987).

The changes in the purposes for reading are clearly illustrated in the various editions of the *McGuffey Readers*. The reading materials changed from McGuffey's original religious intentions to the point where the 1879 revised edition was "severely secularized" (Westerhoff, 1978, p. 19). The fifth and sixth *Readers* were "the first to include a really substantial selection from literature" (Commager, 1962, p. xii), "... a rich repast ... a veritable course in English literature" (Commager, 1962, p. xvi). The change of content in children's school readers paralleled the importance of "good literature" as it was being addressed by society; "... the literary ideal dominated the teaching of reading between 1895 and 1910" (Gray, 1941/1984, p. 8).

A variety of themes was presented in the literature of the turn of the century, including ones about various aspects of morality; however, unlike the overt, superficial messages put forward in the period of author dominance, these themes were often implicit. This shift from the explicit message to the implicit message cast the reader in a very different role in the conceptualizations of reading. Whereas, when the message was explicit, the reader was seen as a passive receiver of the message of the author; as the message of text ("literature") became more implicit, the reader was reconceptualized as a "translator" of text into meaning. Therefore, shortly before the turn of the century, the text itself became viewed as the place in which meaning was located (rather than in the author), and the reader was reconceptualized as a "translator of text" — no longer just the recipient of knowledge or meaning, but active in figuring out the meaning, a "puzzle solver" of textual meaning. With this important shift, we see the near disappearance of author from the "communication," with the text taking over the role previously held by the author. There was a realization that the reader must bring some kind of skill to the act of translating text into meaning. Consequently, the concept of "skill" became an important and hegemonic concept that ruled conceptualizations both of reading and teaching for the next seventy-five years.

In general, readers believed that the message dwelt within the structure and style of the text and that it was the readers' task to seek that message. Instructors provided pupils with knowledge about the text that could then be applied to a new selection in interpreting meaning.

Around this same time, cognitive psychologists began conducting research that involved the act of reading. Although their intentions in research were aimed at finding solutions to issues in the field of psychology (such as the nature of perception), as opposed either to theorizing about the reading process or to improving the instruction of reading in the public schools, they often used reading as the vehicle for their studies (Venezky, 1984).

Beginning with Emile Javel's 1879 publication and that of James Cattell in 1886 (in Venezky, 1984), the two decades between 1890 and 1910 saw over a dozen researchers investigate most elements of basic reading processes (e.g., word recognition, eye movement, memory). In 1908, Huey published his comprehensive text about reading in which he included, among other topics, discussions about meaning, methods of reading, and instruction in reading.

Little of this research, however, had much influence on reading practice or pedagogy, or, for that matter, directly on general conceptualizations of reading. Much more influential was the work done in the measurement of individuals' abilities. This work led to the development of standardized tests of mental ability; objective tests were devised to measure individuals' achievements and progress in many facets of education, including reading. Edward Thorndike published his reading tests in 1914. The next year, William Gray published the *Gray Standard Oral Reading Paragraphs* (Venezky, 1984).

Translation notions of reading, still encompassing a communication model and a conduit metaphor, held major sway in reading for nearly eighty years after the publication of Cattell's early studies on word recognition and perception. It was realized primarily in the "atomization" of reading theory, in an analysis of the skills and subskills necessary for the decoding of print and the figuring out of words and, therefore, meaning from print. A major emphasis, besides being on the assessment of readers' "skills" in reading, was on individual words in a text. Major work was completed during this period on text difficulty as predicted by vocabulary difficulty with the appearance of various readability formulas. Text was seen as an accumulation of the meanings of the individual words, suggesting that the words themselves carried the meaning in a text.

One skill that preceded any discussion of comprehension was the ability to recognize words, meaning notwithstanding—what Goodman has called "recoding" (Samuels & Kamil, 1984, p. 187). For decades, an argument raged concerning whether word identification was best taught by a visual approach, in which children came to recognize whole words automatically by sight, or by a phonetic approach, in which children "attacked" the word, sounding out letters and blending them into meaningful words (Chall, 1983). Regardless of the method used, the conceptualization of reading was clear: the meaning of a passage resided in its constituent words. Reading was a puzzle; it was a reader's task to crack the code and thereby find the meaning that lay hidden within the text.

Later during this period, the first theories of reading and the first models of reading comprehension appeared. Because these theories and models are indicative of the communication conceptualizations of reading, and because they are eloquent examples of the translation notion of reading, we deal with them in some detail.

TRANSLATION THEORIES AND MODELS OF READING COMPREHENSION

The early comprehension models, appearing about the time of the Second World War and immediately thereafter, were derived from an analysis of competent readers' skills: we call these "psychometric/skills models." The later models, appearing in the 1970s, were theories derived from researchers' attempts to account for the results of empirical research on reading comprehension. We call these "text-based models" because they share a set of assumptions that reading begins with the analysis of the features of print. Both groups of models are similar in that they share a similar conceptualization of how reading works: on the one hand, they assume that reading is a communicative act; on the other, they assume that "comprehension" can be achieved through an analysis of the text and a "translation" of that analysis into meaning.

Psychometric/Skills Models

The early attempts to describe the reading process were grounded in statistical analyses of reading behavior. Samuels and Kamil (1984) have referred to these models as "psychometric" (p. 186). In developing psychometric models, researchers measured reading-comprehension behavior using some generally accepted test of reading comprehension, hypothesized what "skills" or "abilities" underlay reading comprehension, devised or selected tests to measure these "skills," and then examined the relationship between these hypothesized skills and reading-comprehension performance. This was done in an attempt to identify the combination of skills that accounted for most of the reading-comprehension performance observed in subjects. Obviously, these were "performance" models. The statistical procedures most often applied were multiple regression analyses or factor analyses, procedures whose purpose was to choose sets of skills whose combination best accounted for the criterion performance (in this case, reading comprehension).

Davis and the Skills-Development Model. An early attempt to define the reading process through this type of psychometric procedure was reported by Davis in 1944. Davis reviewed the literature in reading and selected nine clusters of testable skills for inclusion into his analysis: knowledge of word meanings, contextual analysis, ability to follow the organization of a passage, ability to select the main ideas of a passage, literal comprehension, ability to paraphrase, inferential comprehension, recognition of literary devices, and ability to determine a writer's purpose or point of view.

Davis hypothesized that each of these skills was independent of the others, and that each would make a unique contribution to the totality of reading comprehension. His results from competent readers indicated that two factors, *knowledge of word meanings* and *reasoning in reading* (a component ability made up of the ability to paraphrase and inferential comprehension), accounted for approximately 89% of reading-comprehension performance as Davis measured it.

A number of research problems existed with Davis's original study, such as the reliability of the measurement, the weightings of the factors, and the particular factor-analysis method he chose. This led researchers to reanalyze his data or partially replicate his study (Alshan, 1964, cited in Davis, 1968; Hunt, 1957; Johnson, Toms-Bronowski, & Buss, 1983; Thurstone, 1946) and led to Davis (1968) himself redesigning his testing instruments and completing a study similar to his first with the redesigned instrumentation. This, in turn, led researchers (Davis, 1972; Spearritt, 1972) to reanalyze those data. In reviewing all of these analyses, replications, and reanalyses, Blachowicz (1983) has summarized the results as follows: "No clear evidence emerged across the studies in favor of unique and separable comprehension skills beyond the designation of vocabulary knowledge and the elusive 'something else'" (p. 257). Though this assessment may be a bit harsh, the results of these studies do indicate that beyond knowledge of word meanings and a paraphrase/inference ability, the psychometric approach has given us little information about the nature of actual reading and has not necessarily given us much information on the components that need to be included in the development of models or theories of reading.

Holmes and Singer and the Substrata Theory of Reading. The second major attempt to create a model of reading from testing and psychometric analyses was carried out by Holmes (1953). Singer (1985) suggested that "... previous research in reading had been atheoretical" (p. 630). Although attempts such as Davis's were not atheoretical, they seemed to lack a set of basic underlying principles driving the theory other than the assumption that reading could be broken down into discrete component skills (the translation/ communication notion). Holmes (1953) was not only interested in the component skills of reading, but also in how they operated and how important clusters of skills were in contributing to reading behavior. The development of Holmes' substrata-factor theory and its visual display was an early example of the now-ubiquitous flow charts of the reading process. Holmes began his work by reviewing the literature in reading and selecting thirty-seven factors that correlated significantly with either the speed of reading or what he called the "power of reading" (p. 7). It is important to note here that these thirty-seven factors were derived from research literature that shared a common translation notion of the reading process. The variables were categorized into five clusters: mental ability, linguistic ability (vocabulary, spelling, phonetics, word discrimination, affixes, etc.), small-motor ability, eye-movement behavior, and personality factors (assessed by a number of personality and adjustment inventories). Three criterion tests were employed, two to measure reading speed and one to measure the "power of reading." The power-of-reading test was made up of a set of subtests measuring main ideas, literal comprehension, generalization, and inferential comprehension. These global tests of speed and reading, as well as tests for each of the thirty-seven factors, were then administered to a sample of college students. Holmes used a multiple-correlation technique to select variables that significantly accounted for the criterion performance of speed and power of reading; that is, he statistically decomposed reading speed and power into their component parts.

Holmes was able to account for 56% of reading speed and 78% of reading power. The factors that accounted for most of the reading-speed performance were word sense, word discrimination, and span of recognition. The factors that accounted for most of the reading power were identified as intelligence, vocabulary in context, fixations, and perception of verbal relations.

Subsequent to this college-level study, Singer (1960, 1962, 1965) reported research applying the multiple-correlation analysis to grades 3 to 6, thus hypothesizing a developmental model of reading that would account for the acquisition of reading speed and reading power. A variety of factors accounted for the majority of variance in speed of reading and power of reading at different grade levels and included visual-verbal meaning, word-perception speed, knowledge of the meaning of affixes, spelling recognition, listening comprehension, word recognition in context, matching sounds in words, and blending word elements. Singer (1983) grouped these factors into four "systems" (p. 17) that underlay the power of reading: graphophonemic (matching word sounds), semantic (vocabulary), morphemic (suffix), and reasoning (mental age). He also identified three systems operating for reading speed: speed and span of perception, vocabulary knowledge, and mental age. Two of the systems (vocabulary knowledge and mental age) are common to both speed and power. Singer (1983) suggested that this developmental model could be used as a basis for classroom decisions about curriculum design, grouping of students, and evaluation.

Holmes and Singer (1966) summarized their combined substrata-factor theory as follows:

> The Substrata-Factor Theory holds that general reading is a composite of Speed and Power of Reading and that underlying each component is a multiplicity of related and *measurable factors*. Further, the Theory states that, in essence, excellence in reading is normally an audiovisual verbal-processing skill of symbolic reasoning, sustained by the inter-facilitation of an intricate hierarchy of substrata factors which are mobilized as a psychological working-system and pressed into service in accordance with the purposes of the reader (p. 155) [emphasis added].

The basic assumptions underlying the theory, then, are that (1) reading is a language skill ("an audiovisual verbal-processing skill"), (2) reading is made up of a hierarchy of factors (i.e., not only is there a set of component skills, but these are hierarchically arranged), (3) reading is made up of measurable skills, (4) reading is a composite of speed and power, and (5) the constructs of speed and power are themselves measurable. A further assumption underlying the developmental model is that particular tests are reasonable measures of particular constructs. All these assumptions share a basic translation metaphor.

These skills-development "models" of reading comprehension have driven reading theory and reading instruction with a vengeance (Goodman, Shannon, Freeman, & Murphy, 1988). One need only to review basal reading materials from the past two decades to conclude that, regardless of the shaky empirical base for such an approach, skills lists are the primary basis for instruction in developmental reading. The analysis of reading, not only into component skills, but into subskills (and, at times, subsubskills), has been the model of reading that has dominated materials development in reading. Since both students and teachers generally perceive the reading process as the activities presented in their reading materials (Shannon, 1983), the skills-development model has probably become the most pervasive model of reading espoused by the general public. These skill models have as a basic underlying assumption that meaning resides in text and the role of the reader is to translate that text into its intended meaning.

Text-Based Models

"Text-based" models of reading attempt to explain what a reader does in the presence of text—that is, during the act of reading. We have called these models *text-based* because they place a primary emphasis on the text itself and how the reader breaks the textual "code"—a basic notion of translation. A heavy emphasis is placed on the reader in accounting for all of the visual stimuli (that is, everything that is on the page), and such models are generally unidirectional (from text to meaning). In general, they assume that meaning is determinate, that meaning can be identified and specified and, therefore, a reader's comprehension can be measured objectively, and that, for the most part, meaning resides in the text itself. Their goal is to explain comprehension, rather than interpretation, and they attempt to account for the translation of meaning of the text by the reader.

Gough's One Second of Reading. The first of the text-based, information-processing models to become popular was Gough's in 1972. In many ways, it is the prime example of linear, text-based models that have a translation assumption as their basic underpinning. The model itself has a set of operations that results in a set of subproducts along the linear movement of the reading process. Each operation in the model has associated with it a set of reader knowledge that is employed to complete the operation and results in the next subproduct. The model, then, comprises a string of operations informed by sets of reader knowledge (such as phonemic knowledge, lexical knowledge) performed on successive products that eventually results in comprehension of the text.

Without going into specific detail about the levels of the model itself, essentially the model begins with the text (SUPPOSE THE EYE), which is perceived by the VISUAL SYSTEM. This operation results in the formation of an image in the brain (the ICON). The ICON persists long enough for the brain to scan it for recognizable patterns, and when the letters have been recognized, the DECODER uses the CODE BOOK to translate the visual input into the auditory code (the PHONEMIC TAPE). From the sounds and combination of sounds on the PHONEMIC TAPE, the LIBRARIAN checks the LEXICON for the meanings of individual words. When the meanings have been attached to the words, they are then transferred to PRIMARY MEMORY. Then, an operator, which

Gough calls MERLIN (the little black box), applies SYNTACTIC and SEMANTIC RULES to the input from primary memory. This is the point at which comprehension takes place, so that when a sentence is understood, MERLIN transfers it to TPWSGWTAU, The Place Where Sentences Go When They Are Understood.

At any point in the model, one of the operators may fail to recognize or process the product from the previous step; at that point, the reader goes back in the processing chain, possibly back to the graphic input, to check the veracity of the processing.

Gough's model assumes that the reader begins reading when faced with an actual text and that processing takes place letter by letter. He has stated: "I see no reason, then, to reject the assumption that we do not read letter by letter. . . . [T]he weight of the evidence persuades me that we do so serially, from left to right" (p. 353). The model assumes that the mind is able to process graphic features (features of letters, features of patterns, features of sounds, features of words, etc.) in lightning-quick succession.

The LaBerge and Samuels Automaticity Model. LaBerge and Samuels (1974) developed a model of reading similar to Gough's in that it has a primary emphasis on word identification and the processing of the visual input from text. Feedback loops were added to the model after its original inception and publication. The addition of these feedback loops attempted to account for the interactive nature of reading (that is, that a reader's knowledge can significantly influence how visual information is processed). However, the essential nature of the model was not changed with this addition, and the processing of text flows, in general, from left to right — from text to meaning — in the model.

The model (or processing of text) begins with the graphic input that is perceived by the SENSORY SURFACE. From the sensory surface, information from the print moves through a set of three "memory" systems, generally in a linear order: from VISUAL MEMORY (the reader's knowledge of graphic patterns), to PHONOLOGICAL MEMORY (the reader's knowledge of the sound/symbol relationships), and, finally, to SEMANTIC MEMORY (the reader's knowledge of general information about the world). Semantic memory is the point at which comprehension is completed. Samuels and Kamil (1984) described how comprehension takes place within semantic memory:

> At the risk of oversimplification, the process seems to work in the following manner. In order to make sense of what we are experiencing — or reading — we attempt to match the information coming in from outside the head with the knowledge stored in the semantic memory network. To the extent that there is a good match

between the information coming in from the outside and the knowledge stored in memory, we are able to comprehend and make sense of the world. When there is a poor match between incoming information and stored knowledge, the incoming information seems to be incomprehensible (pp. 205–206).

Each of the memory systems is informed by EPISODIC MEMORY (a reader's recall of specific events). Episodic memory can be a reader's experience with graphic patterns (thereby informing the VISUAL MEMORY system), with sound/symbol relationships (thereby informing the PHONOLOGICAL MEMORY system), or with life in general (thereby informing the SEMANTIC MEMORY system).

Within each of these memory systems (VISUAL, PHONOLOGICAL, SEMANTIC, and EPISODIC), processing usually takes place from smaller units to larger units (for example, in the VISUAL MEMORY system, "spelling pattern codes" are recognized and grouped into "visual word codes"), though this smaller to larger unit processing can be changed or informed by information that comes later in the model. Samuels (1985) discussed how more proficient readers can process information in a more holistic fashion, thereby "skipping over" some of the processing within each stage of the model.

Perhaps the most important aspect of the LaBerge and Samuels models of reading is related to their addition of ATTENTION to the model. The model assumes that the amount of attention that any reader has at any one time is limited. It also assumes that attention is required in order to comprehend, or make sense out of, textual material. LaBerge and Samuels identified two major aspects of reading — decoding and comprehension — and asserted that if a reader's attention were taken up with decoding (that is, with pronouncing letters and words), then the reader would have limited (or perhaps no) attention left in order to comprehend. Samuels and Kamil (1984) described the allotment of attention as follows:

Both tasks, decoding and comprehension, require attention. In fact, we can assert that comprehension, under virtually all situations, requires attention, whereas decoding may require more or less attention, depending on the skill of the reader. ... For the beginning reader, decoding the text is a difficult task. Consequently, the combined demands of decoding and comprehension may exceed the limited attention capacity of the student. When combined demands from these two essential tasks exceed the student's attentional capacity, the tasks cannot be performed simultaneously. In order to overcome this apparent impasse, the beginning reader uses a simple strategy, namely, that of attention switching. ... With time and practice, there is a transition from the attention switching characteristic of the beginning reading stage of reading to the skilled stage where attention switching is not required. The skilled stage occurs when the decoding task can be performed with little or almost no attention. When almost no attention is required, we can think of the student as being automatic at the decoding aspect of reading. Now, the skilled reader, who is automatic at decoding, can do two things simultaneously — decode and comprehend — whereas the beginning reader who is not automatic can do only one thing at a time, either decode or comprehend. The reason the skilled reader can decode and comprehend at the same time is that the decoding task requires so little attention that nearly all of the available attention can be allocated to the task of comprehension (pp. 197–198).

The LaBerge and Samuels automaticity model of reading has had enormous impact on how researchers have considered the reading process. It includes two important features that had been left out of previous attempts to explain the reading process: episodic memory and attention. Both these features of their model aid tremendously in explaining their concept of the reading process, and especially assist in differentiating between the reading of more- and less-skilled readers. On the other hand, a number of problems exist with the model: first, even with the feedback loops added, the model is essentially linear in nature (moving from text to comprehension) and assumes that the reader deals with most or all of the visual information. In addition, it also assumes a passive role for the reader — that of matching incoming information with background experience — and it assumes that text is determinate and measurable. Like Gough's model, it also generally assumes phonological mediation (that is, that visual input in some way is translated into sound either in real or abstract form before comprehension takes place) and does not deal adequately with response and interpretation of text.

Just and Carpenter. A recent attempt to describe the reading-comprehension process has been published by Just and Carpenter (1980/1985) based on an analysis of the eye movements of competent readers. Just and Carpenter analyzed the eye movements and eye fixations of college-level readers, attempting to account for these movements and fixations. Their theory is based on two underlying assumptions: (1) the immediacy assumption, "that a reader tries to interpret each content word of a text *as it is encountered,* even at the expense of making guesses that sometimes turn out to be wrong" (p. 175, emphasis added), and (2) the eye-mind assumption, "that the eye remains fixated on a word as long as the word is being processed" (p. 176). The validity of their model rests on the validity of these two assumptions: that a person attempts to comprehend words as they are encountered (rather than holding comprehension in abeyance until some processing point such as at the verb or at the end of a sentence), and that the eye does not move on to the next word until the first word has been comprehended.

Like the LaBerge and Samuels model, this model has some "interactive" aspects (that is, it is possible for reader knowledge to impact on the act of reading itself). The evidence provided by Just and Carpenter in validation of the model is based on readers' reactions to text, thereby making the rationale for the model, if not the model itself, essentially text-based and an example of what we are calling a translation notion of reading. The model does avoid being strictly linear in including parallel processing and adaptive sequencing. Just and Carpenter pointed out, however, that their model focuses on "processing time [that] has resulted in a theory that accounts for the moment-by-moment, real-time characteristics of reading. By contrast, the theory pays less attention to retrieval and reconstruction, *two later occurring processes* that are important to an account of summarization" (p. 204, emphasis added). This characterization of the model by the authors would lead us to infer that the model is both text-based and, at least on the larger level, linear (i.e., word recognition precedes retrieval and reconstruction, the two later-occurring processes). In summarizing their model, Just and Carpenter suggested the importance of text in their model:

> The current model falls somewhere between the extremes [i.e., between text-based and reader-based models]. It allows for contextual influences and for the interaction among comprehension processes. Knowledge about a topic, syntactic constraints, and semantic associates can all play a role in activating and selecting the appropriate concepts. However, the printed words themselves are usually the best information source that the reader has, and they can seldom be entirely replaced by guesses from the preceding context. Thus the top-down processes can influence the bottom-up ones, but their role is to participate in selecting interpretations rather than to dominate the bottom—up processes (pp. 204–205).

THE IMPACT OF TRANSLATION MODELS OF READING COMPREHENSION

Most of us who have grown up during the period of translation — and that is most of us — have been exposed to the communication/translation notion through our own experiences in public schools in learning to read; in English classes, both at the secondary and university levels; in the explication of literature; and in the methods and materials we have encountered both in psychology courses and in educational study. It is not surprising, therefore, that translation is such a resilient and pervasive notion. In some ways, it is the only notion we have ever had about reading; certainly, the communication contract is the prevailing notion that we have had—until very recently—about language.

In all of the "theories" discussed here, we have identified basic underlying assumptions that (1) reading is a code-breaking or puzzle-solving activity much like translating a foreign language, (2) meaning is determinate, (3) the act of getting meaning (called "comprehension") is measurable, (4) meaning can be extracted from text via the application of skills to the process, (5) the primary direction of the reading act is from text (the code) to the reader (via comprehension), and, finally, (6) reading is seen as a communicative act, the "receptive" side of the author-text-reader contract.

Translation conceptualizations of reading have had a long history from before the turn of this century to recent developments in the 1980s with the appearance of Just and Carpenter's model (1980/1985). By no means is a translation conceptualization of reading dead; it is especially resilient, as is evident in this recent appearance of a model based on the eye movements of readers. It is also particularly resilient in school methods and materials. Toward the end of this period with the development of interactive models, however, conceptualizations have begun to become more cognizant of the role of the reader in the act of reading and have begun to question the supremacy of text as the retainer of meaning.

INTERACTIVE THEORIES OF READING COMPREHENSION: A STEP TO THE FUTURE

Most reading theorists now accept a notion of *interaction* as a primary tenet of the reading process. (Witness the addition of a feedback loop to the original LaBerge and Samuels model.) However, this is a relatively new phenomenon on the landscape of reading and language. Hunt (in this volume, Chapter 4) suggests that we can date this shift from the appearance of Chomsky's *Syntactic Structures* in 1957—essentially a new conceptualization of language that has called into question basic notions of reading as translation. Chomsky's reconceptualization of language learning and use, paired with a renewed interest by cognitive psychologists in the application of psycholinguistics to reading, has resulted in the development of interactive models of reading. This was a fundamental change from traditional translation models in that interaction notions took into account that meaning is molded in light of reader background and knowledge (see Hunt). In some ways, this shift rerecognized the role of the author in the communication contract. Interaction suggests that the author and the reader share knowledge and experience and that these are shared via the structures of the text.

Interactive models of reading have attempted to account for both the information encoded in the text and the knowledge and experience of the reader. All reading theories are, in some ways, interactive in that perception of text is molded by experience, and experience is adjusted to the text. Nonetheless, certain theories have attempted to strike a balance between these two knowledge sources (text and experience) such that neither is necessarily dominant in the acts of reading and processing text. We think of interactive models as attempts to account for the match between reader knowledge and text structure (whether that be orthographic structure or a higher-level structure). Most interactive theorists would suggest that the closer the match between reader knowledge and text information, the better comprehension is; the more disparate the match between reader knowledge and text information, the poorer comprehension is (see Pearson & Johnson, 1984). The assumptions underlying interactive models have been, therefore, that meaning ultimately resides in text and that the good reader is the one whose background knowledge most closely resembles the text itself (that is, the ultimate meaning). They have assumed that meaning is determinate and determinable, based on the analysis of the structure of text.

One of the major strengths of interactive reading models is that they account, in some ways, for how readers come to understand texts when some knowledge base is "deficient" or not fully developed. Stanovich (1980) suggests that the reader is able to compensate for lack of knowledge in one area by hypothesizing meaning based on knowledge from another area. For example, if readers cannot recognize a word by using decoding skills, they may be able to recognize the meaning by employing syntactic or semantic knowledge to compensate for their difficulty. This concept suggests that, although a particular reader may rely heavily on one or another knowledge base as the primary means of getting meaning, if that system fails in some way, the reader is able to draw on other knowledge bases in order to make sense of the text, implying that reading is a sense-making, meaning-getting process. This interactive-compensatory notion draws into serious question models from the translation era that were primarily linear and assumed that earlier operations (such as decoding in Gough's model) must be completed successfully before later, more complex processes (such as comprehension) could operate.

Interactive theories of reading comprehension have most often been associated with a "schema-theoretic view" of the reading process (Adams & Collins, 1985; Anderson, 1985; Anderson & Pearson, 1984). Schema theory has its roots in the work of Bartlett (1932), whose work on the recall of North American Indian folktales suggested that when comprehending, a person is guided and directed into what will be remembered and how important particular aspects of a story are by a set of schema that are present in the reader prior to reading. That is, when readers have a preconceived "script" (Schank & Abelson, 1977) inside their heads prior to reading, comprehension is shaped by that script. This work in schema theory was supported by the work of Ausebel (1963) in advance organizers, Bransford and Johnson (1972), and Bransford and Franks (1973) on the nature of recall and recognition, and Adams and Collins (1985) in comprehension. The interactive nature (as we are using that term in this chapter) of a schema-theoretic point of view is evident in Adams and Collins' description (1985) of it:

> A fundamental assumption of schema-theoretic approaches to language comprehension is that spoken or written text does not itself carry meaning. Rather, a text only provides direction for the listener or reader as to how he should retrieve or construct the intended meaning from his own, previously acquired knowledge. The words of a text evoke in the reader associated concepts, their past interrelationships, and their potential interrelationships. The organization of the text helps him to select among these conceptual complexes. The goal of schema theory is to specify the interface between the reading and the text—to specify how the reader's knowledge interacts and shapes the information on the page and to specify how that knowledge must be organized to support the interaction (p. 406).

Interactive theories of reading comprehension fall into two general categories, *psycholinguistic* models and *interactive-compensatory* models. Psycholinguistic models, at least as conceived in the mid-1960s, emphasized the interaction between cuing systems in text and the reader's knowledge of those cuing systems. Interactive-compensatory models have described the hierarchical nature of knowledge sources and how those were employed in comprehending text.

Psycholinguistic Reading Models

In response to a number of developments in reading and language during the late 1960s and early 1970s a new, and at times seemingly radical, view of reading was being developed, most often attributed to the work done by Goodman[1] (1967) and Smith (1971), which led to a rethinking of the reading process as an interactive act. This view of reading and language processing has been identified as a psycholinguistic point of view and has resulted in theories that have attempted to view reading as a holistic activity (rather than a set of discrete component skills) and that have attempted to account for both the knowledge and the activity of the reader in the act of reading. The earliest model of reading to come out of these psycholinguistic speculations and research was Goodman's (1970). His theory emphasized the redundancies in text and attempted to describe how the competent reader relied on syntactic and semantic cues rather than on the graphophonics (that is, the sound-symbol relationships in the text) during the act of reading. The model emphasized the knowledge of the reader—both linguistic knowledge and world knowledge—in making sense out of print and deemphasized the role of the text itself. Goodman did not discount the role of text in reading, but suggested that the reader "always prefers the cognitive economy of reliance on well-developed linguistic (syntactic and semantic) rather than graphic information" (Samuels & Kamil, 1984, p. 187). Goodman assumed that the author assigned meaning to the text and that the text itself encoded that meaning in three cue systems: graphophonic cues (the graphic symbols on the page), syntactic cues (the syntax of the passage), and semantic cues (the meanings of the words and larger units of the passage). He also suggested that these cuing systems paralleled knowledge systems in both the author's and the reader's head: that is, knowledge of the graphic symbols and their corresponding sounds; knowledge of the grammar of language; and knowledge of meanings, in particular the meanings of words. The way the system worked is that the competent reader relied on the interaction between syntactic cues and syntactic knowledge, and between semantic cues and semantic knowledge, by setting up sets of expectations and hypotheses about what would occur in the text. The visual display (paired with the corresponding graphophonic knowledge) was used to confirm or adjust the expectations and hypotheses developed from syntactic and semantic cues and knowledge, and was used to develop new expectations and hypotheses. Although all three cuing systems and knowledge systems worked in concert with each other, the efficient reader relied first and most heavily on syntactic and semantic cues/knowledge. Graphic cues and sound/symbol knowledge were employed to confirm hypotheses on the one hand or when the reader experienced difficulty in matching expectations with the text itself on the other. The model was a kind of efficiency model that assumed that the efficient readers relied most heavily on what was familiar (what they knew about syntax and semantics) and relied least on what was novel (the text itself).

The psycholinguistic point of view has had tremendous impact on both reading diagnosis and the teaching of reading. Goodman and Burke's miscue analysis (1972) was an attempt to view the reading process of the students by observation of the quality of the "miscues" (mistakes) readers made during oral reading. They suggested that readers' strengths could be identified by the kind of miscues they made. For example, the reader who read the word "mind" for the text "brain" was demonstrating both syntactic knowledge (a noun has been substituted for a noun) and semantic knowledge (the substitution does not significantly interfere with meaning), though the reader was not attending to the specific visual display of B-R-A-I-N. This was seen less as a "mistake" than as an effective use of syntactic and semantic knowledge—an efficient use of textual cues and reader knowledge.

In terms of reading instruction, the psycholinguistic point of view has led teachers away from the teaching of component skills, particularly sound-symbols skills, to instruction emphasizing the background knowledge of the reader—in particular the world (or semantic) knowledge of the reader. It has also led to procedures that familiarize readers with the patterns of language (repeated patterns, rhyming patterns, etc.) and has attempted to take advantage of children's own language patterns in teaching reading (such as a language experience approach in which students learn the "skills" of reading by using their own oral language written down as the basis for instruction).

The popularity of psycholinguistics, in general, has made both educators and reading theoreticians more sensitive to the role of the reader in the act of reading, has led both teachers and researchers to value what readers bring to text rather than to view the meaning as residing wholly in the text itself, and has heralded the development of more sophisticated interactive models of reading.

Interactive-Compensatory Models

Rumelhart's Interactive Model. Probably the best known of the interactive models has been that suggested by David Rumelhart, originally published in 1977 and summarized in Singer and Ruddell's recent edition of *Theoretical Models and Processes of Reading* (Third Edition) (1985). A major feature of Rumelhart's model is that "it appears that the apprehension of information at one level of analysis [e.g., orthographic, lexical, syntactic] is partially determined by higher levels of analysis" (p. 726). That is to say, text perception and comprehension are, in some ways, determined by reader knowledge. The tenets of Rumelhart's theory are as follows (moving up the hierarchical scale from graphic knowledge to semantic knowledge):

[1] The perceptions of letters often depend on the surrounding letters. ... [2] Our perception of words depends on the syntactic environment in which we encounter the words. ... [3] Our perception of words depends on the semantic environment in which we encounter the words. ... [4] Our perception of syntax depends on the semantic context in which the string appears. ... [5] Our interpretation of the meaning of what we read depends on the general context in which we encounter the text (pp. 726–734).

These tenets hold for the majority of early psycholinguistic and later interactive-compensatory theories of reading.

Ruddell and Speaker's Interactive Model. Ruddell and Speaker (1985) have hypothesized a somewhat more complex model, attempting to account for a number of additional factors not accounted for in earlier models, though the tenets of interactive models still hold for it. The model incorporates four interactive components:

1. *Reader environment*, which is the environment in which the act of reading takes place, including the text itself, the communication context, and instructional features.

2. *Declarative and procedural knowledge*, which refers to the reader's knowledge used in processing the text. Ruddell and Speaker refer essentially to three types of knowledge: decoding knowledge (knowledge of the graphophonics and lexical access), language knowledge (lexical knowledge, syntactic knowledge, and text-structure knowledge), and world knowledge (the accumulation of past experiences).

3. *Knowledge utilization and control*, which refers to the processes through which the reader applies the declarative and procedural knowledge to the environment. The product of these processes is the "text representation"—the internal text constructed by the reader based on the information from the environment and from the knowledge sources. Three internal states interact in the reader and are responsible for the activation of information used in construction of the text representation: they are the affective state, the cognitive state, and the metacognitive state.

4. *Reader product*, which refers to those things that the reader produces as a result of the processing that has taken place. These products include comprehension, word recognition, oral output (e.g., discussion of text, oral reading), written output (e.g., journal entries, formal papers), affective state change (e.g., changes in the interests, attitudes, and values of the reader), cognitive state change (e.g., changes in the plans and cognitive processes of the reader), meta-

cognitive state change (e.g., changes in the self-monitoring and self-control of the reader), and new knowledge (e.g., additions to the declarative and procedural knowledge of the reader).

An important aspect of Ruddell and Speaker's model is the interactions that take place between and among these four areas. They describe these as follows:

1. *Environment interaction*, which is the interaction between the reader environment and the knowledge utilization and control. This interaction, according to the authors, provides the basic input mechanism of the model. "Any feature of the reader environment which is to be processed enters the text representation via the Environment Interaction" (p. 773).

2. *Knowledge interaction*, which is the interaction between the declarative and procedural knowledge of the reader and the knowledge utilization and control. During this interaction, the knowledge used by the reader in order to develop the text representation resides in the declarative and procedural knowledge of the reader and is used by the knowledge utilization and control mechanism to develop the text representation.

3. *Product construction and evaluation interaction*, which is the interaction that links the reader's text representation with the products the reader will produce. The products created by the reader during reading are effected by the reader's affective state (goals), cognitive state (plans), and metacognitive state (monitoring and control). In each of these, the text representation is the source of information for the generation of reader products.

4. *The A/C/M control interaction.* Ruddell and Speaker do not discuss this interaction in detail, but describe it in the following way:

   The A/C/M Control Interaction links the Reader Product and Knowledge Utilization and Control. Through this interaction, the reader is constantly modifying the Affective, Cognitive, and Metacognitive control states based on Reader Product. This interaction thus influences the control processes and, in turn, the Text Representation and Reader product(s) (p. 780).

   It appears that this interaction leads the readers to reevaluate the plans, goals, and monitoring systems based on the products they produce, thereby affecting or changing the internal text representation. It is unclear, however, how this can be distinguished from the product construction and evaluation interaction.

5. *New knowledge interaction*, which is the interaction between reader product and declarative and procedural knowledge. This interaction

allows for the products of reading (comprehension, new knowledge, word recognition, etc.) to be integrated in the reader's memory and be retained. It also implies (though this is not discussed by Ruddell and Speaker) that the products of reading can be adjusted by the reader's knowledge without directly affecting the text representation.

Because this model attempts to account for much of the reading act not accounted for by other models (for example, the larger reader environment and the products of reading), it is very complex. It suggests that there are a number of qualitatively different interactions taking place during reading that could account for a wide variation in researchers' observations of the act of reading. The model implies, though it does not explicitly state, a basic tenet of all interactive models: that reading in some ways is compensatory; that is, if meaning cannot be extracted employing one process, another process is employed as an alternative means.

THE IMPACT OF INTERACTION CONCEPTUALIZATIONS OF READING

In this section, we discuss two current and major thrusts in reading comprehension theory that fall into what we call an *interaction conceptualization of reading*. Each of the psycholinguistic and interactive models of reading comprehension share some essential characteristics. First, they emphasize the shared knowledge (between author and reader) that is signaled in the textual features. Text is important in that it stands for a set of knowledge structures resident in the author, reflected in the reader. Furthermore, the communication between author and reader is most effective when experiences, knowledge, structures, schema, signs, and cuing systems are shared by them both. Second, these theories share notions of the reductionist nature of language. Language can only sign or signal or gesture to experiences or meanings or schemata. They are not the reality of the experiences themselves, but they stand as incomplete signals of those experiences. Third, there is a basic underlying notion about the purpose or primary function of language — that is, the communication contract.

The advent of interactive theories in reading comprehension signaled an important rise in the role of the reader in the act of reading and comprehending text. For the first time, perhaps, the knowledge, experience, and interpretive strategies of readers became a central concern to theorists. This movement opened the door to an important step toward valuing the reader in the act of reading that has become more evident in conceptualizations of reading comprehension now being developed and discussed—in the *transactional* and *constructive* conceptualizations of reading that we are theorizing are the wave of the future. Perhaps interactive theories were a necessary step toward more productive notions of reading. Certainly they have revolutionized how we think about reading, and, in many ways, we can date the revolution against the hegemony of formalist approaches from the application of linguistics and systems of knowing to reading comprehension and interpretation.

CONCLUSION

Reading-comprehension theory and research have made tremendous strides over the past two centuries—from a narrow conceptualization of reading as an act of transmission, with the primary emphasis on the author as creator of meaning, to a broader more reader-based conceptualization of reading as the interaction among reader, author, and text. All of these conceptualizations have shared a basic underlying tenet associated with the purpose of reading—for the communication of meaning to the reader, whether that reader was conceptualized as a mere vessel into which meaning was poured, a puzzle-solver of text, or an active participant in the development of the assignation of meaning to the text. Notions about the residence of meaning (with the author, with the text, with the interactions among reader, text, and author) have changed over the period, as well as the kind of knowledge thought important in the act of reading (declarative or procedural). The basic purpose for reading, however, has not changed during this long history. It is only within the past few years that we have begun to question the communicative function of reading, a question that is pursued in Chapter 3.

NOTE

1. Goodman's early conceptualization of the psycholinguistic model of reading is placed in this group of models for a number of reasons: first, because we think that his thinking about reading has changed substantially since the appearance of his early work in cuing systems; second, because he, himself, in response to Keith Stanovich in a letter to the editor of *Reading Research Quarterly* (Vol. 16, No. 3, 1981) states: "My model is thus an interactive model" (p. 477). He goes on to say that "[a]n interactive model is one which uses print as input and has meaning as output. But the reader provides input, too, and the reader, interacting with text, is selective in using just as little of

the cues from text as necessary to construct meaning" (p. 477). Our reading of his "Unity in Reading" article (Goodman, 1985) would lead us to believe that subsequent to the exchange of letters with Stanovich, Goodman has become more constructive in his notions of reading and reading comprehension—and those more constructive views are discussed later in this volume.

CHAPTER 2

CONCEPTUALIZATIONS OF COMMUNICATION IN THE HISTORY OF LITERARY THEORY
Readers Apprehending Texts and Authors

Stanley B. Straw

Unlike reading-comprehension theory and research, literary critical theory has had, as one of its major concerns, the examination of its own history and the movements within the field from era to era. This chapter is not an attempt to rewrite any of those particular histories; rather, it is an attempt to throw additional light on conceptualizations of the act of reading and interpreting literature by drawing parallels between the historical movements in literary critical theory and reading-comprehension theory. The parallels are, it seems, striking in that both fields have shared some basic assumptions about the nature of the act of reading, comprehension, and interpretation. Though the movements in both are roughly parallel, they are not identical, and here the focus is on those aspects that are similar. This chapter, therefore, roughly parallels the previous chapter on reading-comprehension theory. I have drawn heavily on other interpretations of the fields (e.g., Eagleton, 1983; Guerin, Labor, Morgan, & Willingham, 1979; Jefferson & Robey, 1982), identifying the important similarities between the recent history of literary critical theory and the "periods" in reading comprehension.

The history of literary theory in North America is divided into three periods, starting with the appearance of literary criticism as a field of study and continuing through the beginning of the poststructuralist period of about twenty years ago. The discussion in this chapter ends with the appearance of poststructuralism, since an underlying tenet of criticism that had been basic to critical theory took a dramatic change with the appearance of reader-response criticism in North America and reception theory in Europe, a tenet associated with the purpose of reading and interpretation based on the communication function of reading. This chapter attempts to trace the history of this communication notion of reading and interpretation. The terminology of both this chapter and the one preceding has been adopted in order to demonstrate the parallels between literary critical theory and reading-comprehension theory.

This chapter traces three periods of development in critical theory: an early conceptualization of reading as *transmission* that covers the period from the appearance of literary theory as a university subject to the early articulations of New Criticism during the 1920s; a second conceptualization that is called reading as *translation* that essentially covers the formalist period of New Critical thought; and a third conceptualization of reading that is called reading as *interaction* (a term adopted from reading-comprehension theory) that encompasses structuralist thought and the beginnings of the poststructuralist period. All three periods share a common conceptualization—that the purpose of reading is for communication—although many of their other assumptions (e.g., locus of meaning, kind of knowledge important to reading, importance of text) are radically different from one another.

TRANSMISSION IN LITERARY SCHOLARSHIP

The same transmission point of view described in the previous chapter on reading comprehension was evident in literary theory during the nineteenth century. As with reading comprehension, in transmission, the overriding metaphor for reading was a conduit metaphor, a notion of reading in which information, knowledge, or meaning was shunted from the author to the reader via the vehicle of the text (Smith, 1985), suggesting that meaning was transferred from a source (the author), unchanged, to a passive reader, much like pouring lemonade from a pitcher into a glass. The author was valorized as the source and locus of the meaning of text. Underlying this notion of reading was the communication contract—that reading literature was the act of moving knowledge from author to reader by means of text.[1]

This transmission view, however, was more long-lived in literary theory than it was in reading comprehension, lasting until after the

First World War. Prior to the rise of Romanticism in writing and the rise of English studies as a discipline about 1850 (Connors, Ede, & Lunsford, 1984; Gere, 1986), literary theory was embodied in the more comprehensive theory of writing and authorship: either a theory of rhetoric or generalized literacy theory. This is apparent, for example, in the discussions of writer/critics such as Sidney, Johnson, and Pope, and was even apparent in such Romantic writers as Keats, Coleridge, and Shelley. The "reader/critic" as separate from the literate person who was both a reader and a writer did not come into its own until the rise of Romanticism, with its purpose of making literature accessible to the "common man" (Wordsworth in Smith & Parks, 1951) and until the rise of English studies in universities in which the *study* of literature was separated from the *creation* of literature. Even though writers still performed the role of critic (e.g., Matthew Arnold, Edgar Allan Poe, Samuel Coleridge, and the like), there was also the critic who was only a critic. (See Smith & Parks, 1951.)

This division of author from critic, generated out of a view of author *as* critic, led to what was to be the hegemony of the author in critical studies: if the critic was no longer the author, then the purpose of the critic was to come to understand the intentions of the author. The critic became a kind of author *in absentia*. Two major approaches to criticism came together in the nineteenth century to constitute a movement that has been referred to as "positivism." This notion of positivism was an epistemological concept that embodied the nature and genesis of truth—that is, where truth existed and how it was knowable. Gilbert (1987) called these general, positivist approaches the approaches of "expressive realism." She stated: "Expressive realism assumes a communication model, with the text acting as the thread connecting two consciousnesses—that of the author and that of the reader. The author has something to communicate with the reader, and the text acts as a transparent medium through which the author's intentions are actualized. To understand the text, then, is to explain it in terms of the author: the author's ideas, psychological state, social background, and so on" (p. 234).

The two prominent approaches the critic used to come to know the truth of the author's intentions have been referred to as *historical-biographical criticism* and *moral-philosophical criticism* (Guerin et al., 1979). The historical-biographical critical approach assumed that a reader or critic could come to know the "intention" of the author by examining the historical context within which the text was written as well as studying biographical accounts of the author's life. The ideal texts to study for interpretative purposes were the autobiographies of authors, particularly if they chose to discuss the creation of their works. Other important sources of study were the letters and correspondences of an author, an author's journals or diaries, the different drafts of a work that an author revised during the creation of the work, and letters and commentaries from friends and literary colleagues. Under this brand of scholarship and criticism, in order to understand and adequately appreciate a particular piece of literature, a person was expected to come to know the intentions of the author. This meant that the reader must have a rich knowledge of the historical context out of which a work was written, a knowledge of the life and activities of the author, particularly during the time in which a particular piece was being written. Guerin et al. (1979) describe the "hereditary and environmental determinism" of the historical-biographical method in this way: "Put simply, this approach sees a literary work chiefly, if not exclusively, as a reflection of its author's life and times" (p. 25). Since the critic could not *be* the author, then the role of the critic was to "get inside" the author as much as possible. This led to English studies being limited to a small number of valorized authors and to the development of "period" specialties among critics. So a critic might be an important "Milton scholar," or a particularly sensitive interpreter of Pope, or a specialist in Shakespearean poetry, primarily because the critic had done extensive research into the historical background and personal biography of a particular author.

Guerin et al. (1979) have retold an apocryphal story that dramatizes this particular critical point of view. It is about a professor who entered a classroom to discuss Andrew Marvell's "To His Coy Mistress." "He proceeded to discuss Marvell's politics, religion, and career. He described Marvell's character, mentioned that he was respected by friend and foe alike, and speculated on whether he was married." The professor, however, never mentioned the poem itself nor asked his students to read it. The content of the course was not the literary text itself, but rather the historical, biographical, and philosophical "texts" that surrounded the composition of the poem. Morgan (in this volume, Chapter 14) discusses how, in textbooks and teachers' manuals, this point of view resulted in a "technology" that highlighted historical and biographical notes and commentaries and shunted the literature to the background of study.

The historical-biographical point of view was attached to another "traditional" set of critical techniques, generally referred to as the "moral-philosophical" approach (Guerin et al., 1979). The basic tenet of this view of criticism was that the purpose of literature was to "teach morality and to probe philosophical issues" (p. 29). This is the most traditional and classical of all the critical traditions, and its primary examples lie in the attacks on literature mounted by the critics of "poetry" (e.g., Plato, the Puritans) and in the subsequent defenses of poetry (e.g., Aristotle, Longinus, Sidney, Shelley, Arnold).

The moral-philosophical approach takes an interest in nontextual information — usually, pretextual information — similar to historical-biographical criticism. "The basic position of such critics is that the larger function of literature is to teach morality and to probe philosophical issues. They would interpret literature within a context of the philosophical thought of a period or group. From that point of view Sartre and Camus can be read profitably only if one understands existentialism" (Guerin et al., 1979, p. 29). The most famous apologist for the moral-philosophical point of view was Matthew Arnold. In his essay, "The Study of Poetry," first published in 1880 (Kaplan, 1975), Arnold pointed out the poet's ability and responsibility to morally direct the new classes who were developing literacy.

This "moral" critical point of view was nowhere as evident as it was in the school books of the period. Elson (1964), in discussing the texts used in public schools during the nineteenth century, pointed out that authors were required to be read by students because of the "morality" of their own lives, under the assumption that morality would be reflected in their writings. She states:

> Since moral qualities should be paramount in his writings, it was considered entirely proper to inquire into the author's moral behavior in his own life. Scott comes out very well in this respect. More attention is given in several books to his labors to pay back creditors than to his writings: "The sterling integrity of the man shown forth in this dark hour." This portrayal of an honest and industrious man is used as an introduction to and evaluation of his writings. Byron, on the other hand, is to be read with caution. . . . Coleridge's use of opium and the dissipation of Burns interfered with and marred the work of these two writers (pp. 235–236).

Positivist/expressive realism notions of literary theory and criticism held English studies in a choke-hold well into the twentieth century. The implications of these conceptualizations of reading, clearly, were to valorize and deify the author; the locus of meaning was synonymous with authorial intent, and the task of the reader was to look for and find that intent in any text. Text itself was transparent or invisible in that it was equated with authorial intention; *reading the text* was the same as *reading the author*; if there were any problem with the reading, either the reader was at fault or the problem could be cleared away by searching the historical past, the biography of the author, or the moral and philosophical perspectives out of which the text was written. It was ultimately based on a concept of communication in that the purpose of reading and studying literature was to receive the message of the author's intent. Jefferson and Robey (1982) state that nineteenth-century positivists "studied literature almost exclusively in relation to its factual causes or genesis: the author's life, his recorded intentions in writing, his immediate social and cultural environments, his sources. To use a common distinction, it was an extrinsic rather than an intrinsic approach to texts. It was not interested in the features of the literary text itself except from a philosophical and historical viewpoint" (p. 3).

TRANSLATION IN LITERARY CRITICISM: FORMALIST APPROACHES TO TEXT

Translation theories in literary scholarship appeared after the First World War as a violent response to what was seen as the elitism of the nineteenth-century historical and moral-philosophical criticism. With the attendance of a larger proportion of the population at universities and with more literature available to the general public, scholars in literature began to question whether the kind of broad knowledge of history, biography, and philosophy assumed necessary for literary understanding in the nineteenth century was really necessary for the explication and understanding of literary texts. The reactions to nineteenth century critical approaches took two different paths, one on the European continent, another in Britain and North America. On the continent, the response was realized in what is now being called "Russian Formalism." The Anglo-American response was referred to as "New Criticism." Both can be characterized, however, under the rubric of "Formalistic Approaches" (Guerin et al., 1979). They are formalist in that they attempt to define "poetic structure" (Tompkins, 1980, p. 221). Guerin et al. (1979) described the formalistic approaches as follows: "'Formalistic' criticism has for its sole object the discovery and explanation of the form in the literary work. This approach assumes the autonomy of the work itself and thus the relative unimportance of extraliterary considerations—the author's life; his times; sociological, political, economic, or psychological implications" (p. 70). Part of the attempt of this shift from the expressive realism of the nineteenth century to formalist approaches in the twentieth was to direct the reader's attention *away from the author* and *to the text* itself. It should be noted that this response to nineteenth-century criticism was equally positivist in that it assumed that a person could come to know precisely the meaning of a text; a person could come to know the "truth" in the text through examining and decoding its textual features. What was different from the nineteenth century was that the methods through which that knowledge or truth could be attained were radically different (a move from authorial intention to textual information). Gilbert explains it this way: "Wimsatt and the 'new' critics insisted that the words on the page were all that mattered, and search for things anterior to the text became less important" (p. 235).

Russian Formalism focused on the "physical" attributes of the text. De George and De George (1972) described formalism as "focused on the form of the work of art, on the craft of the artist, and on his use of the tools of his trade, in reaction to the traditional emphasis on the content of the work and on matters external to the work itself" (p. xx−xxi). The formalists centered on such things as the series of sounds put together by a poet in an attempt to produce a particular effect. Formalists like Propp also described the textual attributes of folktales, and pursued such textual attributes as rhyme schemes, alliteration patterns, syntactic complexities, often attempting to apply phonological and grammatical descriptions to literary texts (Jefferson & Robey, 1982). Later, this attempt to "systematize literature" led to structuralism, which is discussed later in this chapter under the rubric of interaction models.

The Anglo-American response to the deification of the author in the nineteenth century was a reification of the text in the twentieth; however, the structures pursued were less phonological and syntactic (as in Russian Formalism) than they were semantic. (For a strong discussion of the "semantic theory," see Olsen, 1978.) The critics who espoused this general point of view have been referred to as the "New Critics," and their critical point of view has been referred to as "New Criticism" (though, since most of us learned our early habits of how to interpret literature through these methods, little seems "new" about it these days). The structures of text that the New Critics pursued were the paradoxes, the imagery, the symbols, the ironies of literature rather than the specific textual features. According to the New Critics, these attributes, however, could only be known through "close reading" and an explication of the text. What the reader was expected to do was to examine the text closely, identify the different elements of it, and attempt to account for all its surface features by pulling up their "meaning" within a conception of "organic unity."

A number of names are often associated with New Criticism. The earliest proponents of the movement were I. A. Richards (1926) and T. S. Eliot (1932). The banner of New Criticism, however, was taken up by others, and the names from the 1940s and 1950s in the United States most often associated with the New Critical point of view are Brooks, Wimsatt, Beardsley, Ransom, Tate, and Warren. Guerin et al. (1979) summarize the New Critical movement in this way:

> The New Critics sought precision and structural tightness in the literary work; they favored a style and tone that tended toward

irony; they insisted on the presence within the work of everything necessary for its analysis; and they called for an end to a concern by critics and teachers of English with matters outside the work itself — the life of the author, the history of his times, or the social and economic implications of the literary work. In short, they turned the attention of teachers, students, critics, and readers to the essential matter: what the work says and how it says it (p. 75).

Here are described a number of tenets of the New Critical stance toward text. The first was to make the author not only invisible, but nonexistent. Wimsatt and Beardsley (1946/1954), for example, in one of their most famous contributions to New Critical thought, wrote about the "intentional fallacy"; a major mistake in reading literature, they said, was in attributing the meaning of a work to the intention of the author and in attempting to find that intention. According to the New Critics, it was unnecessary for the reader even to hypothesize about the authorial intention based on any information outside the text. Meaning was *in the text*, not in some supposition about what the author might have meant.

The second major assumption had to do with the role of the reader and the "effect" of the literary work on the reader. The New Critics were unconcerned about the affective effect (the feeling produced in the reader) of the literary work; reading was primarily a cognitive activity, and, as Wimsatt and Beardsley (1946/1954) point out in their essay "The Affective Fallacy," the reader should not be concerned with the emotional effect of the poem or the literary work, but rather should attend to what the poem *says*. This was accomplished by a close reading that emphasized the precision of the expression (for the New Critics, the more precise the expression, the more successful the literature), and with the autocratic triumvirate of *Unity*, *Coherence*, and *Emphasis*. The reader should read the text closely to explicate the unity of the literary work (attempting to account for all the aspects of the work), the coherence of the work (how each of the pieces fits into the whole effectively), and the emphasis of the work (how the unity and coherence highlight particular aspects or meanings within the literary work). Thomson (1987) has observed that "[t]he critical emphasis on coherence and harmony through the integration of parts is designed to leave the reader in a state of contemplative admiration — and contemplative acceptance" (p. 97).

Rosenblatt (1978), in discussing the New Critical movement, has observed that "[New Criticism] fostered the ideal of an impersonal or objective criticism" (p. 41). Young (1987), in summarizing the tenets of New Criticism, has suggested that there was "a concern for the primacy of text, a more objective and scientific approach, and a system of close textual analysis" (p. 9). More importantly, however, was the New Critical concern with "correct" reading. Young has pointed out that in the New Criticism point of view, every reader was a critic. This suggests that somewhere in the world, there is a "correct" reading by a more sensitive critic, leaving every reading as "inadequate" (p. 11). In fact, in the application and instruction of New Criticism, both in universities and in public schools, for decades students played the game of "guess what the teacher is thinking about this particular literary work" based on a conception that the text had one true meaning discernible only by the closest and most sensitive reading of the text.

In actual practice, New Criticism — what Richards has called "practical criticism" (1929) — was played out, according to Guerin et al. (1979) in this way:

> Intensive reading begins with a sensitivity to the words of the text and all their denotative and connotative values and implications. . . . After one has mastered the individual words in the literary text, he looks for structures and patterns, interrelationships of the words [such as referents, grammar, tone, and systems]. . . . When all the words, phrases, metaphors, images, and symbols are examined in terms of each other and of the whole, any literary text . . . will display . . . the logic of metaphor. . . . When that "internal logic" has been established, the reader is very close to identifying the overall form of the work. The context . . . must be identified also (p. 76).

Here Guerin et al. (1979) are referring to what is often called the dramatic situation — the persona of the literary work, the audience that the persona is addressing, and the history of that persona. It is important to note that this is not the history of the author; New Critics would think it inappropriate to equate the persona of a poem (or the narrator of a story) with the author. The persona is IN the text — internal to the literature; the author, on the other hand is external and extratextual. And for the New Critic, all extratextual information was irrelevant. (See Perrine, 1964, for a complete discussion of the dramatic situation and the role of the persona in the text.)

What does the foregoing say about the attitudes and the underlying conceptualization of reading, and, in particular, in the reading of literature, of the period roughly between 1920 and 1960? The first major observation is that the basic traditional concept of communication was still in effect — the shift had merely been made from communication between author and reader (in the nineteenth century) to the communication between text and reader. Rosenblatt (1978), in discussing T. S. Eliot's view of the act of reading, stated: "Eliot is actually concerned with communication" (p. 103). By the same token, John Fekete (1977) discussed I. A. Richards' concept of communication as follows:

> In this context, Richards raises the problematic of communication which . . . becomes so important later on in the tradition. "A large part of the distinctive features of the mind are due to its being an instrument for communication," "the arts are the supreme form of the communicative activity," and "the two pillars upon which a theory of criticism must rest are an account of value and an account of communication" (p. 33).

Finally, in *Practical Criticism*, Richards (1929) stated: "That the one and only goal of all critical endeavors, of all interpretation, appreciation, exhortation, praise or abuse, is improvement in communication may seem an exaggeration. But in practice it is so" (p. 11).

The second observation is that not only has the author lost his authority to the text, in reality, the reader becomes merely a translator of text. Wimsatt and Beardsley (1946/1954) dismiss the role of the reader except as a translator and explicator of text by stating: "The Affective Fallacy is a confusion between the poem and its results (what it is and what it does). . . . It begins by trying to derive the standard of criticism from the psychological effects of the poem and ends in impressionism and relativism" (p. 345). In the terms of Wimsatt and Beardsley, "what a poem is" is what criticism should be about, is what the goal of reading should be; what the poem does is not worth study.

INTERACTION IN
LITERARY CRITICAL THEORY

The tenets of New Criticism began to be questioned during the late 1950s and early 1960s in literary theory. Critics began to consider the role of the reader in the act of reading and reconsider the role of the author. With the publication of Frye's *Anatomy of Criticism* in 1957, a new era of literary scholarship was ushered in with the application of a systems approach to the reading and interpretation of literature (see Gilbert, 1987). This movement culminated in what has been called "Structuralism in Literature" (Scholes, 1985), an era that roughly parallels, in thought, the *interaction* movement in reading comprehension. The new structuralist movement in literature was a fundamental change from the traditional translation models of New Criticism and formalist criticism in that it recognized the role of the author as the encoder of the signs and messages in literature and, more importantly, the role of the reader as the decoder of the signs and messages in literature. It viewed text not as a puzzle to be solved by a reader, but as a complex configuration of symbols infused with meaning—meaning for the author as well as for the reader. It suggested that communication was effective in literature insofar as author and reader shared the sign system of the text.

Interactive/structuralist criticism implied that reading literature was not a one-way transmission of ideas from either author or text to reader, but rather an *interaction* between the knowledge and truth of the author on the one hand, and the knowledge and truth of the reader on the other. This interaction was made possible by what the author and the reader *shared,* not only in terms of experience and perception of truth, but in the systems in which experience and truth were encoded—in the case of reading, the text. In reading comprehension, we think of interaction as an attempt to account for the match between reader knowledge and text structure, whether that structure is the orthographic representation or higher-level structures such as archetypal structures in the case of Frye (1957), or rhetorical structures in the case of Booth (1961), or aesthetic or stylistic structures in the case of Culler (1981), or political structures in the case of Jameson (1971).

Formalism in Europe was much less resilient and long-lasting than formalism in either Britain or North America. Anglo-American New Criticism held sway in literary circles until the appearance of the criticism of Northrop Frye (see Hunt, Chapter 4 and Bogdan, Chapter 5). On the continent, however, formalist thinking began, soon after its rise in popularity in the 1920s and 1930s, to take into account the larger "systems" of language and to apply the principles of structural linguistics to literary criticism. This resulted in the structuralist movement, an application of a systems approach to the analysis and understanding of literature. Structuralism in literary analysis closely paralleled the thinking of schema theorists who wrote later about reading comprehension and language. Structuralist thought grew out of the linguistic principles of Saussure and was the application of structural linguistics to a wide variety of fields. These principles have been referred to as semiotics (Eco, 1976, 1979), and, as such, are closely related to, if not a subset of, the science of semiology (DeGeorge & DeGeorge, 1972; Olsen, 1978). DeGeorge and DeGeorge (1972) identify a number of structuralists in a broad range of fields, though perhaps the movement has been most evident in literary criticism. In an attempt to identify structuralist thought, they state:

> What Marx, Freud, and Saussure have in common, and what they share with present-day structuralists, is a conviction that surface events and phenomena are to be explained by structures, data, and

phenomena below the surface. The explicit and obvious is to be
explained by and is determined ... by what is implicit and not
obvious. The attempt to uncover deep structures, unconscious motivations, and underlying causes which account for human actions ...
is an enterprise which united Marx, Freud, Saussure, and modern
structuralists (p. xii).

One might immediately position Chomsky (1957) in this tradition
with his concepts of *surface structure* and *deep-meaning structure*, and, in
fact, Chomsky can be viewed as a major motivator for North American
reading theorists to encompass structuralist thought into their conceptualizations of reading.

Eagleton (1983) describes structuralist thought in the following
way: "Structuralism in general is an attempt to apply this [Saussure's]
linguistic theory to objects and activities other than language itself.
You can view a myth, wrestling match, system of tribal kinship,
restaurant menu or oil painting as a system of signs, and a structuralist
analysis will try to isolate the underlying set of laws by which these
signs are combined into meanings" (p. 97). This description echoes
the schema theorists' notions about comprehension. Eagleton suggests
how structuralist notions can affect what we think of as the communication contract and why it was seen as a significant advance over
formalist approaches in that it represented a "demystification"
(p. 106) of literature and the reading of literature. It also makes a
substantial jump ahead in that it emphasized the "constructedness" of
human meaning (p. 107). He states: "Meaning [for the structuralists]
was neither a private experience nor a divinely ordained occurrence:
it was the product of certain shared systems of signification ... what
meaning you were able to articulate [as a reader] depended on what
script or speech you shared [with the author] in the first place. There
were the seeds here of a social and historical theory of meaning ... "
(p. 107). In structuralism, we see the reentry of the author into
conceptualizations of the reading process, but an author much changed
over the autocrat who was beheaded under the regime of New Criticism. In structuralism, the author was seen as a person who shared
signs with the reader through the text. The author assigned meaning
to text, the text represented an agreed-upon set of meanings, and the
reader, because author and reader shared the signs with one another,
was able to apprehend the meaning of the text. Text stood in place of
the experience (the meaning) of the author; it also stood in place of
the experience of the reader. The closeness of the match between the
experience of the author and the experience of the reader determined
the effectiveness of the communication — how well the communication
contract was fulfilled.

Thomson (1987) has characterized structuralism as inattentive to the *actual* meanings in literature and only concerned with the *language system* itself. He states that the structuralists saw literature as a particular kind of language organization, and they focused primarily on the ways in which literature's meanings were produced by authors and apprehended by readers rather than on the meanings themselves. Thomson observes that "[t]he structuralists have taught us to think of the literary work not as a self-contained organism as the New Critics think of it, but as something that has meaning because of publicly agreed upon conventions which readers have internalised" (p. 104).

In North America, perhaps the earliest work in structuralism was associated with the archetypal criticism of Northrop Frye (1957, 1963a, 1963b, 1970, 1971/1973). Frye's system, as outlined in both his work on the nature of criticism and his critical practice, was basically a pan-cultural system. He suggested that all cultures have a set of structures that he referred to as "archetypal"—that is, that reflected the hopes, dreams, aspirations, fears, etc. of mankind. These were encoded, culturally, in such structures as myths, heroes, and the genre of literature. Although this systems approach was not developed directly from structural linguistics and may have its appeal in its similarities to structural anthropologists, it still operated as a critical "system" through which the structures of text could be identified and, ultimately, understood.

The processes of working out the meaning of a work and explicating it have a number of realizations in the literature of structuralism and related literary theories. Some of these theories are aesthetic (e.g., Culler's structuralist poetics [1975] or Riffaterre's semiotics of poetry [1984]), some are cultural (e.g., Frye's archetypal criticism [1957]), some are political or social critiques (e.g., early feminist criticism as described by Showalter, 1985, and early Marxist criticism such as Lukacs, 1971), some are rhetorical (e.g., Booth, 1961; de Man, 1969). What all these literary critical methods and critiques have in common is the application or use of a system in order to "unpack" the literature. Culler (1975) uses stylistics as his system for unpacking the text; Riffaterre (1984) uses genre and intertextuality as his system; deconstructionists use binary opposites as their system; Marxists use the principles of the dialectics of class opposition as theirs; feminists employ the response to sexual politics as theirs; psychoanalytic critics use the principles of Freud as theirs; rhetorical critics use the principles or rhetorical unity as theirs. Regardless of the systems approach that any one or group of these critics may use in order to interpret literature, they share a conceptualization of the interpretative process such that structures can be used systematically to reach an interpretation of any particular text.

(Anti)structuralist thought[2] (*anti* because it is based on the assumption that there is a system to react against) essentially falls into this interaction group of critical theories.[3] Perhaps the best-known, and probably the least-understood, example of antistructuralist thought is deconstructionist criticism. (See Bogdan, in this volume, Chapter 7, for a cogent discussion on deconstructionist criticism as well as an example of a deconstructionist reading.) Although deconstruction is, according to Culler (1982), "confusing and confused" (p. 17), he has defined it within the structuralism it has hoped to deconstruct, as has Gilbert (1987). Derrida, a leading deconstructionist, stated: "In a traditional philosophical opposition we have not a peaceful coexistence of facing terms but a violent hierarchy. One of the terms dominates the other (axiologically, logically, etc.), occupies the commanding position. To deconstruct the opposition is above all, at a particular moment, to reverse the hierarchy" (in Culler, 1982, p. 85). Derrida continues in his description to state that this reversal of the hierarchy—the giving of the power to its binary opposite (thereby making the controller the controlled)—is only one step in deconstruction. He states that deconstruction "through a double gesture, a double science, a double writing, put into practice a reversal of the classical opposition and a general displacement of the system" (in Culler, 1982, pp. 85–86). But this displacement is not chaos; it is, in fact, the establishment of an opposing system, a system that is itself open to further deconstruction (an example being deconstructionist critics who unpack the work of other critics). Deconstruction does this metaphysically and aesthetically—that is, it attempts to undermine ways of knowing and, in particular, ways of attaining pleasure. Deconstructionists might argue, furthermore, that the pleasures of text and the pleasures of reading are found in the act of undermining aesthetic values.

A crude example might be: as persons are viewing a pornographic film, they are constructing the morality that is in polar opposition to the structure of the film; in contemplating that morality, furthermore, the viewers become aware of the *pornography of morality*, thus turning the hierarchical relationship around; this realization leads to a reassertion of the *pleasure of morality* over the pleasures of pornography, and so on. Where does all of this unpacking lead? It leads to the contemplation of systems and their opposites, and therein lie the pleasures of text, what Bogdan in Chapter 6 calls "textual hedonism." The aesthetic swirl of understanding and not understanding, the process of unpacking, leads to the insights from text and, therefore, the pleasures of text.

(Anti)structuralism, however, takes other less "aesthetic" and more action-oriented routes as well. One of those routes has been much of the early feminist criticism (Gilbert, 1987). Feminists have severely criticized the hegemony of male-dominated writing and criticism, and, through critical methods, have attempted to expose that hegemony on the one hand, and replace it on the other. Showalter (1985), in her collection of essays on feminist criticism, states that early feminist criticism "concentrated on exposing the misogyny of literary practice: the stereotyped images of women in literature . . . , the literary abuse or textual harassment of women in classic and popular male literature, and the exclusion of women from literary history" (p. 5). Much recent criticism, particularly in France, has looked "at the ways that 'the feminine' has been defined, represented, or repressed in the symbolic systems of language, metaphysics, psychoanalysis, and art" (p. 9). Much feminist criticism has also been concerned with the structures of the male hegemony and how they can be combated (Spender, 1980). These approaches are themselves structuralist approaches in that they hope to identify the system, in this case, the system of misogyny, and either undermine the system or replace it with a new and better system, whether that system be the system of "pluralism" as suggested by Kolodny (1985) or the system of the matriarchy as suggested by Showalter (1985). My point here is that feminist criticism, in critiquing the dominating and domineering male structures (semiology) in the culture are, by default, structuralists themselves. Bogdan points out in Chapter 6 that some poststructuralist feminist criticism is structuralist, even by this definition. It is not my intent to characterize all of feminist criticism as structuralist, but rather to point out that reacting to a set of signs in the culture and critiquing those signs involves essentially an acceptance of the reality—though not the validity—of the structures being critiqued.

A similar case (for the basic interactionist nature of structuralist criticism) can be made, I think, for a number of other critical theories. Marxist criticism, or at least much of the early Marxist criticism in the sixties and seventies, was an attempt to critique one system (in this case, capitalistic endeavors and the resulting literature) by applying it against the yardstick of another (Marxist thought). The earliest Marxists (e.g., Lukacs, 1971) were formalist/structuralists in their attention to the forms of language (e.g., the novel) and the meanings those forms encoded. This tradition has been maintained by later Marxists such as Bernstein (1984), and Jameson (1971). Bakhtin (1973) expressed this point of view when he stated that "the domain of ideology coincides with the domain of signs. They equate with one another. Wherever a sign is present, ideology is present too. Everything ideological poses semiotic value . . . without signs there is not ideology" (p. 10). Frow (1986), in discussing this ideological sign system, points out that "[a] theory of ideology is a theory of semiotic value, because within the symbolic order the position and intensity of values are the index of a mediated tactical assertion, the site of a struggle for symbolic power, and are charged with the traces of that struggle. The ideological structure is coextensive with the semiotic field—with the totality of signifying systems" (p. 64). Many current Marxist theorists, such as Foucault (1988) and Said (1985), have abandoned the structuralist tradition in that they have investigated how aspects of social construction, historicity, and reader input inform the meanings that readers assign to texts, more similar to transactional and constructionist notions of reading than structuralist ones. (These are dealt with in the next chapter.)

The same can be said for early psychoanalytic criticism: it was an attempt to interpret literature in the light of a particular system, in this case, the Freudian explanation of psychodevelopment (see Suleiman, 1980), though current psychoanalytic critics such as Holland (1980) have abandoned structuralist psychoanalytic criticism in favor of a more subjective criticism that is an example of later-developing transactional conceptualizations of reading.

All of these critical stances, because they address how author and reader respond to text as a set of mutually agreed upon signs, are essentially *interactionist*; they address the interaction between author and reader through text. Although the input of the reader or the reader's experience may be violently opposed to the input of the author, they are both interacting with an agreed-upon set of signs. What the reader concludes does not change the fact that both reader and author are gesturing toward the same meanings.

What all of these seemingly disparate points of view represent, from Frye to Booth to Culler to Barthes to Showalter, is a basic belief in the communicative nature of reading and writing, the semiotic agreement about meaning. Suleiman (1980) observed that structuralist approaches, whether they are rhetorical, semiotic, or political, have shared "a model of the literary text as a form of communication. According to this model . . . the author and the reader of a text are related to each other as the sender and the receiver of a message. The transmission and reception of any message depend on the presence of one or more shared codes of communication between sender and receiver. Reading consists, therefore, of a process of decoding what has by various means been encoded in text" (pp. 7—8).

CONCLUSION

It is difficult to draw conclusions about all the activity in literary critical theory. There have been numerous thinkers and critics who are difficult to categorize because of their genius and originality.

However, as played out in schooling—both at the public school level and in universities—a surprising amount of coherence is evident among critics during the three periods previously identified: *transmission, translation,* and *interaction.* Although they have some very basic differences, the three conceptualizations of reading literature have a common assumption: that the purpose of reading is for communication and that reading has as its basis the communication contract either between author and reader or between text and reader. This point of view has defined how reading has been conceptualized and how it has been played out in critical discourse. It has held sway until the past twenty years, when the underlying communicative assumption has begun to be questioned, and the role of the reader has been increasingly appreciated in the act of reading. Many of the observations made by the proponents of these three points of view are still valid observations about the nature of the act of reading literature; however, the assumption that the purpose of reading is communicative is now being seriously questioned and that questioning is having a profound impact on how we conceptualize the entire nature of reading.

NOTES

1. In this chapter the theorists who have discussed the *nature* of reading rather than those who have *practiced* the art of criticism are dealt with. Though those who have practiced the act of reading and written about it may imply certain theoretical stances that reflect their conceptualizations of the nature of reading, they have not always explicated those practices as a description of the phenomenology of reading. I have, for purposes of clarity and conciseness, limited discussions to writers who have explicitly discussed the act of reading and its implications for practice. The discussion is also limited to those authors who have written about reading in particular, rather than aesthetics or perception as a whole. Thus, the discussion in this chapter may appear to ignore a number of thinkers often associated with literary critical practice (e.g., Foucault, S. Langer); it is not that these writers have not had a significant effect on our conceptualizations of reading, but rather that other writers have made their theories more directly relevant to a discussion of reading. Finally, in both this chapter and the next, the discussion is limited to English and North American writers except where writers from the European continent have had significant impact on the thinking of the Anglo-American movement, especially as related to the reader-response movement (e.g., Iser, Jauss).

2. The term "antistructuralist" is used here to distinguish between types of poststructuralist thought. Though deconstructionist thought has often been associated with, or even equated with, poststructuralism, deconstructionist

thought is best categorized as antistructuralist since it is a response to (and thereby bound to) structuralist and semiotic thinking. The term "poststructuralist" is reserved to apply to theories of reading that essentially reject the structuralist notion, not by attempting to react against it, but to create a hermeneutic that either denies the importance of structure at all or employs it merely as one of a number of important elements that impact on the act of reading. This point of view is expanded in the next chapter on "postcommunication" or "actualization" notions of reading.

3. Holub (1984), in discussing the differences between German reception theory and French poststructuralism, suggests that the French are more avant-garde than the Germans in their approach to the dynamic between the reader and the text. My reading of these theorists suggests, however, that, although the German reception theorists subscribe to a notion of communication, the descriptions of the acts of reading by such authors as Iser (1978), Gumbrecht (as described by Holub), and Jauss (1982) are examples of what I am calling "actualization," and that their discussions of communication are an attempt to explain how reader reception *can* fit into a communication model, not that it *must* fit into one. The deconstructionist, however, by attempting to *de*construct text must, ultimately, accept the construction itself. Holland (1980) points out that Derrida's "disbelief . . . mask[s] a disappointed need to believe" (p. 362). Earlier, Holland made the point that "Derrida . . . writes out of a need not to believe, a need to *dis*trust. Yet . . . I feel the absence is itself a presence. Disbelief is itself a belief in disbelief" (p. 362).

CHAPTER 3

CHALLENGING COMMUNICATION
Readers Reading for Actualization
Stanley B. Straw

RETHINKING THE COMMUNICATION CONTRACT

The movement from interactive notions of reading to transactional ones is a significant change in conceptualizations about reading. All three prior conceptualizations of reading, *transmission, translation,* and *interaction,* were grounded in the assumption that "reading was communication," that it was part of a larger language act that included the author as originator of meaning, the text as a symbolic or representative of meaning, and the reader as receiver or reconstructor of meaning. Transmission theories valorized the author; translation theories reified the text; interaction theories substantialized the compensatory negotiation between reader knowledge and text structure. All, however, assumed the purposes of reading were inherently related to a communicative act. When this assumption was questioned by theoreticians and researchers, it undermined the foundations of transmission, translation, and interaction models. This is the essence of the rethinking about reading that is presently being observed in the field of reading—that leads us "beyond communication."

In this chapter, I hope to document the rethinking in both reading comprehension theory and literary critical theory and make some suggestions about the direction of the two fields in the future. In general, I deal with reading-comprehension theory and literary theory as a single field under the rubric of "reading," because I think there are substantial similarities in the assumptions about reading in both fields and in the directions both are taking.

TRANSACTIONAL MODELS OF READING COMPREHENSION

With the renewed interest in the nature of the aesthetic reading process (literary reading) and with the recognition of Louise Rosenblatt's theories in the mid-1970s, reading-comprehension theorists and researchers began rethinking the nature of reading comprehension along *transactional* lines. Rosenblatt (1978) describes the beginnings of reading transactions this way: "The dynamics of the literary experiences include first the dialogue of the reader with the text as he *creates* the world of the work" (p. 69, emphasis added).

In contrast to conceptualizations of reading built on the communication model, transactional models suggest that reading is a more generative act than the receipt or processing of information or communication. From the transactional view, meaning is not a representation of the intent of the author; it is not present in the text; rather, it is constructed by the reader *during* the act of reading. The reader draws on a number of knowledge sources in order to create or construct meaning.

The knowledge sources include the text itself, readers' knowledge of language features (similar to Goodman's cuing systems [1985]), and their background experiences, world knowledge, and worldview. Harste, Woodward, and Burke (1984) also include social, cultural, and literacy experiences as significant knowledge sources.

In contrast to theories of reading based on the communication model, transactional theories suggest that meaning is created by the active negotiation between readers and the text they are reading. It is the generating of meaning in response to text. "Transactional theories suggest that meaning is indeterminate because each reader brings a unique set of background experiences, world knowledge, social experiences, and social identifications to the act of reading." (Straw, 1990). Transactional theories suggest that no two readers will ever generate exactly the same meaning from a single text because they have different sets of background experience. By the same token, the same reader will never generate the same meaning from the same text at two different readings of a text because at different times, this reader's experiences will be different, if for no other reason than that she or he will have experienced the reading of the text previously. Transactional theories have described the central activity of reading as generative. The assumptions about the centrality of the generativeness of language and reading fly in the face of previous assumptions about comprehension—those that suggest that comprehension is knowable in an objective sense, that suggest that comprehension is measurable, and that meaning is a static or determinate reality. This may be because early transactional theories dealt primarily with aesthetic (e.g., Bleich, 1980; Fish, 1980; Rosenblatt, 1978) or literary reading, the reading of texts that have more "implicit" meanings, rather than with reading for information, the type of reading Rosenblatt (1978) calls "efferent" (p. 24). However, Goodman (1985), Smith (1985), Wittrock (1984), and Harste and his colleagues at Indiana (e.g., Harste, Woodward, & Burke, 1984) have attempted to apply transactional theories to all reading circumstances. Though there are some obvious difficulties in doing this (e.g., in explaining how someone learns from text or how someone reading for information assigns significance to text), the work in transactional reading grows out of the rich research in schema theory and the application of background knowledge to the act of reading; for example, Anderson (1985) speaks of a person who could "construct an interpretation of the sentence" (p. 373), and Adams and Collins (1985) discuss how the text "provides directions for the . . . reader as to how he should retrieve or construct the intended meaning from his own, previously acquired knowledge" (p. 406).

I might continue to reference the literature on reading research and theory in order to chronicle the number of times that reading researchers have used the notion of meaning and significance construction rather than more conservative notions of comprehension and reconstruction: that is, noting how there has been a subtle shift from a conceptualization of reader as meaning getter or meaning apprehender to a conceptualization of reader as meaning maker (Straw, 1990). However, in many cases, the use of a constructive conceptualization of reading, a transactional conceptualization of reading, is deeply embedded in interactive and communicative theories of the reading process, so that it is difficult to locate exactly when significant rethinking has occurred. Transactional theories, however, have knowledge generation as the *central* operation in their models. They also acknowledge a substantial contribution of the text to that knowledge construction.

Wittrock (1984) discusses a major aspect of his reading model as "reading comprehension as a generative process" and speaks of the "generative cognitive processes" (p. 77) that take place in any reading. He emphasizes the parallel nature of reading and writing in that they are both generative: "Good reading, like effective writing, involves generative cognitive processes that create meaning by building relations between the text and what we know, believe, and experience. The meaning is not only on the page, nor only in our memories. When we read, we generate meaning by relating parts of the text to one another and to our memories and our knowledge" (p. 77). Wittrock goes on to distinguish his reading model from those of the interactionists: "Generation, the central process of my model of reading comprehension, is not the same as semantic processing, schema building, or discovery learning. Generation is the process of constructing meaning, a representation, a model, or an explanation, for example, of words, sentences, paragraphs, and texts that agrees with our knowledge, logic, and experience, and that makes sense to us" (p. 79).

Although Wittrock's model has a strong decoding aspect and although he implies that decoding precedes comprehension, he views comprehension as the result of the transactions and negotiations between reader and text. He concludes from the studies he and his colleagues have carried out that invoking this generative transaction between reader and text increases comprehension ability and performance. "When readers construct relations between their knowledge or experience and the text, their comprehension and retention also tend to increase" (p. 82). In his studies described in the Jensen monograph (1984), however, presentation of the text generally preceded the generative acts of readers, thereby leading me to believe that the text itself is seen by Wittrock as the motivator of the transaction, rather than as the volition of the readers (as described by Hynds, in this volume, Chapter 10). Nonetheless, this is a substantial movement away from the communication models underlying previous interaction models of reading.

Harste, Woodward, and Burke (1984) have suggested a transactional view of language learning that they have applied informally to reading and have conceived of as a semiotic notion of transaction.[1] Within the field of reading and reading pedagogy, they identify a traditional behaviorist view that is similar to what I have called a transmission view of reading in which the learner (reader) is passive and the meaning resides in the environment (in the reading mode, this is the author and his or her environment); problems in learning and in reading are problems in the vehicle or the delivery system — the text. A second view they identify as "cognitive" (p. 58), i.e., a view similar to the translation and interaction conceptualizations in which reading and learning are dependent on the assimilative schemas of the learner; problems with comprehension, then, are problems with the skills and knowledge of the reader. Their third, and from their position, superior point of view is a transactional one. They suggest that "[m]eaning involves seeing objects as signs which have the potential to signify" (p. 58). They explain this view of language learning and, therefore, reading as follows:

> A transactional view of language ... assumes that meaning resides neither in the environment nor totally in the head of the language learner. Language is seen as open, and meaning is seen as triadic, the result of a mental setting actively attempting to make sense of a print setting (p. 57).

Goodman (1985) attempted to marry his earlier psycholinguistic model (an interactive model based on an underpinning of communication) with a transactional view in his "Unity in Reading." In his attempt to describe a unified theory of literacy, Goodman addressed the writing process, the characteristics of text, as well as the reading process. In his description of the transactional reading process, he states: "Though researchers may take macro or micro views of the reading process, it ultimately must be seen as construction of meaning from text. ... Most research is converging on the view that transactions between reader and text characteristics result in construction of meaning. This view makes the role of the reader a highly active one. It makes what the reader brings to the text as important as the text itself" (p. 827).

Goodman goes on to describe "dual texts," a notion that a reader constructs "a text parallel and closely related to the published text" (p. 827), though he emphasizes that the construction of a parallel text is not the end product in reading, that the end product is meaning. The construction of a parallel text is merely a step toward constructing meaning. Thus, meaning for the reader is mediated by the parallel text generated by the reader while she or he is grappling with the published text. This is not unlike Ruddell and Speaker's notion (1985) of "the text representation" (p. 756).

This parallel text is also very similar to Rosenblatt's (1978) conception of the "poem" (p. 12). She suggests that the poem is the result of the experience of reading, of "what [the reader] is living through during his relationship with that particular text" (p. 25), the implication being that the reader then views the reading experience (the poem) in determining meaning. Both Goodman and Rosenblatt imply that a reader could compare the self-generated text with the printed text in order to evaluate either the text or the experience of reading.

Transactional theories also suggest that the meanings of texts are "hidden away" in the reader, waiting to be drawn up and released during the act of reading. Readers are full of "possible meanings," and reading helps actualize those meanings (Iser, 1980). Bogdan (1986a) refers to these negotiations as a dialectic—a kind of conversation

between text and reader that results in constructed meanings—
syntheses between reader knowledge and text. Rosenblatt (1978)
refers to the creations of the reader as "the poem" (p. 12). Goodman
(1985) describes the transactional view of reading in the following
way:

> In a transactional view, both the knower and the known are trans-
> formed in the process of knowing. The reader is transformed as new
> knowledge is assimilated and accommodated. Both the reader's con-
> ceptual schemata and values are altered through reading compre-
> hension. Since the published text seems to be a reality that does not
> change its physical properties as a result of being read, how can it
> change during reading? The answer is that the reader is constructing
> a text parallel and closely related to the published text. It becomes a
> different text for each reader. The reader's text involves inferences,
> references, and coreferences based on schemata that the reader
> brings to the text. And it is this reader's text which the reader
> comprehends and on which any reader's later account of what was
> read is based (p. 827).

In some ways, the rhetoric of transaction is preceding an actual
change in the thinking about reading. Rosenblatt (1985b) makes this
claim in her article on the differences between transactional and
interactive conceptualizations of reading. She states: "I cannot accept
a blurring of the distinctions between, on the one hand, *transaction*,
transactional, and *transactional theory* and, on the other, *information
processing*, *interactive processing*, and *interaction*. The distinction
between *interaction* and *transaction* is basic" (p. 97). She goes on to
make her point about the differences by blasting the interactive
notions of reading and setting them against her description of transactional notions:

> Instead of trying to plaster over the distinction between the dualistic,
> mechanistic, linear, interactional view, in which the text, on the one
> hand, and the personality of the reader, on the other, can be separ-
> ately analyzed, with the impact of one on the other studied in a
> vacuum, we need to see the reading act as an event involving a
> particular individual and a particular text, happening at a particular
> time, under particular circumstances, in a particular social and
> cultural setting, and as part of the ongoing life of the individual and
> the group. We still can distinguish the elements, but we have to
> think of them, not as separate entities, but as aspects or phases of a
> dynamic process, in which all elements take on their character as
> part of the organically-interrelated situation. Instead of thinking of
> reading as a linear process, we have to think rather of a complex
> network or circuit of interrelationships, with reciprocal interplay
> (pp. 100–101).

Like interactive models and conceptualizations of reading compre-hension, transactional theories may be serving as a step to more productive and generative theories of reading—theories I am calling *constructionist* theories—that place the locus of meaning in reading more firmly with the reader and with the social experiences and social situations of reading. In the same vein, as Goodman suggested similarities between the transactions of author and the transactions of text, we are presently seeing attempts in the field that equate reading and composition—that suggest that there is a single literacy process applied either to the composition of text or the reading of text.

TRANSACTIONAL THEORIES OF LITERARY CRITICISM

The major work associated with transactional conceptualizations of reading has been done in literary critical theory rather than in reading comprehension. The amount of writing associated with these theories is enormous and includes the work done in Germany by reception theorists, in France by poststructuralists, and in Britain and North America by reader-response critics. Though I will not try to chronicle all the writing in this rich field, I will attempt to identify what these writers have in common and why I have identified them as transactionalists.

In the first place, they share a common emphasis on readers' construction of meaning within the context of the text itself. It is unclear whether these theorists see the text as the motivator of this construction or whether the text provides a set of constraints on the possible constructions a reader can make when reading a particular text. What *is* clear, however, is that meaning resides in the *activity* of reading, along with all the ramifications of that activity (e.g., the social circumstances, the background of the reader, the situation in which the reading is taking place).

A second notion that all of these theorists hold in common is related to the purposes for reading. Whereas previous literary critical theories held that reading was an act of communication, these writers assume that reading can have a wide range of purposes and functions, one of which *may* be communication, but that communication is certainly not the only, or, perhaps, not even the major, function or purpose in reading. Communication is only a purpose for reading when the needs of the individual reader are fulfilled by reading for communication. According to these theorists, reading is used to fulfill a personal set of needs of the reader. Holland (1980) puts it this way: "Each reader . . . re-creates the work in terms of his own identity theme" (p. 126) — that is, when reading addresses readers' own needs and actualizes their own themes.

Finally, what many (if not all) of these writers have in common is a pair of concepts related to text and mature reading. What differentiates this group from what I call *constructionists* (which I deal with later in this chapter) is a dependence on the text itself. They all see the text as a major player in the act of reading, a player who restricts the possible constructions of the reader. How these writers reconcile the constraints of the text with the constructive nature of reading is through the development of a kind of "mental text" or "hypothesized text" — a text that is created in the reader's mind during the act of reading, a mental text constructed from a complex interaction between the experience of reading, the situation of reading, and the reader's background knowledge and experience. This "mental text" is then compared to the "real text," and the mental representation is adjusted in the face of the printed text. Although this is, perhaps, an oversimplification of a number of diverse theories, my reading of the literature in this area leads me to believe that it is a common thread through many of the reader-response/reception theory critics. One of the possible criticisms, it seems to me, of this mental text-representation notion is that once that mental text is created, it is open to all the hermeneutic procedures or explications that were carried out on printed texts in earlier eras.

The other related concept shared by a majority of transactional critics is one of the "ideal reader," that is, a reader who is able to successfully unpack the reading experience and associate that experience with the appropriate background knowledge within the context of his or her own purposes for reading. In a general way, this "ideal reader" is the one who, given a personal background knowledge, the circumstances and purposes for reading, and a particular text, comes up with the appropriate transactions. These idealized readers were hypothesized, I think, to escape the charge of solipsism in interpretation and constructing meaning, so that teachers or other critics could somehow decide if one interpretation was more appropriate (more correct?) than another. Fish calls this the "informed reader"; Culler, the "ideal" or "qualified reader"; Riffaterre, the "super-reader" (in Brooke-Rose, 1980, pp. 121–122).

The point of this discussion of mental text and idealized readers is that transactional conceptualizations of literary reading still maintain some conservative notions about the unity and integrity of text and what is meant by an acceptable or appropriate reading. This, perhaps more than anything else, is what distinguishes them from the constructionists discussed later in this chapter.

I have dated the onset of transactional notions at about 1970 based on the publication in the late 1960s and the early 1970s of papers in reception theory by Jauss and in reader-response criticism by Fish. However, transactional conceptualizations of reading have their history in the early work of Rosenblatt with the publication of *Literature as Exploration* in 1938. My dating, however, of 1970 is associated with the time at which reader-response criticism became generally known in North America.

Jane Tompkins (1980) identifies one of the major transactionalists in literary reading as Stanley Fish. She says of Fish's transactional view of reading: "[He] makes the crucial move in reader-oriented criticism by removing the literary text from the center of critical attention and replacing it with the reader's cognitive activity. The decisive shift in focus opens a new field of inquiry. If meaning is no longer a property of text but a product of the reader's activity, the question to answer is not 'what do poems mean?' or even 'what do poems do?' but 'how do readers make meaning?'" (p. xvii).

Briefly, this emphasis on "how do readers make meaning?" has been investigated under a number of rubrics. Suleiman (1980), in her introduction to "Varieties of Audience-Oriented Criticism" (p. 5), categorizes them under six varieties: "rhetorical; semiotic and structuralist; phenomenological; subjective and psychoanalytical; sociological and historical; and hermeneutic" (pp. 6–7). Two of these categories, rhetorical, and semiotic and structuralist, I have identified as belonging to interaction conceptualizations of reading (see the previous chapter), although there are certainly semioticians who qualify as transactionalist; rhetorical criticism, packaged somewhat differently, is making a reappearance as a constructionist conceptualization of reading. For the most part, however, these two categories belong to older and more conservative traditions than the others. The last category, hermeneutic, for me is not a category of criticism at all, although I understand why Suleiman has used the terminology; hermeneutics, either positive or negative (as in the criticism of Hirsch in the first case and in that of Derrida in the second), is an activity related to all criticism in its attempt to make meaning out of the act of reading (either by pursuing its unity or the destruction of its unity).[2] The other three categories, however, fall clearly within transactional conceptualizations of literary theory: (1) *phenomenological*, (2) *subjective and psychoanalytic*, and (3) *sociological and historical*. I deal briefly with the underpinnings of each of these points of view and attempt to identify some of the authors generally associated with them.

Phenomenological

Phenomenological criticism is most often associated with a group of critics from Germany referred to under the rubric of reception theory. According to Suleiman (1980), "Phenomenological critics are concerned with the experience whereby individual readers (or listeners or spectators) appropriate the work or art . . . whereby they *realize* it. The act of realization is what transforms a text . . ." (p. 22). The reception theorists believe that the literary text (as opposed to the printed text) *becomes* literary through the act of reading; this is similar to Rosenblatt's concept (1978) of the *poem*. Iser (1980), perhaps the literary phenomenologist best known in North America, states it this way: "The work is more than the text, for the text only takes on life when it is realized, and furthermore the realization is by no means independent of the individual disposition of the reader—though this in turn is acted upon by the different patterns of the text. The convergence of text and reader brings the literary work into existence, and this convergence can never be precisely pinpointed, but must always remain virtual, as it is not to be identified with the reality of the text or with the individual disposition of the reader" (p. 50). This point of view highlights the phenomenologists' emphasis on the transaction between reader and text, similar to Rosenblatt's description (1978). It also highlights the importance of the printed text in the phenomenological perspective. What Iser (1980) proposes is that the printed text allows for a range of possible meanings for any reader; he suggests, however, that the effective reading of any text must be done within the possibilities allowed by the printed text itself. He describes the act of reading as "an active interweaving of anticipation and retrospection" (p. 57). He then suggests that "the impressions that arise as a result of this [reading] process will vary from individual to individual, but only within the limits imposed by the written . . . text" (p. 57).

Another phenomenologist, Jauss (1982), suggests that reading is made up of three fundamental operations: *poiesis*, *aisthesis*, and *catharsis*. *Poiesis* is, according to Holub (1984), the productive side of aesthetic pleasure such that it is a "cognition dependent on what one can do, on a form of action that tries and tests so that understanding and producing can become one . . ." (Jauss, 1982, p. 51). *Aisthesis*, on the other hand, is the receptive act in reading—aesthetic perception. *Catharsis* is the interaction between art and recipient. Jauss, like many reception theorists, suggests that reading is a complex construct that depends on the perception of the text (*aisthesis*), the interaction of the text with the reader (*catharsis*), and the ability of the reader to actively construct meaning within the parameters set forth by the text (*poiesis*). Though aspects of a phenomenological approach appear to be committed to a communication model, these writers speak of communication as a kind of realization of reader possibilities. Reading is communicative only in that it sets parameters around meaning, rather than determines it, and that within that broad concept of communication, the act of reading is a transactive realization or actualization on the part of the reader.

Subjective and Psychoanalytic

Subjective and psychoanalytic theories of reading and response are most often associated with the writings of reader-response critics such as David Bleich (1980) and Norman Holland (1980). As characterized by Suleiman (1980), these subjective critics are "interested in the influence of personality and personal history on literary interpretation" (p. 27). Holland's work grew out of the traditional application of psychoanalytic theory to reading. In his early work, according to Suleiman (1980), he "sought to reconcile the objectivist assumptions of New Criticism with an orthodox Freudianism" (p. 28). In many ways, however, his later work abandoned both the objectivist assumptions and orthodox Freudianism and, instead, centered on the issue of how "individual readers 're-created' texts according to their own personalities" (Suleiman, 1980, p. 29). Although Holland maintained many of the elements and the terminology of psychoanalysis in explaining how individual readers recreate texts, he abandoned the "structures" of psychoanalysis. According to his present stance, a reader's "transaction" with a text is such that "interpretation [including comprehension] is a function of identity ... all of us, as we read, use the literary work to symbolize and finally to replicate ourselves" (Holland, 1980, p. 126). Holland, then, emphasizes the essentially constructive and transactive nature of reading by positing that reading is an attempt to explain experience through our own subjective point of view, a point of view developed through our prior experiences, which are, by their very nature, subjective.

Bleich (1980) supports this subjective point of view, even though he rejects the psychoanalytic terminology used by Holland (Tompkins, 1980). He suggests that reading is a subjective act and that we must reject our concept of printed text as "objective reality" because reading is not an objective act, that the experience of reading and the development of meaning can only be realized by a reader constructing meaning via background experience, ideology, prior knowledge, and purposes for reading.

In his discussion of the epistemological assumptions in the study of response, Bleich (1980) reviews the underlying assumptions associated with subjective reading and concludes with a discussion of what these assumptions say about language and literature pedagogy:

> When knowledge is no longer conceived as objective, the purpose of pedagogical institutions from the nursery through the university is to synthesize knowledge rather than to pass it along [transmission]: schools become the regular agency of subjective initiative. Because language use and the interpretive practices that follow from it underlie the processes of understanding, the pedagogical situations in which consciousness of language and literature is exercised establish the pattern of motives a student will bring to deal in his own pursuit of knowledge (p. 159).

In my terminology, then, this is a call for schools to help students employ reading and literature to realize or actualize their own subjective purposes.

Sociological and Historical

According to Suleiman (1980), sociological and historical criticism "seeks to investigate reading as essentially a collective phenomenon. The individual reader is seen, in this perspective, as part of a *reading public*" (p. 32). Suleiman identifies Jauss as a major figure in this sociohistorical category, although he can also be identified as a phenomenologist (none of the categories is discrete). She does not, however, identify the major new ideological critics within this area—a group of writers that I feel best fit here. At first glance, one might immediately classify Stanley Fish (1980) as a major sociological critic because of his concepts about the social construction of knowledge and of "interpretive communities" (Fish, 1980, p. 182). However, my sense of Fish is that he is more constructive than the ideological critics; I feel that he belongs, at least in his later writings, to the constructionist critics that I deal with in the next section. The ideological critics, on the other hand, attempt to demystify literature by identifying the ideologies present in text and attempting to get readers to challenge and critique those ideologies. This is usually associated with a "dialectic" (Bogdan, in this volume, Chapter 7) with the text that attempts to tease out the historical ontology and genesis of the text, the sociological assumptions presented in the text, and the reader's response to those things. They argue for readers to challenge the text (a transactional process) rather than be a passive recipient of the text. The most articulate proponents of this type of critical activity are the poststructuralist Marxist critics, notably Belsey (1980), Robinson (1987), and Said (1983), and poststructuralist feminist critics, such as

Schweickart (1986) and some aspects of Kolodny (1985). Bogdan (in this volume, Chapter 7) discusses the entire issue of the relationship between ideology and reading and develops the argument that ideology is central to reading and critical activity. The important aspect here, it seems to me, is to point out that sociological and historical critics, unlike their colleagues in subjective criticism, argue for a detachment from the act of reading (see Bogdan and Morgan, in this volume, Chapters 7 and 14, respectively) — a healthy skepticism about the truth (or even the meaning) of literature as a way of actualizing oneself during the act of reading. Most authors suggest that this self-actualization requires the activity of "dialectic" (Bogdan, 1986), an activity through which the reader can negotiate meaning as a partner in the act of reading rather than accepting tenets thought to be embodied in literature. The reader is, thereby, cast in the role of critic, skeptic, and questioner — clearly transactional notions.

READERS COMPOSING TEXTS: CONSTRUCTIONIST CONCEPTUALIZATIONS OF READING

Predicting future developments in any field is risky business, and I am sensitive to the difficulty in doing this, particularly in a field as rich as reading theory. However, I am going to attempt to hypothesize where I think the field of reading-comprehension theory and, to a lesser extent, literary theory are going in the next decade or so. Two major movements have led me to believe that the field is heading for a notion of how reading processes take place that is more constructionist than transactional. The first of these movements is toward the integration of notions of reading and writing that will lead, I think, to a single conceptualization of a *literacy process*, a single overarching explanation of both reading *and* writing. The second of these movements is toward the "socialization" of reading (see Hunt, in this volume, Chapter 4).

Integration of Reading and Writing

Though the relationships between reading and writing have been investigated for years, researchers have found only weak statistical correlations between the two (see Dahl, 1981; Hopkins, 1981). However, as new thinking about the writing process is emerging, I have been struck by a similarity between the two processes, not in the products each produces (which in some ways was the problem with previous correlational research between reading and writing), but in the hypothesized patterns of how reading and writing operate. This has led me to investigate the possibility of applying compositional models to the reading process. I refer to this notion as "reader as rhetor, text as audience," because it seems to me that reading can be conceptualized as an act in which the reader is a composer of meaning (a rhetor) and employs the text in the same way a writer employs audience awareness—as a litmus test of the appropriateness of the meaning being constructed. I have chosen a rhetorical model because it seems that both the reader and the writer are faced with a rhetorical problem, and not only *a* rhetorical problem, but with the *same* rhetorical problem. If we examine current rhetorical "canons and divisions" (Johnson, 1986, pp. 207−208), we find a close resemblance between the problems facing a reader in constructing meaning and the rhetorical problems facing a writer, particularly in the assumptions about prior knowledge and composing procedures (see, e.g., Beale, 1987; Conners, Ede, & Lunsford, 1984; Johnson, 1986).

In the reader as rhetor notion, the hypothesis-generating/text-confirmation acts of reading are similar, if not identical, to the discovery, organizing, and drafting/revising stages of the writing process as hypothesized by cognitive psychologists or the invention and arrangement categories suggested by rhetoricians. As Lindberg (Newkirk, 1986) has pointed out, "To comprehend what is written requires the same kind of trial-and-error process that produced the writing in the first place ... [They both] require that one be allowed the experience of error and the feedback that accompanies it" (p. 152).

Although the specifics of the models change, when composition or rhetoric is applied to reading, the constructive dynamic in the process of reading is analogous to the constructive dynamic in the writing process. It should be noted here that in this conceptualization, one cannot map the reading process *directly* onto the writing process (or vice versa), because the particulars of each process may be different, and the emphasis that one or another subprocess receives in reading may be different from the emphasis the same subprocess receives in writing. Nonetheless, the *dynamic* remains the same, in that similar activities or processes that lead to both meaning development and text development are the same in both reading and writing. The *productive rhetorical* nature of reading is the same as the *productive rhetorical* nature of writing.

If we accept the construction of a "parallel text" as suggested by Goodman (1985) or the "poem" as hypothesized by Rosenblatt (1978), or any of the other "mental texts" suggested by transactionalists, then it is a short step to a compositional (constructionist) model of reading—in fact, the transactionalist theorists would probably argue that they are already supporting one.

In the first place, both reading and writing are motivated by basic personal purposes for the act of literacy. What the purpose of writing is significantly affects both the process itself and the products generated (Flower & Hayes, 1980; Hillocks, 1986). By the same token, the purposes for reading significantly affect both the process itself and the product of reading (Lavery & Straw, 1986; Vipond & Hunt, 1984). Readers who are reading for information employ significantly different strategies in reading than those who are reading for pleasure. Readers who are reading to reinforce already held beliefs read in significantly different fashions than those who are reading to discover new information. I am suggesting that this basic underlying driver — purpose or intent — is the same in both reading and writing.

Secondly, the knowledge sources that inform reading and writing are, I think, identical. Both draw on the same knowledge bases such as episodic memory, visual memory, syntactic and semantic knowledge, world knowledge, and lexical knowledge. The act of recognition in reading, then, can be conceptualized as the same as the act of generation in writing.

Thirdly, I believe that this overriding "metaphor" of reading as writing cannot necessarily be applied at the letter-by-letter level, or even, probably, at the word-by-word level. An attempt to explain the moment-by-moment act of reading and the processing of letters, phonograms, and words has been one of the major problems of previous models of reading and has led reading researchers into problematic debates about word recognition and processing (e.g., Chall, 1983) rather than more pertinent discussions about how readers assign significance to what they read. It has been problematic because researchers have assumed that if they could account for the moment-by-moment nature of reading (e.g., Just & Carpenter, 1980/1985), they could then account for the larger "meaning-getting" aspects of reading. This appears backwards to me. Since the primary purpose of reading is comprehension (Durkin, 1983) — and this term is really too narrow to account for the unique meaning-generating activities of real readers in real reading circumstances — models of reading have to be powered by the notion of meaning and significance. However, researchers and theorists have become embattled in discussions of decoding and recoding to the point that they have conceived of meaning as the *product* of the process rather than as the *single purpose* in reading and, therefore, the major activity in the act. Work in composition instruction has suggested that in order for meaning construction to drive the act of composing, "editing" activities should be placed near the end of the writing activities, even though it is clear that some level of editing takes place at each "stage" of writing. If reading is indeed a meaning-building process, that is, if meaning construction powers reading as it powers composing, then recoding and word identification should operate in a role similar to editing—it should be delayed in order not to interfere with the meaning construction. Word and letter identification in reading are analogous to activities associated with editing for an audience in the act of composing. That is, the primary activators and controllers of meaning are the purposes with which readers approach text, and their "drafting" of meaning possibilities in text.

Another important similarity that has been observed between reading and writing is that both rely on elaborate monitoring systems that appear to operate in the same way in both processes. These monitoring systems tell writers when the writing is or is not achieving their purposes and give them information as to how to solve the writing problems when they arise. In the same way, readers have monitoring systems that tell them when the reading is or is not achieving their purposes and give them information as to how to solve reading problems when they arise. These processes, though they result in different *physical* products, result in analogous *cognitive* products—meaning.

Without overprescribing what compositional theories of reading might look like, I would like to suggest how each "element" of the rhetoric for writing might be worked out in a rhetoric for reading.

First, the discovery process in writing is probably very similar to the hypothesis-generating and schema-instantiation processes in reading. Writers, in discovering what they wish to say about a particular topic, pull up their "general schema" about the content of that topic and then explore that schema and related schema in discovering what it is that they want to write about. Readers do approximately the same thing: in preparing to read about a particular content, readers pull up the schema associated with that topic and employ it in generating or constructing the meaning of the text. Studies in such prereading activities as advance organizers (Tierney & Cunningham, 1984) and the cultural schema of readers (Reynolds, Taylor, Steffenson, Shirey, & Anderson, 1981; Rogers-Zegarra & Singer, 1985; Steffenson, Joagdev, & Anderson, 1979) suggest that these activities are similar to the initial discovery through which writers go and that they fulfill an early organizing function in reading just as they do in composing.

Second, one of the ways in which writers explore the topics about which they are going to write and probe those topics while they are drafting is through a set of self-questioning procedures. The same appears to be true for readers: at the beginning of a text, the successful reader generates some general questions about the text which she or he will attempt to address in the reading (as related, as in writing, to the specific purposes for reading the text) and then adjusts those questions or generates new ones during the act of reading itself—the reading analog to the drafting process. Readers and writers, further-more, both monitor their own reading and writing and keep adjusting their strategies for meaning construction on an ongoing basis. Both these processes are analogous to what has been described as higher-level revising processes in writing. Writers revise their meaning as they monitor and subsequently work through their text; readers do the same.

In terms of the organizing aspects of writing and how they are parallel in the act of reading, they appear to be very similar in that the writer has at least a general notion of how (at a macro level) the text she or he is generating will ultimately be cast. That is not to say that the final product always reflects that early organizing activity, but without some hypothesis about the overall structure of the piece of writing, the writer probably could not continue to draft. The same is true of the reader. Before approaching the text, the reader has some notion of the overall macro structure of the discourse she or he is reading; the final product may not always confirm that hypothesis, but the reader could not continue to read—to generate or construct meaning—unless there was a general notion of the macro structure of text.

One of the problems in this compositional notion of reading is the role of the text itself. I am hypothesizing that the dynamic between reader and text is the same as the dynamic between writer and audience. That is, as the writer has in mind the audience for which she or he is writing, as the writer says to himself or herself, "What does the audience know?" "What does the audience need to know?" and, metaphorically, at least, as the writer keeps turning to the audience and saying, "Isn't that right?" so the reader has in mind what the text knows, what the text is likely to "need" in terms of meaning, and the reader is turning to the text and saying, "Isn't that right?" Recently at a conference on literacy, Gordon Wells pointed out that audience perception in writing is significantly different from text checking in reading, as I am suggesting it here, in that writers do not check with their audiences with the same regularity as readers check with their texts—that readers are regularly checking with the text and revising meaning during reading, whereas evidence on the writing process suggests that writers check with their own audience perceptions rarely. Competent writers often "put aside" their audiences in the passion of composing and may only come back to them during revision (see Roen & Willey, 1988), whereas competent readers are continually and frequently checking with their texts. Wells's comment is correct—the *frequency* of checking is different between reading and writing; however, I would argue that the *dynamic* is the same. Readers may read with much more text awareness than writers may write with audience awareness, but readers appear to use the text *in the very same way* that writers use audience.

This view of reading suggests that readers really create meaning before encountering the reality of the text, and that readers have "drafts" of meaning in their heads as they proceed during the act of reading; while reading, they are constantly revising that draft (the hypothesized meaning) in light of their audience—the text itself. This delays the particulars of word recognition, phonic analysis, etc. to much later in the reading process than has been hypothesized before—it places "decoding" and "recoding" in the role of the "editing" stage in writing, rather than at the beginning of the process. For me, perhaps a powerful indication of the similarities of these processes is suggested by similarities between the problems encountered by both weak readers and novice writers. Studies of the attributes of novice writers suggest that they are overattentive to their audience and overattentive to the particular forms of writing from which audiences will make judgments about the writer (e.g., spelling, punctuation) and that since they attend to those aspects of writing too early in the composing cycle, they are inhibited in their ability to create and manipulate meaning. By the same token, studies of weak readers suggest that they are overattentive to the particulars of text (e.g., recoding, word identification), and since they attend to those aspects too early in the reading cycle, they are similarly inhibited in their ability to read and interpret text—that is, to create and manipulate meaning (Samuels, 1985).

Recently, while working on this chapter, I was also reviewing recent work in research and theory in composition. With very little difficulty, I found that I could substitute "reading" each time a major concept in composition was used in relation to "writing" or "composing." Concepts such as "rhetorical problem" (Flower & Hayes, 1980, p. 21) could easily be descriptive of the purpose-setting and task-definition activities of mature readers. Descriptions of long-term memory (Bereiter & Scardamalia, 1984; 1987) could easily be discussions of the long-term memory of readers, with the concepts of topic knowledge, audience awareness (Bracewell, Scardamalia, & Bereiter, 1978; Crowhurst & Piche, 1979) and knowledge of writing plans (Flower & Hayes, 1980; Scardamalia & Bereiter, 1985) being substituted respectively with readers' *knowledge of topic*, readers' *knowledge of discourse possibilities*, and readers' *knowledge of reading strategies*. The planning aspect of compositional and rhetorical theories could be adopted almost whole to reading, since generating, discovering, or invention could be analogous to reading's *hypothesis generation*—in particular, predicting topic and accessing schema; concepts of organizing could easily be associated with the concepts of *organizational schema* or *hypothesized discourse structure* in reading. Concepts around goal setting could be related directly to readers' *purpose setting* and the subsequent *choice of a particular reading strategy*, based on an analysis of the *discourse possibilities* and the *hypothesized topic*. Translating (Flower & Hayes, 1981) and transcribing (Moffett & Wagner, 1983) is analogous to readers' *sentence- and word-level predictions* (use of context to make meaning). Monitoring in writing (Bereiter & Scardamalia, 1987) could describe, in many ways, *monitoring* in reading as described by such researchers as Markman (1981) or the situation described by Baker and Brown (1985) as "[r]ealizing that one has failed to understand" (p. 357). Concepts such as reviewing and revising are analogous to descriptions of *metacognitive behaviors* discussed by Baker and Brown (1985) as "what to do when comprehension failures occur." They continue to say that "[t]his involves a number of strategic decisions. The first decision is whether or not remedial action is even necessary, a decision that will depend largely on the purposes for reading. . . . If the reader decides to take strategic action, a number of options are available" (p. 357). Numerous authors, in addition, discuss the role of editing in composition and suggest that editing, like recoding in reading, is embedded in other processes of greater importance hierarchically (e.g., purpose setting).

This attempt to point out the similarities in observations about writing and similar observations about reading is not to say that any particular "model" or "theory" of composition completely describes accurately the activities of all writers in all circumstances, nor do models of reading completely describe the activities of all readers in all reading circumstances. What is striking, however, is that if we stand back from the particular *terminology* of either reading or writing (such as discovery, organizing, schema knowledge, decoding), we find that most, if not all, of the constructs described by composition specialists have analogous or identical constructs in reading. The knowledge underlying composition and the operations that expert writers employ in creating text appear to be similar to the knowledge underlying reading and the operations that competent readers employ in making sense of text.

Tierney and Pearson (1984) have made a case for such a view of analogous processes in their discussion of a "composing model of reading" (p. 33). They state:

> We believe that at the heart of understanding reading and writing
> connections one must begin to view reading and writing as similar
> processes of meaning construction. Both are acts of composing. From a
> reader's perspective, meaning is created as a reader uses his back-
> ground of experience together with the author's cues to come to
> grips both with what the writer is getting him to do or think *and*

what the reader decides and creates for himself. ... Few would disagree that writers compose meaning ... readers also compose meaning (that there is not meaning on the page until a reader decides there is) (pp. 33–34).

Tierney and Pearson have attempted to describe a model of reading that closely approximates a model of composition. They include five similar or identical processes in reading and writing: planning, drafting, aligning, revising, and monitoring. Planning, they say, involves goal setting and knowledge mobilization. These two activities "[t]aken together ... reflect some commonly accepted behaviors such as setting purposes, evaluating one's current state of knowledge about a topic, focusing or narrowing topics and goals, and self-questioning. ... The goals that readers or writers set have a symbiotic relationship with the knowledge they mobilize, and together they influence what is produced or understood in a text" (p. 34). They define drafting as "the refinement of meaning which occurs as readers and writers deal directly with print on the page." They go on to note that "getting started is just as important a step in reading [as it is in writing]. What every reader needs, like every writer, is a first draft" (p. 36). Drafting in reading is the point at which readers begin to compare their hypotheses about text meaning with the printed text itself. This process is also carried out in the alignment process—which includes revision—hypothesized by Tierney and Pearson. They state: "If readers are to develop some control over and a sense of discovery with the models of meaning they build, they must approach text with the same deliberation, time, and reflection that a writer employs as she revises a text. They must examine their developing interpretations and view the models they build as draft-like in quality—subject to revision" (p. 37). They hypothesize a monitoring operation that is similar to the monitoring operation identified by composition researchers—an operation that evaluates the appropriateness or "goodness of fit" of the construction of meaning in light of the text, assigns attention to important aspects that need revision, accesses strategies for revision, and engages the reader with a dialogue with "the inner reader" (p. 42), similar to the dialectical operation identified by Bogdan (1986a). They conclude their article in the following way:

> To reiterate, we view both reading and writing as acts of composing. We see these acts of composing as involving continuous, recurring, and recursive transactions among readers and writers, their respective inner selves, and their perceptions of each other's goals and desires. Consider the reader's role as we envision it. At the same time as the reader considers what he perceives to be the author's intentions (or what the reader perceives to be what the author is trying to get the reader to do or think), he negotiates goals with his inner self (or

what he would like to achieve). With these goals being continuously negotiated (sometimes embedded within each other) the reader proceeds to take different alignments (critic, co-author, editor, character, reporter, eye witness, etc.) as he uses features from his own experiential arrays and what he perceives to be arrayed by the author in order to create a model of meaning from text. These models of meanings must assume a coherent, holistic quality in which everything fits together. The development of these models of meaning occurs from the vantage point of different alignments which the reader adopts with respect to these arrays. It is from these vantage points that the various arrays are perceived, and their position adjusted such that the reader's goals and desire for a sense of completeness are achieved (p. 43).

In Tierney and Pearson's (1984) description of a composing model of reading, we see that, although more traditional concepts of unity and coherence are still proposed, the purposes of reading—actualization rather than communication—have been radically changed from an interaction point of view, and the kind of knowledge needed to be a successful reader has been redefined in the direction of procedural knowledge, procedural knowledge that is similar—if not identical—to the procedural knowledge needed for composing. The locus of meaning, furthermore, is identified with the reader; the text serves the role of meaning arbiter or monitor (much as the audience serves in composing) rather than determiner as in more formalist notions of reading.

Social Construction of Knowledge

Another major movement that I feel is influencing the way in which researchers and theorists approach reading is the current interest in social construction of knowledge, as hypothesized by Vygotsky in learning theory, and by such reading and writing researchers as Bruffee, 1984, Goodman (1985), Harste, Woodward, & Burke (1984), and Vipond, Hunt, & Wheeler (1987). The social construction of knowledge—that knowledge is socially patterned and conditioned, that coming to know is a result of the social experiences and interactions we have had, and that all knowledge and knowledge construction are essentially social acts—fits neatly into the constructionist notions of reading (Bakhtin, 1981). The impact of these on the "literacy process" is that we not only view reading and writing as a single act of literacy, but that our subsequent models of reading attempt to identify where knowledge comes from (from social interactions) and how meaning construction is mediated by social experiences. It further suggests that since all knowledge is socially constructed and that since knowledge of the literacy process is one of those knowledges, literacy is both profoundly constructive and profoundly social. Russ Hunt and Susan Hynds (both in this volume, Chapters 4 and 10, respectively) consider this social construction aspect of literacy and make similar suggestions.

The reader-response critic who most nearly approximates this "socialized" view of reading is Stanley Fish (1980). Fish suggests that readers employ particular "interpretive strategies" (p. 180) in order to assign or construct meaning from text. Fish states, in speaking of himself as a meaning maker, "I am immediately predisposed to perform certain acts, to 'find,' by looking for, themes,... to confer significances,... to mark out 'formal' units.... My disposition to perform these acts...constitutes a set of interpretive strategies, which, when they are put into execution, become the large part of reading. This is to say, interpretive strategies are not put into execution after reading [as is hypothesized by linear models of reading and response]; they are the shape of reading, and because they are the shape of reading, they give texts their shape, *making them* rather ... than arising from them" (pp. 179–180, emphasis added). According to Fish, these interpretive strategies are the mechanism through which readers make or construct meaning out of text. He tells a story about interpretive strategies and Augustine that so illustrates this notion that it is worth quoting:

> [I]t has always been possible to put into action interpretive strategies designed to make all text one, or to put it more accurately, to be forever making the same text. Augustine urges just such a strategy, for example, in *On Christian Doctrine* where he delivers the "rule of faith" which is of course a rule of interpretation. It is dazzlingly simple: everything in the Scriptures, and indeed in the world when it is properly read, points to (bears the meaning of) God's love for us and our answering responsibility to love our fellow creatures for His sake. If only you should come upon something which does not at first seem to bear this meaning, that "does not literally pertain to virtuous behavior or to the truth of faith," you are then to take it "to be figurative" and proceed to scrutinize it "until an interpretation contributing to the reign of charity is produced." This then is both a stipulation of what meaning there is [what meanings are possible] and a set of directions for finding it, which is of course a set of directions—of interpretive strategies—for making it (p. 181).

Where do we learn any set of particular interpretive strategies? Fish answers that question with the notion of "interpretive communities" (p. 182). Interpretive communities are groups of individuals who share the same interpretive strategies, and these particular strategies are either negotiated by the members of the social group (they are socially negotiated) or they are learned by any particular individual as she or he becomes a member of the group (they are socially patterned). Fish makes it very plain, however, that interpretive strategies derived from membership in particular interpretive communities are not strategies for reading texts — "but for writing texts, for constituting their properties and assigning their intentions. In other words these strategies exist prior to the act of reading and therefore determine the shape of what is read ..." (p. 182).

A FINAL WORD

It seems to me that this constructive notion of reading, this compositional view of both the reading and interpretive processes at work, this socially mediated view of literacy, is the direction of the future. The reader has been recognized, finally, in the reading act; it has become clear to me that the act of reading is a meaning-generating activity rather than a meaning-getting activity. The challenge for the future, then, is to adequately describe how readers compose texts.

NOTES

1. It is unclear how Harste and his associates reconcile their semiotic notions of reading with their transactional notions; they have attempted, it seems to me, to marry a structuralist/interactive conceptualization of reading with a transactional one, attempting to serve both masters at once. Though semiotics and transaction are not necessarily anomalous terms, they do suggest a different "contract," a different dynamic, among reader, author, and text. I suspect that they hold a transactional view of reading but have couched it in the terminology of structuralism and semiotics.

2. Hermeneutics is related to methods of interpretation — how a reader interprets a text — and grew out of work in biblical interpretation. Traditionally, hermeneutics was used as a means of interpreting one biblical passage in light of another, a kind of semantic intertextual analysis, and was later used as a means of interpreting passages in light of the social context in which they were written. The term has been adopted by literary critics to describe the process of interpreting any text, and in that way, could be applied to any critical activity, from the historical criticism of the nineteenth century to reader-response criticism. Suleiman (1980) differentiates between positive hermeneutics, which attempts to account for the unity of text (or rather which attempts to ascribe a unified interpretation to any particular text), and negative hermeneutics, which attempts to deconstruct the text.

CHAPTER 4

THE PARALLEL SOCIALIZATION OF READING RESEARCH AND LITERARY THEORY

Russell A. Hunt

THE STORY SO FAR

Gaps between disciplines—like sociopolitical borders of all kinds—are more difficult to bridge than it might seem they ought to be. In a panel discussion at a conference on theories of reading in 1981, for instance, I heard a well-known literary theorist casually observe that, as everyone knew, after all there really were no theories of reading. Had that conference not been determinedly and aggressively inter-disciplinary (that is to say, had its organizers not dragooned into it three or four people from disciplines other than literary theory), I am convinced that no one would have challenged, or even much noticed, that observation.

As it happened, however—and has been recounted elsewhere (Hoetker, 1982)—on the same panel there happened to be a reading specialist from Indiana University, Robert Carey, who pointed out that there were indeed a number of elaborate, thoughtful, and useful theories of reading, and observed that the creator of one of the most important, Louise Rosenblatt, happened to be present at the con-ference. It was not clear from the ensuing discussion whether the literary theorist was convinced that Rosenblatt's (1978) theory of reading—or those of Kenneth Goodman (1967) or Philip Gough

(1972), for that matter—really met his criteria for what might constitute such a theory. It was clear from the coversations over coffee afterward, though, that the almost complete lack of comprehension was mutual. As Carey argued, none of the literary theorists in the room seemed to be aware of the mammoth effort in psychological and educational circles toward understanding the reading process. Neither did they appear to see that it might have anything to do with their own attempt to understand the nature of the literary experience. But by the same token, the few lonely education people at the conference simply did not understand what the literary theorists were doing—how, for instance, they could possibly have such a lack of interest in generalizable conclusions about common patterns, or such a disdain for the hard work of empirical observation and experiment, or why they would show such an interest in unique, individual, irreproducible, and peculiar interpretations of particular texts. It was apparent, in other words, that neither group had any clear idea what the other meant when they used the word "theory."

Since that time (and before it as well), there have been many calls for more communication between the two domains (for one particularly persuasive one, see Weaver, 1985). And some steps have been made: a conference at Carnegie-Mellon University in 1984, for example, celebrated the institution there of a formal program intended to straddle the borders between empirical and purely humanistic, between educational/psychological and aesthetïc/literary, between practical and speculative approaches to the understanding of how people deal with written texts (Waller, 1985; McCormick, 1985).

Even so, any look at the history of this activity makes clear that large gaps remain. Linguists have not, in general, been aware of the work of educational theorists, and vice versa; cognitive psychologists studying reading processes have not known about (or have held in contempt) ethnographic case studies of literacy learners, and vice versa (see Guthrie & Hall, 1984); reader-response critics working in literary theory have rarely heard the names everyone working in discourse theory cites daily, and so forth.

It is hardly surprising that disciplines arising out of such different fundamental sets of assumptions, occupying such different positions in the social structure of universities and the scholarly community, and with such superficially different histories, should have a difficult time establishing regular and fruitful contact. In some ways, it is only an instance of the mutual incomprehension between what C. P. Snow (1959) labeled the "two cultures" of empirical science and humanism. As a graduate student in English literature in the 1960s, I—with all of my colleagues—was imbued with a healthy, dismissive New Critical contempt for the narrow, trade-school practicality of schools of education, and a hostile skepticism toward the behaviorist, rat-maze experimentalism of psychology. I infer that my colleagues in departments of education and psychology were absorbing a symmetrical set of attitudes toward the fuzzy, self-absorbed, and dilettantish aestheticism of the snobs in the English department across campus.

From a more inclusive historical perspective, however, this tradition of mutual incomprehension and hostility is surprising indeed. To study the history of any one of these disciplines over the past third of a century or so is to be struck with some remarkable parallels and similarities. Historically, it is no accident that the two fields in the late 1980s have come to exhibit the similarities so persuasively outlined by Constance Weaver (1985) and by W. John Harker (1987, 1988/ 1989), among others. And, of course, some similarity between their histories is only to be expected. Neither field exists as an island unto itself: both are firmly situated in an intellectual geography whose large geological shifts and political upheavals are felt in every principality, however isolated it may think itself.

It is not, for example, merely an innocent coincidence that two books that had revolutionary impacts on the field of literary theory and language understanding respectively—Northrop Frye's *Anatomy of Criticism* and Noam Chomsky's *Syntactic Structures*—were published in the very same year, 1957. Each of these books can be said to have brought the structuralist revolution home to its discipline (though in quite different ways). The subsequent history of reading-comprehension research, through the gradual abandonment of behaviorist principles and methods, the cognitivist revolution, and the rise of computer modeling and psycholinguistics, parallels in a surprising way the gradual decline of the New Criticism on the one hand, and the rise of deconstruction, semiotic criticism, and reader-response theory on the other.

It is instructive to trace those parallels, paying particular attention to the continuing similarities between the disciplinary revolutions occurring in these two fields in the late 1980s. As reading comprehension moves toward a social model of written language, literary criticism moves toward what is being called "The New Pragmatics." It is equally useful to speculate on some of the benefits likely to ensue as this pair of long-separated twins is at last finally brought together.

The stories of the two disciplines are not unfamiliar ones, but are worth retelling—in part because both are not often equally well known to the same people. If you know much about literary theory and how it has developed in the last half-century, you're probably not very familiar with developments in studies of reading comprehension—and, of course, vice versa. And to contemplate the two stories together is, I think, to encounter some remarkable parallels.

I should make clear that in recounting these stories, I am not attempting an exhaustive literature review; rather, I want to describe some broad patterns with a few illustrative examples. There is a wealth of examples of research studies that fit the pattern I am describing — and there is also, naturally enough, a wealth of examples of other kinds of research going on at the same time. I believe, however, that the general pattern is obvious and powerful.

READING AND LANGUAGE-COMPREHENSION RESEARCH

The history of studies of reading comprehension is in many ways the sketchier of the two, largely because for many years, there virtually were none. It is a common observation among scholars of reading research that following a burst of activity just after the turn of the twentieth century, which included the work of James Cattell (1885), Edmund Burke Huey (1908/1968), and E. L. Thorndike (1917), most reading research was concerned with issues like comparing the outcomes of various instructional strategies (see Gibson & Levin, 1975). In part, this was because a dominant model of reading suggested that there really was not much to understand: it was assumed to be essentially a pretty unproblematic matter of decoding from visual stimuli to aural, and then comprehending that. The central questions seemed to concern the nature of that process of decoding (or recoding, to use Kenneth Goodman's [1971] term).

More important, the overwhelming hegemony of behaviorist models and stimulus-response research in psychology during most of the middle third of the century meant that questions about what might be going on in readers' minds as they read prose were, in effect, simply not askable. In 1960, as Gibson and Levin (1975) sum it up succinctly in their classic text *The Psychology of Reading,*

> [E]xperimental psychologists had shunned this vital field for nearly sixty years. It is true that when Woodworth's classic edition of *Experimental Psychology* appeared in 1938, it contained a brilliant chapter on reading. But S-R psychology won the day, and when the 1954 edition by Woodworth and Schlosberg appeared, reading was out. Few experimental psychologists had touched it in the interval, and there was nothing new to say (p. xi).

In the same connection, it is interesting to consider Bartlett's work on memory (1932), introducing the notion of mental "schemata" used for organizing ideas in memory. His work was drastically neglected during the ensuing years, and, as van Dijk and Kintsch observe

(1983), his ideas only began to experience a revival in the 1970s. What dominated the field in the middle third of this century were studies of single-word processing, word recognition, and assessments of such external and more "empirically verifiable" matters such as reading speed, accuracy of oral reading, and so forth. Questions such as those, involving measurements of behavior rather than speculations about hypothetical mental states and processes, were deemed eminently askable; more "mentalistic" ones were not (Neisser, 1982; see also Bruce, 1985).

What triggered the demolition of the *ancien regime* and opened the door to speculations about what language understanders were doing in the secrecy of their minds was the publication of *Syntactic Structures* and (perhaps more directly) of Chomsky's celebrated review (1959) of Skinner's *Verbal Behavior*. In it, Chomsky thoroughly demolished — or at least substantially crippled — the behaviorist contention that stimulus-response psychology could account for language learning. There is no point in adding here to the overwhelming consensus that the ideas Chomsky's work made suddenly relevant radically affected every branch of scholarship, research, and science that had anything to do with language (the one possible exception being literary theory). It is, however, worth indicating areas in which this "cognitivist revolution" had a particular impact on studies of reading and comprehension. Perhaps the most important of these areas was the discipline of psycholinguistics.

Psycholinguistics was in the air in any case, as Frederick Gollasch has pointed out: "during the mid-1950s, there was a revival of interest in language by psychologists who came to see that human language is very closely linked to understanding, and thus to cognitive processes" (Goodman, 1982, p. xiv). But Chomsky's work was particularly important. He legitimized going beyond observable behavior to study the cognitive principles and mental processes underlying and driving it. This argument was so powerful because his theory of language had built into every joint and connection the assumption that behavior could not be understood in isolation from theories about such mental processes. Indeed, Chomsky's famous distinction between performance and competence — he argued that what people might actually say or write was linguistically important primarily as evidence of what they knew or were capable of — was founded precisely upon that assumption.

Chomsky's theory promoted the invention of the new discipline of psycholinguistics in part, then, because it was so powerfully predictive of mental states, and supplied so many tempting hypotheses which could only be tested by exploring cognitive states and processes. For example, his notion that actual complex sentences represented "transformations" of the "deep structure" of simpler sentences with the same meaning suggested almost immediately that if such structures were actually operating in the minds of language users, it should take proportionately longer to process sentences that represented more complex transformations (Miller, 1962, 1964).

It was through the medium of psycholinguistics that Chomsky's ideas had their most powerful effect on theories of reading. For instance, the influential ideas of Kenneth Goodman (1967, 1982a, 1982b) about reading directly parallel much of the work of psycholinguists with comprehension of oral speech (cf. Cambourne, 1976–1977), and Goodman himself has characterized his technique of "miscue analysis" as "applied psycholinguistics" (1969). Goodman helped us see reading as a profoundly active and constructive activity, in which the reader constructs meaning by hypothesizing, predicting, testing, and sampling from the graphophonic display of the text—and, especially, argued that oral reading miscues offer a "window" on that process. So "cognitive" or "mentalistic" a conception could hardly have evolved without the Chomskyan assumption that there indeed is a mental or cognitive "competence" that underlies the visible behavior, or "performance," of individual language users.

It is apparent, further, that Goodman's work—especially his early work with miscue analysis—shared one important limitation with Chomskyan linguistics: it assumed that language was a set of sentences, and, therefore, that to understand the structure of sentences was essentially to understand language. Just as earlier theorists had held the tacit assumption that language was fundamentally a set of words, so this new view held that it was fundamentally a set of syntactic structures—in written text, structures that were bounded by the capital letter beginning a sentence and the period ending it.

Almost imperceptibly, however, the movement toward considering larger and larger units as fundamental elements of analysis and understanding continued. (Just as it had become clearer with Chomsky and the psycholinguists that words could not be understood outside their syntactic functions in sentences, so it became apparent that a sentence was determined by the discourse and the social situation around it.) This process reached a crisis point somewhere around 1970. De Beaugrande (1980, p. xii) remarks that "around 1968," two related changes had powerful consequences for the way in which we understood written discourse to function: the idea of a linguistics "beyond the sentence" arose, and dissatisfaction with the "transformational" paradigm increased markedly. Within a few years, entirely new, alternative theories of language—examples include the text grammars of writers like van Dijk (1972), the sociolinguistic approach of a William Labov (1972), and the new interest in the pragmatic or "speech-act" theory of John Austin (1962) — were being generated, theories that attempted to obviate what de Beaugrande calls "the context-free abstractness" of the older methods, and to take account of "the importance of social interaction in language groups" (1980, p. xiii).

Similarly, van Dijk and Kintsch (1983) have nominated 1970 as the watershed year, with the recognition about that time that "language studies should not be restricted to the grammatical analysis of abstract or ideal language systems, but rather, that actual language use in the social context should be the empirical object of linguistic theories" (p. 2).

What all these changes meant in practice was that there was a great deal more room for detailed studies of text structure and discourse theory. This included, for example, a revived interest in "story grammars," a concept similar to analyses of Russian folk tales by Propp (1928/1968) and employed (by, e.g., Mandler & Johnson, 1977, and Stein & Glenn, 1979) in the same way transformational grammar had been used, to predict and test mental processes in the understanding of language. It also included text linguistics (as, e.g., the work of van Dijk, 1972), and studies like those of Meyer (1975) on the way in which the structure of the text affects readers' memory of the information "contained" in it.

There was also a new interest in reversing this perspective and looking at the way in which the structure of knowledge and understanding in *readers* affects their understanding of texts — for example, the way in which text understanding depended on readers' activation of relevant knowledge structures (scripts, frames, or schemata) to make the inferences and connections necessary to understand texts, whether narrative or expository. Such cognitive structures seemed to have little to do with the processing or understanding of individual, isolated sentences (much less isolated words), but to have great power over the way readers understood and remembered texts (Anderson & Pichert, 1978).

In other words, the basic unit of understanding came to be not merely the discourse or text, but the dyad of text and reader. It was clear by 1980, as de Beaugrande announced at the beginning of his influential *Text, Discourse, and Process*, that "we cannot treat texts simply as units larger than sentences, or as sequences of sentences. The prime characteristic of texts is rather their *occurrence in communication*" (p. xi, emphasis in original). And, as might be expected, the expansion did not stop there, but continued: the current consensus is clearly that because readers act as participants in social circumstances influencing their goals, expectations, and strategies, any specific instance of reading — and thus, reading in general — cannot be understood except as part of an entire social situation. As James Heap (1980) and David Bloome (1986) have argued, for example, reading in classrooms is as much a function of the social situation of classrooms as of either the structure of the text or the psychological makeup of individual students. Studies by Douglas Vipond and myself have suggested that readers of short stories understand them differently in different social contexts and when the goals of their understanding are different (Hunt & Vipond, 1986; Vipond & Hunt, 1987; Vipond, Hunt, & Wheeler, 1987).

The pattern, then, running all the way from tachistoscope studies of word recognition to observation of how readers make sense of short stories when they are reading them aloud to convey them to listeners who do not know them, is clear: the units of study get larger and the social context becomes more important. The socially communicative function of language becomes more and more a matter of primary concern and not something to be factored out or dealt with later, after the "simpler" problems are solved.

LITERARY THEORY

The tale of literary theory is a slightly more elaborate one. Virtually anyone whose graduate training in English occurred in the middle third of the century came of age in an intellectual context that can perhaps best be compared to the middle stages of the Roman Empire. Although there were many pockets of local culture that differed from area to area (one example was the cadre of neo-Aristotelians around Chicago; cf. Crane, 1952), there was a common language, a very deep and widely shared set of common assumptions about how the world worked, and—most important—a sense of common cause against the barbarians beyond the walls of civilization. When there were disagreements—and there were lots of them, heated ones—they took place within a set of boundaries that we can now see, with the advantage of a generation's hindsight, were remarkably narrow and clearly defined. Everyone, at bottom, was a New Critic.

The construction of the New Critical set of assumptions and strategies, which has endured in classrooms and studies right down to the present day, began as early as the 1920s and 1930s, with the work of T. S. Eliot (e.g., 1920) and I. A. Richards (1925, 1929), though it did not, as Applebee (1974) notes, become the dominant mode in universities until after the Second World War. The specific character of New Criticism owed a great deal to its institutional context; that is, it developed as it did because most of its practitioners were engaged in the business of education, usually in university departments of English. It seems clear, for example, that its most notable feature—the elevation of "the text" out of contexts, the attempt to disconnect it from author, reader, historical situation, and universe and contemplate it as a perfect empedestalled *object d'art*—was conditioned in part by the need to deal with wave after wave of less academically sophisticated students who were ignorant of the author and the historical situation and who were not readers whose responses an academic critic would want to take with a lot of seriousness. William Dowling (1987) has recently noted the way in which New Criticism made the teaching (though not the scholarship) of eighteenth-century literature possible in the sort of context, by downgrading the importance of all the historical and social background that otherwise would have to be directly taught, often displacing the literature itself altogether.

The fundamental nature of the New Critical dispensation has been described (generally with a good deal of hostility) by a number of recent theorists, most notably Frank Lentricchia (1980) and Terry Eagleton (1983). At the risk of summarizing and simplifying outrageously, the fundamental tenets of New Criticism may be said to run something like this: The work of literary art (prototypically, a short poem) exists as an object that can be apprehended, understood, and responded to on its own terms. To assess, understand, properly cherish, and celebrate such a work, one cannot have reference to its creator's intentions or background, because (as was explained most uncompromisingly in Wimsatt & Beardsley's classic essay, "The International Fallacy," 1946b/1954) the only evidence we can possibly have of the creator's intentions are there in the work. If they are not in evidence there, they are not relevant, regardless of what we may know of the author's privately expressed intentions. The test is the text. To study the author and his (very rarely her) intentions is to study something other than literature—biography, history, or psychology. "Critical inquiries," they conclude, "are not settled by consulting the oracle" (Wimsatt & Beardsley, 1946b/1954, p. 18).

Similarly, the individual reactions of actual readers are of little interest. Wimsatt and Beardsley made this point, as well, in a companion piece titled "The Affective Fallacy" (1946a/1954), but its most powerful expression was probably Wellek and Warren's famous warning in their *Theory of Literature* (1949); to study such responses empirically, they asserted, would be to abandon literature in favor of psychology. The text could be evaluated and understood, then, not with reference to any real effects in the world outside it, or to the author's own perhaps grandiose plans and programs, or to its truth or falsity, but on its own, in and of itself. In practice, this focused attention on the verbal structure of the work, requiring a single-minded employment of what Stanley Edgar Hyman (1947) called the "armed vision," and meant that inevitably certain elements of discourse—predominantly, irony (Brooks, 1947), ambiguity (Empson, 1947), and texture (Ransom, 1941)—came to be seen as central.

This in turn, as T. S. Eliot (1920) had noted very early on, meant that the entire canon of literary history had to be rethought. A text not amenable to such close, attentive, analytic reading seemed less important; conversely, a text that had in a previous generation been found to be a powerful expression of a writer's sensibility or of the spirit of an age might suddenly seem less rewarding. Ironic and intellectual writers like Donne replaced in importance more direct and passionate writers like Milton. And those direct and passionate writers were reread to show their ironic complexity, as Cleanth Brooks did so brilliantly with Keats in *The Well Wrought Urn* (1947).

It is paradoxical that although the New Critics were, in general, passionately and sometimes stridently opposed to a scientific-technological worldview, their approach to literature is solidly positivist in its assumption that there is an exterior, theoretically knowable "truth" (the text) *out there*. It is also paradoxical that what was originally seen as a way of making literature available to a wider audience than the historically and culturally initiated became (and was attacked as) an elitist and exclusionary practice engaged in during sophisticated graduate seminars by verbal acrobats. But the most strenuous recent objections to its hegemony have been to the way in which its account of what literature is and how it works left history, human society, and practical considerations entirely out of the picture.

Frank Lentricchia (1980) has argued persuasively that the intellectual *coup de grace* was applied to New Criticism by Northrop Frye in 1957, just as Chomsky and the cognitivists were storming the Bastille of behaviorism in language and psychology. Nonetheless—and in spite of the immediate popularity of Frye's work—graduate students in the 1960s, and undergraduates into the 1980s, and high school students on into the foreseeable future continue to absorb the principles of New Criticism as "common sense."

In the 1920s and 1930s, a teacher who claimed to have no "theory," but to be just "teaching literature," actually embraced an elaborate set of post-Romantic assumptions about literary history and the centrality of the artist's sensibility. In the same way, today a teacher who rejects "theory" and embraces "common sense"—that is to say, almost every teacher of literature—is almost certainly a New Critic. Among those who consciously avow theoretical positions, however, it is difficult to find a practicing New Critic in the 1980s.

What happened? Simplifying again, we can say that the limitations of an approach that was not only centered on, but restricted to, the text, began to be felt among various constituencies. As the New Critical empire collapsed, the invading barbarians reconnected texts to the world in a variety of ways. Perhaps the most powerful force behind the collapse, and the reconnection, was the increasing influence of structuralist thought, then gaining strength in Europe, across a wide variety of academic fields (Culler, 1975; Gardner, 1974; Hawkes, 1977). Just as Chomsky's ideas were clearly part of the fundamental structuralist work in linguistics (Pettit, 1975), so in a sense at least, Frye's work is an application of structuralist "scientific" principles to literary criticism, representing a reconnection of literary texts to each other, if not to the social and physical world, and an attempt to see all of literature as one structurally coherent phenomenon.

Another milestone was the publication in 1961 of Wayne Booth's *Rhetoric of Fiction*. Taking an approach usually thought to be well within a broadly defined New Critical paradigm (it arose out of Chicago neo-Aristotelianism), Booth's book nonetheless signaled a new direction for criticism and theory. It offered two new (and related) directions: it suggested that, as an object of sophisticated, theoretically driven critical scrutiny, narrative was as important as poetry; and it suggested that narrative had a rhetorical dimension. The idea that narrative was rhetorical—that is, embedded at least conceptually in socially structured situations—was, if not new, often new to the academic audience Booth's book addressed, and its publication was in the long run to have dramatic consequences.

These initiatives were overshadowed, however, as Eugene Goodheart (1984, pp. 4–5) notes, by the advent in literary studies themselves of European structuralist ideas, in the work of writers such as Roland Barthes (1970) and Gerard Genette (1966). This was in part because they were prepared to go all the way toward instituting a "science of literature," abandoning altogether the focus on the valuation of individual works of art and looking for larger patterns among art objects as phenomena. As Goodheart phrases it, "structuralism changed or tried to change the goal of literary study from the interpretation of the meanings of literary works to the knowledge of the conditions of meaning" (p. 5). In order to define or understand those conditions, however, it became clear that one had to go beyond the set of meaningful objects (the individual works of art) to consider the circumstances under which meaning was made, and the human beings who made it. One result of this was that structuralists found that it was necessary to consider literary works of art not just in connection with each other, but with all discourse. (This had the ultimate effect, as Frank Lentricchia has pointed out [1980, p. 103], of denying special privilege to literary discourse.)

As the search for general principles of meaning generation

continued, it became necessary to make connections even beyond those among written texts. This led to a further fragmentation of critical theory. The attempt to see and understand texts in connection with language in general, for example, produced what has been called semiotic criticism, and, ultimately (and perhaps more important), under the philosophical influence of Jacques Derrida and others, the deconstructive criticism of writers such as Paul de Man, J. Hillis Miller, and Geoffrey Hartman (Arac, Godzich, & Martin, 1983). The feminist movement, with its compelling argument for acknowledging the connections between gender issues and literature, literary theory, and literary study, has had a remarkable and transforming impact on the field of literary theory (Brown & Olson, 1978; Diamond & Edwards, 1977). Further, the attempt to connect literature to broader social concerns and history has produced what has been termed the neo-Marxian perspectives of writers such as Frederic Jameson (1981) and Terry Eagleton (1976).

The attempt to connect texts with their readers also precipitated the most recent notorious *succès de scandal* in English studies (and perhaps the most compelling force toward making connections with reading comprehension research), the reader-response criticism of writers like Norman Holland, David Bleich, Stanley Fish, and others (for a full sampling of the range of this work, see Tompkins, 1980, or Suleiman & Crosman, 1980). What these critics and theorists have in common is that they deny that texts can be understood without reference to readers. Whether, like Wolfgang Iser (1978), they assume that what the reader does is pretty much at the behest of the text and its structure, or, like Bleich (1975) or Holland (1973, 1975), argue that it is ultimately the reader who controls what the text will be understood to be, all of them agree that texts cannot be understood without readers — that, in fact, texts cannot really be said to exist without readers. In this, if nothing else, virtually all theorists who call themselves poststructuralists would agree: the work of literature can no longer be assumed to exist, sufficient unto itself, in a world separate from the practical, everyday considerations of human action or other forms of discourse.

Most recently, there are hints in a nascent movement sometimes called the "New Pragmatism" (Kamuf, 1986) that literary theory is moving even further in the direction of connecting literature to the social transactions of actual human beings. There is a growing acknowledgment that generalizations about *readers* are as risky as generalizations about *texts*: how a reader will understand and respond to a work of literature depends, it is suggested, on his or her own immediate social situation and goals as much as on any characteristic of the text or of the individual reader. Hassan (1987), for example, argues that literary theory should embrace the "comeback" of American pragmatism and deal with literary texts as William James and Richard Rorty (1982) argue we should deal with all sense data: acknowledge that, like the "truth" about natural phenomena, the "truth" about what texts mean is a social construction, socially arrived at. As James says, "our faith is faith in someone else's faith" (quoted by Hassan, 1987, p. 454). Statements about literary meaning, like statements about other aspects of the universe, can be validated only according to their usefulness to the society in which they are made. Some pragmatists go so far as to reject literary theory altogether (Knapp & Michaels, 1982; see also Mitchell, 1986) on the grounds that "no one can reach a position outside practice" (Knapp & Michaels, 1982, p. 742). They argue that any attempt to treat literature and literary theory in abstraction from the give and take of everyday social relations is doomed by definition.

Here again, the underlying pattern should be obvious: the focus of the lens has widened inexorably for a half century, moving outward from the isolated work to take in other works, other genres, readers, writers, and the social contexts in which readers and writers move, act, and relate to each other through the medium of text.

SOCIALIZING READING RESEARCH AND LITERARY THEORY

It seems clear that both these rather complicated historical narratives can be summarized as parallel movements toward what we might call "socialization."

From 1957, both fields moved decisively away from the positivist notion that the objects of their study (texts, words, language as object) could be understood or dealt with in an artificial isolation from the rest of the world. Both began this movement, under the influence of structuralist thought, by connecting the object of study to other similar objects: words to other words in the case of Chomsky's transformational grammar, literary works to other literary works in the case of Frye's mythic/archetypal criticism. As that structuralist influence grew, both fields began to see that simply widening the focus of study to include more objects of essentially the same kind was not going to offer significant advance. By the beginning of the 1970s, both disciplines were moving to consider the cognitive activities of the perceiver of their language objects; and within a decade, both had begun to move significantly toward taking into account the larger social matrix in which individual language learners conducted their activities.

Both these histories follow patterns that can be extrapolated into the immediate future. To venture such an extrapolation, then: it will become increasingly widely acknowledged, both in reading-comprehension research and in literary theory, that people only read and understand written texts—literary or not—in social contexts and for social purposes, and that what any reader does while reading, and how he or she does it, is heavily influenced—if not determined—by that context and that purpose.

I believe it will become increasingly clear that in order to understand any reading, we need to understand the most complex and engaged, the richest forms of reading—for example, engaged reading of texts that afford literary, aesthetic experience (Vipond & Hunt, 1987). As that view becomes more widely accepted (cf. Dias on reading education, in this volume, Chapter 12), it will become obvious that reading-comprehension research will need to tap the expertise of literary theorists. For example, as reading researchers become increasingly concerned with the reader's construction of the situation and the task, they will realize that they need to study readers engaging in tasks for their own purposes, with naturally occurring, whole texts. This will have a powerful impact on experimental, laboratory-style studies of reading; it will also have radical implications for the processes by which we generalize the results of such studies. It may be that researchers will have to take into account the traditional reluctance of literary theorists to generalize from one instance of reading to another, and their productive sense of the potential richness and variety to be found in occasions when people read will become a rich source of hypotheses to drive research (Hunt, 1987; Hunt & Vipond, 1987).

Similarly, it should become apparent that as literary theory increasingly acknowledges the importance of the pragmatic contexts in which literature is "consumed," the strategies, insights, and assumptions of reading-comprehension research will become more and more important to critics and theorists. As it becomes clearer that reading is a transaction that must be seen not only in, but as part of, a larger context that includes the reader's immediate social situation and goals, and the larger social context, the strategies that educational and psychological research is developing for taking such matters into account will become more important (Vipond & Hunt, 1989; Vipond, Hunt, Jewett & Reither, in press).

As literature comes to be thought of and understood as a social system itself—as Schmidt (1982, 1989) and others in Germany have argued it must—more attention will need to be paid to the actual social circumstances of the creation and consumption of literary works. To look at writers writing and readers reading in productive and useful ways, it is necessary to come to an understanding of the traditions of empirical observation in fields like reading comprehension and the sociology of language.

Whether the two fields manage to stay apart in the face of such similarity of aim, subject, and method will be as much a matter of politics as of substance. And even if a new synthesis eventuates, there is no guarantee that everyone will be happier for the change. Ideas and practices in both fields may suffer and die. The tachistoscope word-recognition test and the interpretive, analytical "literary essay" may die the same death together. Fortunately, however, in matters intellectual, such suffering is rarely altogether bad. Unlike people, there are some ideas and practices we may be a good deal better off without—however difficult it may be to part with them.

THE PHENOMENOLOGY
OF READING

CHAPTER 5

IN AND OUT OF LOVE WITH LITERATURE
Response and the Aesthetics of Total Form
Deanne Bogdan

ARISTOTLE'S "THOUGHT" AND WORLDVIEW

Lately, I've been wondering why I hear fewer jokes being told, and why it is that when they *are* told, not everyone laughs, regardless of the skill of the joke teller. Is it that ours is becoming an increasingly dour society, one in which the imperfection of human existence is taken so seriously that it can no longer function as the context for laughter? Perhaps. My sense, though, is that this problem in joke telling, if there is one, springs from a crisis in what Aristotle in his *Poetics* calls "thought." For Aristotle, "thought" entails the entire constellation of intellectual, moral, social, and political assumptions shared by dramatist and audience that provides the basis for the protagonist's decision making and brings about catharsis. In everyday terms,

The author would like to acknowledge a Research Grant from the Social Sciences and Humanities Research Council of Canada for support in preparing this work. As well, she would like to thank Stanley Straw for suggesting the topic and for the clarity of his perceptions; Robert Boynton for his ebullience; her readers, Patricia Brückmann, Robert Denham, James Moffett, and Jeffrey Robinson for their support and suggestions; her students for their unrelenting dialectical pursuit; and Northrop Frye for his entire oeuvre and continuing interest in her work.

"thought" provides what we might call the "ground" for the joke teller. As one of the three "objects of imitation" (the other two being plot and character) comprising the metaphysical center of a tragedy, thought "is present in speeches where something is being shown to be true or untrue, or where some general opinion is being expressed" (Aristotle, 1967, p. 41). Another way of defining "thought" is as the set of belief systems held in common by author and reader, or as the manner of thinking characteristic of an individual, class, or civilization that enables cultural participation.

"Thought" is Aristotle's term for ideology. In order for a tragedy to do its proper work, to accomplish its goal of raising and purging the tragic emotions, pity and fear, the tragic hero has to be put in a situation in which his strengths work against him. The whole aesthetic mechanism of tragedy presupposes a certain kind of moral failure in the protagonist, and it is the ideological assumptions, the shared "thought" between author/dramatist and reader/audience, that provide the basis for the failed moral decision, lending credibility to the tragic events as inevitable consequences of that failed moral decision. Thus, Hamlet, who has a problem with ambivalence, is placed in a situation requiring singlemindedness; and Othello, wanting in circumspection, is seduced into unreflective wanton action. Their sins are the sins of human nature, but also the sins of tragedy; that is, they are sins rendered "probable" and "necessary" (Aristotle, 1967, p. 45) by virtue of the audience recognizing and accepting—at least for aesthetic reasons, for purposes of enjoying the story—the moral framework (what constitutes moral success and moral failure) within which the story is set. So important is this moral framework to audience response that to reverse the social contexts within which Hamlet and Othello act, to transplant Hamlet into Othello's world and vice versa, would be to create a scenario for comedy not tragedy. Had Othello possessed more caution and Hamlet less, both plays might have ended happily, that is, the protagonists' strengths would have worked *for* them.

That the audience can recognize whether the protagonists' strengths work for or against them within a plot structure, and respond accordingly, presupposes their having a certain awareness and acceptance of the premises upon which the protagonists act, a certain prior knowledge of and consensus about human nature. Only under these conditions can the working through of the dramatic conflict, the intellectual, moral, and emotional dynamics, result in Aristotle's notion of "universal" or "poetic truth" (1967, pp. 43–44), that is, "the kinds of thing(s) a certain type of person will *probably* or *necessarily* say or do in a given situation ..." (p. 44, emphasis added). This universal truth underlies what is generally referred to as the human condition. In short, certain events are brought about because human beings have a tendency to act according to certain moral and psychological laws, which remain more or less the same over time. A tragedy is cathartic rather than pessimistic because, despite the dead bodies strewn across the stage when the curtain comes down, the audience becomes imbued with the serenity arising from their recognizing the inevitability and constancy of how human beings behave. That they die because they behave this way is a truth that everyone born to this earth eventually learns in one way or another. A tragedy helps us to objectify this knowledge and come to terms with it within the safe confines of the imagination. It is this "dramatic" realization that purges the respondent of the "tragic" emotions of pity and fear. But this can happen only if we understand the ideology that prompts their decision making.

To return now to our joke-telling dilemma. Can it be that increasingly joke tellers can no longer presume to draw on the ideological correspondences between them and their audiences that make their jokes work? Is Aristotelian "thought" today so fragmented that the joke is by definition the "in joke" that only those privy to certain beliefs or values upon which the joke turns can appreciate and others will either not "get it" or be offended by it? There just are fewer correspondences now to draw on in an age in which not offending others is itself increasingly becoming part of the ideology of many joke tellers. Let's take, for example, one of my favorite jokes, which usually falls flat, even though I am considered to be a fairly competent teller of jokes. "Question: How many feminists does it take to change a lightbulb? Answer: Only one, but it's not funny." Most often this joke is met either with a shrug of the shoulders, a blank stare, or a hostile glare. Why do so few people laugh?

First, let's examine why I and those who laugh (and they do laugh heartily) think the joke is funny. The response, "Only one, but it's not funny," stereotypes and derides the humorlessness of some feminists about their cause. As well, it anticipates and enacts feminists' censure of sexist jokes, even as it invites the hearer to transcend her own impulse toward humorlessness and censure in the instance of responding to *this* joke. Through stereotyping feminism, the joke demands that the hearer maintain a certain aesthetic distance on her own ideology, something for which feminists are not renowned. The joke asks the feminist to laugh at her own earnestness by recognizing the stereotyped earnestness in the joke. Whether she laughs or not depends upon a number of factors, including how secure she is in her feminism, and how she positions herself in the feminist movement. What is essential, though, what the joke assumes, is that the hearer knows enough about feminism to be engaged by the invitation to laugh about feminism as a bona fide social and political movement based on fervently held pre-suppositions about the eclipsing of gender in the way the world is run. Someone unaware of feminism's history will simply shrug his or her shoulders at the joke; it will go right past them, as we say. Others, who may know this history, may "get" the joke but not consider it funny for reasons having to do with being distanced from the inner dynamics of the feminist cause. They might see the connection but are not sufficiently engaged by the issues to care. There needs to be some kind of identification on the part of the hearer in order for the joke to "take." On the other hand, those who are offended by the joke, those who would contend it inappropriately burlesques the serious revolutionary intentions of the movement, may be so identified with the issues that they cannot separate their emotional response to prejudice against feminism sufficiently to join in making fun of that very inability to stand outside their own cause. For them, to laugh would be to stand back, and to stand back would be to identify against themselves.

What does any of this have to do with reading comprehension and response to literature? In this chapter and the next two, I want to explore some ways in which Aristotle's "thought"—ideology, or worldview—is implicated in how we read, how that ideology connects with processing text, how it influences or at least sets the conditions for the reader experiencing textual pleasure, and, finally, how, under the general rubrics of structuralism, feminism, deconstruction, and Marxism, all of these constitute four different theories and practices of reading. I proceed on the supposition that teachers of literature should be aware of their own philosophy of reading, for it is only by being so aware that we can show students "the codes upon which all textual production depends, and ... [encourage] their own textual practice" (Scholes, 1985, p. 25). More and more, it is becoming accepted that every literature teacher is a literary theorist of sorts, and that the classroom practitioner's responsibility includes a self-consciousness about his or her theoretical position, whether that position is made explicit to the students, as Robert Scholes would have it, or whether students are led inductively to practice a plurality of positions that they ferret out for themselves, as James Moffett (1988b and in this volume) prefers.

Before actually examining these theories, I would like to clarify further what I mean by literary theory and ideology. I do not use ideology in the sense that Gregory Baum (1979) does in *The Social Imperative*, where he defines ideology as "a distortion of truth for the sake of social interest" (p. 19), as though one's social good is some deviation from a single notion of a truth that exists apart from social existence. For the literary critic especially, it is more useful to think of ideology as a system of representations (images, myths, ideas, or concepts) endowed with a specific historical context and functioning within a given society. It is related to the culture (in its sociological rather than humanistic sense) of that society, and to the sum of its pre-judices and preconceptions. In most cases "ideology" is transmitted on a preconscious level, since it is usually taken for granted, considered as "natural," hence neither repressed (unconscious) nor intentionally propounded (conscious) (Roudiez, 1980, p. 15).

Ideology is inscribed on the very fabric of our lives, inseparable from our picture of the world. According to Michael Apple, it is important in dealing with ideology within education not to be dismiss-ive or reductive about it. Apple (1979) writes:

> Ideology cannot be treated as a simple phenomenon. Nor can it be employed merely as a bludgeon with which one hits an opponent over the head (Aha, your thought is no more than ideology and can be ignored) without losing something in the process. Rather, any serious treatment of ideology has to contend with both its scope and its function, with its dual role as a set of rules that give meaning and its rhetorical potency in arguments over power and resources (p. 22).

Theory — in this case, literary theory or a theory of reading — cannot escape ideology except to acknowledge its own imbrication with a particular set of values. In one sense, theory and ideology are identical: they both function according to a set of precepts or system of laws, which operate tacitly or overtly, depending upon the degree of con-sciousness of the reader. One of the commonplaces today in the field of reading theory is the importance of prior knowledge to reading comprehension. Two points about the relationship between ideology and comprehension should be made here. First, ideology is by definition bound up with prior knowledge and will thus necessarily influence comprehension. Whether that ideology is visible or hidden will further affect comprehension. Second, and perhaps more important, in the reading of what we call literature — fiction, drama, poetry — reader identification with literary characters, events, setting, images, and the like produces aesthetic pleasure, which, because of its largely uncon-scious nature, powerfully influences interpretation. That sympathetic identification and the joy of reading are educational givens, not phenomena to be interrogated, form part of the current ideology of language arts. One of my purposes is to explore and render problematic these givens of literature education.

Coopting the reader's sympathies, engaging with the text, has become part of the received wisdom of response to literature theory. Textual pleasure has long been acknowledged as an important motivational factor in developing students' reading ability. Whether it appears as Louise Rosenblatt's (1978) insistence on aesthetic reading as "the lived-through" (p. 26) experience of the text or as a preoccupation with the social relevance of subject matter (to wit, the adolescent fiction industry), the need for readers to project their desires, wishes, and anxieties by way of literary identification goes unchallenged as part of readers' identity formation, both as readers and as human beings. Too often ignored, though, is how vitally and in what manner belief systems and value positions, both collective and individual, connect with this process of identification, how this connection constitutes prior knowledge, and how the engaged reader is led, or "constructed," to interpret, and thus comprehend in certain ways. Literary theory can clarify understanding of this crucial intersection of ideology and aesthetics in the reading process.

STRUCTURE AND THE LITERARY COMMUNICATION MODEL

As stated earlier, my aim in these chapters is to investigate just how ideology interrelates with aesthetics in four theories of reading based on four different literary critical worldviews. The first paradigm, which is discussed in this chapter in its two versions, "the communication model" and "the lightning model," combines elements of universalist, structuralist, formalist, and humanist aesthetics. I use the term "universalist" because this first model turns on the presumption that the values—moral, social, political—comprising what Aristotle termed "thought," when perceived as objectified in a literary form such as tragedy, describe the "universal truth" of a human nature that is transhistorical and transcultural. This model of human behavior is a form of ideology, but it is not so deemed mainly because those who adhere to it tend to regard ideology as a self-conscious partisanship rather than as the set of cultural codes and cues with which a society is freighted.

Northrop Frye's literary theory offers a useful example of a neo-Aristotelian universalist aesthetic at work. For Frye (1985), ideology is subordinated to mythology. Ideology is what myth declines into when anxiety gets the better of mythological expression of universal values or primary human concerns. These are "concerns common to the whole human race: concerns over food, sex, shelter and survival: a freedom without anarchy, a social order without slavery, a happiness without misery" (pp. 14–15). But, according to Frye, "all through history, these primary concerns have had to give way to the secondary demands of ideologies. We want to survive, but we go to war; we want freedom, but live in societies committed to slavery or exploitation; we want happiness, but somehow come to terms with a happiness that depends on the misery of others" (p. 15). Ideology defines our humanity through difference, and operates according to "the thesis-language of law, philosophy and theology" (p. 14). Mythology strains for a unitary, but not uniform, vision of earthly paradise, and always appears as story or *mythos*. The limit of the ideological imagination is the achievable; of the mythological, the conceivable. Frye's critical project is to restore literature to its central role of expressing at the broadest and highest, i.e., the mythological level, of primary human concern a vision of "hope that is focused on a more abundant life for us all" (p. 18).

It is this vision of hope "for us all" through the archetypal story that connects the universalism of the literary communication model to its structuralism, humanism, and formalism. Interpreted in its broadest sense, structuralism systematizes the human imperative to recognize patterns and formal relations. In *Structuralism and Semiotics*, Terence Hawkes (1977) defines it this way:

> At its simplest, [structuralism] claims that the nature of every element in any given situation has no significance by itself, and in fact is determined by its relationship to all the other elements involved in that situation. In short, the full significance of any entity or experience cannot be perceived unless and until it is integrated into the *structure* of which it forms a part (p. 18).

Applied to reading literature, structuralism equips readers with a knowledge of literary convention that would enable them not just to make sense of texts, to interpret, but to analyze, to inquire into the conditions of how texts mean. Structuralism is primarily concerned not with literary "*content*, but with the *process* by which content is formulated" (p. 158). This entails a judicious suspension of value judgments — personal, moral, social, political, and aesthetic — until the work under scrutiny is integrated into the larger structure of human understanding. Thus, the work of literature becomes domesticated, demystified, by breaking down the "strangeness . . . power . . . organ-ization" and "permanence" of "its formal and fictional qualities" (Culler, p. 134, quoted in Hawkes, 1977, p. 159).

In general, structuralists agree that a literary work is not quali-tatively different from other forms of discourse. Jack Thomson (1987) is correct in his characterization of the structuralist view of literature as one that recognizes "literature as a particular organisation of language," one that is simply "part of semiology, a general science of signs, which analyses all cultural artifacts as 'signifying systems.' A literary text is 'just another system of signs like a newspaper article, a comic, a photograph . . . a menu and so on, all to be analysed in the same way to discover how they construct meaning'" (p. 101). But the literary communication model is not structuralist in this sense, for it distinguishes sharply between literary and nonliterary structure, concentrating on literature's "formal and fictional qualities" as something literally made up. This view harkens back to the early structuralists of the Russian Formalist school, the most famous member of which, Roman Jacobson, saw poetry as "a deliberate 'deformation' of ordinary language" (quoted from Hawkes, 1977, p. 71). The effect of such violence is *ostranenie*, or the making strange of reality in order to create it anew. The function of poetry, then, is to stir things up:

> According to Shklovsky, the essential function of poetic art is to counteract the process of habituation encouraged by routine everyday modes of perception. We very readily cease to "see" the world we live in, and become anaesthetized to its distinctive features. The aim of poetry is to reverse that process, to *defamiliarize* that with which we are overly familiar, to "creatively deform" the usual, the normal and so to inculcate a new, childlike, non-jaded vision in us. The poet thus aims to disrupt "stock responses" and to generate a heightened awareness: to restructure our ordinary perception of "reality", so that we end by *seeing* the world instead of numbly recognizing it: or at least so that we end by designing a "new" reality to replace the (no less fictional) one which we have inherited and become accustomed to (p. 62).

The literary communication model springs from the structuralism of Aristotle and Northrop Frye, whose *Anatomy of Criticism* (1957) is, according to Hawkes, "a classic of North American structuralism" (1977, p. 174). Aristotle and Frye conceive of the literary work, or, in Frye's case, all of literature (his "order of words," 1957, p. 17) as verbal entities from which emanate certain correspondences with the structure of the world and of human nature. These correspondences can be communicated to the reader/respondent primarily by perceiving the similarities and differences between literature and life, which then become part of the respondent's storehouse of garnered truths about human existence. It is this process of assimilating the structure of the literary experience with the reader's prior knowledge of self and the world that allows him or her to share in the intense joy of learning we call aesthetic pleasure (Aristotle, 1967).

But the structuralism of Aristotle and Frye is formalist in that it stresses the distinctness of literary form in the structuralist literary experience just described. They both privilege the ontology of literature, its thingness, its being, its metaphysical reality. With this metaphysical focus comes an emphasis on perception, sight, and visual clarity. For these theorists, as for the Russian Formalists, to undergo literary experience, the reader must first *see* the literary object, and in order for that to happen, she or he must be able to distinguish it as itself, as something that is not "life." Literary structure, then, becomes both the means of separating literature from life and of conjoining literature to life once that separateness has first been discerned through what we call aesthetic distance. Horror movies are enjoyable because we know the scary events are not really happening to us. Our experience is real enough, but a different experience from what would be the case if the fictional events were actual. As respondents, we are insulated by our knowledge that the content is a fiction, and that knowledge accrues from our perception of it as objectified, "out there." Yet its true-to-lifeness, the verisimilitude created by the similarity of the content to our own experience or imaginings of life, allows us to participate in the event as though we were actually involved in it. Content draws us in; form distances us. It is through the push-me-pull-you of content formalized that the vicarious nature of literary experience is possible and pleasurable.

Within the aesthetic of the literary communication model, content must be subordinated to form just as ideology must be subordinated to mythology (see Bogdan, 1987a). In Aristotle's terms, the material cause of literature, the "stuff" out of which it is made, becomes appropriated to aesthetic purposes by literature's formal cause, or literary structure. Aristotle (1967) is very clear as to how the mechanism for this appropriation works. Those aspects of a tragedy that point outward toward life — character and thought — "the two natural causes of actions" (p. 39) — crucial though they are to the play's verisimilitude, must bend to plot, the artificial cause, as "the ordered arrangement of the incidents" (p. 39), thereby creating a rational design out of the raw material upon which the action turns. Without this conscious manipulation by the dramatist, there could be no catharsis, no purgation of the tragic emotions of pity and fear through the recognition scene, in which the respondent realizes that "There but for the grace of God go I!" For recognition demands more than sympathetic identification; it requires a simultaneous empathy with and distancing from events so that, emerging from the literary experience, the respondent senses the inevitability issuing from universal truth as probable and necessary. In a tragedy, the playwright cannily plots the inexorable march of events toward the ending, which literally plays out a mechanism intended to confer awareness on experience in a flash of insight cum hindsight, with the knowledge that everything that had to happen did happen. This knowledge, perhaps best illustrated in *Macbeth* just before the "To-morrow and to-morrow" speech, after the last of the witches' prophecies is actualized, comes about as a result of the respondent's being able to encompass the entire vehicle at once, as what Frye (1972) calls "a frozen . . . simultaneous pattern" (p. 4). It is the palpability of the drama as a "total form" (Frye, 1963d, p. 31), "a whole . . . which has a beginning, middle, and an end" (Aristotle, 1967, p. 41), but even more important, its capacity for being recognized as such, that, for Aristotle, makes poetry more philosophical than history, that raises poetic truth to the level of hypothesis or the articulation of "the kinds of things that might happen" (p. 43). In order for the respondent to glean the full benefit of this truth, the drama must be seen in all its structural quiddity or being, appreciated as some "thing" simultaneously made and made up, resembling life but never to be confused with it.

Frye corroborates the Aristotelian subjection of content to structure, and the imperative to separate literature from life as a precondition of literature's subsequent reconnection with life (Bogdan, 1980, 1982b, 1989a). Here he recalls the Russian Formalists. The literary text is fundamentally "an *alien* structure of imagination, set over against us, strange in its conventions and often in its values" (1970, p. 77, emphasis added). This emphasis on form as structure extends to his pedagogy, which in turn relates to his conception of reader response. Teachers should teach "the structure of literature, and the content by means of the structure, so that the content can be seen to have some reason in the structure for existing" (1972, p. 12). Thus the reader perceives the content-as-structure-as-content in order to better appreciate the universal truth of the human condition.

We can see how Frye is at once formalist, structuralist, humanist, and universalist. His foregrounding of structure is similar to New Critical formalism, but by no means can the aesthetic canons of the verbal icon (Wimsatt, 1954) contain the archetypal dimension of Frye's position. Ideological in its very bones, despite his disclaimers, Frye's structuralism bespeaks his fierce commitment to humanism and the educational value of literature, which he sees as "an ethical instrument, participating in the work of civilization" (1957, p. 349). The universalist character of Frye's theory is marked by faith in literature as a "myth of deliverance" in deconditioning habitual, unreflective thought. In his Preface to *The Myth of Deliverance* (1983), he writes about the significance of the study of Shakespeare to his own life:

> One begins by reading or seeing a play like other plays, subject to the conditions and limitations of its own age and to our corresponding limitations in receiving it. One ends with the sense of an exploding force in the mind that keeps destroying all the barriers of cultural prejudice that limit the response to it. In other words, we begin with a notion of what the play might reasonably be assumed to mean, and end with realizing that what the play actually does mean is so far beyond this as to be in a different world of understanding altogether.

What Frye telescopes for us here is the power of literature as a total form to transform consciousness — an expression, some would say, of the liberal humanist ideology that the study of literature effects and sustains social change. (See Apple, 1979, pp. 18–19.)

How is the reader to understand and to experience total form within the literary communication model? There is the short easy way or the long hard way — what I will call stasis and dialectic. (See Bogdan, 1986a, 1986b, 1987c.) Both routes are reminiscent of Plato's lover of wisdom in search of ideal Beauty, who, if lucky enough, attains it by way of an instantaneous mystical rapture (*Symposium*), but most often trudges the arduous path of imperfect understanding and partial vision (*Republic*). If we transplant Plato's pilgrim into the world of literary response, the reader engaged in stasis perceives/receives the literary object through direct insight as a kind of gnostic vision. Most often, though, she or he must tread the lower road of interpretive inquiry, the road that oscillates between engagement with the text and detachment from it. This second path to total form I discuss later (se pp. 129–133) under the heading "Total Form as Dialectic," but for now let us look at response to total form in the first mode, stasis.

STASIS AND THE LIGHTNING MODEL

The condition of stasis may be defined as that state of imaginative identity with the literary object, typified by the fusion of intellect and emotion that literature teachers often aim at but only rarely succeed in triggering. When it does occur, stasis often takes place unexpectedly and outside the classroom. An intensely personal and private experience, perhaps best manifested as silence, it is usually marked by a recession of cognitive faculties and a near paralysis of linguistic powers. In his dialogue *Phaedrus*, Plato (1973) rather poignantly describes this state of aesthetic engagement as a "type of madness, which befalls when a man, reminded by the sight of beauty on earth of the true beauty, grows his wings and endeavours to fly upward, but in vain, exposing himself to the reproach of insanity because like a bird he fixes his gaze on the heights to the neglect of things below" (p. 56). Teachers can readily empathize with students rapt in a state of what Plato would call "divine possession" (p. 56).

The most compelling example of stasis I have witnessed occurred with my own daughter, whose name happens to be Stasia. We were traveling by air on a winter vacation during which she had some "English homework" to do. There she was, wired up to the headset, deeply ensconced in one of her reading anthologies. Some minutes later, as I glanced over at her, I noticed her eyes welling up. When I asked what she was reading, she could only sputter, "You see, there was this woman who was very poor, and she had to go to a ball, and so she borrowed her friend's pearl necklace . . . and then . . . and then . . . ." Here the best pedagogy seemed to be no pedagogy at all, but rather the intimate sharing of mutual experience. I simply acknowledged that I, too, knew the de Maupassant story, and joined her in dumb savoring of the moment.

It is difficult to know whether Stasia's tearful inarticulation was a manifestation of sentimentality or her intuitive grasp of the reason for the content existing in the de Maupassant story. Because of its clear outline, the story's total form, the inextricability of form and content, its *mythos* and *dianoia*, could easily have been apprehended by her in a single participating response. If she *was* experiencing stasis, she would have undergone the full brunt of the Aristotelian recognition scene, in which the pain of the irony became contingent on and coterminous with apprehending the symmetry of the author's design. With a "genuine primitive," i.e., "an ideal reader or listener," one unencumbered with any awareness of literary convention (Frye, 1976, p. 131), the communication is instinctual rather than intellectual; but it is there, testimony to the writer's art, to how language in narrative fulfills the laws of its own inner coherence, enacts "the ordered arrangement of events" prior, at least logically so, to bestowing on the respondent universal or poetic truth.

Stasis, then, is the simultaneous perception and experience of the total form of a literary work, however fleeting that glimpse may be. As the apotheosis of textual engagement or the participating response to art, it can be thought of as the overcoming of T. S. Eliot's dissociation of sensibility. In his essay, "The Metaphysical Poets" (1975), Eliot observes that the English dramatists of the sixteenth century and their successors, the poets of the seventeenth century, "possessed a mechanism of sensibility which could devour any kind of experience" (p. 64). But ever since Milton and Dryden mastered the art of integrating sensibility, language and feeling became divorced in the history of English literature. In general, "while the language became more refined, the feeling became more crude," and there grew up either sentimentality or cerebration. In the nineteenth century, continues Eliot, we see "traces of a struggle toward unification of sensibility. But Keats and Shelley died, and Tennyson and Browning ruminated" (p. 65).

Frye (1963a) has modified the concept of dissociation of sensibility to signify the virtual psychological impossibility of simultaneously participating in and being consciously aware of experience (see pp. 31, 81–82). The reader's habitual mode of responding to literature is some form of imbalance between thought and emotion: we either overintellectualize, lacking feeling—or sentimentalize, lacking truth (see Bogdan, 1986b). To strike a balance would be akin to coalescing Louise Rosenblatt's two kinds of reading, aesthetic and efferent (1978), thus enabling the reader to bring away from the reading the consciousness of the poetic experience itself. This would be a rare, if not impossible occurrence; for if Frye (1963b) is correct, the state of engagement in fact lowers and debases consciousness (see p. 123). Stasis perceives total form through a kind of gnosis or direct apprehension, and the integration of sensibility it represents occurs at a level of experience not yet brought to consciousness. Thus, it functions more as reception than perception, more as insight than cerebration. This reception, or "lightning model," has enormous implications for both ideology and pedagogy.

First, pedagogy. To hope for overcoming dissociation of sensibility in the teaching of literature comes with the territory. Most teachers, motivated by a humanistic, even romantic, ethos about the educational value of aesthetic experience, want students to share in those rare instances in which sign and signifier are felt as one. In his introduction to Paul de Man's *Blindness and Insight: Essays in the Rhetoric of Contemporary Criticism*, Wlad Godzich (1983) uses the analogy of a flash of lightning to describe

> a perfect congruence between the expression and that which is expressed. Lightning cannot be said to be hidden before its manifestation, but rather expresses itself ... fully in the instant of its illumination. In fact, it suspends the difference between the manifest and the manifesting, producing in its instantaneity a moment of perfect presence (p. xx).

Moments of perfect presence are spiritual experiences that readers desire to recur. Yet the dark side of lightning, so to speak, is its brevity and randomness. When applied to reading literature, the lightning model, a kind of compressed communication model, has severe limitations. First, it is simply unreliable; its elusiveness must be counterbalanced and supplemented by the disciplined training of perception, as Godzich (1983) notes, "to ensure that lightning does strike; ... [and] even more formidably, that it strike repeatedly, at will, in the same place and with the same intensity" (pp. xx—xxi; cf. Frye, 1963b, p. 145). Godzich would corroborate Frye's admonition not to trust to "the gambling machine of an ideal [literary] experience" 1971/1973, p. 29), but rather to turn to the training of perception through literary criticism, which makes up for the absence of stasis. Stasis is constellated by a virtually identical match between the perceived reality of the respondent and the received reality of the text. This event would seem to be serendipitous, but would be at least in part precipitated by an intersection of the author's and reader's worldviews. The feeling of having come to know the truth about the world and oneself coincides through the intermediary of the text. Stasis, then, can be taught *for* but not taught; that is, teachers may wish to set the stage for stasis, but should not seek to orchestrate the conditions under which it might occur, or interfere with its effects. That is what I think Frye (1957) means when he says we cannot teach literature, only literary criticism (see p. 11).

Next, ideology. The appeal of stasis is due partly to the role of Beauty in a kind of collective rescue fantasy. Frye speaks of art as a consolation for the imperfections of "ordinary existence" (Bogdan, 1980, 1982b); George Steiner (1974) would call it part of "nostalgia for the absolute." One of the most provocative descriptions of the phenomenon I have called stasis comes from Jeffrey Robinson in *Radical Literary Education* (1987), where he defines aesthetic experience in terms of its original connection with Beauty:

> The experience of beauty requires the suspension of the critical faculty, the transcendence of a comprehending response to the world, the suppression of the fantasy life except for idyllic fantasies. Beauty, in this tradition, is largely defined in terms of its healing powers: it heals the psyche's wounds by providing a vision of peace and unity. Mind, in its analytical, critical capacity, acting only as a fallen instrument of ordering life in a fallen world, ceases to act in the presence of beauty and, as Keats says, ends in speculation or wonderment (p. 14).

In trusting the poem to rescue the reader from confusion and misery (p. 15), the reader makes a Faustian bargain with the poem, which ultimately controls, in the sense of taking hold of, the reader. This stupefaction or wonderment in the face of total form, for Robinson, is double-edged in another sense. On the one hand, the "consoling view of literature is very powerful and valuable. To the extent that it offers moments of coherence and hope, it serves us well. But when a reader imagines that beauty in art demands for its existence society's 'bad present' from which to escape, then it has ceased to function positively" (p. 26). In other words, the recognition of universal truth in the aesthetic "Aha!" response, as in "There but for the grace of God go I!" or, as Maxine Greene (1986) has put it, "This is just how things are, and I didn't know it" (p. 240), is never morally innocent. And, Plato's notion of the naive respondent gazing upward like a bird, insensible to the things below, has material consequences. According to Robinson, the poem itself is alive: it seems "insulated by contemplation," but envisions "a particular audience to live and act with its principles and preferences ..." (1987, p. 21).

In the literary communication model, readers collude voluntarily with the ideology of the author in order to experience beauty; but in the lightning model, the wholly engaged reader loses the detachment that comes from standing outside the literary event. Literature swallows life, as Frye (1963c) tells us (see p. 33). Humanists have always thought this a good thing. What of Frye's "exploding force in the mind that keeps destroying all the barriers of cultural prejudice that limit response . . ." (Frye, 1983, Preface)? Isn't reading literature *per se* a way of expanding consciousness (see Moffett, 1988a), or is believing that it does simply part of the ideology of total form? Have we come full circle to Plato's dictum that the seductive charm of poetry compels assent to the poem's postulates? Robinson (1987), for one, says as much. Is reading for pleasure to be deemed an activity for consenting adults, as it was for the Greeks? (See Jaeger, 1943, p. 214.)

PARTIAL FORM: STOCK, KINETIC, AND SPECTATOR RESPONSES

With stasis we encounter the reception of the literary object as total form. Stasis calls forth the deepest recesses of human desire and gives the illusion of its fulfillment by conferring a sense of plenitude of being on the reader. Such profundity of response raises with it the larger question of the social effects, the ideological ramifications, of literary experience, particularly important for stasis because of its intuitional, essentially precritical, nature. Setting aside for the moment this larger question, which I will deal with more fully in the next chapter, I would like to consider now the various manifestations of partial form within the aesthetics of total form.

If total form through stasis overcomes dissociation of sensibility, partial form embodies it by way of stock, kinetic, and spectator responses, each of which represents an excess of either engagement or detachment. Stasis, as the reception of total form, reveals itself as primitive (in the sense of "prime" or "primary") response *in bono*. With it we have the perfection of engagement with the text, the reader intuitively apprehending the total form of the text and re-creating it on its own terms. Here, the precritical nature of stasis is no impediment to total form. However, we see the dark side of precritical response — primitive response *in malo* — in stock and kinetic responses. While stasis is uncritical but neither superficial nor egocentric, the other two are unthinking and narcissistic, at least within the aesthetics of total form. Stock and kinetic response are passive kinds of automatic reflex reinforcing preexisting prejudice, the former with respect to the content of a work, the latter, to its form. Both mistake the part for the whole.

Stock Response and "The Search for Truth"

Stock response reads a poem or novel according to its moral and ideological anxieties, ignoring what we have outlined as the metaphysical reality of the text, that is, *mythos* and *dianoia* seen in terms of each other. Less a response than a reaction (usually an initial reaction), stock response interprets and values a text solely according to whether the work in question seems to reinforce or countervail the welter of ideas, values, and feelings that go to make up the reader's conscious or unconscious worldview. Left to its own devices, stock response is interested only in the pursuit of a particular kind of truth, and culminates in, according to Frye (1963b), "the social consensus we call the mob" (p. 128).

As already mentioned, stock response reinforces preexisting prejudice with respect to the content of a work by reducing the meaning of literature to its extraliterary terms, usually some historical, moral, or social analogue of the work itself.[1] Privileging literariness over propositional statement, Frye (1957) reminds us of the metaphysical status of the literary work as a "self-contained verbal pattern" (p. 74). For Frye, the poem is preeminently "a structure of imagery" whose "conceptual implications" can never "serve as a full equivalent" of its mythological meaning (p. 136). Frye's objection to the literary "search for truth" is not just that literature becomes subject to the laws of the disciplines, but that the work ends up being "translated" and *reduced* to its "conceptual implications," into what we know or think we know about its ideational content. Here a little learning becomes a dangerous thing because without close attention to the text, personal biases and ideological predilections cloud literary judgment. The following anecdote might serve to illustrate searching for truth outside literary context.

A few years ago, when I was teaching high school English, I was commended by my principal, a Catholic priest, for including in my course of studies, Robert Bolt's play, *A Man for All Seasons* (1960, 1963). It was, he thought, an appropriate choice for today's teenagers, who, engulfed in a world of moral relativism, as he put it, sorely needed a prototype of transcendent values. At the time I was conducting a curriculum experiment in "Values and Literary Criticism" (Bogdan, 1978, 1980; see also 1982a) with my thesis supervisor, who is an unabashed utilitarian. *His* view of the play was the polar opposite of the principal's. My thesis supervisor worried that it could be psychologically unhealthy for young people to view martyrs as heroes, for altruism can set up unrealistic ethical expectations that can instill needless guilt in students about the level of their own morality, as well as preclude the possibility of compromise in solving everyday moral problems.

Within a universalist aesthetic both these valuations are needlessly and dangerously one-dimensional. But the premises upon which they are founded are precisely notions about literary theory and the psychology of response that perpetuate the current preoccupation with social relevance in the literature curriculum. When the questions asked about the works in our courses are *primarily* aimed at whether they are written by Canadians or project a contemporary image of women, for example, the sociological assumption that literature functions solely as a role model of attitudes and values directly transferable to life predominates. Within such a context, literature is regarded as either an escape from, or extension of, ideology, a kind of counterindoctrination; and response to literature, simply as precritical identification with fictional worlds, rather than critical recognition of them as the means to *conscious* life (see Frye, 1980, p. 6).

Affirmative action curriculum and censorship both are off shoots of the search for truth as the primary goal of literature education. That is, adding or subtracting works on the basis of subject matter alone would be a move toward galvanizing students' precritical response at the expense of critical reflection. To lobby for curriculum change, as for example, Priscilla Galloway (1980) has done in her book, *What's wrong with high school English? ... it's sexist ... un-Canadian ... outdated*, on the presumption that a literary education should provide modern, Canadian, and feminist images with which students can identify, comes uncomfortably close to recommending that *The Merchant of Venice* or *Oliver Twist* be jettisoned because of their racism. Identification cuts both ways, that is, it can be either uplifting or alienating, depending on whether the "truth" being pursued and discovered squares with the values of the seeker (see Bogdan 1988, 1989b). Searching for a particular kind of truth as the ultimate aim in literature education reifies the stock response, and simply turns the open-ended probing of literary ambiguity and complexity into a reconfirmation of the reader's mind-set prior to approaching the text.

Kinetic Response and Desire

Although kinesis is by definition a kind of action, like stock response, it is essentially passive action, born of a compulsion to react directly to a verbal or imagistic stimulus and to judge its worth on the basis of its immediate impact. Kinetic response is really a form of the reader's unleashed desire for emotional gratification.[2] The reader who says,

"Lord of the Flies is a great work of literature because I've always wanted to live on an island by myself," would be grounding response in a sort of phony primitive. Stock and kinetic response can be thought of as the two horns of dissociation of sensibility: stock response thrives on clichéd thought; kinetic response, on pseudofeeling. To reject a work of literature because it gainsays instant reader satisfaction, or, conversely, to laud it because of its capacity for raising gooseflesh, is to adopt a "fingers-up-and-down-my spine" or warm-bath theory of literature[3] on the assumption that literary works turn us into nice people by making us feel good.

Earlier I said that kinetic response turns on reinforcing prejudice with respect to literary form. At its core is the blurring of convention and reality that impels readers to view fictional characters as real people and fictional events as real life, without due attention to the configuration of *mythos* and *dianoia* that constitutes a work's total form. Because of the failure to retain the aesthetic distance requisite to making the appropriate comparisons between the fictive and the actual, textual pleasure is conflated with other emotional states; thus is ignored the unique blending of intellection and emotion that go to make up the domain of the imaginative. When applied to the classroom, the warm-bath theory shows up as an emphasis on motivational tricks to "turn kids on" to literature, and, conversely, as the excision of works that are thought to be outdated or devoid of emotional impact. Kinetic response raises the pleasure principle to a critical axiom of literary interpretation; that is, the reader evaluates the work according to whether it packs a whollop or falls flat. The following characterization of response to Ernest Hemingway's short story "The Killers" furnishes us with a good example of kinetic response in operation.

"The Killers" is a work of literature in which intensity of feeling is often dependent on recognition of its formal structure. Yet students may not get the chance to become familiar with literary structure in this story because of a misplaced emphasis on sympathetic identification. Teachers may decide that, say, in a post-Godfather era, students would not be in tune with Hemingway's understatement of gangland terror. Admittedly, students rarely like the piece on a first reading. They complain that nothing happens, that Nick and George are bland characters, and that the story just "stops." Usually, the more perceptive and honest members of a class will propose that its "greatness" as a "classic" perhaps has something to do with Hemingway's reputation as a stylist, but that in the end, style can't make up for a story that begins to pall as soon as we learn that Ole Anderson is not coming to the diner. The tale may have worked in its time, but the theme, which probably is related to the passing from innocence to experience, just does not come off in the late 1980s.[4]

These fairly typical sentiments are sincere, precritical reactions to the Hemingway work. Stock response assumes that literature is the attempt to deliver a message, to "say" something about reality through the fictive replication of figures like ourselves, while kinetic response assumes that the main objective of reading literature is to further the reader's enjoyment. In realistic fiction, for example, the criterion of reader pleasure or pain is usually how "true to life" the content and the characters are represented. If students don't instantly "connect" to the material, it is often not thought to be "relevant" for classroom use.

Kinetic response can preclude any holistic relationship between literary experience and analysis. The integration of analysis and literary experience presumes an appreciation of the story that is impossible so long as it has been treated only in terms of whether students can "groove" on its subject matter. For example, the editors of the school anthology (see Ross & Stevens, 1967) that had included "The Killers" for study attempted to have students explore literature-to-life issues in their questions at the end of the story.

> Nick says, "I'm going to get out of this town." Does his experience in the story represent a defeat or victory for him in his development toward manhood? Justify your view.

And

> Hemingway excludes any author's comment on the significance of the events that he relates; yet he has led the reader to make certain judgments. What are your conclusions regarding the society that is suggested by his story? (p. 51).

If students simply don't care about Nick and George, or if they regard as unconvincing the moral judgment Hemingway may be making about America forty years ago, they will not be helped by such exercises, which in the end only exacerbate the circularity of locking students into a content-oriented approach to literature. The teacher of literature guided by kinetic response is unreflectively committed to a curriculum and teaching methods that "work" or "don't work," and would reject "The Killers" because of a preconception that today's students would not "relate" to Nick and George. She or he might substitute for this story of literary "quality" a Judy Blume ego-massage that bypasses the literary dimension altogether in favor of fictionalized indoctrination into contemporary mores attained primarily by means of precritical conflation of literature and life. Admittedly, caution about kinetic response and the pull of desire entails allegiance to a kind of formalism redolent of New Criticism; however, the aesthetics of total form goes beyond adherence to narrow formalism in that it regards literary structure as a container for literary experience. As we shall see in the next section, engaging the reader was not a priority for New Criticism.

Spectator Response and Literary Knowledge

Central to this chapter is a major tenet of total form: except for rare instances of stasis, which are altogether gratuitous and unbidden, literary values are earned. Its corollary is that the literature teacher's mandate is to lead students to the perception and experience of literature's total form through a process of identification and recognition. In stasis, the process is catalyzed and experienced as a gestalt of seismic proportions. Since dealing with it explicitly and in the moment is not, I believe, the proper province of the classroom, the teacher should pursue total form by fostering in students a critical detachment through aesthetic distance to balance textual engagement by way of an ongoing dialectic between text and reader. But it is incorrect to assume that critical response should be equated with imaginative withdrawal from the text. Indifference to the emotional and imaginative dimension of a literary text I call spectator response, the demonic form of literary criticism, so to speak.[5] An example of this occurred in a second textbook question on "The Killers," which asked students to divide the story into four stages (see Ross & Stevens, 1967, p. 50), without combining that analysis with the vital imaginative inhabiting of the story's fictional world. Inquiry into structure can have imaginative force to the student only if it can be meaningfully linked to content questions, and that can happen in this story only if we give up looking at Nick and George as real people, or even as protagonists, and begin to view them as devices of the plot, the rational element of design (see p. 133). To reiterate Frye (1972), "the content [must] be seen to have some reason in the structure for existing" (p. 12).

Spectator response has prevented many literature teachers from even countenancing the critical process as part of their methodology. Indeed, revulsion against spectator response may account for the current romanticizing in literature education of the precritical and the personal as the beginning and end of response to literature. (Pendulum swings have a way of being extreme.) Naturally, students and teachers abhor the endless "naming of parts," the unremitting fragmentation of literary works (usually in accordance with the tenets of the now old New Criticism) that so often dessicates a poem or short story in the minds and hearts of the unsuspecting. Spectator response heralds the triumph of positivism in the literature class. Nothing counts except what can be weighed and measured by mechanical quotation or formula essay. Under the tyranny of spectator response, literature study ceases to be part of the humanities and becomes indistinguishable from the ugliest excesses of social science. Just as stock and kinetic responses indulge in the phony primitive, spectator response does so in the phony technical. We hunger for at least a choral reading to "knit up the ravell'd sleave of" cant.

Teaching methods that tend to separate analysis from experience and so produce spectator response are those, for example, that stem from interdisciplinary units of study sometimes based upon conceptions of literature as historical or social documents only, or from a single interpretation or pedagogical approach, such as examining the story according to the tenets of I. A. Richards' practical criticism (1929). In these cases, response might be reduced to looking for and gathering specific kinds of literary "evidence." The best defense against spectator response is to become aware of a plurality of critical viewpoints, but always with an eye to engaged reading of the text. Knowledge *about* literature should never be "an opaque substitute for literary experience" (Frye, 1981, p. 13).

TOTAL FORM AS DIALECTIC

Stock, kinetic, and spectator responses typify those reactions to a literary work that reflect Eliot's dissociation of sensibility; as such, they constitute partial form. Each of these three responses isolates and reifies one aspect of a full literary response: stock response, the search for truth; kinetic response, desire; spectator response, knowledge about literature. But dissociation of sensibility is a perfectly normal way of responding to art, at least initially, and its place in the attainment of a full literary response should not be devalued. If the reader is truly a maker of meaning, if the psyche is really crucial to the reading act, then a literary response without reference to the reader's worldview would not only be illogical but undesirable. Literary response as dialectic accepts dissociation of sensibility as a fact of normal reading life, however, and endeavors to actualize the total form of a literary work through the alternation between engagement or participating response, and detachment or critical response. Instead of longing for stasis, and trusting to "the gambling machine" of an ideal experience, the reader turns to literary response as dialectic, which legitimates and capitalizes on the responses of partial form by building on whatever emotional and intellectual raw material presents itself at a precritical level in such a way that response can be deepened, refined, and enriched by standing back from the text. Literary dialectic transcends the impulse to limit response, viewing the literary work neither as an object to be dissected nor an analogue of personal experience, ideas, or values, but as a separate reality, an "alien structure of the imagination," a verbal universe whose self-containment logically precedes its referential function. Through exploration of the poem as a construct of otherness as much as a reflection of experience, wants, and desires, the reader comes to recognize the self as part of the larger pattern of the human condition. Thus, the transformation of consciousness and the transmutation of literary knowledge are interdependent, actualizing Frye's myth of deliverance.

In what follows, I shall outline briefly the movement from partial to total form in literary interpretation. (As already suggested, in stasis, the reader escapes partial form, like Plato's mystical lover of Beauty in his intuitive grasp of its total form.) But first I want to elaborate on my reservations about what I have called the lightning model, or total form as stasis.

We have already acknowledged that innovative pedagogical methods in literature education today, in their efforts to reclaim personal response, are directed toward remedying the stultifying effects of purely text-based New Critical analysis. In an effort to reconnect literature with students' lives, teachers now concentrate on the enjoyment of reading, the social relevance of literary content, the imaginative recreation of the text, and their combined potential for psychic and social growth. While these are salutary objectives as far as they go, they devolve around a notion of literary experience as the feeling of having come to know some "truth" about oneself, the world, or both. The very power of this kind of knowledge renders it both profound and dangerous. This ideal experience, which I have described as stasis, precious in itself, is risky business when it is taught — for ideological, pedagogical, and ontological reasons. We have already seen, if we follow Jeffrey Robinson, that the pleasure dome of aesthetic wonderment conceals a hegemony: beauty demands assent, at least for literary purposes, to the ideas and values embodied in the work. (In the next chapter, I will demonstrate how complying with Aristotle's "thought" is a prerequisite for stasis, and how experiencing stasis would be an impossibility for a reader with ideological proclivities counter to those demanded for aesthetic enjoyment.)

Pedagogical and metaphysical objections to stasis are directly related to ideological ones. We recall Wlad Godzich's account of the deficiencies of the lightning model on the grounds of randomness and unreliability, as well as my own claim that it threatens to invade the spiritual life of the reader, which should remain private. These are problems real enough when the model works, that is, when total form, as I have been describing it, is actually perceived/received in stasis. However, we have already seen that not integration, but dissociation of sensibility, is the usual mode of response, and that stock or kinetic response can be expected at the precritical level; and, further, that these responses should/must be honored if response is to remain authentic. Literary response as dialectic is the pedagogical tool designed to approximate in the "ordinary life" of reader experience the ideal literary experience of stasis.

Dialectic aims to build on precritical intuitive responses by means of rereadings. Knowledge about literature and imaginative recreations of the text, exercises in detachment and engagement, so to speak, bring to consciousness the insights and feelings typified by stasis. Such a process, of course, entails a certain attenuation of experience necessarily accompanying the very act of verbalizing literary response. It is through criticism that students can mourn the loss of the paradisal bliss of the genuine primitive, compensating in reliability and consciousness for what has been sacrificed in sheer intensity. Literary response as dialectic demystifies the aesthetics of total form, bringing it into the realm of study and the quotidian.

It is not my intention here to provide a curriculum model for literary response as dialectic.[6] Instead, I want to reconsider the two works referred to in our discussions of stock response and kinetic response, Bolt's *Man for All Seasons* and Hemingway's "The Killers," in the light of the potential of dialectic to shore up these particular manifestations of partial form, to help readers negotiate the journey through literature. (See Frye, 1976, p. 186.)

First, *A Man for All Seasons*. Literary response as dialectic would attempt to come to literary understanding by utilizing literary criticism as a tool for interpreting the play comparatively free of the strictures of ideological bias, literally to "recognize" its total form on the play's own terms. (That such an undertaking is possible, valuable, and advisable, of course, constitutes part of the ideology of the aesthetics of total form.) But what does this dialectic look like in the actual interpretation of a particular work? Am I suggesting that it would be incorrect, for example, to study the play in terms of Bolt's Preface (1960, 1963), in which he expounds his individual brand of existentialism? Not if we resist substituting the play's philosophical context for the play. There is an important difference in the aesthetics of total form between regarding the play as a *statement* of Bolt's existentialism and as an *exploration* of it. We should beware of facile readings that define the theme as "the importance of being true to one's principles" by counterposing Sir Thomas More and "the adamantine sense of self" (Bolt, 1960, p. vii) Bolt attributes to him with the "crassly opportunistic" Common Man. Admittedly, the play is an indictment of crude pragmatism, with its adulation of common sense, convenience, and expediency, as personified by Richard Rich, who betrays More for his own advancement. But the Common Man is much closer to More than many might admit. If we study the play through its literary structure, we cannot reduce it to anything so neat as "Spiritual values are better than temporal values." Rather, we would say that, for example, the land-and-water imagery literally incarnates the interdependence between the spiritual and the natural dimensions of the human condition (see Atkins, 1967).

The association of land metaphors with earthly, immovable, and invariable elements such as law and security, on the one hand, and water metaphors with the fluidity and precariousness of spiritual concerns, on the other, furnishes the symbolic framework for viewing More and the Common Man. Both More and the Common Man have an aversion to water; that is, they are both trying to square the rational with the transcendental through a search for self. The reciprocal relationship between More and the Common Man can be established by observing that they are both survivors; they will serve two masters if they can; neither wants to be a martyr, and both have an "adamantine sense of self." That one finds it in the words of an oath and the other in his own survival is not to equate the saint with the machiavel, but rather to identify the apprehension of God with self-knowledge (Atkins, 1967). This is neither a reinforcement of the narrow definition of Christian altruism espoused by my former high school principal nor the pragmatism of my thesis supervisor, but a richly complex synthesis of the two: a "figuring forth" (Sidney, 1966, p. 54) of the attempt to overcome alienation in becoming fully human. The essentially ineffable nature of such a notion resists any prescriptive transcription of literary content. We can only glimpse the fullness of literature through the tension of literary form, through the delineation of its *dianoia* or theme by means of its *mythos* or structure. When the resulting response challenges the passive acceptance of conventional morality, as it does in this case, literary criticism can be said to be a subversive activity. At the same time, however, it also represents a powerful conditioning to assent to the agnostic existentialism of Bolt's own endorsement of convictions of individual conscience over duty to family and government—testimony indeed to how "thought" intersects with the aesthetics of total form. (See Bolt's Preface.) Other readers may have come to similar kinds of readings about the Bolt play without recourse to critical articles such Atkins'. And this is not to say that the previous interpretation is the only "correct" one. Total form as dialectic expects that knowledge *about* literature gleaned through literary criticism can enhance, not diminish, enjoyment. Engagement can be deepened and enriched by appreciation, but appreciation entails sufficient detachment from personal biases in order to apprehend the text in as complex and complete a response as possible.

How might dialectic operate in "The Killers"? We recall the problem of two kinds of partial form in this story: a reverse kind of kinetic response (students were bored with the story because of their inability to attain easy sympathetic identification) and spectator response (the question in the anthology invited students to carve up the story into four sections ostensibly without relating it to their interpretation or experience of it). In point of fact, this exercise is important to the *conscious* perception of the story as total form, and it is surely derived from R. S. Crane's neo-Aristotelian interpretation of "The Killers" found in the second volume of his *Idea of the Humanities and Other Essays, Critical and Historical* (1967). In this study, Crane demonstrates persuasively that regarding Nick and George as functions of the plot is crucial to making the imaginative leap in seeing Ole Anderson as the real focus of the narrative. But, it should be stressed, Ole is not a character with whom readers are expected to identify any more than they are expected to identify with Nick and George. All three characters are devices for objectifying the "reality" of the fictional world. Nick and George act as elicitors of information about the personalities of the killers and about the strange passivity of Ole's submission to what he has decided is to be his fate. This occurs in the two deliberately long "disclosure scenes" in the diner and in Ole's bedroom (Crane, 1967). The boys' "spectator" personalities are essential to the bizarre nature of the evil being unveiled. Ideally, in subsequent readings, questions of character development, suspense, social values, and even moral conflict will take on a new dimension as students experience the grotesquerie of the discrepancy between appearance and reality woven into the very fabric of the story, as they come to understand the way Hemingway juxtaposes the illusion of normalcy through concrete diction, casual conversation, uneasy humor, and the spare use of metaphor with the relentless progression toward inevitable death, which we never see:

> "I wonder what he did?" Nick said.
> "Double-crossed somebody. That's what they kill them for."
> "I'm going to get out of this town," Nick said.
> "I can't stand to think of him waiting in the room and knowing he's going to get it. It's too damned awful."
> "Well," said George, "you better not think about it" (p. 50).

It is only by appreciating the economy of Hemingway's style and dramatic method that readers usually realize the full horror of the ending. With this reading, kinetic response can be transformed into a truly experiential recognition scene.

TOTAL FORM:
NOW YOU SEE IT, NOW YOU DON'T

In the picture of literary response as dialectic that I have been sketching, I have been subscribing to the dictates of Northrop Frye's admonition not to trust to the gambling machine of an ideal literary experience through stasis, but to realize the total form of a literary work through alternating states of engagement with and detachment from a literary text, reading according to the "autoreferential nature" of a literary text (Stierle, 1980, p. 101). This means, at most (some would say "at worst"), having recourse to interpretive guides of literary critics whose analytic expertise is schooled in total form; at least (some would say "at best"), it would simply mean rereading the story. In any case, what is important to understand is "that the schematized views of fictional texts do not correspond to those of everyday life" (p. 101), as well as the painful but inevitable truth that literary experience is only a facsimile of "real" experience, that aesthetic pleasure, despite its power, is qualitatively different from the emotions of "normal" existence. At least, these would be the claims of the structuralist/universalist/formalist/humanist aesthetic underpinning total form. Central to this aesthetic is insistence that the jury must remain out on ultimate evaluations of the work until the reader can surpass his or her experience of the text's linear structure, suspending judgment until this "textual linearity [can] . . . be viewed in relation to the hierarchic conceptual [Frye would add "imagistic"] organization of the text as a whole" (Stierle, 1980, p. 95).

Why, within the aesthetics of total form, do I think it important for classroom teachers to be aware of the distinctions I have been drawing between total and partial form, stasis and dialectic? First, because reading as a personal act of enjoyment has social and political consequences; and, second, because I believe that part of the literature teacher's job is to help students appreciate and evaluate a literary work in terms of both its literariness and its political implications. Students need to make sense of the literary dimension of their reading experience and to relate it to their extraliterary experience in complex and subtle juxtapositionings between the world of the imagination and the "real" world, between the ideology of the text and that of the reader's sense of self. This need renders problematic the notion of engagement with the text. What tends to be forgotten in debates about literary analysis versus personal response (itself a false dichotomy) is the function of psychological projection in literary response. With stasis and stock, kinetic, and spectator responses, literary experience is in part a projection of unsatisfied needs, desires, and longings clamoring for fulfillment, which have been objectified by and in the text as parts of the reader's self yet to be realized. In this sense, literary experience as the interaction between text and reader strikes me as something like falling in love. It is a primary datum, a given, something that "happens." In literary response, this precritical state, being in love with the text, is crucial as a *first step* in literary knowing; but stasis needs to be brought to consciousness; and stock, kinetic, and spectator responses need to be balanced and brought to completion. The limitations of these forms of literary experience can be described as the distinction between the rapturous *feeling* of being in love and the act of *will* involved in committing to a love relationship.

The aesthetics of total form does not denigrate the authenticity of the feelings that literary experience precipitates; to the contrary, it attempts to clarify a conception of literary experience as feeling so as best to see its implications for classroom practice. That readers respond as they do is the inescapable given of reader response theory and practice. But somewhere along the line, even at its most sublime, as is the case with stasis, the respondent must *come to terms* with the basis of the feeling part of literary experience, of what constitutes the gestalt. As in life, when human beings move from falling in love to really loving, the projection is withdrawn and the relationship undergoes a crisis. Eventually, the real question is whether the lovers can accept each other as they really are. This, as we all know, takes work. (See Johnson, 1983.)

Within the aesthetics of total form, stasis and the responses of partial form turn upon an aesthetic mechanism in which feelings of unity, identity, or identification are produced associatively, at least in part, by assent, conscious or unconscious, to the "thought" embodied in the work. Not to unpack the relationship via the critical act is to practice a kind of Pygmalion pedagoguery (Bogdan, 1984); it is to trade on verbal mystification. The aim of this chapter has been to recognize the work of literature on its own terms, as related to life, but distinct from it. Without this recognition, students can remain semiconscious reading subjects unable to distinguish convention from reality.

We might now relate students reading literature within the aesthetics of total form to the anecdote of the feminist joke at the beginning of the chapter. Students will never be able to "get" the joke unless they come to see, to be fully conscious of what it is, unless they can "constitute" the text as object (Miller, 1980, p. 15). In the next chapter, I will argue for the importance of readers becoming fully conscious of not just the literary text as object and themselves as subjects, but of themselves as both subjects and objects of their reading.

This might be equivalent to appreciating the humor of the joke even if one were offended by it, and to know why some laugh and others do not.

Teachers of English are particularly susceptible to being cathected or "hit" by poetry, to being in love with books. Perhaps it is this touch of Peter Pan that generates envy in our colleagues from other disciplines who do not regard doing what one loves as real work. Real work for literature teachers, I think, includes having the courage to question the metaphysical significance of the joy of reading, and ultimately to fall out of love with literature long enough to withdraw their projections once they have been undergone, and ultimately to understand them. This is emphatically not to deny these projections, but to build on them, to move, like lovers who finally really *see* each other, from the aura of sublimity to the reality of a dialectical relationship, characterized not by stasis, but by ambivalence of identity that lies at the heart of both human and textual reality.

Total form as dialectic is literary experience as work, which, through dialectic, may just turn out to be identical with play. When labored and played at long enough, literary experience can culminate in the connected knowing of what Marion Woodman in *The Pregnant Virgin* calls "experiential realization" (1985, p. 158). This is no flash of lightning in response to a nostalgia for the absolute in search of a consolation for existence — to mix the metaphors of Godzich, Frye, and Steiner; for the essence of literariness, as I hope to show in the next chapter, is repudiation of the myth of *unmediated* verbal expression (de Man, 1983).

For Marion Woodman (1985), experiential realization mirrors the birth of a new attitude of self-consciousness of the reading subject that enables action on felt truth; it is an articulated reintegration of Eliot's dissociation of sensibility, of which stasis is a harbinger. As total form, experiential realization represents the union of — or disjunction between — text and reader through finding one's way and one's own voice. Experiential realization leads out of stasis, out of Longinus's (1967) conception of "the sense of vaunting joy, . . . *as though* we had ourselves produced what we had heard" (p. 107, emphasis added), to actually producing it.

In the absence of experiential realization, what we have to choose from is either the gambling machine of stasis or the ambivalence of dialectic — either being in and out of love with literature or working with literary texts. If there is a third alternative, it would have to be found outside the aesthetics of total form described here. There total form would be conceived less in terms of vision, as some "thing" beheld, bestowed from without, than as act, something to be done, of one's own, in which the goal is the journey, study and enjoyment one, and aesthetics and ideology interdependent aspects of reading.

NOTES

1. Frye terms this approach to literary interpretation "the centrifugal fallacy." (See Frye, 1971/1973, p. 32.)

2. Frye terms this approach to literary evaluation "the centripetal fallacy" (1971/1973, p. 33). For a fuller discussion of the centrifugal and centripetal fallacies see Deanne Bogdan, 1981, pp. 33–40.

3. This physical manifestation of kinetic response is often indistinguishable from that of stasis; to wit, my daughter's tears on reading "The Necklace." The difference between these responses has to do with whether or not total form has been perceived. Here only the reader knows for sure, but that she suspended her response until the end is a good indication that the response was informed by the apprehension of *dianoia* as *mythos*.

4. Ironically, it is the very opposite perception of the nature and evidence of violence in this story that has been the cause of recent attempts in Newfoundland to prohibit its use in the schools. On July 1, 1989, the Toronto *Globe and Mail* reported that objections to "The Killers" were based on the "violent language" spoken by the gunmen. In response, one politician defended the story by invoking literary context: "... it's the killers that speak in a violent language. Obviously Hemingway did that so the readers could judge for themselves that people whose language was uncontrolled and violent were evil. It's an extremely moral study." A further irony is that this interpretation is as much an example of stock response as that of the would-be censors. Within the aesthetics of total form, the "moral" nature of the story devolves around the recognition scene, the full horror of which in turn presupposes being able to *perceive* that the killers' language is in fact very much controlled and understated. But the predisposition to holding such a perception is a question of worldview. The difference between seeing the killers' language as controlled and as uncontrolled depends very much on whether the reader shares in the intellectual and moral assumptions constellated by the story's "thought." (See "Censorship Cries Heard As Province Changes Textbooks." The *Globe and Mail*, July 1, 1989; also Bogdan, 1987b, 1988, 1989b.)

5. My spectator response differs markedly from that of James Britton, who defines it in terms of a detached literary response that is also engaged. My spectator response, however, is a deliberate drawing back from textual engagement; as such, it is an incomplete response. (See Bogdan, 1986a, 1988b, 1987e; Gambell, 1986, pp. 127–128.)

6. For a developmental approach to teaching John Updike's short story "A & P," see Deanne Bogdan, 1985a, pp. 43–49; 1987b, pp. 13–32.

FROM MEDITATION
TO MEDIATION
Breaking Out of Total Form

Deanne Bogdan

STASIS DECONSTRUCTED:
WHAT IS IT, ANYHOW?

It is Sunday afternoon, Valentine's day, and I am not supposed to be writing this chapter yet. According to my "plan," I am still to be marshaling my "authorities," awaiting the inexorable dawn of Monday morning when the writing imperative will descend like the threat of impending doom — and gloom. I break for lunch, treating myself to one of my favorite records, a collection of Purcell Songs by counter-tenor Andrew Dalton. At the same time, I pick up an old *Harper's* that has been sitting around on the coffee table since before Christmas. Randomly I open it to an article by Peter Freundlich titled, "Gazing into Bergdorf's Window: Reflections on the Higher Shopping" (1987). As I begin to read and the first Purcell song runs its course, I sense that the lunch break will be restorative; the music flows over me like a warm bath and the Freundlich piece promises to be just the right diversion.

Something else is happening, though. I realize as I sink back into the rocker by the sun-flooded window that my preoccupation with stasis is a direct expression of my own metaphysics, my version of Descartes' *cogito* being "I hanker after the absolute, therefore I am."

This does not present itself to me as a new awareness, however. I have known for a long time that musical experience has always been prototypical of the ineffable for me. Perhaps because of a very early intense musical education (I could read music before words), I have always felt that meaning at its most profound resides in an essentially wordless universe. Language for me has served to ground experience, music to expand it. The act of naming itself I find a deeply ambivalent enterprise.

Yes, there is something about these Purcell songs, especially as they are rendered by Dalton, that exactly embodies, and elicits, what I mean by stasis: paralysis of thought and action coupled with a paradoxical blend of satiety and frustration of desire. I listen transfixed, unmindful of the songs' titles and deaf to their lyrics. That makes sense, doesn't it? In vocal music, content is only a function of form, I have always believed.[1] That is why I never bother to read the translations of German lieder. What counts is the exquisite, almost immaterial — certainly ungendered — "tracing of the mechanism," as Wittgenstein (see pp. 13–17) has put it, of the aesthetic experience itself. In these songs, it has a lot to do with apprehending the pattern of rising minor thirds and falling perfect fifths. My savoring of them seems to embrace the aesthetics of total form.

Out of curiosity, I eventually do attend to the words. The first line of the first song, "Music for a while shall all your cares beguile," speaks precisely to my sense of music's palliative and curative powers. The second and third songs, even more ethereal, are, respectively, odes to presence and absence. Both taken from Purcell's "semioperas," his adaptations of plays, the first, titled "Fairest Isle," is intended to be Venus paying tribute to Britain, "all isles excelling,/Seat of pleasure and of love." The second, "Since from My Dear Astrea's Sight," addresses a character who does not actually appear in the play. The entire song exudes a bittersweet longing endemic to stasis:

> Since from my dear Astrea's sight
> I was so rudely torn,
> My soul has never known delight,
> Unless it were to mourn.
>
> But oh, alas! with weeping eyes
> And bleeding heart I lie,
> Thinking on her whose absence 'tis
> That makes me wish to die.

At this point, my more fervent poststructuralist colleagues would probably want to wrench me out of this "humanist" reverie, quick to point out that these three songs juxtapose the aesthetic with the political, auguring hegemonies of the worst sort. Reluctantly I would agree, but would want to reassert my claim to the province of the aesthetic as at least addressable on its own terms even if it is no longer sacrosanct (yes, I know, pleasure is never innocent). Bringing me to consciousness about the ideological implications of these songs might be able to bracket out, but would never blanket over, the fact that the ongoing desire for recurrence of aesthetic experience will persist. In one of the more useful conceptions of aesthetic experience, Paul Valéry (1972) concludes that what distinguishes it from mere sensation is its inexhaustibility,

> the need to see again, to hear again, to experience indefinitely. The lover of form never wearies of caressing the bronze or stone that excites his sense of touch. The music lover cries "encore" or hums the tune that has delighted him. The child wants the story repeated: "Tell it over again! . . ." (p. 29).

To understand the properties or dynamics of such experience is not to dissolve the category. Decomposing aesthetic experience into extra-aesthetic terms, as some contemporary theorists tend to do, simply begs the question of the *need* for aesthetic experience, even if that need is reduced to the most primitive of psychological terms. As feminist filmmaker Yvonne Rainer comments, "Why else do we go to see narrative cinema than to be confirmed and reinforced in our most atavistic and oedipal mind-sets?" (quoted in de Lauretis, 1987, p. 122).

But to return to the *Harper's* article. The irony of my thoughts about stasis and the content of the Purcell songs is deepened by the topic of Freundlich's article, which, we recall, I just stumbled upon. In reflecting "on the higher shopping," the author relates the refined state of current consumerism to a kind of nostalgia for the absolute incarnated. It is startling to compare the tropes of yuppiedom with the rhetoric of stasis. Freundlich (1987) writes:

> We were ordinary folk once, our dreams simple: a few chickens, a tarpaper shack to call our own, an extra pair of overalls into which to change on Sundays, a crystal radio. But now something new has been loosed among us . . . Instead of being satisfied with a ham sandwich, we want for a snack goat-cheese pizza with sun-dried morrels; instead of all-cotton, we wear our tennis athletic socks of lapin fur; instead of refrigerator ice, we plop hearts of glacier cubes into our Cartesian well water.
>
> How did we get from there to here? What fantastic dream dreamed by the world's merchants—by . . . automobile salesmen lost in transports of nocturnal greed—revealed to the multitude the wonder of the higher shopping? By what pure act of will did the dream become flesh? How did the divine word turn first into a fat wallet, clay-soft so that it could tease and stretch itself into a Giacometti-like human being? . . . (p. 73).

Freundlich continues his tract on the consumer as "the dream buyer," with Swiftian lists of how

> the *made* world . . . is being fashioned for *him*. Look you everywhere, and see! The search now is for the very best, the most rare, the empyrean, the nonpareil. We need not ask anymore who or what it is that has inherited the earth: we *know*. It is the walking wallet with the coal-black eyes, in search of underwear handwoven by Tibetan virgins, in search of silk foulard toilet paper, badger-bustle johnny-mops, . . . (p. 73).

At first glance, the comparison between consumerism and stasis seems invidious. Stasis is the aesthetic expression of a spiritual yearning for perfect presence; consumerism, the infantile demand for instant material gratification. Yet even in the prose just cited, we note the conflation of the art world with narcissistic self-image ("Giacometti-like human being"); we observe, too, the pervasive language of Longinian *ecstasis* ("fantastic," "dream," "transports," "revealed," "wonder," "higher," "divine"). Common to these seemingly two disparate realms is flight from the quotidian, rejection of the mundane, ardor for nicety, and aspiration to the authentic:

> I tell you we are discriminating ourselves out of existence. If our hankerings become any more refined, we shall die of hunger and go naked and unhoused. We are incapable of settling anymore, incapable of compromising . . . We are like Geiger counters calibrated for preciousness, our hearts clicking harder, faster in the presence of the rare (pp. 73–74).

Here the signifiers of the sublime ("hankerings," "refined," "preciousness," "pressure," "rare") are counterposed with zeal for the nirvanic quest.

What begins as a diatribe ricocheting its caricatures of connoisseurship ends as a sober diagnosis of a major ailment of our *fin du siècle*, the aware consumer as visionary *manqué*. It turns out that yuppies are not "genuinely in love with the stuff of which the world is made," after all (p. 76). They are really "symbolists . . . blind to the material itself, mindless of the coming of gold by sweat and hatred and death out of the ground," revelling less in their material possessions than in the knowledge that they have reached "the point toward which the striving restless riches of the world tend" (p. 76). Freundlich's characterization of this Utopia Gained is "a new Romanticism . . . Where once Tennysonians swooned, . . . on the banks of peaceful rivers, soul-struck by the perfection of a world not dependent in the least on man, now we swoon over artificial beauties. We would have 'Ode to a Mercedez-Benz' now or 'Upon First Looking into Bergdorf's Window'" (p. 76).

Whether Freundlich's cynicism about the excesses of an aestheticism run amuck is well or ill founded does not concern us here. More important is how we can utilize his observation that above the religion of stuff, of artifacts exotic and pristine, hovers some kind of spiritual hunger. My surmise that Freundlich's pinpointing yuppiedom as a demonic form of aestheticism undergirded by a nostalgia for the absolute akin to stasis may not be the act of committing heresy on my own work that it may at first appear to be. For I have already suggested in the previous chapter that all is not well with stasis; out there in the black void, like a distant diamond, stasis simultaneously beckons and lies in wait.

In the last chapter, I suggested that stasis as the precritical intuitive apprehension of total form must be sacrificed on the altar of consciousness. It is only by giving up the illusion of fulfilled identity, by falling out of love with literature and committing to the clear-eyed state of working *with* literature, that is, by alternating between reading for pleasure and rereading for awareness of what it is we are confronting, that aesthetic experience can be the true joy of *learning* as Aristotle's recognition scene, rather than the usurping of cognitive faculties that has worried theorists from Plato to Jeffrey Robinson. Plato feared that falling in love with the word, with logos, as it became aestheticized and thus concretized through poetry, would seduce the respondent into false resting places. As Iris Murdoch (1977) has noted so wryly about Platonic aesthetic theory, "[t]hose who want to be saved should look at the stars and talk philosophy, not write or go to the theatre" (p. 60).

Disengaging not from literature, but from attachment to whatever truth, bliss, security, or escape literature may promise or point to, moves the reader, as I suggested in the last chapter, from the naive condition of being in love to the maturer state of loving, from surety to ambivalence. Harold Bloom (1982) invites readers to become metaphysicians of their reading by asking, "What do we mean when we think we love poems, and what does that love defend, or defend against?" (p. 17). This question can first be answered by acknowledging that reading, "as an art, depends upon fundamental previsions of what is being read, so that in order to read a poem you necessarily start with an idea of what a poem is, or can be" (p. 31).

But we already know, from the previous chapter, what a poem is, or can be — an aesthetic verbal object cannily crafted by its author, which when seen in the totality of its rational design, when meditated upon with sufficient expertise, will disclose a universal truth about the human condition. This act of perception can be made instinctively through stasis (as with the Purcell song) or dialectically through alternating states of engagement with the text and detachment from it, the preferable mode being the latter slower but surer process, which brings with it a heightened consciousness of the poem's metaphysical reality. Not so for Bloom. In the first place, metaphysics is the wrong category. Poems are not products; they aren't even processes; they're hapennings, "pragmatic events" (p. 41). So is literary criticism. We must ask, "What is a poem *for* anyway? . . . Poetry and criticism are useful not for what they really are, but for whatever poetic and critical use you can usurp them to, which means that interpretive poems and poetic interpretations are concepts you make happen, rather than concepts of being" (p. 39).

This unseating of the metaphysical reality of the poetic object marks one aspect of the critique of the aesthetic of Aristotle and Frye recounted in the previous chapter; one of the by-products of this critique is the discrediting and demystification of stasis. And so we come full circle to the *Harper's* article. Is it possible that Freundlich has unwittingly given us a picture of the yuppie as a seeker after stasis in a universe that has nullified total form? Desire, thought, and action, fused in stasis as the rapturous act of contemplation, have in Freundlich's hands, been brought down to earth with a thud. Demolition of the aesthetic artifact removes with that object the possibility of the meditational engagements acting as moments of perfect presence. Not only is *God* dead, but so is spiritual communion by way of the kind of aesthetic pleasure that comes from believing in literature as a structure to be understood and undergone (Moffett, 1988b).

Within the aesthetics of total form, stasis promises to be the link between literature and life by fashioning the reader into a more morally aware member of the human community. Through the quite literal stoppage of desire, action, and the search for truth—truth is attained, desire fulfilled, action made redundant to the "static state"— stasis eventuates in the inspiration to live life as well as we can, reading the reader in a kind of Rorschach test of the sublime. Dialectic performs the same task on earth that stasis does in heaven, bringing the entire process of literary response into the arena of intellection. But both stasis and dialectic rely on a conception of the literary work as object, and response to literature as the best approximation of that object in the reader's consciousness. Poststructuralist literary theory seeks to change all that.

In this chapter, I will be exploring the relationship between the aesthetic and the ideological through three theories of reading literature helmed by three critical worldviews that can loosely be called poststructuralist: feminism, deconstruction, and Marxism. I say "loosely" because while the term "poststructuralist" includes Marxist criticism and deconstruction, it is not descriptive of all forms of feminist criticism. Just as "structuralist" does not adequately define the aesthetics of total form I have outlined in the previous chapter (total form is also humanist, formalist, and universalist, but not all of structuralism can be defined in those terms), "poststructuralist" is also a somewhat impure term for the breaking down and out of total form I am undertaking in this chapter. However, it does provide a useful reference point for what has been happening in contemporary literary theory over the past two to three decades as a backdrop for my inquiry into the intersection of aesthetics and ideology applied to reading literary texts. In making my way through this inquiry, I will not attempt a detailed rehearsal of poststructuralist literary theory; rather I will stress only those tenets of poststructuralism that serve to highlight the breaking out of stasis and total form encouraged by poststructuralism. What follows represents my effort to stand total form on its head in the light of three of the most influential ideologies in contemporary literary theory, each of which in its own way vindicates as critical principles the three varieties of partial form — stock, kinetic, and spectator response — described in the previous chapter.

Poststructuralist aesthetics inverts the aesthetics of total form. The literary search for truth, desire, and action, formerly anathematized by total form as the progenitors of partial form (see Bogdan, 1986a, 1986b, 1987c) become, within poststructuralism, aesthetic critical principles *sui generis*. As to the fate of stasis in all this, the feminist can't have it, the deconstructionist doesn't need it, and the Marxist doesn't trust it.

We recall that stasis epitomizes the fusion of thought, desire, and action in an instant of perfect identity with the literary object, and that somehow this fusion represents a spiritual transcendence — the attainment of wholeness as an irreducible human need. Partial form is a deviation from stasis, the inevitable playing out by mere mortals possessing imperfect faculties, of the perfect balance of intellect and emotion symbolized by imaginative identity. I use "symbolized" advisedly because, except for rare occasions, stasis is really only a metaphor for this identity. Partial form is the best we can aspire to in a fallen universe (Frye, 1971/ 1973). I see poststructuralist theory as a way of bringing stasis down to earth without the incompleteness or loss that comes with partial form, of making material what within total form can only be metaphorical, of articulating its unconscious apprehensions — rendering visible its unseen presence, giving voice to its mute reality.

Poststructuralist theory divides total form into its component parts, liberating the search for truth, desire, and action, each to go its own way, thus enabling the reader to overcome the either/or polarization of the engagement/detachment dichotomy. In this chapter and the next, I hope to illustrate how feminist literary theory rescues stock response from partial form by restoring the legitimacy of the search for truth to literary response, how deconstruction does the same for desire and kinetic response, and Marxist criticism does it for action and spectator response: in short, how the reader moves from meditation to mediation, from contemplating the text to creating it in the return of literature to life.

THE POSTSTRUCTURALIST CRITIQUE OF THE LITERARY COMMUNICATION MODEL

As stated earlier, the phenomenon of stasis is tied to a "lightning model" of literary interpretation (see pp. 119–123), itself a kind of compressed communication model, in which the text can be regarded as "an invisible thread leading from the author's subjectivity to the reader's" (Belsey, 1980, p. 127). The impact of the work is made possible mainly by virtue of the complicity between author and reader, who share certain ideological assumptions, what Aristotle called "thought." Attendant upon this literary communication model are other assumptions about the ideology of readers and reading, having to do with belief in universal values, poetic truth, determinate response, textual stability, univocal, "correct" meaning, and the idea that a rational "self" participating in an invariant human nature propels the act of reading. These assumptions turn on a theory of language in which thought and experience, deemed anterior to language, are expressed or reflected by language.

Uniting the various forms of poststructuralist theorists is their belief that language does not reflect reality but produces it, and that the subjectivities of the author and reader, presumed in the communication model to be innate, unified, and fixed, are, rather, constructed by language. Thus, the subjectivities of author and reader are not presumed to be entities threaded together by a coherent text, but the "site of disunity and conflict, central to the process of political change and to preserving the status quo" (Weedon, 1985, p. 21). "Poststructuralism" is itself a term with a plural meaning, referring to a range of theories embracing reader-response theory, deconstruction, feminist, psychoanalytic, and Marxist criticism. Though they overlap considerably, each proclaims its own gurus and its own emphases. All, however, are suspicious of a "common sense" view of the world and the assumptions underlying it. In a single paragraph, Catherine Belsey (1980) sniffs/ snuffs out the ideologies endemic in the linguistic appeal to experience, the bedrock of the literary communication model and the aesthetics of total form:

> Common sense proposes a *humanism* based on an *empiricist-idealist* interpretation of the world. In other words, common sense urges

that man is the origin and source of meaning, of action, and of history (*humanism*). Our concepts and our knowledge are held to be the product of experience (*empiricism*), and this experience is preceded and interpreted by the mind, reason or thought, the property of a transcendent human nature whose essence is the attribute of each individual (*idealism*). These propositions, . . . constitute the basis of a practice of reading which assumes, whether explicitly or implicitly, the theory of expressive realism. This is the theory that literature reflects the *reality* of experience as it is perceived by one (especially gifted) individual, who *expresses* it in a discourse which enables other individuals to recognize it as true (p. 7).

A number of difficulties arise for poststructuralists from the communication model of literary interpretation. First is the romanticization of the creative process. Literary artists are larger than life, and literary objects come about by a sort of magic. For example, the poet and critic, Robin Skelton, in his book *Poetic Truth* (1978), tells us that "poetry, in as far as it is consciously experienced, is experienced as magic" (p. 110) because of the primitive quality of the metaphorical habit of mind. Belsey contests this romanticizing of the creative process as "a mystical and mysterious occurrence conceived rather as a state of mind than as work" (p. 127). What should be highlighted, according to Belsey, is not the author's presumed "qualities of insight and understanding," but "the labour of producing out of the available signifying system of language and literature an intelligible fiction" (p. 127). In dismantling the communication model, Belsey asserts that this "intelligible fiction" is not a literary artifact to be meditated upon, not a finished product to be gazed at by an awestruck reader who imbibes the author's genius (p. 127). The metaphysical reality of the text presumed by the aesthetics of total form is apparently an illusion, as is the feeling of coming to know some universal truth about oneself and/or the world. That these are fictions constructed by the interworking of language and ideology is the primary tenet of poststructuralism.

In the aesthetics of total form, what allows the literary object to be communicated is a set of dynamics that begins with a preexistent meaning or intention that is deemed authentic because it is guaranteed by the author's subjectivity, moves to being "translated" into words, and then "transmitted" to a reader, its meaning intact, channeled by the complex of Aristotelian "thought" uniting them. Eventually, if the reading is "correct," the reader becomes imbued with a "sense of plenitude, of a full understanding of a coherent text" that "moves inevitably and irreversibly to an end, to the conclusion of an ordered series of events, to the disclosure of what has been concealed," i.e., to be communicated (Belsey, 1980, pp. 104–105). In what follows, I hope to show how three poststructuralist approaches to the text break out of the aesthetics of total form and topple the communication model. I am suggesting that in the feminist critical project, the search for truth surfaces as the preeminent critical value; in the deconstructionist one, it is desire; and in the Marxist approach, action. Within the aesthetics of total form, these were each aspects of partial form: the search for truth was identified as stock response; the impulse of desire, kinetic response; and the withdrawal of engagement, spectator response. In the remainder of this chapter, I will sketch out how each of the poststructuralist approaches to the text rebels against the constraints of total form. In the next chapter, I will attempt to demonstrate how each can reclaim total form through a redefined dialectical process between text and reader.

FEMINIST CRITICISM: STOCK RESPONSE AND "THE SEARCH FOR TRUTH"

Earlier, I suggested that poststructuralism annihilates stasis: the feminist reader can't have it; the deconstructive one doesn't need it; the Marxist doesn't trust it. These dispositions can serve as a way of orienting our discussion of the three theories of reading of which I am undertaking to give an account. As a focus for our discussion, let's use Sinclair Ross's short story (1971), "The Painted Door." In this story, Ann, the wife of a Canadian prairie farmer several years her senior, is left alone during a fierce blizzard by her husband John, who sets out on foot to assist his father with some chores at his farmhouse, ten miles distant. Hurt by John's allegiance to his filial duty taking precedence over his concern for her, Ann broods about her sense of isolation, the tedium of her marriage, and the steadfast but colorless character of her husband, as she begins to paint their bedroom in order to pass the time. Ann's loneliness and anxiety are assuaged by a visit from Steven, a neighbor and family friend much younger than John. Ann and Steven became aware of their mutual sexual attraction and sleep together, though through the night Ann is wracked with guilt and haunted by the image of John's face. Sick with worry because he has failed to return, Ann realizes too late her deep love for her husband.

> Already it was long past midnight; either John had lost his way or not set out at all. And she knew that in his devotion there was nothing foolhardy. He would never risk a storm beyond his endurance, never permit himself a sacrifice likely to endanger her lot or future. They were both safe. No one would ever know. She must control herself—be sane like Steven.

For comfort she let her hand rest awhile on Steven's shoulder. It would be easier were he awake now, with her, sharing her guilt; but gradually as she watched his handsome face in the glimmering light she came to understand that for him no guilt existed. Just as there had been no passion, no conflict. Nothing but the sane appraisal of their situation, nothing but the expectant little smile, and the arrogance of features that were different from John's. She winced deeply, remembering how she had fixed her eyes on those features, how she had tried to believe that so handsome and young, so different from John's, they must in themselves be her justification.

In the flickering light they were still young, still handsome. No longer her justification—she knew now, John was the man—but wistfully still, wondering sharply at their power and tyranny, she touched them a moment with her fingertips again.

She could not blame him. There had been no passion, no guilt; therefore there could be no responsibility. Looking down at him as he slept, half smiling still, his lips relaxed in the conscienceless complacency of his achievement, she understood that thus he was revealed in his entirety—all there ever was or ever could be. John was the man. With him lay all the future. For tonight, slowly and contritely through the days and years to come, she would try to make amends.

Then she stole back to the kitchen, and without thought, impelled by overwhelming need again, returned to the door where the draft was bitter still. Gradually toward morning the storm began to spend itself. Its terror blast became a feeble, worn-out moan. The leap of light and shadow sank, and a chill crept in again. Always the eaves creaked, tortured with wordless prophecy. Heedless of it all the clock ticked on in idiot content.

They found him the next day, less than a mile from home. Drifting with the storm he had run against his own pasture fence and, overcome, had frozen there, erect still, both hands clasping fast the wire.

"He was south of here," they said wonderingly when she told them how he had come across the hills. "Straight south—you'd wonder how he could have missed the buildings. It was the wind last night, coming every way at once. He shouldn't have tried. There was a double wheel around the moon."

She looked past them a moment, then as if to herself said simply, "If you knew him, though—John would try."

It was later, when they had left her awhile to be alone with him, that she knelt and touched his hand. Her eyes dimmed, it was still such a strong and patient hand; then, transfixed, they suddenly grew wide and clear. On the palm, white even against its frozen whiteness, was a little smear of paint.

Within the aesthetics of total form, this story almost invariably induces stasis as the flash of lightning wherein thought and feeling coalesce. The reader sustains a powerful shock of recognition that John indeed *had* returned home, and after seeing the two in the bedroom, slipped away back into the storm. There results a suffusion of aesthetic pleasure, arising from the immediate impact of *dianoia* perceived as *mythos*, and *mythos* perceived as *dianoia*. Simultaneity of expression and illumination become both a function and enactment of the interconnection between the reader's feelings and awareness of the author's craft.

Against the previous reading, let's put a feminist interpretation, in which the reader foregrounds her heightened consciousness of gender bias both in literature and in life. It can be safely assumed that such a reader of "The Painted Door," even if she were to accept the notion of total form, is not likely to be swept away by stasis or divine madness. She probably would just get mad — angry that the mechanism allowing the story to work at an aesthetic level presumes and perpetuates a value system inimical to women. Within the ideology of total form, this would be regarded as a stock response, for a genuine literary response would require accepting the story on *its* terms, rather than the reader's. But let's take a further look. The conjunction of *mythos* and *dianoia* precipitating stasis in this story resides in the final recognition scene, where the "little smear of paint" performs two major functions: first, it fuses plot and character, revealing in graphic terms the tragic consequences of Ann's moral choice; second, it ascribes the burden of guilt for John's death unequivocally to Ann, who assumes responsibility for the fatal painted door, literally and metaphorically. Here the poignancy of ironic reversal — Ann's coming to realize her love for her husband too late — devolves upon author and reader sharing certain moral and intellectual assumptions, certain tenets comprising Aristotle's "thought," that is, ideology.

This reading of "The Painted Door" entails accepting a certain "given" about "women's place" in sexual relations, viz., marital fidelity is a moral good that supersedes the exploration of a woman's sexuality or the expression of doubt about her marriage. There is simply no dramatic interest in the story unless this dictum is in some way contravened; and in order for it to *be* contravened, author and reader must first mutually accept the validity of patriarchal constraint on female sexuality, at least for purposes of "enjoying the story." In short, the mechanism of plot and character (Aristotle's other two objects of imitation; 1967, pp. 33, 41–43, 51–52), eliciting stasis, demands that Ann make a moral choice that goes against her. She acts out her feelings in order to know, quite literally under pain of death (both John's death and the death of her own happiness as realized, too late, in her marriage). For stasis to work at all, author and reader must be in agreement about the nature of her moral choice. If Ann had resisted Steven (been a good and faithful wife), there would have been no story. That she succumbed to her sexual desire brings about the death-dealing reversal and with it the realization — and acceptance — that "[t]his is just how things are, and I didn't know it" (Greene, 1986, p. 240).

There is, however, a great difference between the sense of "how things are" under the assumptions of total form and "how things are" under feminist criticism. Within a universalist perspective, the realization of "how things are" devolves upon the truism that "[d]eath is the price of human knowledge"; within the feminist purview, upon the observation that "[d]eath so often seems to be the price of *women's* knowledge."

For feminists, one of the problems with total form as stasis, as a literary gestalt, is that its "totality" presupposes a universal human condition derived from male life experience and an aesthetic effect derived from male reading experience.

> The classic line of literary theory has hardly acknowledged the existence of two sexes let alone the possibility that women might read and interpret literature in some way of their own. From Aristotle to Northrop Frye, women are assumed to be a subspecies of men (Lipking, 1983/1984, p. 86).

There is no way of enlisting total form in the service of the feminist reader within the aesthetics of total form without making women or women's reading a subspecies of men or men's reading. In his book, *Sinclair Ross: A Reader's Guide* (1981), Kenneth Mitchell reiterates the "universalism" of the story's appeal:

> The ending employs an unexpected twist of plot, yet its impact is totally convincing. Ann is left . . . facing an indescribably tormented future of guilt, for her one lapse of conviction. It is a tough moral world that Ross's characters occupy (p. 16).

But it is precisely this conjunction of the unexpected ending (which seems so true-to-life and, in hindsight, inevitable) with the "tough moral world" of Ross's characters that, according to Mitchell, make the story so "convincing." To enjoy the story in this way, to take its "point," to appreciate it as craft, or to experience stasis, the reader must resonate with the ethos of the fictional creation (see Bogdan, 1987a), must collude with Ross in setting up the "thought." To do otherwise, to read with a feminist agenda in repudiation of such "thought," within the aesthetics of total form, is to read as a stock responder, as an ideologue who goes to the story, as Sir Philip Sidney (1966) would say, "looking for truth" (p. 53). The feminist as ideologue would be, according to a structuralist such as Frye, doomed to circular argument, locked into continually lining up the belief systems thought to be contained in the story with "a set of associations that [she] already has or at least knows about" (1965, p. 131), much like my former principal and thesis supervisor in dealing with Bolt's *Man for All Seasons*. After all, a work "has to be understood as well as read" (Frye, 1985, p. 3), i.e., "read" understood as the undergoing of literary experience.

Within the aesthetics of total form, a reading is considered literary in direct relation to the suspension of moral or aesthetic value judgments. Frye (1985) puts it this way:

> In reading a work of literature, no process of belief, in the ordinary sense, is involved. What is involved is a continuous process of acceptance. We accept every word given us in the text without question (unless we are textual editors), and withhold our response until the end (pp. 5–6).

Frye is so unequivocal on this point that he uses it as the distinguishing feature of literature's metaphysical reality. "Literature differs from descriptive or factual verbal structures in the degree of emphasis it places on this postponing of response" (p. 6). Paralleling this distinction is that between the mythological and ideological as primary and secondary expressions of social concern. Ideology adopts the rhetorical form of the thesis, and mythology of narrative. "A story, unlike a proposition," argues Frye (1985), "cannot be refuted or argued about" (p. 14). That isn't to say it cannot be interpreted in different ways, but only that it cannot be denied or proved false in the sense that $2 \times 2 = 4$ can.

Within this framework of literary reading as suspended judgment, feminist literary criticism would appear to be a contradiction in terms, for the very lifeblood of feminist reading has been its *refusal* to suspend belief. Ideology is its motivating force. In *The Resisting Reader*, Judith Fetterley (1978), echoing Adrienne Rich, invites the female reader to "re-vision" texts, that is, to engage in what Bloom (1975) calls "strong" readings or misprision, deliberate reading against the grain of a universalist perspective. For both Fetterley and Bloom, the notion of total form as contingent upon separating interpretation from worldview is a fallacy to be exploded by a resistant reader. "The true critic . . ., knows that criticism, like poetry, cannot be an escape from personality" (Bloom, 1975, p. 48). Here Bloom attempts to reconnect literature to the author despite the persistent moves of criticism to keep them disconnected. Fetterley's concern is to reestablish the tie at the reader's end, to engage in "re-vision" as an act of survival that aims at nothing less than changing the world (p. xix). While Bloom is resigned to the loss that comes from falling out of love with literature in the process of revisioning (and feminist incursions into universalist assumptions do entail a loss to masculinist values), Fetterley is determined to reclaim for women readers an entire heritage of (American) literature denied to them on the premises of universality and tangibility espoused by an aesthetics of total form.

> One of the main things that keeps the design of our literature unavailable to the consciousness of the woman reader, and hence impalpable, is the very posture of the apolitical pretense that literature speaks universal truths through forms from which all the merely personal, the purely subjective, has been burned away or at least transformed through the medium of art into the representative. When only one reality is encouraged, legitimized, and transmitted and when that limited vision endlessly insists on its comprehensiveness, then we have the conditions necessary for the confusion of consciousness in which impalpability flourishes (p. xi).

I have reproduced a fair chunk of Fetterley's Preface here because it encapsulates so justly the *bouleversement*, the upsetting of my taxonomy of total form described in the last chapter. Fetterley is challenging on its own ground the uniting of *mythos* and *dianoia* by a "thought" based on universal values. For her, what purports to be total form is in fact partial form by dint of a totalizing mechanism that defines the universal as the not-female. Fetterley's language here is even neo-Aristotelian ("design," "consciousness," "forms," "transformed," "medium," "representative," "comprehensiveness"). She is not so much inveighing against total form as pleading for its actualization by way of an aesthetic principle that would not require fifty percent of readers to identify against themselves in order to embrace it. Searching for truth is redundant in the aesthetics of total form because "truth" is already there as the assumption of universal values. The feminist must find her own textual truth beyond the strictures of patriarchal reading.

This is a tall order for a feminist reader ill content to be relegated to the twilight zone of partial form. As reading metaphysicians, feminist readers are not satisfied with what Lorenne Clark (1976) calls "the ontological basement." For them, the task would be to construct an interpretive theory equal to the perspective of Frye's, that is, one in which literary structure is subsumed under the widest possible category of human concern: happiness over misery, good over evil, freedom over anarchy. Strong reading against the grain is one thing; devising a conceptual framework for it is another. In order to transcend the hierarchical relationship of mythology and ideology within total form, then, Aristotle's universal truth must be redefined in feminist terms as the ground for "how things are."

A possible solution comes to us by way of Susan Aiken (1986), whose work helps to overcome the metaphysical problem posed for feminist criticism by total form. In her inquiry into the marginality of women writers in the literary canon, Aiken raises to Frye's archetypal level the relationship between the subjugation of female sexuality and the cultural order by making a convincing argument that the history of western civilization trades on male ownership of discourse and "the exchange of women in exogamous alliances" (p. 294). That is, the cultural order itself is contingent upon "female chastity and strong taboos against adultery" (p. 294). When "thought" changes from the puritanical "tough moral world" inhabited by Ross's characters (a world the reader must also inhabit for literary purposes) to, say, the locking in of women within a power structure that victimizes them through guilt in sexual relations, stasis becomes a response that is well nigh impossible in "The Painted Door." Total form cannot be perceived/received so long as the reader opposes the sociological grounds of its aesthetic mechanism. The union of *mythos* and *dianoia* constituting the recognition scene is precluded by feminist consciousness itself, which by definition turns facts and assumptions of the patriarchal social order into contradictions. As Sandra Lee Bartky (1979) reminds us, "Feminists are not aware of different things than other people: they are aware of the same things differently" (p. 254).

One way a feminist reader might attain stasis in this story would be to suspend belief in feminist doctrine for "literary purposes." (See Kolodny, 1985, pp. 154 ff.) But for the feminist, aesthetic response cannot be legislated in this way without capitulation to masculinist paradigms. Moreover, the reader's assent to "thought" is especially crucial in "The Painted Door" because of its realism, a literary genre in which the aesthetic fabric is acutely dependent upon the illusion of reality that "thought," as the "sociology" of the piece, conjures up (see Bogdan, 1987b). In the next chapter, we shall look at how a feminist reader, working with an awareness of the way in which the imbrication of plot and "thought" perpetuates sexist ideology in literary realism, engages in a dialectical process that moves the reader from total form as experience to total form as activity. But for now, let us turn to deconstruction and how it validates the kinetic response and the reader's desire for textual pleasure.

DECONSTRUCTION:
KINETIC RESPONSE AND DESIRE

If feminist criticism can be said to recast stock response as a legitimate impetus toward "looking for truth" in interpretation, then deconstruction and Marxist criticism can be said to do the same for desire and action, respectively. We recall from the previous chapter that the main objection to kinetic response within the aesthetics of total form was that it presumed a misguided conception of aesthetic pleasure based on the immediate impact of a literary work (see pp. 125–128). If "kinetic" pertains to motion, kinetic response is a form of motion based on the laws of pleasure and pain, a reflex reaction to text in terms of "I like it/don't like it." In my simulated reading of "The Killers," students mistakenly believe they are supposed to identify with the characters as real people rather than perceive them in their Aristotelian roles as structural devices of the plot. In literary response as dialectic (see pp. 129–133), knowledge about literature becomes a prerequisite of literary enjoyment in that literary knowledge acts as a corrective to the partial vision eclipsing total form and encumbering the process of attaining imaginative identity with the literary object through the recognition scene. Within the aesthetics of total form, wariness of kinetic response denotes a kind of textual Calvinism in which the reader is continually on guard about the conditions under which she or he should be experiencing pleasure.

Textual Hedonism

Circumspection about surrendering to the delights of reading issuing from kinetic response resembles that of the feminist reader's caution about stasis. But whereas kinetic response is regarded as an aberration of the aesthetics of total form, it is the very conception of total form itself that makes the feminist reader suspicious of stasis. Both stasis and kinetic response are concerned with metaphysical distinctions between the literary text and "objective" reality as sources of textual pleasure. In short, the reader is asking questions about just where this pleasure is coming from, and why and how it produces its effects. The literary theory of deconstruction obviates the necessity for such distinctions, its major tenet being that reality is not anterior to language: "There is nothing outside of the text" (Derrida, 1977, p. 158). Thus, the "metaphysics of presence, that is, the conviction that words are only signs of a real substance which is always elsewhere" (Weedon, 1987, p. 85) — the difference between textual and "real" reality — is an illusion. The only expedient for the deconstructionist, then, is to forget such worries and submit to the "chaotic processes of textuality ... in the reifications, the personal pleasures, of reading" (Leitch, 1983, p. 122).

In *The Pleasure of the Text* (1973/1975), Roland Barthes, an early proponent of deconstruction theory, springs the reader free from the tyranny of the "should's" to the point of textual hedonism. His project is to reconnect literature to life at the level of desire on an initial reading. Barthes' idea of textual pleasure is far more dynamic than stasis. Whereas stasis represents a kind of stoppage or paralysis, Barthes' *jouissance* (translated somewhat feebly as "bliss") is veritable orgasmic experience. *Jouissance* transmutes the randomness and unpredictability of the lightning model into a critical principle:

> Everyone can testify that the pleasure of the text is not certain: nothing says that this same text will please us a second time; it is a friable pleasure, split by mood, habit, circumstance, a precarious pleasure. . . .
> The bliss of the text is not precarious, it is worse: *precocious*; it does not come in its own good time, it does not depend on any ripening. Everything is wrought to a transport at one and the same moment. . . . Everything comes about; indeed in every sense everything *comes — at first glance* (pp. 52–53).

Barthes repudiates the delayed gratification of the recognition scene in favor of a *carpe diem* theory of reading, in which literature and life are collapsed into "textuality." Gone is the *ostranenie* of the Russian Formalists (Hawkes, 1977, p. 62), the Aristotelian "object of imitation" with its "beginning, middle, and end," setting off the text as a separate reality. For Barthes, the "important thing is to equalize the field of pleasure, to abolish the false opposition of practical life and contemplative life" (p. 59). With the joy of fusing literature and life comes an inversion of the hierarchy between the precritical and critical responses that we encountered in total form. For Barthes, criticism is a lower road than just plain reading, for the best a critical reading of a text can produce is a *plaisir* in tune with the culture. Following critical conventions for Barthes simply reinforces culture; it is the *jouissance* of an *initial* reading that brings true rapture. But this *jouissance* is, curiously enough, contingent upon first experiencing the very kind of disappointment a story, say, like "The Killers" precipitates; the kind of "text that imposes a state of loss, the text that discomforts (perhaps the point of a certain boredom), unsettles the reader's historical, cultural, psychological assumptions, the consistency of his tastes, values, memories, brings to a crisis his relation with language" (p. 14).

Paradoxically, boredom is the very opposite of engagement, but for Barthes, boredom becomes "a major theoretical category with a role in any theory of reading" (Culler, 1983, p. 99). Why is boredom a precondition for *jouissance*? Because it is only through boredom, through "the motions of ungratified sucking, of an undifferentiated orality," through the "frigid text" that desire and neurosis can form in it. Why neurosis? Because neurosis connects the subjectivities of the writer and reader of language, who engage in a mutually engaging dance of seduction: "Thus every writer's motto reads: *mad I cannot be, sane I do not deign to be, neurotic I am*. The text you write must prove to me *that it desires me*" (Barthes, 1975, p. 6). This is, of course, precisely the way in which Hemingway's spare style works in creating the tacit violence in "The Killers." But in a Barthesian reading, the words do not *disclose* the violence; there is nothing unforeseen that is to be subsequently *revealed*. This would be what in *S/Z* (1974) he calls a readable (*lisable*) text, a piece of merchandise to be consumed. Rather, the text must be made writable (*scriptible*), that is, broken up into its multifarious entry points, whose tracings through become polyphonic, as in a musical composition.

Music is all-pervasive in Barthes' work as that art form that most resists fixed meaning and the metaphysics of presence. Barthes prefigures the kind of textual atheism (see pp. 157–161) we see operating in Derrida, by proclaiming himself a heretic in the religion of the text as God. In *Image, Music, Text* (1977), Barthes engages in "what may be called an anti-theological activity, . . . truly revolutionary since to refuse to fix meaning is, in the end, to refuse God and his hypostases—reason, science, law" (p. 147). Hypostasis as the unique essence of the Godhead recalls stasis as the respondent's fusing with the unique essence of a literary work. Barthes banishes such ideas to the point where he insists that the author as guarantor of textual meaning must die in order to give birth to the reader (see p. 148).

As textual hedonist, Barthes enjoins the reader to become a metaphysician of reading very different from that within the aesthetics of total form. His is unabashedly a poetics of engagement, enacting with the abandon of a *roué*, all the hidden delights of kinesis. Through the free range of textual play, readers give over their bodies to the textual enterprise in a kind of stream of consciousness game of verbal associations, but always with an awareness that the readers themselves are repositories of literary convention and agents of its application (Culler, 1983), always remembering that the "most interesting or most valuable literature is that which most vigorously exercises the reader, challenging and calling attention to the structuring activity of reading" (Culler, p. 82). In this sense, the pleasure of the text entails its own kind of detachment, but one that never loses its irreverence for what seems to be engraved in stone.[2] For Barthes, textual pleasure is primarily bodily pleasure.

Textual Atheism

It is, however, with Jacques Derrida that deconstruction comes to full flower in its inversion of what the text explicitly says. Pleasure in the text comes at the expense of the face value of words. Derrida "takes" textual pleasure by continually undermining the philosophical presuppositions upon which the words on the page rely. Derridean deconstruction, complex and often downright irritating in its refusal of anything remotely resembling conventional hermeneutical strategies, pushes textual play as critical principle to the point of nullifying the categories of oppositional thought that have characterized traditional western philosophy: form/content, head/heart, concrete/abstract, inner/outer, existence/essence, ideal/real, and so on. Crucial to Derrida's conception of language and reality is the dissolution, rather than the resolution, of these oppositions in approaching a theoretical or interpretive problem.

As an illustration of Derridean verbal inversion, let's take his deconstructing the notion of a promise, which occurred during the course he gave at the International Summer Institute for Semiotic and Structural Studies at the University of Toronto in the summer of 1987.[3] By keeping to as internal a reading of the text as possible (even though he acknowledges that a *purely* internal reading is impossible), Derrida attempts to demonstrate how the very naming of an idea or concept entails a corruption of its own definition. If we try to tease out what we mean by "promise," for instance, we end up with its opposite. The chain of reasoning goes something like this: When we ask what the word "promise" entails, we tend to think, first, in terms of fulfillment and then in terms of the recipient's recognition of the promise. A promise is a gift. It is itself already a gift before it is even made, but the origin of this gift must be acknowledged by the second party. That acknowledgment in some way binds the recipient of the promise, though the promise was freely given by the one uttering it. The tacit contract that has been struck contradicts the idea of the sheer gratuitousness of a promise. The very structure of a promise—an act toward another demanding recognition of its nature from the other—already enters the circle of indebtedness, thus requiring that the other enter the circle of exchange. Exchange in the sense of giving something for getting something is anathema to the idea of promise in the sense of something freely offered. But that, according to Derrida, is the way language works. The act of naming itself entails the obverse of what it intends to point to. This kind of tension inherent in all language is what Barthes means by the neurotic nature of language, especially writing. Language itself, then, may be said to be making a promise it can never keep by setting in motion the dynamics of a tension between desire and fulfillment that is eternal, to wit, the consumer seeking stasis in a world plagued by false resting places.

Derrida infuses a logic into the relationship between Barthesian *jouissance*, death of the author, and denial of presence by pushing to its most extreme the notion *of writing as untruth*. In this sense, deconstruction ensures the death—and burial—of the communication model; and it does so by exposing as language games all philosophical pretensions to uncovering truth. Once it is accepted that the text is important for what it does *not* say, that the assumed correspondence between words and truth is a myth, that indirection is the way of the language world, then it becomes clear that Dionysiac linguistic play, the essence of literariness, reigns supreme in the verbal universe. Northrop Frye (1988) has said it already in his contention that "logical thinking . . . seldom does more than rationalize metaphorical visions" (p. 187, see also Bogdan, 1985b, p. 246).

Derridean deconstruction calls for the freeing up of critical reading from categories of history and philosophy at the same time that it calls into question "the traditional values of sign, truth, and presence" (Leitch, 1983, p. 170). With Derrida, not only are God and the author dead, but the referent too. Leitch sums it up nicely in a logic that begins with the assumption that "language serves as ground of existence," and ends with the celebration of misreading:

> [T]he world emerges as infinite Text. Everything gets textualized. All contexts, whether political, economic, social, psychological, historical, or theological, became intertexts; that is, outside influences and forces undergo textualization. Instead of literature we have textuality; in place of tradition, intertextuality. Authors die so that readers may come into prominence. In any case, all selves, whether of critics, poets, or readers, appear as language constructions-texts. What are texts? Strings of differential traces. Sequences of floating signifiers. . . . Sites for the freeplay of grammar, rhetoric, and (illusory) reference. What about the truth of the text? The random flights of signifiers . . . offer truth under one condition: that the chaotic processes of textuality be willfully regulated, controlled, or stopped. Truth comes forth in the reifications, the personal pleasures, of reading. . . . No text utters its truth; the truth lies elsewhere—in a reading. Constitutionally, reading is misreading. Deconstruction works to deregulate controlled dissemination and celebrate misreading (p. 122).

Such a resurrection of the reader is all very well. But teachers of reading, duly affected because of the enormous burden of responsibility that accompanies this kind of validation of their life's work, might want to know just why they should believe Derrida, especially if they have been well conditioned by the aesthetics of total form. How does he come to hold such a position? To my mind, the most compelling account of the premises of deconstruction is to be found in Derrida's meditation on Plato's own dialogue on writing, *Phaedrus*, which Derrida analyzes in his long essay, "Plato's Pharmacy" (1981, pp. 61–171). Here Derrida takes seriously Plato's reservations about the capacity and function of writing to lead to truth; but instead of denigrating writing, as Plato does, Derrida nullifies the notion of truth in Platonic terms. He does this through the metaphor of writing as a *pharmakon*, a medicine or "philter, which acts as both remedy and poison" (p. 70). Its nature is alchemical, functioning as both substance and non-substance in the search for truth.

For Derrida, the relationship between the *pharmakon* and medical science typifies that of writing to truth. The *pharmakon* defies all laws of physics and logic: its potency is directly correlated to its illegitimacy, its untenableness in scientific terms. Working through a kind of magic, the *pharmakon* cures despite, or because of, its unorthodox methods. It is the emblem of the occult, the esoteric. Having no business in medical practice, it nevertheless cannot be ignored because it works. Thus, it establishes itself precisely by dint of its marginal status to orthodox scientific mehod. So, too, with the relationship of books to living knowledge. Books, i.e., writing, are all myth. This relationship between writing and truth in terms of the incapacity of written language to correspond exactly to "the truth of being" or "idea" (p. 134) is precisely what Plato is worried about in the *Phaedrus*. Socrates' first argument against writing is that it

> is not a good *tekhné*, by which we should understand an art capable of engendering, pro-ducing, bringing forth: the clear, the sure, the secure. . . . The truth of what is: writing literally hasn't a damn sight to do with it. It has rather a blindness to do with it. Whoever might think he has pro-duced truth through a grapheme would only give proof of the greatest foolishness . . . (pp. 134–135).

Derrida turns into a virtue Plato's anxieties about the unreliability of writing and its power to seduce to false resting places. Readers live, but writing is dead. All writing can do is repeat without knowing; it makes us gaze upward like a bird, insensible to the things below (*Phaedrus*, see p. 119), thereatening to sweep us into stasis. Instead of defending writing against this charge, Derrida turns the tables on Plato. Building on Plato's insight that the "incompatibility between the *written* and the *true*" resides just in this textual pleasure, the predisposition for readers to "become absent from themselves, forget themselves and die in the thrill of song" (p. 68), Derrida seems to be saying, in effect, "Yes, and therein lies the only form of truth we can get. Truth is myth; the truth of what is untruth."

Writing is indeed a repeating without knowing; but, as such, it "defines the very approach that leads to the statement and determination of its status" (pp. 74–75). Plato complains that writing "is not the object of a science, only of a history that is recited, a fable that is repeated" (p. 74). Precisely. As Derrida notes later in the essay, the "order of knowledge" is not ontological, "not the transparent order of forms and ideas ... it is the antidote" to that order. Knowledge as presence, certainty, identity, or any other entity is a "pharmaceuticals force," i.e., a *pharmakon* that works against itself (p. 138). "Nontruth is the truth. Nonpresence is the presence. Differance, the disappearance of any originary presence, is *at once* the condition of possibility *and* the condition of impossibility of truth" (p. 168, emphasis added). In other words, as soon as a word presents itself as itself, it doubles as its own negation.

Derrida's use of "differance" in the last quotation, to convey the inversion of predictable meaning in interpreting a text is the basis for his theory that meaning resides between the lines, as we say. While *"differance"* refers to what is signified by the whites and gaps, *"difference"* refers to the necessity for the perpetual delay of gratification that readers must practice at the site of truth. We might well ask how such an infinite regress can constitute any form of readerly pleasure. The answer lies in the creative nature of such *difference*. Through this operation reading becomes productive; it transmutes into writing:

> If reading and writing are one, as is easily thought these days, if reading *is* writing, this oneness designates neither undifferentiated (con)fusion nor identity at perfect rest. The *is* that couples reading with writing must rip apart.
> One must then, in a single gesture, but doubled, read and write (pp. 63–64).

As teachers of reading, we are impelled to ask, "How?" and "Why?" Does deconstruction move strictly according to the joyous free play of word association? No. It must follow a "logic of *play*," be guided "by the necessities of *game*" (p. 64). Not anything goes. Deconstruction is not destruction, but *"disfiguration"* (Leitch, 1983, p. 189). In the next chapter, we shall examine deconstruction as a dialectical critical practice, but for now let's turn to the final stage of our effort to break out of total form—Marxist criticism.

MARXIST CRITICISM: SPECTATOR RESPONSE AND ACTION
Marxism and Deconstruction

In stasis, we see fused the stoppages or endpoints of the search for truth, desire, and action: all come to rest in the state of imaginative identity, the apogee of textual engagement. We have seen how feminist criticism legitimates stock response by refashioning the search for truth as literary exploration along ideological lines that are explicitly professed. Similarly, deconstruction vindicates kinetic response by raising the pleasure principle to the highest form of critical deliberation, in which the reader is empowered to overturn all imperatives of the text to control meaning. What deconstruction does for kinetic response and desire, Marxist criticism does for spectator response and action. If deconstruction advances a poetics of the liberated, Marxist criticism champions a poetics of the oppressed.

Spectator response represents a disengagement from the text based upon textual criticism unintegrated with any kind of imaginative re-creation of the text. Spectator response typifies all that literature teachers hate most about literary analysis. To reclaim spectator response under a poststructuralist mantle would seem to be impossible, if not downright repugnant. Somehow restoring the search for truth and textual pleasure, both principles of engagement, to the act of reading seems a worthier project than validating a self-conscious literary detachment. And, in reclaiming spectator response, there is yet the leap to be made between the disengaged reader and restoring action to reading. Before attending to these problems, however, let us briefly look at Marxist criticism and deconstruction in terms of each other.

Marxism and deconstruction at first glance appear to be strange bedmates. In contrast to the deconstructionist suspension of belief, Marxist critics fervently adhere to belief in the "necessary relationship between conceptual apparatuses and political institutions" (Ryan, 1982, p. 8). This belief in the material force of ideas, i.e., the consequences of the word, is what makes Marxism, for Ryan, something other than a philosophy; it is the commitment to action in the world, to changing the reality of human lives, that distinguishes Marxist criticism from deconstruction. As a worldview, Marxist criticism is a *praxis*. Ryan is optimistic about the potential for Marxism and deconstruction together to break "the coercive power of a norm of transcendental 'science' conceived as absolute knowledge" (p. 8). Deconstruction, after all, is primarily the attempt to show the fictive nature of all constructs, textual and otherwise, by teaching readers to attend to gesture of exclusion, and showing them how the antithesis of any proposition is contained within its own premises. According to Ryan, this tendency of deconstruction to provide critical openings whenever and wherever it senses a gap at the center of a cohesive structure paves the way for revolution. "To affirm the abyss deconstruction opens in the domain of knowledge is politically to affirm the permanent possibility of social change" (p. 8).

Textual Materialism

Marxist approaches to texts are inherently deconstructive of the aesthetics of total form in attending to the process, mode, and materials of textual production (hence the expression "textual materialism," which heads this section) rather than to the vision of an individual author in the heat of inspiration, to the unseating of determinate meaning, and to what the text excludes rather than what it is "in itself." Both Marxism and deconstruction reject literary values such as harmony, coherence, integration, organic unity, and the notion of an authoritative reading, in favor of discontinuity and contradiction; both regard the text as "open to rereading, no longer an object for passive consumption but an object of work by the reader to produce meaning" (Belsey, 1980, p. 104). (See pp. 148–154, 168–194 for my discussion of feminist criticism within poststructuralism). But Marxist criticism is unique in its focus on locating literary products and processes within their specificity of time and place, Fredric Jameson's injunction, "Always historicize" (1981, p. 9), having become the battle cry of the Marxist critic. And battle cry it is, for within Marxist ideology, textual interpretation is nothing less than power struggle. In denouncing the myths of universal value and the moral neutrality of art, Jameson transforms the tendency to conflate literature with life into a critical principle. Jameson asks:

> [H]ow is it possible for a cultural text which fulfills a demonstrably ideological function, as a hegemonic work whose formal categories as well as its content secure the legitimation of this or that form of class domination—how is it possible for such a text to embody a properly Utopian impulse, or to resonate a universal value inconsistent with the narrower limits of class privilege which inform its more immediate ideological vocation? The dilemma is intensified when ... it is suggested that the greatness of a given writer may be separated from his deplorable opinions, and is achieved in spite of them or even against them (pp. 288–289).

Thus, the slide from life to literature, of which Frye is so wary (see 1963c, p. 7), for Jameson becomes a political necessity. Separating the author's politics from the work in Marxist terms

> is possible only for a world-view—liberalism—in which the political and the ideological are mere secondary or "public" adjuncts to the content of a real "private" life, which alone is authentic and genuine. It is not possible for any world-view—whether conservative or radical and revolutionary—that takes politics seriously (Jameson, 1981, p. 289).

The bleaching out of politics from literature, insisted upon in the aesthetics of total form, along with the utopian ideal guaranteeing the moral inviolateness of art—both tenets of Northrop Frye's *Educated Imagination* (1963c)—represent, according to Marxist critics, not only the failure to historicize, but the failure to be socially responsible. Frye's version of transferring "imaginative energy from literature to the student" (1963c, p. 55) is for Marxist critic John Fekete a dereliction of duty. Contemplation is not enough. As a matter of fact, Fekete (1978) contends that Frye's transcendental humanism (see p. 118) betrays his own noble purpose. What in *Anatomy of Criticism* (1957) Frye deems the mythical project of literature, its function as the moral "dialectic of desire and repugnance" (p. 106) that tells a society what it wants and doesn't want, ends up turning in on itself. For Fekete, it is Frye's pervasive structuralism that renders his aim of transforming brutish nature into civilization a self-betrayal to the establishment. Fekete delivers a harsh rebuttal to Frye's claims for the imaginative as opposed to "real" life, what Frye (1963b) calls "the source of both the dignity and joy of life" (p. 156). The world according to Frye, Fekete continues, is Heaven or Hell, depending on whether the beholder's imagination is awakened or repressed. This assumption Fekete (1978) hotly contests:

> It can be argued, by contrast, that a truly awakened social imagination would not be content to preserve the actuality of the world. Instead, it would see it as a contradictory man-made Hell with potentials for Heaven. . . . A humanism that depends on inwardness to control meaningless empirical experience capitulates to the given society and renounces its claims to humanism by effectively denying humanity to the vast majority of mankind. Frye's rationalism ignores that there are humanly objective (object-mediated intersubjective) conditions of existence independent of the *individual* will, and, ultimately, his theories reinforce the passivity he deplores (p. 127).

So, it would seem that Frye's conception of total form perpetuates a kind of living-in-your-head that in a way replicates Plato's metaphysical idealism. Both Plato and Frye reverse the order of the actual and (capital R) Reality: Plato, by forsaking the world of the senses for the immaterial World of Forms (*Republic*); Frye, by denigrating "ordinary experience" (1963c, p. 32) in favor of imaginative identity. The paralysis of action induced by stasis, so highly prized in my taxonomy, amounts to nothing more for Marxists than a deflection from the real work of social change because of the bleeding off of psychic energy into the realm of dreams. Literature is not for meditating on reality, but for mediating the materiality of that reality. In other words, literature, either through engagement or detachment, must have a social use. Otherwise, the *litterateur* is open to the same charge that drove Shelley to write his *Defence of Poetry* a century ago (Jordan, 1965).

Is literature only "the mental rattle" Thomas Love Peacock said it was in his diatribe against poetry, *The Four Ages of Poetry* (Jordan, 1965)? Is Peacock right, that literature is a frill in a sophisticated society, that we have outgrown our need for it, that "for the maturity of mind to make a serious business of the playthings of its childhood, is as absurd as for a full-grown man [sic] to rub his gums with coral, and cry to be charmed to sleep by the jingle of silver bells" (pp. 18– 19)? We have thus come full circle to the relationship between stasis and the misplaced romanticism of the yuppie that began this chapter. Marxist textual materialism challenges readers to become metaphysicians of their own reading by inquiring into how desire for literary experience, for the feeling of coming to know the truth about ourselves or our world, and the fulfillment of that desire through reading literature, can have a social use. Freundlich's yuppie (1987) in search of stasis moves blindly from one consumer product to the next, unaware of the nostalgia for the absolute propelling desire. Conscious readers of literature, on the other hand, especially literature teachers committed to the educational function of their discipline, interrogate the conditions of their desire and seek a dialectical practice to help their students do the same. In the next chapter, we shall attempt to sketch out the ways in which such a practice might approximate the aesthetics of total form poststructuralist literary theory seems so thoroughly to have leveled.

NOTES

1. The nineteenth-century musicologist Eduard Hanslick argued that the essence of music lay not in its capacity for representing specific emotional states, but for arousing "unspecified feeling," of which I believe stasis to be the apotheosis. Music's "lack of conceptual definiteness" poses a logical problem for music to be representing anything. Music does bear a relationship to "the dynamics of feeling," but it does so by embodying "the *motion* of feeling . . . abstracted from . . . what is felt" (emphasis added). Thus, music's emotional appeal is inherent in music as an autonomous form. Even though vocal music is a decomposable "amalgam" of the perfect fusion of words and music in which it is "impossible to assay any of its individual constituents," and even though some vocal music compositions do attempt to portray specified feelings, "the most relentless fitting of music to feeling in such a musical portrait

generally succeeds in inverse proportion to the autonomous beauty of the music. . . ." This is, I feel, precisely what was happening with the Purcell songs. In the pages cited, Hanslick recounts numerous examples of the same music "portraying" radically different emotional states (1986, pp. 16–22).

2. Jonathan Culler observes that too much has been made of the distinctions between Barthes' structuralism and his poststructuralism. More important is Barthes' proclamation of himself as "hedonist" (Culler, 1983, p. 90).

3. See also Christopher Norris (1982, pp. 110–111) for a similar deconstructive account of cashing a check.

CHAPTER 7

READING AND
"THE FATE OF BEAUTY"
Reclaiming Total Form

Deanne Bogdan

With poststructuralist literary theory as we have been discussing it, we see an assault on the aesthetics of total form outlined in Chapter 5. The state of imaginative identity typified by stasis is both broken and broken out of in rebellion against the primacy of the text as an object controlling the reading process. We saw how three poststructuralist literary theories—feminist, deconstructionist, and Marxist—transmuted the three aspects of partial form—stock, kinetic, and spectator responses, respectively—into critical principles foregrounding the reader in literary interpretation. Feminist criticism attempts to legitimate stock response by reclaiming the reader's search for truth about "the way things are"; deconstruction does the same for kinetic response by validating the reader's pleasure in the text; and Marxist criticism attempts to rescue spectator response by showing how awareness of the conditions of readerly engagement can appropriate literary response to the project of social change. All three transformations of partial form by poststructuralist theory turn on rejecting a model of literary interpretation as *direct* communication between author and reader. In this chapter, we will examine how the reader can redefine total form from the feeling states of stasis or resistance to it to the ongoing dialectical interplay between text and reader as indirect communication—from the condition of being in or out of love with literature to working with literary texts.

The conception of total form as dialectic in this chapter differs sharply from that in Chapter 5, which is a shoring up of partial form through knowledge *about* literature to clarify literary structure. This structure is apprehended in alternating states of engagement with the text and detachment from it, in which the reader uses the literary text as a meditation on life. In this chapter, I show how the shift in focus from text to reader synthesizes engagement and detachment into a dialectical process that empowers the reader to mediate reality by examining the conditions of literary response itself.

I should perhaps stress here that "total form," as I use it, has deep roots in Frye, its signification going far beyond New Critical notions of the verbal icon. I mean total form to indicate the holistic recognition of the entire text, insofar as such a recognition is possible, in terms of both the text and reader. This recognition of the entire text can be either a gestalt, as in stasis, in which case it is intuited and, in a sense, acritical—a falling in love with literature—or it can be the dialectical working through of engagement with the text (absorption, involvement, identification) and the conscious deployment of critical strategies—loving literature.

In this chapter, I will be talking about the "feminization" of total form, a metaphor for my attempt to detotalize total form, so to speak, to resituate the conceptualization of total form from notions of wholeness and determinacy (as either stasis or dialectic) to awareness of the constructed nature of total form in all its manifestations. This awareness acknowledges—and celebrates—the partialness of all actual apprehensions of total form, irrespective of how "total" they may seem to the reader, on the presupposition that the "totality" of both the text and the reader's "self" are productive of any single reading act. In that sense, total form is both illusion and reality—illusion in that there is no such thing as a text or reader "as they really are"; reality, in that the meaning produced in the reading act constitutes a genuine and significant form of knowledge for the reader.

FEMINIST CRITICISM:
"THE SEARCH FOR TRUTH" AS DIALECTIC
Feminist Alternatives to Stasis

In the previous chapter, I suggested that feminist criticism elevates stock response to a critical principle of the highest order by regarding the search for truth as a legitimate aspect of the reading act. I did this on the grounds that the mythology informing western culture is bound up with patriarchal assumptions about female chastity and taboos against adultery, and, further, that the cultural order itself turns and trades on these assumptions (Aiken, 1986). We saw, first, how total form as the perception of *mythos* as *dianoia* is a literary phenomenon that rests on a definition of the human condition feminists find suspect; and second, how stasis, the aesthetic experience emanating from it, catapults the ineffability of the private spiritual quest into the arena of public values. Not only does the personal become political, but aesthetic and religious, too. The feminist critical project, by unseating the universality of poetic truth, relativizes total form and renders stasis morally accountable. A feminist's aesthetic pleasure is rarely innocent, as the example of the lightbulb joke in Chapter 5 attests.

We have already seen that stasis constellates an asymmetrical relationship between text and reader resembling the psychological projection of falling in love. (See pp. 135–136.) The reader, cathected by the work, is enthralled because what is seen and felt is primarily a filling out of her own psychology. This is what constitutes the Longinian sense of "vaunted joy" in her ineluctable search for truth. However, since the kind of knowing signified by stasis is yet to be brought to consciousness, it matters greatly to the feminist what readers are cathected *by*. Content counts. A feminist reader stands in a painfully paradoxical relation to stasis. Continually on guard about the conditions of her cathexis, she finds herself in the double bind of someone under the spell of romantic love—helpless yet responsible. The feminist reader of "The Painted Door" described in the last chapter may be said to undergo the ethical and ontological shock so characteristic of someone coming into feminist consciousness itself. (See Bartky, 1979.)

We also saw that one way feminist readers seek to resist this double bind of stasis in a patriarchal literary universe is by reading against the grain of a text. (See pp. 150–154). Resistant readers can engage in the act of misprision; that is, they can deliberately undo the intention of a work of literature so as to avoid having to buy into an ideology, a form of Aristotle's "thought," feminists find repugnant (Bloom, 1975; Fetterley, 1978). The palpable anger of the feminist reading of "The Painted Door" in the previous chapter escapes the charge of stock response thanks to a critic such as Aiken and her conceptualization of feminist ideology as a literary critical principle contesting the notion of universal truth. From that point of view, the reading is poststructuralist.[1] Feminist criticism justifies the search for truth on the grounds that its "universality" must be relativized and recognized for its hegemonic implications. An "angry" reading against the grain is a right step in the direction of breaking out of total form. Yet anger as resistance is a counterreaction to stasis. As such, it threatens to entrench the humanist literary communication model that stasis turns on. To say the opposite of something reconfirms the very premise one is trying to deny. Reading against the grain for the sake of implementing a new "truth," to counter the humanist security blanket in so overdetermined a manner, simply reinforces textual power. Such violent wresting of control from the text by Fetterley's resistant reader, as played out, for instance, in my feminist interpretation of "The Painted Door," is in danger of creating a Big Sister "text watch" in place of the paternalistic poetics of Big Brother. Not much is gained by us as metaphysicians of reading in claiming a "feminine" universal truth to replace a "masculine" one.

Hankerings after stasis characterize humanist pursuits of any truth swathed in serenity, security, inner coherence, unity, or some kind of resting point in literary experience. This would include the suspension of *belief*, that is, putting ideology on hold for aesthetic enjoyment (Kolodny, 1985), an enterprise that is probably as much of a psychological impossibility as Eliot's integration of sensibility. It would also include feminist longings for stasis, the desire to fuse with "safe" texts offering a kind of political and/or emotional oasis, where feminist readers could bathe in aesthetic pools of feminist ideology with impunity. I do not wish to denigrate the feeling of this kind of unified experience; fusion has been the *raison d'être* of my literary agenda, as my preoccupation with stasis has witnessed. But stasis grants an omnipotence to text that works against rendering aesthetic pleasure suspect, or at least contingent on the politics of "thought." Feminist poststructuralists would be wary of any feeling of having come to know the truth about "how things are" as its own endpoint.

What, then, can a poor girl do? On the one hand, suspending belief, sacrificing ideological commitment on the altar of aesthetic pleasure, is morally and psychologically debilitating; on the other, jettisoning the potential for emotional growth through sympathetic identification with spiritually nourishing literary characters and events is a political cop-out. Even within the feminist shelter, stasis exacts a price. There is a sense in which the swept-awayness of stasis and its flash of lightning do operate as a kind of phallus. Ravishment of soul, even when politically correct, still poses problems for *conscious* knowing. At some point, the ecstasy of psychological projection must be withdrawn, if only to "tell" about the experience. Plato was right when he insisted that poetry be "a dream for *awakened* minds" (Frye, 1957, p. 111, emphasis added).

Feminist Criticism as Dialectic

Both stasis and anger are engendered by what Patrocinio Schweickart (1986) calls "issues of control and partition" (p. 55), reinforcing, as they do, the humanist ideology that reading literature discloses a universal truth that is there for the taking. Schweickart offers as an alternative a dialogic mode of reading similar to the alternating states of engagement and detachment described in Chapter 5. Here the reading psyche voluntarily splits itself in two, one-half imaginatively and emotionally engaged with the "safe" feminine, and the other detached from the "dangerous" masculine. In this way, the feminist reader would appear to have it both ways, her political radar always attuned to the complicity of aesthetic identification with hidden hegemonies, her hunger for emotional connection satisfied by imaginative recreation of "women's texts." Thus, she gleans the best of both the worlds of engagement and detachment without compromising her ideological integrity or aesthetic pleasure.

Yet the dialogic model Schweickart offers is not without its political and aesthetic problems. Politically, it succumbs to what feminists call the essentialist fallacy, the belief that there is a set of truths, values, or conditions of being human that is intrinsically feminine, that there is one true feminist way applicable to all women for all time (Moi, 1985; Weedon, 1987). Aesthetically, it commits the sin of "reflectionism" (Moi, 1987, pp. 45−46), the assumption that language functions as a transparent window on reality, that literary creations express or radiate better or worse pictures of the world existing prior to or apart from their linguistic embodiment, and that these pictures of the world are self-evidently true or false according to whether they are "reaffirmed as part of the large body of common-sense knowledge upon which individuals draw for their understanding" (Weedon, 1987, p. 79).

On the whole, feminist criticism has turned stock response into a literary theory by validating the feminist's charge of sexual oppression as an intrinsic and legitimate condition of engaging in the very act of reading. Thus, the reader moves from the position of a disinterested meditator on a set of givens to a self-interested mediator on her own behalf. Yet feminist criticism risks degenerating into stock response so long as its engaged search for truth rests content that this "truth," however persuasive and consoling, has indeed been *found*−in the form of a dogma, datum, or proposition. In order to escape this trap, feminist readers, including those following Schweickart's dialogic model, must be ever mindful of the symbolic nature of language and the power of ideology to construct language. As Belsey (1980) reminds us, "Language in an important sense speaks us" (p. 44). What transforms the partial form of stock response into the dialectical process of interrogating the assumptions of the literary communication model is the continuous awareness of the constructedness of all verbal artifacts, even when, and especially when, the ideology it appears to represent matches the reader's. This requires regarding the "truth" one is searching for as a premise for interpretation, not as a foregone conclusion about it. In what follows, I hope to show how using feminist ideology as a premise challenges two assumptions of the literary communication model, namely, fictional realism and the reader as a unitary consciousness with an undivided self.

In *Realism and Consensus in the English Novel* (1983b), Elizabeth Ermarth contends that realistic narrative creates a totalitarianism because it

> implies a unity in human experience which assures us that we all inhabit the same world and that the same meanings are available to everyone. Disagreement is only an accident of position ... the uniformity at the base of human experience and the solidarity of human nature receive confirmation from realistic conventions. All individual views derive from the same world and so, with enough good faith, enough effort, enough time, problems *can* be solved, tragedies *can* be averted, failures in communication *can* be overcome (p. 65).

Ermarth argues convincingly that literary form, specifically the narrative structure of realism, constitutes a kind of authoritarianism. To challenge the prevailing social ethos of a realistic literary work would be a contradiction in terms because the dramatic interest itself is propelled by conflict between individuals and a "formal consensus" about ideology. In a realistic work, any existence of "multiple agreements," i.e., divergent points of view about the premises upon which moral choices are to be made destroys "the representational illusion" and with it "the ontological status" of the story. There must be "a common denominator" (1983a, p. 9) of social thought; to privilege one value system over another is to destroy the body of unified belief animating the aesthetic movement. In "The Painted Door," of course, this body of belief, what might be called a Calvinist-Jansenist worldview (see Sutherland, 1971), coheres in the narrator, who operates as the voice of "the collective nature of human consciousness" (Ermarth, 1983b, p. 65).

Like our feminist reader of "The Painted Door" in Chapter 6, Ermarth (1983a) is interested in the issue of female casualties in realistic fiction. For Ermarth, as for Aristotle, the fates of women such as Emma Bovary, Tess Durbeyfield, and Anna Karenina have been literally "plotted": their deaths, physical and/or psychic, are necessary because their functional (realistic) worlds cannot contain them without dire consequences. Thus, acceptance of a piece of ideology—the fact that in women like them self-actualization wreaks havoc—is prerequisite to the reader's aesthetic "Aha!" response, "This is just how things are, and I didn't know it" (Greene, 1986, p. 240). The reading below indicates just how the feminist search for truth discloses the patriarchal conspiracy between plot and "thought" in a work of realism.

Ann of "The Painted Door" does not die of starvation or suicide, but she will doubtless eke out her existence loaded down with the opprobrium of her isolating self-discovery. And, like Tess and Anna Karenina, "her persecution is tied explicitly to her sexuality" (Ermarth, 1983a, p. 12). Ann escapes the split psyche and physical death of the other two heroines because her male author makes her tidily remorseful for her adultery *before* she discovers the "little smear of paint." Physical death becomes redundant for one ultimately redeemed by the Calvinist-Jansenist worldview of Sinclair Ross's tyrannical narrator.[2] Like Tess and Anna, though, Ann's attempt to recover from loneliness with a friend/lover is a "fragile," "unsupported," and doomed exercise (pp. 13−14). Not only is her competing vision of reality disallowed in the story, but she assumes Steven's guilt as well as her own, absolving him from blame by reason of his very *lack* of passion and responsibility, the fullness of which *she* exemplifies as a fully adult human being. Her moral choices are as bleak as the narrow circumscription of the grounds upon which she is permitted to act. And when she *does* act, the "little smear of paint" condemns her while exonerating her consort and martyrizing her husband.

Ermarth (1983a, 1983b) successfully critiques the way in which aesthetic pleasure is manipulated by the interworkings of ideology and literary convention from the standpoint of presumed continuities of mind between narrator and reader in realistic literary forms. She concentrates on how the narrator in realism corrals the reader into agreements about characters' moral choices, in short, how the conventions of literary realism can work only by presuming "a unity in human experience" that makes the same meanings available to everyone (1983b, p. 65). To put it another way, in order to experience the aesthetic pleasure of a realistic work, the reader must share in the worldview created by its narrator, and in order to do *that* she or he must accept a fixed (patriarchal) definition of "the way things are" perpetuated by the very convention that demands reader compliance with that view, if the story is indeed to be understood and undergone.

The result is a vicious circularity between human consciousness and a fixed conception of the so-called objective world. This gives the narrator enormous power over the reader. The reader submits to the narrator's vision of the world "as it is"; all viewpoints support this vision, producing a "realistic . . . consensus," which in turn is reinforced by the "objective" world that the text is seen to reflect (Ermarth, 1983b, p. 77). The only escape for a dissenting reader is either to reject the objective, universal nature of the single collective consciousness embodied in the "ontologizing power" (1983a, p. 4) of the narrator, as Ermarth has done, or to reject the idea of the single individual consciousness of the reader. It is to the latter that we now turn.

Both stasis and anger are feelings of the reader's having come to know some "truth" about the world—different feelings and different truths, each influenced by its own ideology: stasis, by the belief in a universal human condition; anger, by belief in patriarchal subjection of women's desire. Both responses are informed by a notion of the reader as possessed of a psyche that is stable and unique, along with a consciousness that is rational and fixed. Here, all the faculties are engaged in a moment of felt truth. Poststructuralist feminism sets over against "this irreducible humanist essence of subjectivity . . . a subjectivity which is precarious, contradictory and in process, constantly being reconstituted in discourse each time we think or speak" (Weedon, 1987, p. 33). For feminist poststructuralism, the changing face and place of language decentering the subject from its position of certainty about "the way things are" is crucial to militating for social change. The illusion of a stable self tends to make of knowledge a "thing," and this reification of knowledge works to preserve the status quo. On the other hand, the unstable, shifting, often incoherent and contradictory subject makes way for real transformation because of its inexorable movement into its own power. As a result, readers are freed from the either/or of being in or out of love with literature, of static swept-awayness or angry refusal. As Weedon (1987) puts it:

> The political significance of decentering the subject and abandoning the belief in essential subjectivity is that it opens up subjectivity to change. In making our subjectivity the product of the society and culture within which we live, feminist poststructuralism insists that forms of subjectivity are produced historically and change with shifts in the wide range of discursive fields which constitute them (p. 33).

It is the importance of readers' understanding of how their subjectivities are constructed that links poststructuralist feminism to deconstruction and to Marxist criticism.

DECONSTRUCTION: DESIRE AS DIALECTIC

Feminist poststructuralists differ about the usefulness of deconstruction to the feminist political project. Some are more sanguine than others about the possibilities of textual atheism and its infinite regression of horizons of meaning to alter patriarchy. A critic such as Weedon (1987) cautions against deconstruction's ahistorical framework and the tendency of indeterminate meaning to eclipse the real hierarchies of power inscribed in all linguistic forms. Yet other feminist critics consider what I have called textual atheism, Barthes' repudiation of "the text as God," i.e., attention to what lies outside explicit verbal expression, a valuable political tool. Plurality of meaning and the decentered reader, central to deconstruction, is fundamental to foregrounding contradiction in the radical reading of literary texts, which is in turn prerequisite to the political ends of feminist criticism (Belsey, 1980). What is most politically significant to the feminist search for truth in deconstruction is the search itself: readers must ever be pilgrims in pursuit of whatever hidden ironies, ambiguities, and dissonances lend a healthy skepticism about being in full possession of any one "truth," feminist or otherwise. To rise above feminist ideology as a stock response is to use feminist criticism as a life skill in ferreting out what might lurk between the whites and gaps of readers' own apprehensions of any text and what it might be saying about "the way things are." Deconstruction ensures that the dialectic between readers — of any ideological bias — and their own definitions of truth remains open-ended.

Deconstruction is, above all, the redefinition of close reading (as perceived by New Critics) from one based on the teleology of coherence, in which all the textual elements conspire to produce a controlled meaning, to one based on "scrupulous attention to what seems ancillary or resistant to understanding" (Culler, 1982, p. 242). The reader looks to whatever patterns in the text are valorized, then strives to "unpack" them. In "The Killers," of course, what immediately strikes the readers is the aura of normalcy in the heartland of middle America. Deconstructors of "The Killers" might reverse the importance of the two "disclosure" scenes (see p. 133), the first in the diner, the second in Ole's bedroom, and concentrate on what is suppressed in the two seemingly less important scenes, the one with Mrs. Bell at the rooming house (p. 49), and Nick and George's final mutual recognition scene (p. 50). In so doing, they might find that the text does not in fact "hide" the evil lurking below the patina of normalcy, but rather that the atmosphere of routine life is a condition of the latent evil.

How might this "logic of game" apply to a deconstructive reading of "The Painted Door"? Crucial to a deconstructive reading is the fracturing of continuity between *mythos* and *dianoia* assumed in the literary communication model. In more traditional interpretive procedures, such as those pursued in the aesthetics of total form, the narrative organization and thematic unity culminating in the recognition scene control meaning. The shock of recognition proves, in a sense, that Sinclair Ross has constructed a successful literary form that, when read appropriately, produces a desired effect. Since deconstruction is a form of "exegetical labor" (Culler, 1982, p. 256) that

> treats any position, theme, origin, or end as a construction and analyzes the discursive forces that produce it, deconstructive writings will try to put in question anything that might seem a positive conclusion and will try to make their own stopping points distinctively divided, paradoxical, arbitrary, or indeterminate (pp. 259–260).

My earlier feminist reading of "The Painted Door" was poststructuralist because it resisted the Calvinist-Jansenist "thought" that holds the story together within the aesthetics of total form. But feminist ideology is not necessary to a *deconstructive* upsetting of the hierarchies that allowed the story to work in my initial neo-Aristotelian reading. All that is required in deconstruction is to read "from the margins," to bring to the surface the "hidden articulations" (Culler, 1982, p. 247), to expose as blindnesses the premises upon which such a reading is founded (*differance*), and to keep up the dialectic between text and meaning indefinitely (*difference*).

What might this look like in "The Painted Door"? In my first "coherent," humanist reading, Ann's guilt and self-recrimination become preconditions for the reader's coming to feel that she had been responsible for her husband's death. Within "ordinary" logic, Ann's guilt presupposes John's innocence. Within the "logic of play," i.e., *differance*, which would invert the categories of guilt and innocence, John would become the transgressor and, *ipso facto*, the author of his own death, in just retribution for his neglect of Ann. In the first "humanist" reading, maintaining the coherence of the ending required that John be cast as the blameless victim of Ann's carnal knowledge — an interpretation that seemed to be reinforced by the final image of him as a kind of Christ figure, his palm nailed by the "little smear of paint." Suggested here is an icon of the Pieta, with Ann as the Mater Dolorosa lamenting over the body of her dead son. John becomes Ann's son, in a way, because she has "mothered" his awareness of her lack of fulfillment in their marriage. Her susceptibility to Steven was, of course, created in part by John's persistent inattention to her. A deconstructive rereading of the story presents a certain absence at the center of the humanist reading, a gap that prevents that interpretation from "holding." Evidence of John's complacency about his relationship to Ann pokes holes in the neatness of the recognition scene. Different bits of text leap up from the page when the reader seeks to undo the principles of signification upon which a prior reading has been based. Ann's remark at the beginning of the story, "It isn't right to leave me here alone. Surely I'm as important as your father" (p. 96), is a telling example. Her "sin" springs from an honest confrontation of her needs; John's "virtue," from his naive pride in her, "his trust and earnestness" (p. 98), a means of control over her. John brings about his own death by his irresponsible refusal to know his wife. Ann knows herself through carnally knowing Steven. Only by losing both can she gain mastery over herself, yet her guilt will always haunt her. The text, then, works both for and against Ann as a character through a set of contradictions that produces a situation of "undecidability" or "unreadability" (see Culler, 1982, pp. 80—82), in which the reader finds it impossible to come to a synthesis.

In the prior reading, what the story is thought to mean is *undermined* by the *way* it means (see Culler, 1982, p. 238). A deconstructionist might ask, "How does the image of the Pieta militate against an interpretation based on Ann's responsibility for John's death?" One way of approaching the problem might be to delve further into the symbolism of the Pieta itself. In Jungian terms, for example, mother love for the firstborn is "perhaps the most powerful instinctual attachment of the human psyche" (Edinger, 1987, p. 109). For Jungians, maternal mourning of this loss constitutes a crucial step in the process of psychic growth. Thus, Ann, in the very act of recognizing the consequences of her action, catalyzes her own maturation by passing through this necessary mortification "phase of the alchemical process of transformation" (p. 109). Her carnal knowledge brings with it life born of the death of self-ignorance, but her liberating knowledge itself is contingent upon her marriage as a kind of living death.

So much for *differance*; but what of *difference*, the continual delaying of interpretation? Diligently pushing back the insights of their "new" readings, deconstructionists are careful not to capitulate to the need for false resting places; they literally defer to exploring the logic of further "forces and structures that recur in reading and writing" (Culler, 1982, p. 260). Thus, appealing though it may be, the previous reading could never be regarded as definitive. Curiously enough, though, dedication to this kind of language game is itself an affirmation of faith in the text. Even if deconstruction eschews the false resting place of the finality of one's own reading, "the distinctions between truth and falsity, blindness and insight, or reading and misreading remain crucial" (p. 275). In the end, textual atheism deconstructs into a kind of textual faith, a kind of new New Criticism. Deconstruction shows how the pleasure principle upon which kinetic response is premised, when brought to its logical conclusion, leads right back to our departure point, the text, the text, and nothing but the text! Barthes' *jouissance*, within Derridean deconstructive practice, becomes the Longinian *ecstasis* of rewriting the text, the sense of "vaunted joy" that comes from doing it yourself.

MARXIST CRITICISM: ACTION AS DIALECTIC

We ended the previous chapter with the Marxist challenge that litera- ture must have a social use, that it stand up and be counted as benefitting the real lives of readers. We also rendered problematic engagement with the text; i.e., we considered aesthetic pleasure as possibly counterproductive to the "real work" of individual and col- lective growth (see pp. 163–165). In this section, I want to look at how meeting these problems head on might convert the latent power of literary engagement to a dialectical process that is at once instructive, delightful, and transformative.

Within the aesthetics of total form, the evils of spectator response reside in partitioning off literary analysis from any sense of imaginative literary experience. Spectator response marks the scientization of lit- erary knowledge by an unengaged reader (see pp. 128–129). The respondent in the spectator mode is so distanced from the vitality of the text, the text has become so objectified, that any kind of relation it might hold to life is effaced by obsession with treating it as an artifact. Spectator response is an abuse of total form in that it seeks only separation from, not eventual reunion with, the literary object typified in total form's recognition scene. Imprisoned in the head space of their own detachment, spectator respondents are literally ossified.

In the previous chapter, we saw how Marxist criticism turns spectator response into a critical principle by interrogating the con- ditions of literary engagement as a way of restoring to reading its potential for action in the world. The method of doing this was to disengage from engagement itself in a highly self-conscious way, in short, to push the spectator response to its logical conclusion, to make readers acutely aware of the actual consequences of aesthetic pleasure taken in the imaginative verbal universe. Marxist criticism, then, legitimates the spectator respondent's refusal to regard literature as a kind of magic that works *on* readers. More precisely, it takes seriously the fact that literature works on readers, that readers *undergo* literary experience, that literature seduces readers into falling in love with it. But what the aesthetics of total form accepts as a given, Marxist criticism adopts as a premise for inquiring into the social implications of the relation between this "magical" literary force and the life that it purports to influence, a relationship that, for the most part, persists in remaining untheorized in the current practice of English studies in the schools.[3]

Literary critic/educators Catherine Belsey and Jeffrey Robinson recapitulate the Marxist position on the potentially noxious effects of the kind of aesthetic domination so highly prized within the aesthetics of total form. Both Belsey and Robinson are concerned with what is eclipsed by fixing on transcendent states: for Robinson (1987), it is the imperfection of the "real" world, upon which this transcendence trades; for Belsey (1980), "the labour of producing out of the available signifying systems of language and literature an intelligent fiction," which is ignored in the face of the author's presumed "qualities of insight and understanding" (p. 127). For both critics, the aesthetic "Aha!" response simply reproduces the world as it is. Maxine Greene's "[t]his is just how things are, and I didn't know it" (1986), instead of signaling transcendence of reality, rather indicates how aesthetic experience compensates for literature's impotence to effect social change within the aesthetics of total form. For Marxist critics, Aristotle's recognition scene, if recognized at all, would indeed constitute a false resting place in the reading act. Again, meditation on the text must give way to mediation of the real world.

Robinson (1987) applies the Marxist critical principle described before to his own undergraduate teaching, in rebellion against one of the lessons he learned from his own literary education at Harvard, i.e., that "what's to be preferred is not experience but rather the spiritualization and internalization of experience, of erotic life and desire" (p. 26). Devotees of stasis (Freundlich's yuppie included) would agree. But for critics such as Robinson, students pay too high a price for literary heaven. Robinson draws a direct homology between the illusion of satiety in stasis and the capitalist dream that "happiness can be bought" (p. 5):

> Theodor Adorno's comment that "life has become appearance" is nowhere more dramatically obvious than in the college literature classroom where young people and their teacher talk about losses and restoration, grief and desire, revolutions and tyrannies, form and content, in ways that satisfy the hunger for order and coherence and the chaste idyll of beauty. Yet this particular satisfaction rarely bridges the gap between the pastoral play inside the classroom and the life outside of it. Indeed, it only further divides the student from his or her sense of the present and future. Today the effect of this

gap seems, ironically, to support the student's fantasies about security: if I make enough money or marry into wealth, I can acquire for myself a version of the idyll of literary experience (pp. 4–5).

Now, for someone with my aesthetic predilections, this idea seems as farfetched and offensive as the notion that the kind of delayed gratification intrinsic to sonata form is a capitalist plot. On the other hand, I did myself make the comparison between consumerism and stasis at the beginning of the last chapter. Robinson's position gains credence as he draws convincing correspondences between the asymmetrical relationship of the reader in love with a poem and the late adolescent caught tightly in the grip of a rescue fantasy. For Robinson, the oppression of beauty lies in the paralysis of will issuing from student readers who have been robbed by literary experience-as-consolation of the effulgence of their own psychic growth. Literature teaching "at present generally operates between the mutually reinforcing poles of grandiosity and helplessness, both being fantasies of human power that have as their source the single fantasy of salvation" (Robinson, 1987, p. 15). Literature study, by promoting the illusion of fulfilling human desire (which Frye would say is its proper function), through submitting to a kind of aesthetic despotism, encourages students to abandon themselves to the "mysterious and bewitching" poetic object, thus rendering their desire passive (p. 95). As a result, the very promise of human development traditionally claimed by humanists for literature students is denied them, for they have no chance to work through "the fullness of fantasies of desire and aggression" as real adolescents, to have these fantasies "known and integrated into social life" (pp. 170–171). Thus, student readers would seem to be left in a state of perpetual puberty.

Robinson's prescription for this dilemma is to take students where they live, right in the middle of their desires and aggressions, and submit them to a regimen of studying a poem that appeals directly to their complex of needs — material security, spiritual yearning, altruism, coherence, beauty, as well as rebellion. Wordsworth's "Ode: Intimations of Immortality from Recollections of Early Childhood" is a poem of contemplation students readily fall in love with, and Robinson devotes an entire academic term to moving student readers from awestruck wonderment to a Paulo Freirean education for critical consciousness (see Freire, 1969). This exercise can be seen as my spectator response converted to dialectic: study becomes the conscious act of withdrawing from engagement. But instead of dissecting the *poem*, the students analyze the conditions of its production as well as the processes by which they are, first, seduced by its appeal; second, are complicitous in the playing out of the set of projections comprising their thralldom; and, finally, are freed from the limitations of engagement by integrating literary experience with knowledge of literature and knowledge of themselves. Such an undertaking is a tall order, but Robinson is a master teacher determined to address the pedagogical implications of the intersection of the aesthetic and the political at the site of its materialization—the consciousness of the student reader.

Following theorists such as Theodor Adorno, Walter Benjamin, and Michel Foucault, Robinson designs a curriculum that forces students ultimately to ask themselves, "What for me is the fate of beauty?" (Robinson, 1987, p. 17):

> The object of a "pedagogy of the oppressed" applied to Wordsworth's "Ode" is to gain critical consciousness of this system or of, as Freire might call it, a set of "codes" which education is at pains to transmit and which we readily embrace (pp. 13−14).

What I find compelling about Robinson's "model" is that it demystifies without debunking, without succumbing to the either/or of engagement/detachment. Unlike many contemporary literary theorists, such as Terry Eagleton (1983), Peter Widdowson (1982), and even Chris Weedon (1987), who, in their drive to raise consciousness about the sociological implications of reading literature, feel that they have to construct an enemy out of the aesthetic, Robinson has sufficient memory of, and appreciation for, his own literary education to prevent him from throwing out the proverbial baby with the bath water. What is more, he shows enormous respect for students and their own capacity to engage in dialectic, so to speak, without missing or dismissing the joys of stasis. His method is so successful that in a sense through it dialectic approximates stasis by integrating study with enjoyment in such a way that students' mourning the loss of their aesthetic captivity eventuates in a depth of felt poetic understanding of which any humanist professor would be proud. More than this, though, Robinson's dialectic allows the student to stand inside and outside the poem at the same time, to undergo Marion Woodman's (1985) "experiential realization" (p. 158) mentioned at the end of Chapter 5 (see pp. 136−137), and to attain the kind of detachment that enables understanding of just how this undergoing has been achieved, without diminishing the poem.

Proceeding on the assumption that "wonderment" is only "part of the point" of studying literature (p.104), Robinson sets out to educate his students' historical imagination by sequencing the study of the processes and modes of the text's production, in fine poststructuralist fashion. Students are lured away from literature-as-consolation by learning the history of the ode as a genre, becoming privy to Wordsworth's own revisions of his poem, immersing themselves in his biography, and finally by reading the critical commentary of William Hazlitt, Wordsworth's contemporary, on Wordsworth's masterpiece. Study is, of course, carried out by the usual research methods, there being no real substitute in all this for trips to the library. But crucial to the process are class discussions and copious amounts of journal writing, in which students ponder the various correspondences between history, literature, and their own psychological development, all the while becoming destabilized from the rescue fantasy of stasis. The final stage of the process, encounters with Hazlitt's criticisms of the poem, is of utmost importance, for he becomes a kind of surrogate parent, providing students with a point of both identification and recognition of one who can love and be detached at the same time. In this way, students can more easily come to terms with the maturer state of ambivalence to the text mentioned in Chapter 5 (see pp. 135–136) that comes when the will to love replaces the feeling of being in love.

Journal writing and informal discussion also serve to help students connect their study of the creative process in "the greats" and in themselves. For instance, by exploring Wordsworth's revisions to his text, they come to see "that every stage of thought has its own substantive reality and is not merely an imperfect manifestation that will self-destruct before the next, more perfect realization" (p. 113), both in Wordsworth's creation and in their own. As to the inevitable problem of how such an enterprise is to be evaluated, Robinson sets a final paper that asks the single question, "Can one best describe Wordsworth's 'Ode' by what it excludes?" (p. 185). The answer, it is hoped, would knit up scholarship and interpretation, knowledge about and knowledge of the poem, engagement and detachment, the creative and the critical, the text as it is and as it is not, and, of course, the political and the aesthetic. This is no spectator response, to be sure, but rather the reinfusing of action into literary experience, creating text even as one receives it—mediating verbal and psychic reality as the first step in changing the world.

One would be hard pressed to devote a whole term to "The Painted Door" using Robinson's method, though a good deal could be done within a Marxist critical framework. I would see the major pedagogical project for this story, poststructurally speaking, as less one of constructing a historical imagination (Canadian English classrooms are already replete with attention to at least the *Canadian* historical imagination) than exposing the realistic fallacy that propels the reader into stasis (see pp. 172–174). We have already seen how this can be done with the feminist critique of the Calvinist-Jansenist ideology being played out among the characters (see pp. 151, 154, 172). But one can go still further in disengaging engagement, if you will, through a kind of genre study similar to that used by Robinson with his students—not history of the short story, in this case, but inquiry into narrative as a conservative literary convention. This seems almost as surely to kill aesthetic pleasure as appreciating Beethoven's *Ninth Symphony* in terms of how it paid that month's rent. Isn't "storying," as we now call it, the very lifeblood of English education? (Rosen, 1984). Isn't narrative "'a primary act of mind'"? (quoted in Thomson, 1987, p. 109). But, as noted in his volume, and by Hanssen, Harste, and Short in this volume (see Chapter 11), in order for a story to be constructive of the reader's reality, it "must be verbalized, it must be told" (Rosen, 1984, p. 14). In short, it must be brought to consciousness.

Narrative, sympathetic identification, and engagement with the text have become sacred cows in English education today, without their having been sufficiently theorized. Taking up with students the political implications of what it means to be an engaged reader contributes to their becoming objects as well as subjects of their reading. To ask Robinson's question, "What for me is the fate of beauty?" is to make students metaphysicians of reading. Such a probe can bring to consciousness the advance toward psychic wholeness believed to be so much a part of engagement with the text. It is this consciousness that makes aesthetic reading a critical enterprise, and critical reading a personal pleasure. And it is this consciousness by which readers change the world.

TOTAL FORM AS A MOVEABLE FEAST
Dialectic

Jeffrey Robinson's pedagogical experiment integrates study and enjoyment, scholarship and experience. Here student readers are led through exploration of the productive processes of the text and of the conditions of their own psychic growth to a form of literary knowing that overcomes Eliot's dissociation of sensibility. I want to suggest that the kind of experiential realization or connected knowing inherent in a dialectical process such as Robinson's, in which engagement and detachment are not alternating states, as they necessarily are within the aesthetics of total form, but a true synthesis of feeling, intellection, and imagination through insight into *how* literature is undergone, into ways in which texts work on readers, constitutes part of the "epistemological shift" (de Lauretis, 1986, p. 10) in cultural studies today. My redefinition of the aesthetics of total form would move the student reader from Logos, the god of knowledge who proclaims, compelling compliance, to Sophia, the goddess of wisdom who creates, inviting transformation (see Cady, Ronan, & Taussig, 1986).

Robinson has taken a giant step toward Sophia in providing a theory and pedagogy that addresses the politics of the engaged reader by taking seriously the consequences of falling in love with the poem. Crucial to this contribution is his consideration of developmental and psychoanalytic elements in a conception of literary experience that attempts to bridge the gap between engagement and detachment: the student is demystified about the "objectivity" of the text and the "subjectivity" of the self, coming to understand just how both text and self have been constructed, but in such a way as to deepen appreciation for knowledge *and* experience. Robinson's "model" admirably resolves the tension between the aesthetic and the political in literary reading by having students analyze their own dialectic of engagement and detachment. But he has left out an important factor in his otherwise comprehensive approach, and that is the unavoidable one of gender.

The shape and scope of this study has not been able to accommodate as a separate investigation the major influence of psychoanalysis in poststructuralist literary theory. But in a real sense, the psychoanalytic element is the most important for literature education. In this final section, I want to review briefly some salient points about the feminist critique of Freudian theory, a critique that perhaps speaks most directly to my overall purpose — to transform partial form into total form without splitting off feeling from thought, heart from head, in the act of reading. This objective, what might be called "the feminization of literary knowing," seeks to impart to the reader the fruits of understanding the undergoing of literary experience. I want the reader to have it both ways: to enjoy the benefits of total form without falling victim to its totalizing bid to colonize the soul. Plato would chide me for demanding the best of both the worlds of poetry and philosophy, contending that we must choose between the total form of rational dialectic and the partial form of response to literature. Patricia Jagentowicz Mills, however, in *Women, Nature, and Psyche* (1987), says we *can* have it both ways — through critical theory. Critical theory (I would substitute "literary theory") "undoes reified universals by tracing them back to the experiences from which they arise; simultaneously, it carries partial insights forward into a universal reflection" (pp. 208–209). What Mills underscores here is the difference between naming within Logos, wherein we conform to some external determination of what *is*, and naming within Sophia, wherein we reform the memory by naming for *ourselves*, in full knowledge that our articulation can never capture the immediacy or intensity of the original experience. The plenitude and frustration of this naming-theunnameable I envision as the dialectical alternative to stasis, that is, communication as *indirection*, total form as a moveable feast that can begin anywhere, and, through the search for truth, desire for pleasure, or imperative to action, end unendingly as the ongoing practice of readers rereading readings. As individual "isms," poststructuralist theories can threaten to break down into sectarian corners on the market of literary interpretation. But each of the three critical world-views under scrutiny in these chapters offers the possibility of a new conception of total form if the reader cares to follow the laws of their internal logic. Taken together, these theories promise a joyous dialectical interplay that can reclaim total form as the "universal reflection" through the "partial insights" envisioned by Mills — the overcoming of Eliot's dissociation of sensibility that the dialectic of the taxonomy in Chapter 5 failed to accomplish within any single reading act.

In order to get some idea of how this symposium of literary communication as indirection can come about, it is necessary to understand the impact of feminist critiques of psychoanalysis on the actual psychology of literary reading. We have already seen how gender is implicated in the relationship between ideology and mythology (Aiken, 1986), plot and Aristotle's "thought" in realism (Ermarth, 1983a, 1983b), and the identification process (Fetterley, 1978; Schweickart, 1986). These challenges to the aesthetics of total form have chipped away at the communication model and its thrust toward coherence and stability in literary interpretation. We have also witnessed the demise of this model at the hands of two other feminist poststructuralists in their accounts of the constructed nature of texts and readers (Belsey, 1980; Weedon, 1987). Interestingly, perhaps one of the most cogent expositions of psychoanalytic influences of the reading process comes from a film theorist, Teresa de Lauretis.[4] In what follows, I shall attempt to sketch out de Lauretis's feminist poststructuralist analysis of narrative structure, and the transformative effects of the reading process itself as favoring male psychodynamics, after which we shall consider their implications for total form as a "moveable feast."

In stunning fashion, de Lauretis unpacks the masculinist bias inscribed in fictive narrative representation through cinema, where the moving camera coopts the viewer most forcibly in its capacity "to reconfirm our expectations, hypotheses, and knowledge of reality" (1984, p. 63). Challenging Barthes' assertion that narrative is a universal human construct ("it is simply there, like life itself"; quoted from de Lauretis, 1984, p. 103), she cites Laura Mulvey (another film theorist), who understands narrative as a kind of sadism in its unrelenting demand for "making something happen" (p. 132). For de Lauretis, the process of narrative commits the violence of genderizing the fulfillment of desire in the reading act. The result is a theory of reading based on sexual difference — not sexual deference with respect to subject matter (Fetterley, 1978) or to the interdependence of plot and Aristotle's "thought" (Ermarth, 1983a, 1983b), but to the very structure of the recognition scene as a moment of vision and what it does to readers, male and female. It is this emphasis on vision, on clarity of insight, that we remember from Chapter 5 constitutes the essence of the literary communication model. De Lauretis (1984) argues trenchantly that the thrust toward fulfillment of desire by way of progression from beginning, middle, to a climactic end, wherein the hero's sense of loss is restored by a renewed vision of how things are, is a male paradigm (see pp. 120 ff.).

One might object that de Lauretis draws too close a correspondence between aesthetic forms and human processes, a correlation that I abhorred earlier with respect to the Marxist hypothesis that sonata form is a capitalist plot (see p. 180). Yet at least one male critic, Robert Scholes (1979), has already staked out narrative as a male preserve primarily because of the structure of delayed gratification built into it (cited by de Lauretis, 1984, p. 108). De Lauretis, though, goes further. For her, making sense of the world through story, an activity that ideally moves the reader as mental traveler (see Frye, 1976, pp. 185−186) from one level of consciousness to another — this very idea of human transformation that literature educators have traditionally claimed as literature's unique and august educational province — is seen to be inseparable from the psychosexual process of becoming a man. In Freud's view, continues de Lauretis,

> Femininity and masculinity . . . are positions occupied by the subject in relation to desire, corresponding respectively to the passive and active aims of the libido. They are positionalities within a movement that carries both the male child and female child toward one and the same destination: Oedipus and the Oedipal stage. That movement . . . is the movement of narrative discourse, which specifies and even produces the masculine position as mythical subject, and the feminine position as mythical obstacle or, simply, the space in which the movement occurs (1984, p. 143).

If brought to its logical conclusion, the foregoing provides the metaphysical ground for literary education, construed in terms of the passage from ignorance to knowledge as the *overcoming of an impediment to insight*. Knowers become male "selves" in search of a female "unknown." What results, according to de Lauretis, is an endless reconstruction of a drama in which the female or feminine can only be conceptualized in terms of a "personified obstacle" to "civilized man" — a purely symbolic other, such as "a grave," "a house," "a woman" (p. 133).

De Lauretis's critique of the genderization of consciousness through narrative structure proves useful in accounting for the hegemony of coherence underlying the literary communication model. If we think back to the initial reading of "The Painted Door" upon which stasis was predicated (see pp. 149–151), we recall that "the little smear of paint" effected the recognition scene that knit up *mythos* and *dianoia* into Frye's "frozen simultaneous pattern" (see p. 118). Within de Lauretis's conceptualization of narrative, this pattern, irrespective of its content, can be apprehended by the reader only within the teleology of male desire. In archetypal terms, the reader as mental traveler enacts the Freudian search for identity by infinitely replicating Oedipus asking the riddle of the Sphinx, to which there can be only one answer, one meaning, "one term of reference and address: man, Oedipus, the human male person" (p. 133). Accordingly, a female reader as mental traveler can attain fulfillment of her desire, can complete her story solely as "a question of *his* desire" (p. 133, emphasis added). This usurping of female desire by literary convention is more elusive than the intersection of plot and "thought" we saw operating in Ermarth's analysis (see pp. 172–173), in which the feeling of identity depended upon the reader's compliance with the shared body of moral and intellectual assumptions between author and characters. In that sense, aesthetic pleasure turned on ideology as a kind of content. But de Lauretis enunciates a conspiracy between ideology and aesthetics all the more powerful (and, some would say, insidious) because of its invisibility and inseparability from the act of processing the text. Here, then, the very drive for identity, a fundamental principle of literary reading, is gendered. This means nothing less than the dissolution of the hierarchical relationship between mythology and ideology outlined in Chapter 5: the genderization of narrative form renders mythology itself ideological; *mythos* frozen as *dianoia* becomes the recognition of a masculine identity pattern.

Implications of the previous for total form as a moveable feast are unmistakable in that the principle of noncorrespondence between language and reality as the informing principle of literariness, of indirect meaning, within the psychodynamics of reading becomes reaffirmed. This noncorrespondence can be viewed as the key to reclaiming for total form the search for truth, desire, and action, petrified through stasis and unleashed through the three critical world-views discussed in these chapters. More precisely, noncorrespondence between language and reality coalesces the three elements of total form into a dialectic that is self-creating and self-renewing, dynamic rather than static, based on the awareness and acceptance that no knowledge or insight can ever be more than partial. Thus, inherent in the act of reading is a recognition scene, not of identity, but of nonidentity, or as de Lauretis says in *Technologies of Gender* (1987), "a double or self-subverting coherence" (p. 116), whose dialectical strategies celebrate the "profoundly cleft, inherently contradictory" nature of a "*recognition of misrecognition*" (pp. 122, 124). This feminization of dialectic, so to speak, allows the reader to begin wherever she or he is and to stop anywhere so long as she or he realizes that the resting place, though not false, must be temporary. Ensuing from this is a recognition scene that actualizes the "vaunted joy" of Longinian *ecstasis*, in which the reader uses the misrecognition to create a new genre of nonliterature. De Lauretis rejects the category, literature, conceived as "the novelistic" in favor of a

> new textual form, where the rational historical inquiry is continually intersected by the lyrical and the personal, the subject is at once writer and reader, performer and audience. . . . The text is produced and meant to be received as the intersecting of the personal and the social, a process articulated dialectically on subjective codes and on objective realities (1987, p. 92).

Here are dissolved distinctions between knowledge and experience, the fictive and the real, as readers become metaphysicians of reading by writing their own texts.

Stasis

Total form as a moveable feast reconfirms Victor Lokke's assertion (1987) that "*taxonomies are never innocent*" (p. 3); that is, they are dangerous if understood as reified ontological realities. Rather, they must be "context-dependent" (p. 3), indispensable in themselves as hypothetical paradigms, but open to manipulation, begging to be dismantled, reassembled, literally moved around. The taxonomy described in Chapter 5, imposing and imposing *on*, is clearly not user-friendly. My poststructuralist revision of it has been an attempt to break down and out of its pristine metaphysical grandeur. However, the *logic* of my poststructuralist textual strategies as the *uses of criticism*[5] comprises only a part of my feminization of total form. Poststructuralist theory captures well the idea of dialectic as Act; but the feminization of total form entails also dialectic as Being, as the *magic* of plenitude found in "true ecstasy" (Göttner-Abendroth, 1985, p. 90), of which stasis has been the precursor. True ecstasy transmutes stasis, predicated on vision, and *jouissance*, predicated on desire, into a synthesis of creative thought and material presence.

De Lauretis's creative use of misrecognition as the basis for the reader's rewriting her own text constitutes true ecstasy as dialectic, in which the reintegration of theory and fiction, reading and writing, art and life, can be thought of in its exegetical or interpretive mode—the "logic" of true ecstasy. True ecstasy, though, also has its participatory or liturgical counterpart—its magic. In "Nine Principles of a Matriarchal Aesthetic," Heide Göttner-Abendroth (1985) outlines her version of true ecstasy as celebration, as "the *spontaneous* meshing of all human forces" (p. 90, emphasis added)—which can be evoked but not directed. Hers is a definition of true ecstasy that would bring de Lauretis's integration of reading and writing, the fictive and the real, from the realm of *understanding* the creative act of naming—study, dialectic— to that of simply undergoing the act of creating in everyday terms. This would be to bring magic to the quotidian. Göttner-Abendroth also banishes the fictive. For her, there is no distinction between theory, meditation, speech, and the joyful getting on with life. What results is a magical ritual dance, at once fiercely erotic and wholly disciplined, through which is enacted the interdependence of personal feeling, human relationship, symbolic meaning, and social change.

But does this revivification of stasis as true ecstasy dispense with the "old" form of stasis described in Chapter 5? I want to argue that it does not. Stasis in that sense has its own place in the metaphysics of reading. The feminization of total form described before conceives of desire in terms of its fulfillment, in terms of the actualization of being, as true ecstasy, as Sophia, the knowledge of the goddess who connects through difference (See Cady et al., 1986, p. 74), creating the world anew. Who could ask for more? I could, for my own subjectivity has been constituted by the original taxonomy, and I am ambivalent about paying the price for the new one, if that price is rejection of literature as a category, and the future possibility of falling in love, yet again, with the poem. The synthesis of logic and magic presaged by the redefinition of stasis as true ecstasy does not obviate my present need to account for the human awareness of the "existential gap" (Frye, 1971/1973, p. 104) between what we have and what we want. This acute sense of a void in human consciousness many would argue accrues simply from the material effects of a world run by patriarchy; we need a new way predicated on a feminine psychodynamic, in which desire is conceived as fulfilled, not frustrated. The substance of this chapter, I hope, has been testimony to that promise. But the imperfect nature of what we *have* still speaks to the need for filling the void, for closing the gap, for literature as art, that recalls Valéry's notion of recurring desire quoted in Chapter 6 (see p. 141), a de- sire admittedly Romantic in its harkening back to the hierarchy of the fictive over the real. But this desire should not, I think, be trivialized as escapist. Paul de Man (1971/1983) describes it as tran- scending "the notion of a nostalgia or a desire, since it discovers desire as a fundamental pattern of being that discards any possibility of satisfaction" (p. 17). For de Man, the need for poetry goes beyond the

> desire of something or for someone; here, the consciousness does not result from the absence of something but consists of the presence of nothingness. Poetic language names this void with ever-renewed understanding, ... never tires of naming it again (p. 18).

Perhaps unwittingly, feminist poststructuralist theory has supplied one of the most persuasive justifications for literature as art in its revisioning of desire from void or lack to what Jessica Benjamin (1986) calls "A Desire of One's Own." Benjamin's clinical experience with women coming to terms with their own desire discloses the search for a new kind of recognition, a recognition of identity *and* nonidentity as an "intersubjective reality" grounded in desire for "freedom to be both with and distinct from the other" (p. 98). Springing not so much from de Man's consciousness of nothingness but from "a place within the self," this form of aesthetic *"inner* desire" (p. 97) Benjamin regards as the source of a new dialectic between self and other. I would hazard that stasis, as conceived in the "old" aesthetics of total form, speaks to this kind of desire in respect of its receptivity to what is "other," its openness to being in the world.

In my original conceptualization, stasis is true ecstasy *in potentia*, the not-yetness of fulfillment of desire, Being as the holding of oneself open to being. Stasis betokens a vulnerability to the other as strange but not alien; it is the willingness to be and let be, the antithesis of self-assertion. In *What Are Poets For?* Martin Heidegger (1971) calls this openness "the unconcealedness of beings" (p. 98). The poet undertakes to name this "unconcealedness." Stasis as the "Aha!" response to "The Painted Door," is, we recall, that curious blend of satiety and longing for completion; it is *ecstasis in potentia*, the not-yetness of fulfillment of desire. I suggest that this "Aha!" response is both an internal and external manifestation of the Heideggerian poetic mode of living in the world. Neither stasis nor unconcealedness can exist alongside full consciousness conceived of in terms of self-assertion or guardedness. That is the paradox of Frye's "primitive" respondent, the reader who goes to the poem without any critical preconceptions (see p. 120). In general, the genuine primitive must remain a metaphor for the reader in direct, unmediated contact with the poem, for poststructuralist theory has disabused us of the possibility of unmediated verbal expression (de Man, 1983). There is only total form as moveable feast, as indirection, as creative dialectical interplay between text and reader. Is there, really? At the risk of undermining everything I have said thus far, I still want to retain the value of the susceptibility of stasis to imprisonment by Beauty, for in that imprisonment lies the freedom and strength that completes the inner desire Benjamin speaks of as *both* the magic and logic of the heart. Heidegger invokes the poetry of Rainer Maria Rilke to illustrate reading poetry as response to the unconcealedness of being in a "logic of the heart" (1971, p. 133). This is a difficult task, according to Heidegger, because of the metaphysical cast of Rilke's poetry, and the fact that we "are not experienced travellers in the land of the saying of Being" (p. 98). We must therefore go slow. Heidegger undertakes the reading of one of Rilke's more obscure poems "as an exercise in poetic self-reflection" (p. 100), and through it comes to an understanding of poetic language as the saying of Being. Heidegger conceives poetry as indistinguishable from the nature of language and, indeed, of thinking itself. Language tells us how to dwell in the world poetically by encountering and revealing the ineffability of consciousness of the unseen through the logic of the heart.

What is this dwelling in the world that poetry bestows and how does it relate to the magic of stasis? Language points the way to dwelling in the world poetically, that is, to remaining open to "the plenitude of all [its] facets" (p. 124), not by signifying or representing, but through the reader's inner recall of objects, events, persons. The mere act of saying calls forth the presence of existence as pure song. Response to song is simply listening in openness to all being, living and taking appropriate measure of the world (see Hofstadter, 1971, p. xiv), what Frye would call a scholarship of the ear, in which we are "constantly listening for phrases" (1965, p. 23) — ultimately to be alone and silent in connectedness. This is to become Sophia in the Rilkean moment, whole, bright, deep with understanding, but aware of the painful contradiction that connectedness of this sort entails the ambivalence and virtual impossibility of simultaneously proclaiming and surrendering identity. Stasis as the *static* aspect of *ecstasis* represents for Heidegger that most interior quality of openness, which he calls *Da* ("here") as the standing *in* being (see Orr, 1981, p. 84). For me, stasis most purely typifies immanence in presence, the feeling state of listening to Purcell sung by Andrew Dalton. It is a state altogether outside the dimension of language and Aristotle's "thought." In reading literature, it is the sense, as Frye has put it, of standing "inside the structure of literature" (1966, p. 141), where the surround of art lends the aura that this is what existence is all about, and "the way things are" transmogrifies into "the way things can be." In *A Natural Perspective* (1965), Frye speaks of a condition in which

> experience would be contained, not expressed or, expressed at most by a single symbol ... a mystical unity of consciousness in which

music would be represented by what Milton calls the "perfect dia-
pason" of a tonic chord, painting by Giotto's O, literature by the
syllable *Aum* (p. 31).

Or, as Heidegger (1971), by way of Rilke, would say, "Song is
existence" (p. 138).

Stasis and Dialectic: The Feminization of Total Form

Having come full circle to stasis, we must ask where the trek through
these chapters has led. The relationship between language, art, and
cosmic consciousness may answer the yearnings of the gazer into
Bergdorf's window, but what about the lightbulb joke that started us
off—do we laugh at it or not? Also yet to be dealt with is the status of
the taxonomy in its original disposition, and whether total form as a
moveable feast makes any difference. I suggest that these issues cannot
be resolved to anyone's satisfaction, least of all to my own; however,
I wish to conclude by relocating ourselves within Frye's literary theory.

With the feminization of total form, we have seen the importance
of naming for ourselves (see Mills, 1987) the *understanding* of our
own undergoing of the poem. With matriarchal aesthetics (Göttner-
Abendroth, 1985), we have seen the simultaneous explosion of
connected knowings and experiential realizations (see Belenkey et al.,
1986) in the dissolution of all boundaries between art and life—the
sacramental honoring of the sheer giftedness of reality, which is
reflected in the worldviews of Heidegger and Rilke. It is also what
Frye points to in his conception of "a third order of experience"
(1971/1973, p. 170), a utopian vision with which he ends virtually
every book he has written. Explicit in this vision is his idea that
in a world without lack there would be no need for the notion of
"literariness" to annihilate lack. But we have seen from de Man,
Benjamin, Heidegger, Rilke—and Frye asserts it himself—that in
whichever ways desire is constituted by ideology, it remains a fundamental category of being human as the irreducible movement toward
wholeness. It is the aesthetic impulse that attempts to address desire
directly. Whether conceived as de Man's void or Heidegger's consciousness of the plenitude of Being, desire presupposes the ambivalence of the principles of identity and nonidentity with which human
beings are both plagued and blessed (see Frye, 1957, pp. 105–106).

My poststructuralist re-vision of the taxonomy from static splendor
to moveable feast is intended to reinforce the constructive possibilities
of lack inherent in the fact that language both says and does not say
what we mean. Yet the poststructuralist emphasis on nonidentity is in
the end a structuralist notion. That language only points to things in

the world, that it is primarily self-referential, is one of the basic tenets of formalism, which Michael Fischer in his book *Does Deconstruction Make Any Difference?* (1985) has accused deconstruction of simply solidifying. Fischer notes rightly that "Frye's assertion that even discursive writing owes its form to literature becomes in deconstruction the crack that opens his self-contained literary universe" (p. 94). So, as early as *Anatomy of Criticism* (1957), Frye was saying, "No, Virginia, there *is* no difference between a literary and nonliterary verbal structure!" (pp. 74, 331). If that is correct, then how can ideology be subordinate to mythology?

In "The Dialectic of Belief and Vision" (1985), Frye suggests that the hierarchy between ideology and mythology is in the end a moveable feast. Though ideologies are derived from mythology, inasmuch as a *mythos* or story tells a society what it needs to know about itself, Frye acknowledges that "mythology generally comes to a society already in some form of ideology" (p. 14). I have tried to show how feminists have theorized that at present that prevailing ideology is patriarchy, and that so-called gender-neutral notions, such as universal values, narrative form, and the transformative process itself have been kidnapped by the male imagination and handed over as containers for female experience uncontainable by them. My reading of Frye (1967) would suggest that he would call such a masquerading of mythology as ideology a "closed mythology" (p. 16). A closed mythology reduces the range of mythological vision from the conceivable to the achievable by way of rationalizing its claim to social authority; it is a system bound by belief without imagination, in which conclusions are entailed by their premises—a definition well served by the current state of male domination. By contrast, the "open mythology" is a mythology without a canon, "a reservoir of possibilities of belief," otherwise known as "free discussion" (1967, p. 115). This reservoir of the possibilities of belief has prefigured "the epistemological shift" in cultural studies referred to by de Lauretis (see p. 183) as well as "an altered metaphysical position" heralded by some feminist philosophers in their attempt to overcome the duality between subject and object by creating a truly "relational epistemology" that would change the face of educational transformation (Stone, 1989, p. 192). In Frye's open mythology, the knower espouses a position, but is ready at any point to suspend his or her version of the truth as definitive, i.e., to move beyond stock response. In *The Critical Path* (1971/1973), Frye articulates this concept of the "open mythology" as the "educational contract" (p. 162):

> the process by which the arts and sciences, with their methods of logic, experiment, amassing of evidence and imaginative presentation,

actually operate as a source of spiritual authority in society ... a
free authority, something coherent enough to help form a community,
but not an authority in the sense of being able to apply external
compulsion (p. 163).

The openness of the educational contract entails the *recursive*
operation of engagement and detachment as one long and complex
continuous dialectical process[6] on the assumption that "No idea is
anything more than a half-truth unless it contains its own opposite,
and is expanded by its own denial or qualification" (Frye, 1967,
p. 116). Relational knowing emphasizes "the social, interactive and
connective construction of knowledge" (Stone, 1989, p. 193). This is
the lesson that the interplay of stasis as certitude of truth and dialectic
as skepticism about that truth has for education. Literariness, the
principle of the identity and nonidentity of language and reality, is
both assertion and hypothesis—knowing and questioning in relation.
Literary reading invokes the realm of "This seems true; if it is, then.
... " Applied to what we normally think of as conceptual thought,
stasis and dialectic together say, "I stand here, but am open to moving
there." Is it possible that the taxonomy and its revision are variations
on a theme, that, after all, humanism does retain "the capacity to
encompass critical thinking in the presence of the seductive idyllicism
of beauty" (Robinson, 1987, p. 10)? Yes and no. Yes, if Frye (1988) is
correct that the "final aim of studying works of literature is, in some
way, the absorbing of their verbal power into oneself" (p. 140). No, if
that final aim ignores the importance of creating social and political
conditions in the classroom conducive to the absorbing of verbal
power into oneself. There must be a *predisposition* to reading new
stories in new ways. As Carolyn Steedman (1987) reminds us, stories
cannot be told if "there is not the vision that *permits* the understanding of
[the] new connections" (p. 138) wrought by the myths and metaphors
of literature. Perhaps, then, the teacher of literature should be there
to encourage students to name for themselves the profound tensions
in the undergoing, understanding, and the understanding of their
undergoing, of literature through reading and rereading: the joy of
being in love with literature, the pain of being out of love with it, the
desiring search for truth in working with it, and the more active
involvement in the world because of it. As to the lightbulb joke and
whether or not we should laugh? It's funny—but it's not funny ...

NOTES

1. None of the "readings" in these chapters is an actual reading. They are
construals of readings, in which I have tried to simulate interpretations in
accordance with the theories they are intended to illustrate.

2. It should be noted that the authoritarianism of realism varies according to the subtlety of the author's craft and the quality of her or his moral imagination. For Martha Nussbaum, realistic works of literature can become moral achievements in their own right to the degree that they attenuate moral obtuseness in their characters, and engender an intense and striving *"quality* of bewilderment" in readers. The richer the moral perceptions drawn by the author, the more morally conscious the reader will become. But confining "ourselves to the universal is a recipe for obtuseness" (Nussbaum, 1985, pp. 528, 526).

3. In general, this issue has increasingly become part of the literature curriculum in colleges and universities. At the school level, the rise in parental objections to literary content has forced educators to deal with the practical effects of the relationship between literature and life without the benefit of a theory other than the traditional humanist assertion of the educational value of literature.

4. Poststructuralist literary theory seems to have made its greatest impact in the schools through "Media Studies."

5. See Jonathan Culler's "four tasks" for "the future of criticism" (Koelb & Lokke, 1987, p. 40).

6. In *The Great Code* (1982, p. 226), Frye reiterates the active nature of reading more explicitly than he does in his earlier work. (For a discussion of his theory of reader response before and in *The Great Code*, see Deanne Bogdan, 1989a.)

READING COMPREHENSION
Readers, Authors, and the World of the Text

Robert J. Tierney & Michael Gee

Within the world of the text, there are the images and the voices of characters interacting with one another. At the same time, there is the intermingling of the voices of the authors and readers. If these voices are not heard or these images are not seen, reading and writing may represent mere shadows of the experiences they could be. In this chapter we discuss two facets of a reader's experience: engagement in the world of the text and the author-reader relationship.

AUTHOR-READER RELATIONSHIP

In "Learning to Read like a Writer" (1984), Frank Smith offered the following exhortation:

> To read like a writer we engage with the author in what the author is writing. We anticipate what the author will say, so that the author is in effect writing on our behalf, not showing how something is done but doing it with us (p. 53).

The notion of readers and writers working together has prompted many of us to draw parallels between reading and writing *and* conversation. Perhaps we should conceptualize reading and writing not as a straightforward exchange of information, but as a negotiation. Readers don't just absorb ideas, they "engage with" authors—reflecting upon what they are saying and why.[1] For instance, Tierney and Lazansky (1980) cited Gricean Cooperative principles of conversation to suggest that there exists a reciprocal agreement between readers and writers that defines what is expected by writers of readers and by readers of writers. Nystrand (1987) has extended these notions of collaboration, or as he calls it, reciprocity:

> The expectations for reciprocity in discourse is important because it means that the shape and conduct of discourse is determined not only by what the speaker or writer has to say (speaker/writer meaning) or accomplish (speaker/writer purpose) but also by the joint expectations of the conversants that they should understand one another (producer-receiver contract). Of these three forces that shape discourse, moreover, the contract is most fundamental: without a contract between writer and reader, both meaning and purpose are unfathomable at best and untenable at worst (p. 48).

Tierney and Pearson (1984) proposed a model of reading that draws the salient parallels between the composing nature of both writing and reading. This model identifies four facets of composition that are also present in reading comprehension. In brief, the reader is planner, composer, editor, and monitor. The four roles the reader plays are not distinct and linear, but rather recursive and conjoined in any number of ways in the negotiation of meaning among author, reader, a reader's projected view of an author, and the reader's "other self."

The planning role has to do with establishing goals and purposes for reading and how these are aligned with what readers perceive as their goals and the author's goals and purposes. The composing role deals with the model or world of the text readers build as they read. This entails filling in gaps, making the pieces "fit" as the shape of the whole develops, and refining the meaning negotiated. In the editor role, readers examine their developing interpretations as they restructure, redefine, reformulate, or review their understandings. The monitor function drives and orchestrates the other three roles and helps the reader determine when best to play which role.

A number of us have argued that discerning the readers' expectations of themselves and the writer's goals for the reader is at the heart of understanding the nature of that negotiation. From the readers' side, the readers' goals, prior experiences, expectations, and perceptions (of the author) have a significant impact upon the ongoing understandings readers develop (Austin, 1962; Grice, 1975; Rosenblatt, 1978; Searle, 1969; Winograd, 1976).

Let us illustrate some of these processes with some of the responses we acquired from actual readers. We recently asked two adult readers to share how their understandings unfolded for the "Tell-Tale Heart" (a macabre story by Edgar Allan Poe involving the anxieties experienced in conjunction with an attempt to plan and cover-up a murder), "A Lamp in the Window" (an episode by Truman Capote, involving a rather unusual lady with some strange quirks, including keeping her deceased cats in a freezer), and "The Million Year Picnic" (a Ray Bradbury story of a family coming to grips with the end of planet Earth and relocation on Mars). The purpose of pursuing these responses was to use them as the basis for reflecting upon and illustrating the factors involved in reading comprehension.

Our readers' comments reflected a recurring pattern of formulating expectations. From the very beginning of reading these texts, our readers were hypothesizing, using a prediction-confirmation process in meaning making. Tentative possibilities were later confirmed or discarded as they seemed to fit or no longer fit with the reader's new expectations. One reader, for example, reported in her reading of "A Lamp in the Window":

> I remember the thought crossing my mind that she was . . . maybe it was supernatural, maybe she was supposed to be a ghost and after he had his night's rest, then it would all go away. I just remember thinking that at one point.

The same reader was almost reluctant to let go of the prediction she had made in response to Capote's pinpointing a new deep freeze in the shabby kitchen when she suspected that the freezer held the woman's dead husband:

> My first thought was, I bet her husband's in there. I never thought about there being a bunch of cats, but it made as much sense as her husband being in it.

The other reader in response to reading "The Million Year Picnic" stated:

> Well, it kind of threw me when I got to the paragraph . . . when I found out that it wasn't just going to be a fishing trip, cause when I first started reading it I just thought they were going on a fishing trip here on earth. Then when the paragraph came . . . where it says they had landed on their small family rocket all the way from earth, right then I knew this wasn't going to be just. . . .
>   I wanted to see, get to the end so I could find out what was going to happen. . . .
>   . . . except I kept wondering, well, what happened on earth and the thought crossed my mind that if I read this whole thing and they

still don't tell you what happened. Because that was the only thing that interested me and kept me going through it.

This response points up, too, the implicit contract that this reader has formulated with the author: "I'll hold off on understanding the whole thing as I go through it but I'd better understand it at the end." Readers will place themselves in alliance with the author, willing to suspend judgment, and reserve final confirmation until sometime later.

The past experiences of readers shaped expectations and subsequent understandings. When asked to talk about "The Million Year Picnic," one reader deliberately chose not to explain the story ("I don't think you can."), but would only characterize the story as being "about a distorted value system." Further elaboration of response to the story was possible, but an overriding value system was evident in those responses:

> Maybe it's just because I'm a Christian that I see it that way, but it's like people got caught up too much in things and not each other, that once they let things run their lives the things destroyed their lives.

Another reader connected the same story to contemporary issues despite discovering the time span of over forty years since it was first written:

> What man is doing, we're creating all these star war things that we're just building up to destroy ourselves instead of protect ourselves . . . it has a lot do with war.

The past experience of readers extends to their past experience with authors. One of our readers reported her fear of being asked to read "The Tell-Tale Heart": "As soon as I saw that it was Edgar Allan Poe, I panicked. I thought oh, no, Edgar Allan Poe." On the other hand, a reader can value a piece because of an author:

> . . . I just like the homey style of writing of Truman Capote, he makes you feel like you're sitting down and talking with him and he's relaying this story over a cup of coffee to you. "You know what happened to me the other night? I was stuck in the forest. . . ."

One reader felt disconcerted because the text did not match her expectations for an author:

> . . . Well, knowing it was Ray Bradbury I knew it was probably, after I thought about it, I thought it was probably science fiction, but then they seemed so normal in the beginning it was hard for me to put the two things together.

Sometimes the relationship with the author that emerges is more straightforward — the reader is trying to take advantage of what can be gleaned about an author or "a comfort zone" alongside perceptions of the author. As one reader stated, "I focus on what the author is trying to say." Or, as the other reader remarked about "A Lamp in the Window": "After I started reading it I tried to find out who wrote it so I would have an idea of what I was going to get into again. ..."

Both readers postulated guesses about the psychological state or motives that may have played a part in the author's writing "The Tell-Tale Heart":

> Maybe people thought he was mad and that he had to keep explaining himself, but yet he had, um, maybe had strange thoughts going on in his mind that he couldn't explain to anybody else.
> If you think people can't write based on things they haven't experienced, then maybe he was insane too. Maybe he had that kind of mind.

It should not be assumed that readers ever acquiesce entirely. The reader's role in constructing meaning is *always* central. This is notwithstanding the possibilities that, at times, readers will appear to sometimes follow along and other times embark upon their own excursions. One reader, in response to the Capote text, seemed to maintain the belief that the woman's husband was still involved: "... then I knew she had a freezer full of cats, but I still thought her husband might be lying under the cats"; or in line with her overall framework that the Bradbury story is about a distorted value system, the same reader lays out for our consideration:

> ... it made me think, well, they were the Martians on earth because they were so different from everybody else, separate from everybody else that they were strange ... that just came out to me in the end, but that they were Martians in their own civilization.

Whether Bradbury intended that as his message or his purpose in writing this story, we don't know, but for this reader, her sense that that message was a viable interpretation is certain.

So how important is it for educators to support the view that readers should regard comprehension as a collaboration with authors? Several educators and others speak to this issue. The hermeneutic philosopher, Gadamer (1976), suggested texts remain mute unless readers approach them from the perspective that they are engaged in a dialogue with another person. Slatoff (1970) echoes this when he posits that "an important part of our experience of almost any literary work is the sense that we are being talked to by someone" (p. 93). Bruce (1984) has argued, for example, that a reader's "failure to understand the author's intentions can cause problems for all levels of comprehension from 'getting the main idea' to the subtle insights expected of skilled readers" (p. 380). Calkins (1983) maintains that students who approach text with an understanding that the text was produced by somebody, rather than something, read with a "more critical eye" (p. 157).

In terms of the research on reading comprehension, a limited number of studies have looked at the effects of knowing who the author is and other author-related information (e.g., author's purpose) on reading comprehension. These studies suggest that even very young readers are sensitive to who wrote what, that better readers tend to be more sensitive to authorship than poorer readers, and that this sensitivity to authorship is related to improved comprehension. Graves and Hansen (1984), for example, observed that very young readers were able to discuss the craft of stories written by peers and professional authors and that these discussions appeared to enhance comprehension. In a series of studies, Tierney, et al. (1987) found that readers who approached text with an understanding of an author's intent recalled more information and read those texts more critically than students who were not sensitive to author's intent. Unfortunately, apart from these four studies, research exploring a reader's sensitivity to authorship is rare.

On the one hand, the research confirms the saliency of the author-reader relationship in reading and writing. The research shows rather convincingly that a reader's performance is affected and, more importantly, may be enhanced by a consideration of authorship and readership. On the other hand, the dearth of research in this area leaves a number of issues relative to the nature and role of reader-writer relationships undetermined.

For instance, most studies have looked only globally at the nature and effects of a sense of authorship and readership. They have failed to examine the effects of a sense of authorship and readership upon particular processes. They have not addressed whether heightened sensitivity to authorship as well as readership endures or transfers. Nor have many studies dealt with the complexities suggested by these broad notions of authorship. While literary theorists have debated this issue at length, research has provided very little feedback on just what is the nature of a sense of authorship in different situations associated with different interpretations. Furthermore, a host of social factors that overlap with a sense of authorship as one reads has not been explored. For example, there are teachers, and classmates, whose own interpretations and views may be influencing an individual reader's or writer's experience. And, at the same time, one must not forget that the reader or writer is immersed in the world of the text—

the characters, images, events, and themes they are exploring. It is to this issue we now turn.

THE WORLD OF THE TEXT

Oftentimes, when readers or writers are asked to discuss their understandings of a text, what will come to the forefront is a feeling of immersion. The writer, Enid Blyton, in her letters to Peter McKellar (1957), talked about being present in a cinematic world while she wrote. As he read, D. W. Harding (1967) referred to himself as a "ghostly watcher" (p. 12). Even very young writers will talk about "being there," "seeing things," "entering a cocoon where things happen around me." Tolkien (1964) referred to this as a world inside another world or a "secondary world" (p. 36). Wallace Stevens (1959) captured the flavor of these experiences when he wrote:

> The house was quiet and the world was calm.
> The reader became the book; and the summer night
> Was like the conscious being of the book.
> The house was quiet and the world was calm.

In many ways the readers' or writers' involvement in this secondary world can be quite vicarious and intense—even from an early age. We are reminded of a student who was reading one of Laura Ingalls Wilder's books and suddenly shouted, "No! No! Get away!" as he imagined a pack of wolves had surrounded the house that he found himself in.[2] Students at a very young age have the ability not only to discuss events as if they were there, but also to exhibit enormous empathy for characters and project themselves to be among them or identify with them.

If you consider our readers, there were times when their comments afforded us a glimpse of their engagement in the secondary world prompted by the story. For example, both of our readers appeared to become participants, or at least onlookers, in the closing of "A Lamp in the Window." Their reactions to the freezer opening suggested that they felt as if they were as onlookers beside the narrator. Here are the comments of one of our readers:

> Then when he walked up to the door, I thought that it strange that the woman greeted him so, in such a friendly way, and the other odd thing, then I started thinking about maybe she didn't really exist, maybe it was all his imagination, or that she was supposed to be a ghost or something. Then I think, I remember thinking if she was so well read, why was she so poor? Why did she live out in the

woods? I mean she seemed to be in touch with herself, all these thoughts about "this is what I'd do" and her religious values and I thought, what's she doing out there and all the time wondering why she wasn't a little bit afraid of somebody strange coming and then inviting them to stay in her house, that was, you just wouldn't find that in Columbus, Ohio or any other city. And then when he came down, the rest of it I think I took in as information until the minute he went into the kitchen and said that there was a new freezer. And then I thought, I bet she has her husband in it. And then when she said, then I knew just before she said it was stacked with cats, when he said he didn't have the heart to get another cat when his cat died and she said, "Well, then maybe you'll understand this" then I knew she had a freezer full of cats, but I still thought her husband might be lying under the cats.

A facet of a reader's involvement in this secondary world also involves other dimensions such as feelings of suspense. One of our readers, in discussing "The Tell-Tale Heart," suggested that "it was kind of building up like an excitement." She spoke of the story as "being unpleasant but stimulating . . . your heart would start racing. It made me feel like I was real."

Unfortunately, the nature of readers' involvement in these secondary worlds, including the affective dimensions, has been largely overlooked by researchers and theorists. As Spiro (1980) suggested, the work in the schema-theoretic tradition has focused on "the structure of knowledge that must be analyzed rather than on the texture that must be felt" (p. 273). Moreover, very few researchers have tied together the perspectives that readers achieve (including character identification), the affective dimensions of the perspectives, and their interpretations. It is as if engagement has been viewed as peripheral when it may be at the very heart of our understanding of the meanings readers negotiate. Indeed, work on several fronts seems to lend support to such a view. In several studies, for example, the type of engagement readers attained explained the responses readers had to authors and the understandings to which they subscribed (Dorfman, 1988; LaZansky, 1988).

The research on the influence of perspective taking by Anderson and Pichert (1978) suggests that students induced to adopt a perspective of character related to the world of the text generate more ideas in response to the text than those who are not so induced. Research by Jose and Brewer (in press) suggest that a reader's orientation toward and identifications with characters have a significant impact on their involvement in a story and whether they liked or disliked a story. The work by Jose and Brewer and by others provides some basis for understanding how such involvements are achieved and how they might contribute toward comprehension. For example, social psychologists have been interested for many years in how children, especially children of preschool and infant school ages, achieve a perspective on what others think, see, feel, or do. Oftentimes, they have explored this issue in the context of having children read or listen to stories. In general, this research suggests that to achieve an understanding of others, individuals need to refer to their own experiences rather than try to immerse themselves in the experience of others. By referring to their own experience, they may generalize about others and use partial external information to either infer deeper, internal motivations or achieve perspectives on what they are seeing, doing, or feeling. In accordance with this view, they find that individuals oftentimes fail to achieve perspectives: (1) if they do not have a sense of their own perspective or (2) if they have difficulty relating their perspective to those of others because of anomalies between their experiences and those of others. (For a review of this literature see Schantz, 1983.)

The findings from social psychology parallel the assumptions underlying what some drama theorists contend are essential for preparing to be a character. Stanislaski (1936), for example, argues that to achieve the role of a character, an individual must first discover himself or herself: an actor prepares by fitting "his own human qualities to the life of this other person, and pours into it all of his own soul" (p. 14).

A recurring notion in this literature is that individuals must be able to build bridges from their own experience. The reader or writer is the creator, using her own experience to supply the building blocks for these other worlds. Rather than being told how to relate, readers and writers must find, from within themselves, the seeds of creation. And within these creations, there exists the possibility of suspended belief as the reader or writer wanders these secondary worlds. While the feeling of being lost may be real, it is key not to really lose oneself.

As beliefs are suspended and/or readers and writers enter secondary worlds, a question arises: Is learning enhanced by such engagements? There is little direct support of the enhancement of learning as a result of readers' or writers' involvement in the world of the text. Studies have shown the impact of the activation of readers' or writers' past experiences upon their comprehension and composition, but very little has been done in the way of correlating these understandings with the precise nature of readers' and writers' involvement in these secondary worlds. Studies have demonstrated the positive effects of suggestions to visualize, or of using texts which might prompt images of a more vicarious relationship to the subject matter, but, again, engagement with the secondary world has been presumed rather than verified. (See Sadowski, 1983.)

Several studies point to the fact that the impact of engagement will vary depending upon the nature of this involvement. Some researchers have argued that both comprehension and composition may suffer when a reader's or writer's engagement is overly egocentric (Galda, 1982).[3] Some theorists contend that facility with shifting viewpoints is more the issue than egocentricity (Slatoff, 1970; Tierney & Pearson, 1984). A shift in perspective, they suggest, is achieved through simultaneously being detached and involved or adopting different angles on the same topic. For example, in Brechtian theater (Willet, 1959), this might be achieved by creating a commentary alongside a character (using perhaps a clown to offer asides on a crime victim's behavior as the victim recounts the events).

According to these notions, alienation facilitates a fuller understanding of a character's motives and actions, at the same time as it forces the audience to detach itself sufficiently to achieve a perspective on the perspective it was taking. Obviously, there are various ways alienation of shifts in perspective can be achieved. Many times readers will talk about approaching the rereading of texts solely for the purpose of exploring different perspectives or events. William Hurt, in preparing for his role in "Kiss of the Spider Woman," described the use of perspective shifts as he struggled to achieve his character. After struggling with his role as Molina, Raul Julia and Hurt decided to switch roles for a rehearsal. Hurt claims the perspective this afforded him was integral to achieving a new and more vital interpretation of his role (Kroll, 1986).

To summarize, then, we are suggesting that reading and writing involve engagement in the world of the text. To achieve this suspension of disbelief, readers need to relate to characters and events from their own experience. To take full advantage of these involvements, they need to keep in mind their own responses and to explore shifts in perspective.

The notion of shifting perspective and alienation seem crucial since the ultimate goal of any exploration is to achieve perspectives on one's own perspective taking; alienation or shifts in perspective are directed toward achieving this goal.

The key tenet underlying this chapter is that we must view reading and writing as involving negotiations along several continuums simultaneously. As Slatoff (1970) said,

> The single most important thing to observe about our emotional transactions with a literary work is that they do not occur along single continuums ... Even the most limited reader is capable of maintaining several simultaneous states of relation and feeling toward a work. ... We can share the experience of Gulliver, say, feel the experience, and at the same time view him with detachment and view with detachment the part of us that is identifying (p. 38–39).

For example, whether a reader is trying to understand an author, to follow a writer's set of directions, or to read for himself or herself, readers are involved with multifaceted engagements with their "selves" and the text. These transactions involve negotiating meaning within the context of the world suggested by the text (allowing oneself various levels of involvement with the concepts, characters, events, and settings) and negotiating meaning with the author (as critic, coauthor, observer, or participant). As Fillmore (1974) stated:

> A text induces the interpreter to construct an image or maybe a set of alternative images. The image the interpreter creates early in the text guides his interpretation of successive portions of the text and these in turn induce him to enrich or modify that image. While the image construction and image revision is going on, the interpreter is also trying to figure out what the creator of the text is doing—what the nature of the communication situation is. And that, too, may have an influence on the image creating process (p. 4).

CLOSING REMARKS

Our view of readers has changed from a tendency to consider the reader's participation in meaning making akin to a scribe recopying a text. At present, we recognize that the subjectivity of a reader's responses is not just the residue of understanding, but the very fuel of meaning making. Overly text-based accounts of interpretation have given way to multifaceted considerations of the subjectivity of meaning making and shared understandings held by communities of readers. New emphases in reading comprehension will have to take into consideration the two central issues we have considered in this chapter. Consider if you will what the following issues may mean for researchers and practitioners who understand the convergence of reader-response theory and reading comprehension:

1. The reader rather than the text is at the heart of understanding meaning making. A task for teachers is to change their orientation and the orientation of their students. They no longer have to feel compelled to transform the readers they work with into some elusive "ideal" reader. They can move away from holding their students accountable for matching an "ideal" reading or interpretation of texts.

2. Students should have opportunities to explore the variety of relationships that a reader can have with authors in making meaning from reading a variety of texts. Recent studies (e.g., Marshall, 1987; Rogers, 1988) suggest that teachers and students

are overly text bound in their views of interpretation and response. That is, students hold in abeyance their reactions or perspectives; teachers direct students to do so. What is needed are approaches to comprehension that prompt the students to fuel their meaning making with their ideas.

3. As we proposed in this chapter, engagement in the world of the text can shift from being a peripheral element of reading to a central element in the reading program. The affective side, a major part of readers' prior knowledge, will have to be fore-grounded in reading instruction and for an understanding of reading comprehension. The emotions, images, feelings, and idio-syncratic associations that arise when readers negotiate meaning in texts may be at the heart of what we want to develop in-structionally with students.

4. Within the literature in reading exists an increasing list of tech-niques that teachers can employ to assist students in constructive meaning making. These techniques may be modeled or demon-strated to students. However, the real concern comes with the change from teacher-controlled to self-controlled strategies so that students can monitor their own comprehension. The ultimate goal is that students will use reading for their own purposes from their perspectives as they grow in their own sense of themselves as learners.

One of the overriding issues in this new view of reading compre-hension and instruction is for readers to accept the notion that any text is not a fixed entity: that rather than being finished, the author worked until he or she had to stop (for whatever reason) or that a text can take on new significance as the reader's association with that text changes. Reading-comprehension experiences are tied together and require examination across time. Kenneth Burke (1969) suggests that reading might be viewed as unending conversation. To illustrate, Burke offers an extended analogy — a description of a cocktail party:

> Imagine that you enter a parlor. You came late. When you arrive, others have long preceded you, and they are engaged in a heated discussion — too heated for them to pause and to tell you exactly what it is about. In fact, the discussion had already begun long before any of them got there, so that no one present is qualified to trace for you all of the steps that have gone on before. You listen for a while, until you decide that you have caught the tenor of the argument; then you put in your oar. Someone answers; you answer him: another comes to your defense; another aligns against you, to either the embarrassment or gratification of your opponent, depending upon the quality of your ally's assistance. However, the discussion is

interminable, the hour grows late, you must depart. And you do depart, with the discussion still vigorously is progress (pp. 110−111).

NOTES

1. Lavery and Straw (1986) discuss the reflective nature of response. They suggest that reflection is a crucial activity in developing readers' ability to create theme in literary reading.

2. Bogdan (1986a, 1986b, 1987c), in her taxonomy of literary response, refers to this physical involvement in the constructive reality of the text as the "kinetic response." It is a kind of reflex to the action taking place in the world of the text.

3. Bogdan (1986a, 1986b, 1987c), again in the taxonomy, refers to this egocentric response as "stock response," *a response that reinforces the worldview* of the reader and is particularly associated with identification.

Three decades ago, Walker Gibson (1980/1950) suggested that there were two kinds of readers—actual readers and inner readers—involved in any literary experience. The actual reader is the externalized person reading the text; the inner reader is a kind of homunculus or "mock reader" (p. 4)—a fictitious reader through which the literary work is experienced. The notion of "mock readers" ties in with the view that our goal as educators is to develop in readers facility with adopting perspectives and reflecting upon the nature of those perspectives and their interface with interpretations. This is consistent with Gibson's view of the development of "literary sophistication." As he stated:

> ... Is there among my students a growing awareness that the literary experience is not just a relation between themselves and an author, or even between themselves and a fictitious speaker, but a relation between such a speaker and a projection, a fictitious modification of themselves? The realization on the part of a student that he is many people as he reads many books and responds to their language worlds is the beginning of literary sophistication in the best sense (p. 4).

CHAPTER 9

THE CREATIVE DEVELOPMENT OF MEANING
Using Autobiographical Experiences to Interpret Literature

Richard Beach

In John Updike's story "A & P" (1966), Sammy, a check-out clerk in a grocery store and narrator of the story, describes the routine nature of working in a grocery store, a routine interrupted by three bikini-clad females. When I ask my students to respond to this story in their journals, they often remark on the familiarity of Updike's descriptions of working in a store, noting that the story evoked memories of their own work experiences. In some cases, they may then describe a particular experience — coping with their own boss, reacting to bizarre events in the store, and the like.

These autobiographical responses are often viewed by teachers with suspicion, as frivolous, solipsistic digressions from the need to interpret the text. However, as I hope to demonstrate, evoked autobiographical experiences provide useful analogies between texts and experiences, what Van De Weghe (1987) defines as "analogic conceptualization."

Building on earlier work on autobiographical response (Bleich, 1978; Petrosky, 1982), this chapter examines the specific processes involved in using autobiographical experience to interpret texts. And, moving beyond traditional reading researchers' conceptions of knowledge, it explores how autobiographical response as a form of narrative helps readers construct knowledge and beliefs, and ultimately, to reconstruct their self-concept.

LITERARY-RESPONSE THEORY AND READING-COMPREHENSION RESEARCH

Composition researchers have recently turned to examining how writing about texts enhances knowledge and clarification of beliefs (Spivey, 1984; Stein, 1987; Tierney & McGinley, 1987). This research assumes that, rather than simply reproducing knowledge contained in the text, readers are discovering knowledge and clarifying beliefs through their writing. As students learn to elaborate on information about topics in texts, they clarify their knowledge about those topics (Stein, 1987). For example, Salvatori (1985) found that, over the period of a semester, as one student developed an increasing confidence in expressing her autobiographical responses, she developed a clearer sense of her own beliefs. And, in writing a series of essays about stories by J. D. Salinger, high school students were able to formulate and test out their ideas *through* their writing, resulting in posttest essays judged to be at a higher level of interpretation than was the case for students who wrote responses to short-answer questions or who did no writing (Marshall, 1987).

In Marshall's research, knowledge is conceived of as constantly evolving. A comparison of the conceptions of knowledge inherent in traditional reading-comprehension research, reader-response theory, and composition research suggests that comprehension research often rests on somewhat more static, limited conceptions of knowledge than the other two.

Much of reading-comprehension research builds on schema theory—the idea that readers draw on their cognitive scripts, frames, scenarios, or mental models to comprehend information in texts (Anderson & Pearson, 1984). Using analysis of recall protocols, researchers have demonstrated that readers, given different schemas, recall information from a text consistent with those schemas (Armbruster, Anderson, & Ostertag, 1987).

These reading researchers are, of course, concerned with basic comprehension of information. However, there are several limitations associated with focusing exclusively on comprehension of information, as opposed to larger ways of knowing about the world. Much of this research has conceived of the text as simply a repository of information and the mind as a computer-search mechanism. Schema theory, as Beers (1987) argues, conceives of the reader's mind as an information-processing "machine-model." In this model, the text as "input" is defined in relatively fixed, stable terms. For example, researchers presuppose a defined "gist" for a text. Moreover, in the "machine model," memory, as implied by the metaphors of "slots," "frames," "terminals," "default values," is conceived of in terms of "a container of discrete and stable traces of past experience" (p. 372).

Beers' critique of schema theory portrays schema in a somewhat restricted manner as applied, preexisting knowledge structures rather than as a process of creating and applying schema, a shift described by Whitney (1987). However, Beers rightfully argues that schema theorists often focus on knowledge as a static, articulated set of propositions or frames rather than as evolving from a transaction between a reader and a text.

In focusing on information or knowledge contained "in" the text, Dorfman (1985) points out that schema researchers have not fully examined how readers' beliefs shape their understanding of texts. In Dorfman's model, readers use their beliefs to attribute positive and negative qualities to characters and to story resolutions. For example, in reading "The Tortoise and the Hare," a reader may assign a positive value to the prodding, persistent tortoise and a negative value to the hare. By assigning a positive value to the tortoise winning the race and linking the positive resolution to the positive conception of the tortoise, a reader extracts an interpretation of the story—that "hard work pays off." Rather than assume that the beliefs are contained "in" the text, Dorfman argues that readers' ability to apply their own beliefs is essential to understanding stories. (See Bogdan's discussion of worldview, in this volume, Chapter 5.)

For example, as Janice Radway's (1984) analysis of women readers' responses to romance novels indicated, women's traditional beliefs in the value of the housewife's nurturing role are reinforced. As the women in Radway's study learned from their voracious reading of romances, in the romance novel, the impersonal, occasionally violent male confronts the more emotional, nurturing female, who transforms the male into a relatively more caring person, all, as Radway points out, within the context of a patriarchal belief system. These readers, therefore, used their knowledge of genre and social beliefs to interpret these novels. More importantly, their knowledge of the romance narrative served as a way of organizing and verifying their social, patriarchal worlds. Thus, in a more dynamic conception of knowledge, readers use their "intertextual" knowledge of narrative as a way of knowing.[1]

NARRATIVE AS A WAY OF KNOWING THE WORLD AND ONESELF

In *Actual Minds, Possible Worlds,* Jerome Bruner (1986) argues that there are two basic ways of knowing about the world. The "logico-scientific" or "paradigmatic" mode employed in logic, mathematics, and various sciences involving formal description, explanation, categorizations and generalization. Schema theory is an example of this paradigmatic mode. In contrast, the narrative mode of knowing focuses more on "the vicissitudes of human intention" (p. 16). In responding to a narrative, a reader becomes engaged in a character's unique construction of reality as built on desires and intentions, not for what *is* the case, but for what *may be* or *could be* the case. For example, to become engaged in Gatsby's "rags-to-riches" Horatio Alger vision of power and success is to envision his desires.

Bruner defines this as "subjunctivizing reality," as "trafficking in human possibilities rather than in settled certainties" inherent in a character's unique consciousness or construction of reality. He argues that this "subjunctivization" is conveyed through what Todorov defined as transformations in the language of the story. A character "must, might, could, or would" commit a crime; "plans, intends to, hopes to," commit a crime, etc. These transformations shift the focus from "factivity" — what is — to the "subjunctive" — what could be (p. 30).

In an analysis of readers' retelling of stories, Bruner found that, as they progressed into the retelling, the readers were more likely to adopt a more subjunctive mode, noting that a character "wants to do x" or "is going to do x" regarding certain plights. And, through the retelling, the readers begin to empathize with characters' plights as representing their own plights. While they initially assumed on omniscient, detached stance as evident in language such as "he said," where the "he" is the author, the readers shifted to the subjunctive mood as evident in language such as "she wants to x,' 'she remembers when x,' 'she thinks what else she wants to x' . . ." (p. 33). The reader is therefore empathizing with the characters' experiences through the very process of recreating the text.

Thus, drawing on Iser and Barthes, Bruner argues that narratives invite the readers' performance or creation of a virtual text, and, through that performance, ultimately the readers make the texts their own:

> The virtual text becomes a story of its own, its very strangeness only a contrast with the reader's sense of the ordinary. The fictional landscape, finally, must be given a "reality" of its own — the ontological step. It is then that the reader asks the crucial interpretative questions, "what's it all about?" But what "it" is, of course, is not the

actual text—however great its literary power—but the text that the reader has constructed under its sway. And that is why the actual text needs the subjectivity that makes it possible for a reader to create a world of his own. Like Barthes, I believe that the writer's greatest gift to a reader is to help him become a writer (p. 37).

In relating personal experience, the teller may discover a sense of his or her own emotional stance or voice. Paul John Eakin, in *Fictions in Autobiography* (1985), argues that autobiography involves not only recalling the past, but the very act of recreating the past is itself an attempt to discover and invent the self. The writer is "reaching back into the past not merely to recapture but to repeat the psychological rhythms of identity formation . . . an integral and often decisive phase of the drama of self-definition" (p. 226).

Eakin demonstrates that autobiographers often portray past experiences involving instances of articulating a new language or self-concept, what Nabakov defines as the "'inner knowledge that I was I'" (p. 217). Eakin cites Elizabeth Bruss's contention that defining a sense of self requires "the capacity to know and simultaneously be that which one knows. . . . Indeed to be a 'self' at all seems to demand that one display the ability to embrace, take in, one's own attributes and activities—which is just the sort of display that language makes possible" (p. 218). In narrating one's past experience, a teller is socially displaying a language that portrays self.

Developing this sense of self involves not only the articulation of experience but also the capacity to hear one's own emerging voice in that articulation. In their study on women's development, Belenky, Clinchy, Goldberger, and Tarule (1986) found that the majority of the women were moving from thinking dominated by male authority figures and absolutist thinking to relating their own experiences. By articulating about their experiences, such as their jobs, their marriages, their relationships, these women entered the stage of the "subjective voice," an awareness, for many women, of a new way of knowing. As one woman noted, "There's a part of me that I didn't even realize I had until recently—instinct, intuition, whatever. It helps me and protects me. It's perceptive and astute" (p. 69). As the investigators noted, "[a]long with the discovery of personal authority arises a sense of voice . . . to which a woman begins to attend rather than to the long-familiar external voices" (p. 68). By being increasingly aware of their own voices in their own stories, they began to clarify their own identities.

Tellers' attitudes toward themselves and the world are revealed in how they attribute actions or resolve their narratives. They may relate their acts or the resolution of problems in a manner that portrays them as "heroic," or as "a loser," or as "a victim," etc. In

Updike's story, what might have been Sammy's heroic "knight-in-shining-armor" version, Sammy as hero would have rescued the girls as "damsels in distress" and restored "justice" to the store, a version reflecting his own masculine desires. Similarly, in identifying with a main character, a reader may adopt the attitudes shaping the portrayal of acts and resolution of problems. As suggested by Radway (1984), romance readers' sense of self as "nurturing wife" is verified through triumph of the nurturing over the impersonal.

Thus, in experiencing narrative as a way of defining attitudes and organizing experience—as a way of knowing—readers are provided with the subjunctive vision of desired possibilities. At the same time, readers also experience the ultimate limitation of desires. Through telling his more realistic version of unfulfilled desire, Sammy perceives a limited side of himself and recognizes that life is hard. In his analysis of narrative, Peter Brooks (1984) argues that desire (e.g., status, power, love, success, identity) underlies basic plot development. For example, in early folktales such as "Jack the Giant Killer," "the specifically human faculty of ingenuity and trickery, the capacity to use the mind to devise schemes to overcome superior force, becomes a basic dynamic of plot" (p. 38). At the same time, Brooks argues, "the realization of the desire for narrative encounters the limits of narrative, that is, the fact that one can tell a life only in terms of its limits or margins" (p. 52). While the teller has the desire to "tell all," and to engage and seduce the audience, the teller will never be able to completely understand an event. However, as Brooks argues, "the performance of the narrative act is in itself transformatory ... life-giving in that it arouses and sustains desire" (pp. 60−61). (See Bogdan in this volume for a discussion of transformation through narrative, Chapter 7.)

A teller portrays characters' desires as resulting in some violation of norms or conventions. According to Labov's (1972) and Pratt's (1976) theories of narrative, by dramatizing the violation of norms through various storytelling or linguistic devices, a teller endows the story with "tellability"—the fact that it is worth telling, that it has a point; it is not pointless. Understanding the fact that a violation has occurred requires a shared understanding of the social conventions being violated. Wearing a bikini in an A & P store in a relatively staid small town in the 1960s could be perceived by some as a violation of conventions. Thus, in order to develop the point of a story, Updike describes in detail the social context—the A & P and the customers who frequent the store—as constituted by certain social conventions.

In developing their own autobiographical responses as narratives, cued by the text, readers develop a social context enveloping the narrative events. In writing about their own experiences working in a grocery store, the more they develop the social context, the more they may understand the conventions constituting their own autobiographical world. And, in developing their actions as violating those conventions, they may then clarify their understanding of the point of their own experience. Rather than basing their experience on a predetermined point, through elaborating on the details of their experience, they create that point.

Tellers, then, through the act of telling stories, and by reflecting on the implied purposes and roles, define their social beliefs. As Harold Rosen (1986) notes, "to tell a story is to take a stance towards events and, rather than reflect a world, to create a world." And, the teller is, according to Rosen, quoting from Bakhtin, engaged in "'no simple act of reproduction, but rather a further creative development of another's discourse in a new context and under new conditions'" (p. 235). In telling their story, tellers develop a new way of knowing just as the women at the "subjective voice" stage did (Belenky et al., 1986). These women go beyond reproducing the world to creating a world infused with a point — the idea that their experiences were not pointless, but symbolic of an emerging sense of self.

The text, therefore, serves to cue readers to conceive of their own autobiographical experience in terms of a point. Having experienced Sammy's recognition of the point of his experience, a reader may then infer the point of his or her own experience. Readers, however, may vary in their ability to infer the point. Being able to infer the point requires a particular cognitive stance or orientation toward experience (Hynds, 1985; Lavery & Straw, 1986; Vipond & Hunt, 1984). Hunt and Vipond (1985, 1986) define this orientation as the ability to conceive of discourse as "point-driven." Based on research on readers' responses (Hunt & Vipond, 1985, 1986; Vipond & Hunt, 1984), they find that readers adopt one of three orientations in reading: "information-driven," "story-driven," and "point-driven." In adopting an "information-driven" orientation, readers read simply for the information provided — for example, attempting to determine the name of Sammy's grocery store. In adopting a "story-driven" orientation, readers are reading a text primarily for the enjoyment of the story. And, in adopting a "point-driven" orientation, readers are conceiving of the text in terms of its point.

Readers may switch their orientations as they move through a text. While reading a story, readers read primarily for information or enjoyment, and, only after they've completed the text and can detach themselves from their emotional involvement with the text, do they reflect on the point of the story. Straw's research (1986) on small-group discussions found that through sharing responses, high school students learn to define the point of stories collectively.

It may also be the case, that, in telling a story or in their evoked autobiographical narratives, tellers and readers do not necessarily begin with a point, but, through the telling itself — as they convey information and become emotionally engaged with a text — they discover the point of their story. All this suggests that, consistent with much current composition research, "coming to the point" evolves over time *through* articulation and reflection. However, when faced with difficulties in understanding texts, some readers give up prematurely (Newkirk, 1984). Rather than reaching a premature closure, by continuing to reflect on the text, a reader discovers the point.

In one of their studies on college students' responses to "A & P," Hunt and Vipond (1985) found that the majority of the students adopted either an "information-driven" or a "story-driven" orientation. As a result, many of the students had difficulty understanding the story, viewing it as "pointless." A number of the students were perplexed by Updike's use of descriptive details in portraying the social context. Because they were not able to conceive of Sammy's actions as violating the conventions of the social context, they had difficulty inferring the point of the story.

This review of theory and research suggests the following.

1. In responding to literature, readers adopt the social and cultural perspectives portrayed in the text in order to define or reconceive their own attitudes, beliefs, or social roles.

2. Readers also infer the point of literary texts by determining the unusual, extraordinary nature of characters' actions or story events by noting how they violate social or cultural conventions.

3. The more readers elaborate about the details of actions or events, the more likely they will be able to define these violations.

4. Similarly, the more readers elaborate on their own autobiographical experiences evoked by a text, the more likely they will be able to define the point of their experience.

RESULTS OF A STUDY: COLLEGE STUDENTS' USES OF AUTOBIOGRAPHICAL RESPONSES TO INTERPRET

These theories of narrative and constructive reflection suggest that readers' own autobiographical responses might be useful for interpreting stories. In his study of written autobiographical responses, Petrosky (1982) found wide variation in college students' ability to use their autobiographical writing to interpret a text. Students in his study who were more likely to elaborate on their experience were, in turn, more likely to use their related experience to interpret. As I have argued, by elaborating on their experience, the students may be more likely to develop the social context or conventions to be violated, which, in turn, are related to the point of the experience. And, having inferred the point of their own experience, they may then use *that* point to understand the text.

This suggests that the degree of elaboration of one's experience may be related to the level of interpretation of the story. In order to determine if the degree of elaboration of the experience is related to the level of interpretation of that experience, which, in turn, is related to the level of interpretation of the text, I am currently analyzing high school and college students' journal responses to a number of assigned poems and short stories. In some cases, after reading the texts, the students were simply asked to respond to the texts without any directions as to how to respond. In other cases, the students were prompted to respond to the text, to cite related autobiographical experience, and to relate that experience to the text. Although the prompted assignments generated much more sustained autobiography than the unprompted assignments, in the unprompted assignments, students did cite related autobiographical experiences.

As one part of this study, in order to examine further how experienced readers — preservice and inservice English teachers — used their experiences to interpret, I analyzed the journal entries of forty-nine students in two literature methods courses at the University of Minnesota in response to one poem and four stories. I was interested in determining the following:

1. The relative frequency of students' use of various response strategies and the relationships between the use of these strategies: "Interpreting," "Connecting (autobiographical experience)," "Engaging," "Describing," and "Judging."

2. The relationships between:
   a. level of story interpretation, as determined by a four-point rating (1 = low, 4 = high) for degree of "point-drivenness" for students' interpretation of the story;
   b. level of autobiographical experience interpretation, as determined by a four-point rating (1 = low, 4 = high) for degree of "point-drivenness" for students' interpretation of their own experience;
   c. degree of elaboration of the experience, as determined by the number of continuous t-units within a journal entry devoted to describing the autobiographical experience.

3. The types of links students use in connecting the texts and their experiences.

Analysis

Each entry was analyzed by two judges according to the following:

1. *Response strategies*: percentage of t-units in each of the following categories: "Interpreting," "Connecting (autobiographical experience)," "Engaging," "Describing," and "Judging."

2. *Level of interpretation*: scale of 1 to 4, 1 = low, 4 = high, in terms of degree of "point-drivenness."

3. *Degree of experience elaboration*: number of t-units employed.

4. *Link types*: similarity in terms of "Feeling," "Setting," "Social convention," "Character," "Goal," "Story," "Theme," "Author," and "Genre."

The interjudge agreements were relatively high—within a range from 0.80 to 0.85 (Pearson-product moment correlations).

Results

Use of response strategies. Analysis of the use of response strategies indicated that across all texts, 39% of the t-units were devoted to interpreting, 23% to connecting, 15% to engaging, 18% to describing, and 5% to judging. These percentages were relatively consistent across the five texts, with students consistently devoting approximately one-fourth of their entries to "connecting" (autobiographical) responses.

Relationships between use of strategies. Correlations between the frequency of interpreting and the frequency of other strategies indicated that frequency of "connecting" was related only to the frequency of "interpreting," $r = 0.33$ ($p < 0.01$). The frequency of "engaging" was related to the frequency of "describing," $r = 0.29$ ($p < 0.05$), and the frequency of "connecting," $r = 0.49$ ($p < 0.001$). Thus, the degree of engagement with a text was related to the degree to which subjects described the text and cited related experiences. And, the degree to which they cited related experiences was related to the degree of interpretation.

Level of interpretation. As previously noted, the text response and the autobiographical experience were both rated on a four-point scale for the level of interpretation or "point-drivenness." And the degree of elaboration for the cited experiences was determined by simply counting the number of t-units devoted to a "stretch" of cited experiences.

Across all stories, for the first "stretch" of cited experience, with

Table 9–1
Percentages of Types of Links between Texts and Experiences Employed for Each of Two Related Experiences for Five Literary Texts

Link Types	"Mushrooms"		"A&P"		"My Side of the Matter"		"This is My Living Room"		"Private Greaves"	
	1st	*2nd*	*1st*	*2nd*	*1st*	*2nd*	*1st*	*2nd*	*1st*	*2nd (none)*
Feelings	26%	25%	16%	19%	13%	0	14%	0	28%	
Setting	21%	12%	13%	14%	29%	43%	23%	11%	21%	
Convention	26%	0	16%	0	29%	0	45%	16%	21%	
Character	26%	12%	37%	29%	16%	31%	14%	51%	21%	
Goal	0	0	6%	0	4%	0	0	0	0	
Story	0	12%	10%	19%	0	13%	5%	11%	8%	
Theme	0	12%	0	19%	0	13%	0	11%	0	
Author	0	0	0	0	4%	0	0	0	0	
Genre	0	25%	0	4%	4%	0	0	0	0	

mean t-unit length of 4.4, the level of interpretation was related to the level of experience interpretation, $r = 0.27$, and the degree of experience elaboration, $r = 0.32$. The level of experience interpretation was also moderately related to the degree of experience elaboration, $r = 0.30$. For the second "stretch" of cited experience, with a mean t-unit length of 2.5, the only significant relationship was between level of experience interpretation and degree of experience elaboration, $r = 0.71$. While there was some variation in these correlations across different texts, these results suggest that the extent to which students elaborated on their experience was related to the level of "point-drivenness" of the experience.

Use of link types. The percentages of various link types employed are presented in Table 9–1.

While there was some variation in the types of links employed, the most commonly used links for the initial "stretch" of cited experiences consisted of feelings, settings, conventions, and characters/persons. For the second cited experience, students were more likely to employ links involving story, theme, author, and genre. This suggests that readers in their initial responses are most likely to be reminded of related experiences in terms of relatively immediate links — feelings, setting, conventions, or characters. In subsequent responses, readers are more likely to employ links involving similarities in story lines, themes, other authors, or genres.

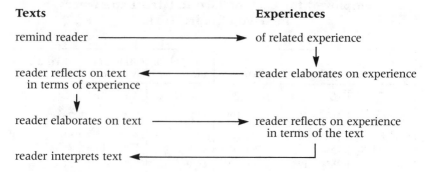

Figure 9-1
Processes Involved in Relating Texts and Experiences

Texts	Experiences
remind reader ⟶	of related experience ↓
reader reflects on text ⟵ in terms of experience ↓	reader elaborates on experience
reader elaborates on text ⟶	reader reflects on experience in terms of the text
reader interprets text ⟵	

THE PROCESSES OF RELATING TEXTS AND EXPERIENCES

In addition to this empirical analysis, I also read over the journal entries, attempting to discern the various processes involved in relating texts and experiences, processes illustrated in Figure 9-1.

As Figure 9-1 illustrates, readers move recursively back and forth between the text and their experience, using one to reflect on the other. For example, in reading "A & P," a female reader may recall her own experience of working as a check-out clerk. She then elaborates on her recollection, recalling the fact that she hated her job because she disliked her authoritarian boss and his many rules and regulations. She then elaborates on her memory, noting that the rules and regulations were demeaning, implying that she may have been prone to cheating her customers. She then applies her recollections to the story, noting that Sammy's boss, Lengel, was also authoritarian and that Sammy was, like herself, critical of demeaning rules. She also notes that Sammy, like herself, believed that he was capable of being more that just a check-out clerk, that he had the capability of doing heroic deeds. She then further reflects on the text in terms of this new reflection, recalling that she too wanted to "break out" of her role, yet, at the same time, realized that she was constrained by that role. She then infers a possible point of the story, that roles and conventions are constraining to the romantic, unconventional side of our personality.

These processes need not occur in this linear, chronological order. However, thinking about these processes in terms of this particular order helped me determine the point at which students failed to extend their thinking. For example, students often described their own experience, but, because they didn't elaborate on that experience, they never used their experience to illuminate the text. They might recall working in a grocery store, but because they would only recall a "bare-bones" version, they never extracted any of their own attitudes and beliefs about that experience. So, the potential for using their experience was never realized.

With these processes in mind, let me now examine some of the phenomena affecting readers' successful and less successful use of these processes.

CONCEIVING OF PAST EXPERIENCES IN TERMS OF VIOLATING NORMS

Texts may revolve around violations of norms and expectations. Bikini-clad girls don't walk into grocery stories all the time. In recalling past experiences, a reader may be reminded of instances involving previous, similar violations of norms and expectations (Shank, 1982).

Roger Shank's model of memory is based on the idea that we recall previous instances of failure to achieve certain goals. Given certain goals, for example, to defrost some frozen chicken using a microwave oven, we recall previous instances of programming the microwave to the defrost level. However, if our programming instructions fail, and the chicken doesn't defrost, then we revise our knowledge of act/goal relationships, and establish a new programming procedure. Then, the next time we try to defrost chicken, we may recall the new procedure. Thus, Shank argues, reminding is based on recollection of violations and failure to achieve goals.

In responding to a character's violation of norms or conventions, readers may also recall instances involving their own violations of expectations or conventions. For example, in responding to "A & P," many of the students recalled previous instances of deviant behavior on their job—in which they or their managers violated certain conventions.

The fact that the recalled experience concerns a violation of norms—an unusual or extraordinary event—is related to understanding the point of the experience. As I have argued, the motive behind a violation is often a character's desire, for example, Sammy's need to assert himself against those norms, the point being that the norms either are or are not viable. Readers, in empathizing with these desires, may then apply the point of the character's experience to an understanding of their own experience. Thus, the text triggers what is potentially a point-driven perspective or orientation for conceiving of the reader's own experience.

For example, the experience of reading about Lengel, the manager in "A & P," reminded one student of her own heavy-handed manager:

> There have been times I could have murdered my bosses for a stupid move or decision they have made. For example, I have worked under a manager who would play favorites with his female employees. I was miserable when he played favorites between us. I thought of quitting but instead I talked to him about the way we felt about his favoritism game. Although from that day I was never his "favorite" again, he never expected me to brown nose because he knew how I felt and why I felt that way.
>
> I'm glad I was honest. I maintained both a job and the respect I deserved by thinking before acting.
>
> Sammy's heroic gesture seems silly because of what he risks — loss of his college money. This isn't worth making a point to his boss and impressing some girls in a swimming suit. If Sammy had such a problem with his manager, he could have talked to his manager or even talked to the girls about his feelings, but to quit was irrational and immature.
>
> I realize what he stands for as a character. Sammy is something that I am not — the heroic, romantic worker. He puts himself into his job and stands for what he believes.

This student shares Sammy's desire — to rebel against a boss. However, in thinking about her own attempts to negotiate with her boss, she infers what she believes is the point of the story — that one's job is more important than one's beliefs. She also is able to distinguish between her own and Sammy's perspective, which reflects a degree of cognitive complexity useful for interpreting literature (Hynds, 1985, 1988).

Another student had a similar perception of her boss in responding to another story, "The Fourth of July" (Brancato, 1985). In that story, a teenager, Chuck, wants to seek revenge against his former friend, Jack, who stole Chuck's money, but was not found guilty in court. Chuck is still angry that Jack was never punished. When Jack shows up at the gas station where Chuck is working on the Fourth of July, Chuck contemplates tossing a firecracker into his gas tank, but decides against doing that. Instead, he pretends to fill up Chuck's tank so that, when Chuck left, he would run out of gas.

Another student uses her perceptions of Chuck's desire for revenge to evoke her own sadistic fantasy involving her revenge against her boss:

> I used to work for this man who was verbally abusive; he had no control of his temper. I would get so furious so I developed this little fantasy where I would be taking a letter from him, and he would

have a heart attack and I would just watch him die slowly. I would just sort of walk around him and consider whether I should call the ambulance or not. Then when I was pretty sure that there was no chance for him to live, I would call the ambulance. Somehow having the fantasy really helped.

This student then admits that "I know I wouldn't really let that happen," a realization of the limitations of her own fantasy versions, her own desires. By realizing the limitations of their own desires, readers may then infer the point of the story—that one's desires have limits. It is through the telling itself, as Brooks (1984) argued, that both expresses one's desires and, in having to end the narrative, simultaneously realizes the limitations of desires. The student then applies this realization to explain Chuck's own reluctance to carry out his revenge by blowing up Sager's car:

> I don't know that Chuck will ever not feel mad at all about Sager, but he'll always have that feeling of having been crossed and then I don't really think there is a way of getting back. On the other hand, if you do something that's going to cost you a lot, then you're stepping over the line into their territory and you're doing something just as low. Afterwards you're going to hate yourself by having acted like that and so revenge in moderation is OK.

In writing about their feelings about their managers, both these students begin to entertain optional perspectives, envisioning the "other side" of their desires. The first student, albeit to save her own skin, recognizes the need to take her boss's perspective. The second student draws back from her own initial perspective to recognize the limitation of that perspective. Thus, through their autobiographical responses, these students achieve a detachment, which, as Bogdan (1986a, 1987c) argues, helps them interpret the story. This detachment helps students infer that revenge can be self-destructive. These readers define violations of norms, particularly as fueled by their desires, through the process of elaborating on past experiences. They can then use their own experiences of violations to define the point or theme of the texts.

Students varied in the level of their thematic interpretation. This variation depended on the level of goals recalled—low- versus high-level. Shank (1982) argues that our memory is organized according to a hierarchy of these goals, with lower-level, immediate goals subsumed under higher-level, social or thematic goals. For example, in recalling their own experiences of working in a grocery store, readers might associate experience with an immediate, short-range goal of "pleasing customers," as opposed to a larger thematic goal of "serving the capitalist system." Thus, story events associated with high-level story goals may remind students of events associated with high-level goals in their own experience.

My own research indicates that college students are more likely to infer long-range goals than are secondary students (Beach, 1985; Beach & Wendler, 1987). Rather than conceive of characters acting only according to immediate, short-term goals, college students are able to conceive of characters' actions and plans in terms of long-range goals such as discovering the motives for a murder.

However, in experiencing a character's own attempts to fulfill their long-range goals, readers may conceive of their own experiences in terms of similar long-range goals. In this way, applying the character's long-range goals to their own experience helps them evoke or reconceive of their own experiences in terms of those goals.

One of Sammy's goals in "A & P" is to demonstrate to the girls that he is "a hero" who will stick by them against the heavy-handed manager. Students in my study used this goal to review their previous experience and to organize their own narratives. For example, in response to "A & P," one high school student wrote:

> I was standing in Monticello one night and these girls were by me. One of them threw a McDonald's bag full of garbage on the ground. About two minutes later, a cop pulled up and said one of us better say who had done it. Me, being the "He-Man" that I am, took it upon myself to say that I had done it. After throwing it away and receiving my lecture, the cop left, but so had the two girls. Once again I was left alone.

This student organizes his narrative around the goal associated with "being the 'He-Man.'" The student conveys this point by using cues that signal the unusual, extraordinary nature of the event—the use of "was standing," "about two minutes later," and "once again," cues that point to the fact that his goal of impressing the girls had failed.

Stories often revolve around conflict based on competing or countergoals. Thus, readers may conceive of their own experiences in terms of conflicting goals. In the following example, a high school student uses Sammy's goal of asserting himself and the manager's countergoal of maintaining order to recall his own experience of working for his father:

> While I was reading this it reminded me of how my dad acts sometimes when he sees some of his employees do something he doesn't like.
> I'll be working right along with these people and we do something he doesn't like, maybe fool around or make a joke about someone. He's worried that someone might see us do this and he might get a bad reputation.

When the day is over, he will come and talk to us all at once — he never says anything when people are around. He will start lecturing, telling why we shouldn't be doing whatever we were doing. Most of the time we all laugh at him. When we laugh, he tells us if it happened again there will be consequences to face.

The thing is that even if we knew we were wrong no one would admit it because you want to be like your fellow workers. If you would say something to them, they would all talk about him and not want to work with you.

I think that this was what happened to the boy. The girls were his age so he stuck up for them. He probably felt down inside that they were wrong.

While the manager in "A & P" may have initially reminded him of his father's own authoritarian manner, as he writes about the experience, he shifts his focus to his co-workers' motives for not tattling on each other — the need to stick together. Thus, through writing about his own experience, he developed the idea of sticking together, which he then uses to explain Sammy's actions.

For these two high school students, conceiving of their own experience in terms of the story's higher level, thematic goals encouraged them to reinterpret their own past experience in a new light.

EMPATHIZING WITH A CHARACTER'S PERSPECTIVE

As the empirical analysis indicated, one of the common links between the text and the experience was "feelings," often in the form of a reader's empathy with a character's perspective. In empathizing with a character's perspective, some students simply described a similar emotional experience without reflecting on the nature or meaning of their own or the character's perspective, as in this student's response to the descriptions of Sammy:

I felt I was behind the counter — I could "see" exactly how the store looked, the sun coming in, the floor — everything. I thought the way he noted the girls' tan lines and swimsuits — even their bodies — was very effective, because it was what he thought.

While this student describes Sammy's perspective, she doesn't interpret the meaning of that perspective. In contrast, another student is able to stand back from her empathy with Sammy's perspective to distinguish between her own and his perspective:

Everything in the story seems familiar; I've been in both Queenie's and Sammy's situation. Being insulted for something just as nominal

(or so I thought) as wearing a bathing suit in an A & P store. I also
have also looked through Sammy's eyes—classifying people as he
did, solely on appearance.

It's funny how the mind magnifies things. Sammy really is the
center of his universe. To us—a kid quitting his job for a sale to a
pretty stranger seems little more than foolish. To him, it decides his
destiny.

When you get into trouble, things seem to take on giant proportions; your mind becomes hypersensitive; your stomach aches.
Maybe that's what Sammy felt in his impending sense of dread.

By distancing herself from Sammy's perspective, this student is
clarifying her own perspective, an important developmental step
toward defining "self." Part of that process involves recognizing that
one is projecting one's own perspective onto the text, resulting in
clarifying the nature of that perspective. As Alcorn and Bracher (1985)
argue, from a psychoanalytic perspective, the "re-information" of self
involves the "denial of fulfillment of the infantile wish." In recognizing
the limitation of one's perspective as conflicting with the character's
perspective, the experience with the text functions to "resist and
undo the reader's projectives and the corresponding introjections
from which they derive" (p. 347).

By empathizing with the text, the student recaptured the experience of being emotionally overwrought. Having recaptured and defined
that experience through her response, she then can distinguish her
own perspective from Sammy's perspective.

Other readers, particularly female readers, not only distanced
themselves, but were also disturbed by and resisted Sammy's sexist
perspective: "The descriptions made me defensive (the crescents, the
bees buzzing around in the women's heads)." "The word sexism
came to mind and evoked experiences that I had in my own life—like
being gawked at by some guy or being called a dumb blonde."

These readers refused to accept and be appropriated by what
Karen Kaivola (1987) perceives to be the traditional cultural distinction
between masculinity as the projection of desire, and femininity as the
object of masculine desire. Accepting this false cultural opposition,
Kaivola argues, places women in the position of having "to model
ourselves as the object of masculine desire to be the blank screen"
(p. 30) onto which the male projects his desires (Bogdan, 1988,
1989b).[2]

In most cases, citing their own autobiographical experiences helped
these readers distinguish between their own and the character's perspective, and, in some cases, recognizing the limitations of the
character's perspective prepared them to interpret the text.

EMPLOYING NARRATIVE, STORYTELLING STRATEGIES

Another phenomenon influencing students' use of storytelling strategies is their ability to use the devices of setting the scene, building up suspense and conflict, and moving toward a resolution in elaborating on their own experience. And knowing the principles of narrative organization means that students can pattern their telling of their own experiences, using the organizational blueprint of the literary text. Similarly, in a conversation, one story triggers a string of related stories (e.g., about travel, birth, drinking), all told in a similar style or format, each text shaping subsequent texts.

For example, in responding to a story about a boy's attending his mother's funeral with his father and developing a new-found relationship with his father—"In the Heat" (Cormier, 1985)—a student used the story to organize his own recollection of his father.

> I come from a large family, and I never spent a lot of individual time with my Dad.
>
> I remember one time with my father quite vividly. It was a hot July day, and I was with my Dad at the camera store buying my first batch of photo chemicals. I was only eleven years old, but my interest and involvement in photography was already quite strong. I was a little worried when the salesman rang up the order. $7.56! At eleven, that price seemed like an enormous sum.
>
> We left the camera store in silence and walked through the hot streets to the car. I broke the silence by telling, not promising my Dad that I'd pay him back. He stopped and looked at me.
>
> "Don't worry about it," he said. "Your brothers are all into sports and I pay for that. If you want to get into photography, I'm more than happy to help you out."
>
> I was ecstatic. My Dad had affirmed for me that I was OK—that I wasn't a jock. He was supporting me and we understood each other at that moment.

This student used the narrative structure of "In the Heat" involving the movement toward an improved father-son relationship to organize his own narrative. As the student noted, "we both knew where our fathers were coming from. At times there is a father-son bond that seems very strong." Moreover, the point of that enhanced relationship was developed by the initial, context-setting sentence, "I come from a large family, and I never spent a lot of individual time with my Dad," a situation that mimics the situation in the story.

Students also used certain key ideas portrayed in the stories as springboards for their own narratives. As illustrated in the following reponse to Chuck's quandary as to how to take revenge in the story, "Fourth of July," a student uses the idea of desire for "revenge" and the conflict between Chuck and Sager to shape his own narrative.

> It's a hot summer day in 1976. I am pitching a Babe Ruth baseball game against Plainville, arch rival of *any* athletic team from Cary. The score is close, and from the start, there is an intimidating game of "burn-back" the hitters escalating between myself and the opposing pitcher. He is seventeen; I am sixteen. We were both throwing as hard as we probably ever will. By the fourth inning, contact is finally made, and my second baseman takes a fastball on the hip. I have known him since I was five years old, my team was two runs ahead, and there is no doubt in anyone's mind what my obligations were . . . revenge . . . an eye for an eye, a hip for a hip.
>
> When I take the mound, I am uneasy. . . . I really do *not* want to hurt a batter. But I have little choice. Everyone, from my fielders to my coach to the moms and dads in the aluminum lawn chairs, are waiting for poetic justice, for our collective revenge.
>
> I plant my first pitch on the ribs of their pitcher and he walks stiffly down to first base. It all seems fair, until I try to pick him off first base, and then I accidentally hit him *again*. This time, to the disgust of my infield, I have to say, "I'm sorry, I did not mean it that time." Two years later, that pitcher and I were the best of friends.

In telling his story, this student develops the inner conflict, the drama of the event, by moving back and forth between the action and his thoughts about the action. He employs certain cues designed to enhance tellability — "we were both throwing" (use of tense), "I really do *not* want to hurt a batter" (the negative), and "then I accidentally hit him *again*" (repetition) — the extraordinary nature of having to seek revenge and accidentally muffing it. And, he creates a social world — two small towns, Plainville and Cary; the "moms and dads in the aluminum lawn chairs . . . waiting for poetic justice . . . ," forces that condone revenge. And, through the telling, he builds up his desire for revenge to the point that "it all seems fair," only to discover, as did Chuck, that he cannot totally follow through on his revenge. He then reflects on the meaning of his narrative:

> As for revenge, it can be most satisfying if you singly *know* you can enact it. My experience was different because I sought revenge, yet I did not feel good about it at all. My firecracker was the baseball; I lit it. A "burn-back" should have been as effective.

This student used the idea of "revenge" to elaborate and reflect on the meaning of his experiences. Then, through telling his baseball story, he clarifies his own attitude toward revenge. Because he deliberately sought revenge, he "did not feel good about it at all," a point he discovered through his ability to tell his story.

Thus, students' ability to employ narrative strategies affects the extent to which they can use their experience to illuminate texts.

ADOPTING A "REFLECTIVE ORIENTATION"

Another factor influencing students' use of experience is their ability to adopt a "reflective orientation," the ability to reflect on the value or significance of their experience, adopting what Britton (1984) defined as the "spectator stance." Those students who did reflect on their own experience often experienced a tension between their own "familiar" perspective or "self" and alternative perspectives encouraged by their experience with the text.

This dual perspective is effectively illustrated by a scene in The Great Gatsby in which Nick Carroway leaves a party with Gatsby and his friends and goes out into the street to look up at the lighted room where the party continues. He then experiences the sense of past involvement in the party—mesmerized by Gatsby's aura—and his awareness of his own disenchanted, moral self that sees through the shallow ethics pervading Gatsby's world.

Nick, in reflecting on the party, perceives his other "self"—one defined by allegiance to Gatsby's values as distinct from his newly emerging "moral self." Similarly, Sammy, as the narrator in Updike's short story, stands backs from his "knight-in-shining-armor" perspective to entertain a darker, cynical version of his heroic events. As Steven Mailloux (1982) demonstrates, a reader may be swept up by a character's idealized versions, driven by desires of fame and fortune, only later, with the character, to realize the limitations of those desires. By applying this dual perspective to their own experience, readers then experience a basic theme of autobiography—the tension between past and present, old and new perspectives.

Rather than adopting this more "reflective orientation," many of the students in this study adopted what could be described as a "descriptive orientation"—expressing their responses primarily in terms of factual details, an orientation that reflects Hunt and Vipond's (1986, 1987) "information-driven" orientation. As a result, some of the students assumed that evoking related experiences was irrelevant to a "correct reading" of the meaning as found entirely "in" the text, rendering any "outside" related experiences irrelevant.

This "descriptive orientation" is evident in the following student's description of his own reading process:

> I try to get everything right in my head—where everything is in relationship to who's who and what they are doing as if I'm directing this movie. When I have problems reading, I usually miss some-

thing—like where did he come from and I have to go back and put him into my picture of where it was supposed to be. I don't very often bring in anything from the outside world. It's more of a distraction if I'm thinking—oh, that guy reminds me of somebody else—then it gets confused for a bit so I try and keep everything locked in on what the story is trying to show me. I try to take as much as I can from what's there. You know he's wearing the red t-shirt and the blue hat and I try and picture him with a red t-shirt and blue hat.

This student is adopting what Hunt and Vipond (1986, 1987) define as an "information-driven" orientation. He is primarily interested in simply extracting information. It may certainly be the case that, as readers move through a text, they may be primarily interested in determining the basic story line. But, after completing the story, and in writing a journal response, if this continues to be the primary orientation, they may foreclose any subsequent possibility for switching to a more point-driven" or "reflective" orientation (Lavery & Straw, 1986).

In adopting this "descriptive orientation," this student assumes that autobiographical responses are irrelevant to the text unless his own initial experience matches identically the experience in the text. (Similarly, when asked to infer "intertextual" connections to other texts similar to the texts they were reading, students were reluctant to recall related texts unless they were identical in structure [Rogers, 1988]). This assumption presupposes that, rather than discovering a possible link through exploring an evoked experience, readers already know that the text and real-world experience are carbon copies of each other.

Some students also assumed that they needed to recall a past experience in as objective a manner as possible—"as it really happened." When they couldn't achieve what they believed was an accurate recall of their past experience, they failed to elaborate on that experience. This assumption represents a failure to suspend their disbelief, resulting in a tendency to directly map their own experience onto the world of the text.

In the following response to "A & P," a high school student judges the various characters as failing to live up to her assumptions about appropriate behavior in stores.

> In the first place, I don't think the girls had the right to walk into the grocery store with just bathing suits on. They should have had enough sense to put more clothes on over the suit.
> Next, I think the manager could have treated the situation with a little more tact. He was kind of rude with the girls, which I thought was unnecessary.
> Lastly, I think that Sammy was just trying to get them interested in

him. So, he really wasn't doing anything for them. He was just thinking about himself.

So, the girls were wrong, the manager was wrong, and Sammy was wrong.

In failing to suspend her disbelief and to recognize the world of "A & P" as representing one version, this student blocked the potential for reflecting on and entertaining different versions of her own experience, reflecting a low degree of "cognitive complexity" (Hynds, 1985). Thus, students' willingness to adopt a "reflective orientation" sought to define the significance of their own experience and the text.

In conclusion, this study found that students' degree of elaboration of their experience was significantly related to their level of interpretation of stories. From these results, I extracted a recursive model of the processes involved in using the text to reflect on experience and the experience to reflect on the text. Analyses of individual students' responses indicated that students who were successful in using their experience to reflect on the text were able to recall previous experience in terms of violations of norms, empathize with the characters' perspectives, employ narrative strategies, and adopt a "reflective-orientation."

USING AUTOBIOGRAPHICAL RESPONSE TO ENHANCE INTERPRETATION: IMPLICATIONS FOR TEACHING

The results of this study have a number of implications for teaching. A major implication of this study is that autobiographical response, while not necessarily a cause of enhanced interpretation, is related to enhanced interpretation. By prompting students to explore their own related experiences, teachers can help students gain insights into their reading.

However, as the study suggests, the extent to which autobiographical responses are useful depends on students' willingness to reflect on the text and on their own experiences. In some cases, students may need no specific prompts for reflecting, while other students may need a more systematic series of prompts.

Teachers could ask students some of the following questions for use in either evoking or assessing their experience for each of the five phases:

1. *Evoking related experience*:
   What are some of the characters' feelings? Have you had any similar feelings? Do those feelings remind you of any experiences?

What are the characters' underlying desires? Do you recall any experiences in which you had similar desires?
What are some of the characters' goals? Have you had any similar goals? Do those goals remind you of any of your own experiences?

2. *Narrating about one's experience*:
   Have you included information about the setting and your feelings, attitudes and beliefs?
   Have you told the "whole story" about your experience?

3. *Using the experience to reflect on the text*:
   What did you learn about life from your experience? What does the point of your own experience suggest about the point of the text?
   How were you conceiving of the experience? What attitudes or beliefs influence your conception? Compare your own perspective with a character's perspective.

4. *Using the text to reflect on one's experience*:
   What does a point of the text suggest may be a point of your experience?
   In what ways did the organization of the text help you shape the portrayal of your own experience?

5. *Interpreting the text*:
   Is there any difference between the character's and/or your own past and present perspectives? What does this difference suggest about what the character and/or what you learned about life?
   From responding to the text, in what ways did your own attitudes and beliefs change?

Teachers could employ a number of other activities. By being encouraged to share their autobiographical experiences, students may acquire the ability to employ narrative strategies. In some cases, teachers may need to ensure anonymity to students who may be reluctant to share their own personal experiences with a teacher. If, however, students are willing to share their autobiographical responses to a text in small groups, each shared narrative could trigger subsequent narratives (Rogers, 1988; Straw, 1989). Some of these narratives, if well developed, could serve as models for others' narratives. And, in comparing the narratives, students could discuss differences between the perspectives, attitudes, and structures of the different narratives and thereby relate their own experiences to the text.

Students could also write longer "phase-autobiographical" essays in which they portray a particular event in their own life. Teachers could then use these essays to discuss or model differences in the degree of elaboration through use of descriptive detail, recognizing, however, the developmental differences between students' ability to develop their narratives (Beach, 1987).

Having cited their own autobiographical experiences, students could also define the relationship between their portrayed self and the characters or world of the text, noting, for example, the extent to which they were, say, "close to," "apart from," "distant from," "part of" the character or world. Students could also draw maps or diagrams visualizing these elements in texts and/or their own experiences, with, for example, circles as characters and lines between circles to represent relationships. They could then define their own alignments with these elements by including "self" as a circle, and, as they move through the text, move the "self" circle to portray shifts in their alignment with the characters, worlds, or resolutions, explaining the meaning of shifts in spatial relationships.

In addition to defining links between their experience and texts, students could also define links between the text and other texts. Unfortunately, teachers often treat each text as a novel experience, rather than linking responses back to previous experiences and other texts. By continually linking back, teachers may encourage students to build on and develop their "intertextual" know-how, know-how that is central to developing the ability to interpret.

All of this rests on the notion that understanding texts is not a static process of simply comprehending predetermined meanings. It is a dynamic process of discovering meanings through relating literature and life.

NOTES

1. Radway's results were based on questionnaire data from forty-two women and interviews with sixteen women who were avid readers of romance novels. The questionnaire and interview data were analyzed according to those attitudes and themes evoked by the novels and according to most- versus least-liked characteristics of the novels.

2. Deanne Bogdan (1988, 1989b) makes a similar case in describing the reaction of feminist graduate students to Updike's "A & P." Despite their literary critical sophistication, they were enraged at having to undergo in literature an experience too familiar to them in life.

CHAPTER 10

READING AS A SOCIAL EVENT
Comprehension and Response in the Text, Classroom, and World
Susan Hynds

In recent years, and repeatedly in the twentieth century, there has been a public outcry over illiteracy in America and the need to "return to the basics" to insure that students acquire literacy skills. Policymakers, researchers, and school personnel at all levels have responded by scurrying about to define and impose the basics, mandate more testing, and insist on more hours of teaching. In research, we have sought to isolate skills to better quantify their measures, and we have given attention to the contexts in which those skills are learned only as a variable and not as the frame for learning which it is. We have given only nodding acknowledgment to the touchy question of "what is the context for learning *literate behaviors*, as distinct from learning *literacy skills*.

Shirley Brice Heath
Being Literate in America

The research reported in this chapter was supported in part by a grant from the Syracuse University Senate Research Committee. The author is also grateful for the helpful advice of Richard Beach, Deanne Bogdan, Peter Mosenthal, and Stan Straw in the drafting of this work.

In distinguishing "literate behaviors" from "literacy skills," Shirley Brice Heath (1985) argues that political and educational reforms have been premised on the notion that giving readers competencies will somehow guarantee a literate populace. Views of reading competence are as disparate and diverse as the pedagogical and research perspectives that underlie them. Is "reading competence," for example, defined by scores on standardized tests, understanding of great literary works, enrichment of one's personal life, of functioning within society? As Heath suggests, if such definitions can be formulated, how then can literacy skills be isolated, tested, and taught apart from an understanding of the social contexts within which readers must be or become literate? Assuming that such competencies can be taught, there is little information on how or whether readers transform literacy skills into literate behaviors.

In light of these issues, I will argue that there are serious problems with this competency-based model of literacy. I will begin by exploring the many views of competency set forth by researchers and scholars in reading and in response to literature. Second, I will examine some assumptions about the relationships among competence, performance, and literacy, demonstrating how readers learn to read and become literate within a complex system of social influences. Finally, I will suggest a social model of reading that attempts to explain how readers develop the intellectual and social competencies to function as readers and literate persons within the realm of the text, the classroom, and the world.

THE TYRANNY OF COMPETENCE IN READING AND RESPONSE

Competence Models of Reading

Although different in their assumptions about the meaning-making process, scholars in reading and response to literature have sought to discover and describe what it means to be a competent reader. Reading research since the 1960s has looked to the reader, the text, and the social context in order to explain the reading process. This section will explore and consider the limitations of reading-competence models derived from schema theory, motivational and attitudinal research, text grammars, and sociolinguistics.

From a reader-oriented framework, schema-theoretic views of reading have demonstrated that readers develop and activate knowledge structures (schemata) that enable them to recall and make inferences about texts (Anderson & Pitchert, 1978; Anderson, Spiro &

Anderson, 1978; Bransford & Johnson, 1972; Clark & Haviland, 1977; Grice, 1975; Pitchert & Anderson, 1977; Reynolds & Anderson, 1982). While some studies have explored the role of cognitive schemata in reading, others have demonstrated that a variety of motivational factors such as readers' attitudes, parental expectations, reading materials in the home, teacher and peer influences affect achievement, educational attainment, and reading performance (Athey, 1976; Bloom, 1976; Entwisle, 1979; Purkey, 1970; Resnick & Robinson, 1979; Wattenburg & Clifford, 1964).

From a text-oriented framework, reading researchers have looked at the underlying structures of prose that influence recall and inferential processes (Frederiksen, 1975, 1977; Graesser, 1981; Kintsch, 1974; Kintsch & van Dijk, 1978; Meyer, 1975). Story grammarians have generated a set of rules and relations by which particular genres of stories operate. Such grammars have been used as a descriptive tool, as well as a predictor of such reading processes as memory and recall and story comprehension (Mandler, 1978; Mandler & Johnson, 1977; Rumelhart, 1977; Stein, 1979; Stein & Glenn, 1979).

Reading researchers working from a sociolinguistic framework have begun to explore the role of culture (home, school, society) on reading achievement, skill development, and access to literacy events. In a sociolinguistic view, reading operates within a mutual system of influences, in which language establishes a social context, and that social context, in turn, influences language learning. Some studies have focused on the influence of context or culture on competence measures such as reading achievement and development, memory and recall, and comprehension (Green, 1977; Mosenthal & Davidson-Mosenthal, 1982; Mosenthal & Na, 1980). Another body of sociolinguistic-based research has explored how teacher perceptions and student communication styles influence readers' access to literacy events (DeStefano, Pepinsky, & Sanders, 1982; McDermott, 1976; Michaels, 1981). Related research has demonstrated that home-school-community relationships influence the ways in which students are evaluated or misevaluated as literate individuals (Cook-Gumperz, Gumperz, & Simons, 1981; Heath, 1982a, 1982b; Michaels, 1981; Scollon & Scollon, 1981, 1982). Thus, reading research has not only explored how reader or text factors influence comprehension, but how a variety of cultural influences affect readers as they develop and gain access to literacy skills.

While such models of reading have contributed to our knowledge of comprehension, recall, and reading achievement, they have been based on certain assumptions about the relationships between reading competence and literate behaviors. Information-processing, schema-theoretic, and text-based models of reading have been premised on the notion that if readers develop certain competencies (e.g., prior knowledge, attitudes and motivation, understanding of text structures), they will put them to use in reading, and, consequently, become literate citizens. This competence model has also dominated socio-linguistic approaches, which focus on the role of culture in either developing competence or providing access to competence. Further, reading research has focused on one type of competence (comprehension) and largely neglected other more personal or affective responses. Reading researchers who study affective processes in reading (e.g., Jose & Brewer, 1984) have done so with the intent of understanding how these processes (for example, character identification) function in students' comprehension of text.

In addition, reading research has measured competence according to how well students recall or comprehend determinate information in texts, which are typically created and controlled in order to tease out various aspects of comprehension and memory. Thus, there is little accounting for variation in response, or for factors other than cognitive ones, with the possible exception of affective factors explaining readers' abilities to comprehend or recall information about texts.

Reading researchers have traditionally conceptualized reading as a "problem to be solved," without considering the ways in which that problem has been conceptualized or framed by various theoretical perspectives (Mosenthal, 1987). Research and public policy decisions have thus been aimed at problem solving, with little attention to problem setting (Reddy, 1979), or to the ways in which the "problem" of reading has been defined by various constituencies. Citing Donald Schön (1979), Mosenthal urges reading researchers to reconsider their notions of reading as a problem of "storage and retrieval" of information from texts:

> By adopting the storage metaphor in reading research, we have assumed, without questioning, that the problem of reading is a problem of storage, i.e., the problem of boxing, transferring, retaining, retrieving, and unboxing text information. ... To preserve our capacity to define not only what reading is but what reading ought to be, we need to seriously reconsider our metaphors of reading in light of our new age (1987, p. 84).

Thus, as Mosenthal suggests, metaphors that underlie theoretical and research models must be frequently examined to ensure that such models can incorporate an ever-changing populace and knowledge base. Just as the "storage-and-retrieval" models of reading research must be examined for their limitations and assumptions, a variety of implicit or explicit assumptions must be examined in models of response to literature. Although models of reading and response are fundamentally different in a variety of ways, they share some common assumptions about the nature of reading and literacy.

Competence Models of Response to Literature

Just as reading researchers have explored factors in the reader, text, and context that account for reading competence, researchers in response to literature have explored the role of textual features, reader differences, instructional techniques, and cultural factors in the sorts of responses and interpretations readers make.

One important distinction between the fields of reading and literary response is in their definitions of "meaning making." While reading theorists study readers in terms of their abilities to comprehend predetermined information in controlled-stimulus texts, reader-response criticism and research focuses on the ways in which readers evoke a variety of meanings from a literary text. In a later edition of her landmark 1938 work, *Literature as Exploration*, Louise Rosenblatt (1985a) described her emergence into what would later be called "Reader-Response Criticism," and her break with more determinate models of reading. In Rosenblatt's view, after the publication of I. A. Richards' *Practical Criticism* (1929), two essentially different approaches to criticism and scholarship emerged: The New Critical stance (which concentrated on close reading and technique) and Reader-Response Criticism (which focused on the variety of potential responses to literary texts).

The move from text to reader in literary criticism that Rosenblatt (1985a) describes was more than simply relocating the source of meaning in reading. It represented a shifting focus from sources of misinterpretation in a literary work (a determinate model) to the variety of possible responses within any community of readers (an indeterminate model).

Thus, in contrast to more determinate notions that underlie reading research and formalist criticism, early studies of response to literature sought to uncover the *variety* of responses to texts—affective and personal, as well as interpretive and descriptive (Purves & Rippere, 1968; Squire, 1964; Wilson, 1966). Further, reader-response theory, in contrast to more linear models of reading, envisioned reading as a transaction (Rosenblatt, 1978, 1985a, 1985b; Holland, 1968, 1973, 1975), in which readers not only act upon texts, but are acted upon in some way. In reading-comprehension models, readers bring prior knowledge and understanding to relatively static determinate texts. In transactional theories (as opposed to transmission theories) of response, readers constantly reformulate their own personal value and identity systems as they encounter and transfom literary works. Thus, no two experiences with a text are ever the same, even for the same reader.

While reader-response theory is premised on the individuality of response, models of response and reading comprehension are similar in that they both focus on implicit or explicit definitions of what constitutes a "competent," "mature," or "ideal" reader. While definitions of competence may differ between the two fields (i.e., "reading skills" versus "response processes"), reading-comprehension and response theories focus on explanations for how these competencies are attained or put into play. To avoid reducing their particular views of response to a solipsism (i.e., "all theories are subjective, including this one"), most response theorists offer some sort of explanation for how similar meanings can recur from one reader to the next. Within these explanations are implicit or explicit definitions of competence.

Johnathan Culler's (1975) notion of "literary competence," derived from a structuralist view, posits that readers must internalize the "'grammar' of literature" (p. 114). Such competence requires linguistic understanding, along with a knowledge of literary conventions. For readers who have "mastered the system," a "range of acceptable meanings" is possible (p. 120). Culler's "ideal reader" must appropriate such knowledge in order to "read and interpret words ... in accordance with the institution of literature" (p. 124). Similarly, Stanley Fish's "informed reader" (1970) possesses linguistic and semantic competence for understanding texts. This competence, Fish argues, is developed through membership in "interpretive communities" (1976).

In contrast to theories of response that focus on the influence of socially constituted discourse communities, the theories of Bleich (1978) and Holland (1968, 1973, 1975, 1985) focus more on the subjective aspects of readers' unique personality orientations. However, both Bleich and Holland imply definitions of competence and attempt to explain recurrences of meaning among readers. Bleich, who argues most strongly for the subjectivity and individuality of response, proposes that readers gain "intersubjective knowledge" through participation in the "thought collective, or community in which the reading takes place" (1986, p. 418). Bleich's "thought collective" is similar to Fish's "interpretive communities" and Culler's "institution of literature" (1970). Thus, while Bleich is perhaps the most "subjectivist" of all reader-response theorists, he appears to offer certain social explanations for how readers come to agree on what constitutes a competent or acceptable reading.

From his psychoanalytic viewpoint, Holland argues that readers must be able to recreate a version of literature in keeping with their psychological adaptive strategies. Without this matching, Holland argues, "the individual blocks out the experience. With it, the other phases of response take place" (1975, p. 817). Thus, before a complete evocation of a text can take place, the reader's psychological defenses, in Holland's terms "must be bribed into tranquility" (1975, p. 817).

To some degree, both Iser (1972, 1980) and Rosenblatt (1978, 1985b) offer explanations for the transactions that occur between reader and text. Iser, citing the phenomenological theory of art, posits that "the literary work cannot be completely identical with the text, or with the realization of the text, but in fact must lie halfway between the two" (1972, p. 279). Similarly, Rosenblatt argues that "[t]he human being is not seen as a separate entity, acting upon an environment, nor the environment acting on the organism, but as both parts or aspects of a total event" (1985b, p. 98).

Although both view the reading process as transactional, Iser concentrates more heavily on the influence of text than does Rosenblatt. He argues that competent readers must actively fill in the gaps or "indeterminacies" in a literary work by construing a "cognitive correlate of the text" (1980, p. 333). Through a continuous process of "forming and overturning illusions" (1980), the reader maintains a "wandering viewpoint" (p. 334) during the reading, and is able to competently participate in the meaning-making process.

Rosenblatt (1978) focuses more heavily on the reader's role in the literary transaction, distinguishing readers according to the stances they take toward texts. She compares "efferent reading" (focused on what the reader will learn or carry away at a later time) with "aesthetic reading" (focused on what is happening at the moment [p. 25]). In order to "evoke" literature aesthetically, Rosenblatt's reader must assume a readiness to read with near-total absorption, continually setting up structures and revising them.

Similarly, Poulet (1980) suggests that an "I who thinks in me" (p. 46) takes over as readers are temporarily able to suspend their own identities, allow themselves to be displaced by the work, and "think the thoughts of another" (p. 44). According to Poulet, the reader must assume a stance that allows temporary immersion in the author's way of thinking—a "humble role" (p. 47) that allows a submissiveness to another consciousness.

Thus, whether implied or explicit, the reader-response critics set forth a variety of explanations for how readers become competent, and how recurrences of meaning arise. The notion of reader as constituted by social systems is reflected in Fish's "interpretive communities," Culler's "institution of literature," and Bleich's "intersubjectivity." Holland, Iser, and Bleich set forth a view of reader as constituted by cognitive or psychological processes, including inferences, text strategies, identity themes, values, and beliefs. Rosenblatt's "aesthetic reading" and Poulet's "displaced consciousness" define a reader as constituted by aesthetic/identification processes. Finally, the reader as constituted by textual understanding is reflected in Fish's "linguistic and semantic competence" and Culler's "grammar of literature." These constructions of the reader argue implicitly that as readers gain membership in interpretive communities, make inferences, become aware of their own identities, submit to, and understand the conventions in a literary text, they will experience a more complete evocation of a text.

Research focusing on reader differences has demonstrated that literary response and understanding are influenced by such factors as readers' cognitive and social-cognitive abilities, psychological predispositions, values, and personal beliefs (Applebee, 1976, 1978; Beach, 1972, 1985; Beach & Brunetti, 1976; Dillon, 1985; Golden & Guthrie, 1986; Holland, 1973, 1975, 1985; Hynds, 1985, 1987, 1989; Lester, 1982). Other studies have demonstrated that how literature is conceptualized and taught in the classroom or the larger culture affects readers' responses and understandings (Hickman, 1980, 1981; Peters & Blues, 1978; Purves, 1986; Svennson, 1985). Researchers have demonstrated the influence of teaching techniques, such as class discussions and written activities, on student response and understanding (Hillocks, 1980; Lucking, 1977; Marlow, 1983; Marshall, 1987; Straw, 1986; Trimble, 1984). Still other studies have shown that textual factors, such as irony, humor, genre, and tone, influence the response and interpretation process (Rubin & Gardner, 1985; Zaharias, 1986). Researchers exploring the "transactional" nature of reading have studied how reading itself influences readers' responses, attitudes, and values (Culp, 1977, 1985; Shedd, 1976).

So many views of the competent reader have been proposed by reader-response critics and researchers that, in the words of Alan Purves, the "composite reader" that emerges "resembles the camel of the story; he or she is a person made up of the self-projections of all those who talk about the reader" (1980, p. 229).

In their particular "views of the camel," reading and response theorists diverge and converge. Reading-comprehension research and theory are based on a determinate conception of meaning; response research and theory are based on a more indeterminate conception. While reading-comprehension researchers are interested in the cognitive frameworks that influence correct comprehension of texts, researchers in literary response are interested in the psychological, attitudinal, and cognitive attributes that contribute to the varied responses of readers. Thus, competence in reading is generally conceptualized in terms of memory and recall, prior knowledge, inferential processes, and text understanding; competence in response is defined by such factors as membership in interpretive communities, knowledge of language and literary conventions, and understanding of personal identity.

CONDUIT METAPHORS IN READING AND RESPONSE PEDAGOGY

Reading and response theory are united in the assumption that the development of certain competencies will somehow translate into performance, and, just as magically, it seems, create a literate populace. Such a conception of literacy seems to operate out of what Reddy (1979) calls a "conduit metaphor" for language learning.

In describing the conduit metaphor underlying conceptions of language, Michael Reddy (1979) cites such expressions as "getting thoughts across," "giving ideas," and "feelings coming through to someone." Such statements, Reddy argues, sound "like mental telepathy or clairvoyance, and [suggest] that communication transfers thought processes somehow bodily" (p. 286). In citing the impact of Reddy's conduit metaphor on reading research, Mosenthal has argued:

> With this metaphor in full force, the goal of reading becomes one of increasing readers' ability to extract large amounts of representative meaning from large text containers. ... Hence, under this metaphor, the larger goal of education becomes the problem of information transfer, shifting information from text containers to mental containers and back again (1987á, p. 341).

Response theorists would disagree with this "container" view of reading, in that they posit the essential uniqueness of each reader's response. Yet the conduit metaphor operates in both reading and response pedagogy, in that both operate out of the implicit assumptions of a "competence-performance" conduit, a "pragmatics-performance" conduit, and a "performance-literacy" conduit. The next section will describe these three prevailing metaphors as they apply to the teaching of both reading and literary response.

The Competence-Performance Conduit

Despite what the reader-response critics tell us about personal and aesthetic aspects of reading, their ideas are not often translated into curricula. In schools, students are most often taught and tested according to determinate models of reading and response. The underlying assumption is that, by giving them access to comprehension and interpretation skills, we will make them "better readers." This is not always a safe assumption, however. In my current research, I am uncovering evidence that readers operate out of a variety of social perspectives that influence their conceptions of how to read, respond to, and demonstrate understanding of literary texts. In some recent case studies of adolescent readers (Hynds, 1989), I found differences in the ways these students viewed reading for school as opposed to reading for self. Despite the best hopes of their English teachers, none of these readers approached literature from a "point-driven" orientation (Hunt & Vipond, 1986; Vipond & Hunt, 1984). When they read for pleasure, they were "story-driven," motivated most often by an engaging plot or interesting characters. Perhaps predictably, "reading for school" (often conceptualized as "reading for the test") was largely "information-driven."

These perceptions of what reading "ought to be" had to do with how these readers construed their teachers' assumptions about "good reading." Many students held negative reductionistic impressions of their teachers. For example, when asked what they would tell English teachers if they could, these students remarked:

> Lay off the one-pathed channel of thought and open your mind to different attitudes about a play or story and don't try to discourage them. If a student's style of writing is different from yours, don't take it out on them. As long as they present information effectively, let that person be.

> Let us just enjoy the story — not force us to understand it and to worry if we interpreted it right. If you get a feeling about the meaning of a story, like a poem, it's not wrong if you can't find proof for it!

> I don't think English teachers have any cause to get mad when we state our opinions of some literature. Not everyone is the same and we don't have to love literature to be a success in life!!!

> Try not to act as if you are God. You may have mastered the English language but many of you haven't mastered life. Live a little!

> I'd like most of them to strive to become close to their students. That way a teacher can understand what kind of writing suits that person; therefore that student can have a choice to write that way and get a good grade rather than be forced to write a certain way and do awful!

The teachers I interviewed saw themselves as equipping their students with valuable skills for reading and for life. Yet, the stress on "reading-as-testing" made some readers so apprehensive that they were unable to demonstrate their true competence in formal papers, quizzes, or impromptu class discussions. One student, for example, said,

Writing is not, I don't feel it's my strong point. If I could write on something I liked writing about I could write a real lot. But the stuff they give in English—I don't like writing.

Another student said,

If I haven't like gone over a story or something really carefully and I had most of the information in my head, I just haven't sorted it out enough to deal with it. ... And then there's a quiz or something. I'm like trying to write down everything without answering the question.

By giving their students necessary skills, their teachers assumed that these students would "perform" better. Unfortunately, definitions for "performance" were directly tied to each teacher's unconscious, and often idiosyncratic, beliefs about what a "good reading" ought to be and how "good reading" ought to be measured. Considering that teachers and students often operated out of different assumptions about competence, the connection between competence and performance was hardly absolute but was undeniably there.

The Performance-Pragmatics Conduit

Sometimes teachers thought they were measuring "performance," when they were really measuring whether readers had the pragmatic skills to "second guess" that particular teacher's underlying biases and assumptions about reading. Thus, "performance" was often confused with "pragmatic" understanding of what was acceptable or unacceptable in the classroom.

Reform reports and competency assessments continually operate out of assumptions about what constitutes acceptable performance in reading. Unfortunately, the resulting standardized tests often measure test-taking abilities, rather than reading competence in any real world sense (Heath, 1985). Students learn quickly that in order to survive in the classroom and in life, they must learn to "do school" (Dyson, 1984). Successful performance in school demands far more than the development of literacy skills. Students must quickly develop what I will call a "pragmatic" sense, or the ability to demonstrate competence within the standards of the teacher, test, or school system. As they fit within these implicit definitions of competence, they gain entrance into approved discourse communities (Bartholomae, 1985; Cooper, 1986; Pereleman, 1986). This pragmatic sense emerges from an elaborate process of social construal, in which readers, in order to be successful, must learn to infer what is in the head of significant adults such as teachers or test makers.

Unfortunately, in literature classrooms, "competence" is often defined by what is teachable or testable. Teachers often misevaluate readers as "incompetent" when they fail to perform in *those teachers'* preferred modes of response. Hal is a case in point (Hynds, 1989). Until his senior year, he had been shunted along as a mediocre student in a basic English class. His teacher remarked that Hal's shyness had prevented him from realizing his potential until his senior year of high school. Over the previous semester, when she switched from formal papers to response journals, she discovered Hal's competence for the first time. In her words, "The way [Hal] reads is the way I think literature is to be read and to be enjoyed. . . . I would say that he found the secret a long time ago." Somewhat regretfully, she remarked that "if somebody, let's say . . . in junior high, had asked him to respond to literature and had seen what he was capable of, he would have been in 'honors' right down the line."

While Hal had difficulty expressing himself in formal papers, Cathy had trouble in on-the-spot quizzes and class discussions. Although her planned written work indicated a great deal of competence, she was so terrified of participating in class discussions that she frequently failed to demonstrate her true interest in and competence for reading. Despite the fact that she was an avid reader who demonstrated a strong interpretive capacity in her planned written work, her teacher described her as "in the middle" of the rest of her classmates. "I don't know," her teacher said, "Maybe she's just a snob. I have no idea" (Hynds, 1989, p. 45).

To Cathy and Hal, school-sponsored reading was a test they often felt incompetent to pass. Because they lacked the pragmatic sense of how to demonstrate competence in their teachers' preferred response modes (i.e., formal papers, quizzes, and class discussion), both were perceived by some teachers as average and uninterested in reading. Cathy and Hal were slipping through the cracks of a hidden curriculum that, in their eyes, defined the teaching of literature as "skill building." For these two readers, the stress on skills and reading for information reinforced a view of reading as "test taking" (i.e., divorced from real life, not an enjoyable experience in its own right). Yet, reform reports and competency assessments continually call for more testing and skill building, as though these activities in isolation would guarantee better and more avid readers.

The Performance-Literacy Conduit

According to Shirley Brice Heath (1985), literate behaviors result when people learn to think and behave as literate persons. These behaviors can only be engendered in a situation that moves beyond skill building, and promotes in all people the desire to be or become literate. Heath's distinction calls into question automatic assumptions about a "performance-literacy" conduit that seems to underlie thinking about reading and writing.

In schools, teachers and curriculum builders often assume that training better readers (i.e., raising scores on competency tests) will result in a more literate populace. As a result, teachers constantly remark, "I don't have time to let the kids read and write what they like. That won't be on the competency exam!" Reform reports set "minimal standards of literacy," assuming that once such standards are met, people will become more "literate," and by implication, more prosperous, God-fearing, or morally upright. Yet this standard setting and testing has not addressed the problem of what Feldman and Woods (1981) call "the illiteracy of the literate," or the astounding percentage of Americans who *can*, but *don't* read anything more than an occasional magazine or television guide.

My studies of adolescents revealed that readers can be competent and can demonstrate that competence in the classroom, yet fail to see themselves as "readers," and, consequently, seldom read for their own pleasure. Consider, for example, the case of Jay (Hynds, 1989). Because he had performed in the top one-quarter of his class on assignments and papers, Jay's teacher, not surprisingly, thought that he liked to read and liked English classes. Jay, on the other hand, reported disliking all of his English classes, and speculated that if his present behaviors were any indication, "I probably won't read that much" after graduation.

Jay had developed "literacy skills," but not "literate behaviors." He was capable of comprehending and demonstrating competence to his teacher when a grade was involved. However, he rarely saw reading as an end in itself, and only occasionally put his competence to use in understanding and identifying with literary characters. Because his teacher defined competence as performance on class assignments, she was not totally aware that Jay was perceiving literature as a springboard to something else (success in school), and lacked the motivation to read outside the classroom.

In an earlier study (Hynds, 1985), I looked at adolescent readers' use of "personal constructs" (Kelly, 1955) or reference axes for representing people (e.g., "good−bad," "godly−ungodly") in their reading of stories. I found that students who demonstrated strong relationships between personal constructs in their impressions of peers and personal constructs in their impressions of story characters were those who read considerably outside the classroom. By contrast, students who reported little outside reading had very weak connections between personal constructs in their peer and character impressions. It appears that readers who bring what they know about people in the real world to reading also tend to read more outside the classroom.

Such findings call into question definitions of "competence" that are limited to cognitive skills or memorization of text information. In order to fully understand literature, readers must invoke not only cognitive competence, but "social competence" as well. Such competence involves the social-cognitive ability to explain the actions and motivations of literary characters, as well as an empathic ability to identify with them in all their struggles and circumstances. Thus, beyond Iser's notion of a "cognitive correlate of the text," readers must also develop the ability to become momentarily absorbed in the thoughts of another (Poulet, 1980), or, in Rosenblatt's terms, to evoke literature "aesthetically," as opposed to "efferently" (1978). Unfortunately, such aesthetic and empathic processes are seldom included in public-policy statements or definitions of literacy. In this light, "conduit" models that conceptualize a linear or one-to-one relationship between competence, performance, and literacy will be reexamined and reconsidered in the following section.

THE LITERACY SYSTEM: CREATING A SOCIAL MODEL OF READING

We might begin by conceptualizing literacy as a system of mutually influential social forces. Readers operate within a context of social perspectives, including their conceptions of teachers' expectations, the value placed on reading by peers and significant adults, and their own notions of themselves as readers. Paralleling these social construal processes in the classroom and world, readers also learn to construe the underlying motivations and thoughts of characters in the text world.

In demonstrating competence to their teachers, readers develop the pragmatic skills to fit their responses into their perceptions of the teacher's expectations for what constitutes a "good" reading or response. Part of this involves learning how to master a particular teacher's preferred discourse form for demonstrating competence (i.e., formal papers, journals, essay tests). Competence and pragmatics alone, however, are no guarantee that readers will envision themselves as "literate" or continue to read outside of the classroom. Volition plays a part in every aspect of this literacy system. Such a system of mutual influences is conceptualized in Figure 10−1.

It is important to note that no direct linear path to literacy exists, and that all elements of the system exist in a transactional relationship to other aspects. As readers are positively reinforced for classroom performance, they learn to develop competencies and view themselves

Figure 10−1
The Literacy System

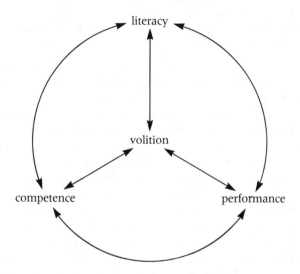

as literate. The development of increasingly sophisticated competencies, in turn, reinforces the system. Finally, no matter how sophisticated the curriculum or the classroom library, readers must *want* to read and must see the value in becoming readers before they view themselves as literate.

On the text level, readers must be engaged by some element of plot, characterization, or meaning in a particular literary work. In the classroom, they must not only see the value of reading, but must also be willing to demonstrate reading competency within their particular teacher's or test maker's preferred assessment mode. In the larger culture, they must develop the will not only to read, but also to develop literate behaviors. As readers develop the will to read in the classroom, text, and world, they will presumably seek out and master the necessary competencies.

We might now explore the ways in which competence, pragmatics, and volition function within the literacy system.

Social Competence in the Text World

[T]he desire for self-understanding and for knowledge about people provides an important avenue into literature. The young reader's personal involvement in a work will generate greater sensitivity to its imagery, style, and structure; this in turn will enhance his understanding of its human implications. A reciprocal process emerges, in which growth in human understanding and literary sophistication sustain and nourish one another. Both kinds of growth are essential if the student is to develop the insight and the skill needed for participation in increasingly complex and sophisticated literary works (Rosenblatt, 1985a, p. 53).

In discussing the interplay among self-understanding, social understanding, and textual knowledge in the reading process, Louise Rosenblatt suggests that "literary sophistication" cannot be taught in the absence of the reader's personal or social understanding. Unfortunately, what has come down to us from the political sector and large-scale testing programs has largely defined reading as a cognitive process, neglecting the "social-cognitive" competence underlying the personal and social understandings that Rosenblatt envisions. George Kelly (1955) has argued that a knowledge of people requires a sophisticated repertoire of "personal constructs," or reference axes for representing and understanding others. Interestingly, the complexity of someone's interpersonal construct system has not been related to general intelligence or verbal abilities (see O'Keefe & Sypher, 1981, for a full review). Thus, it is possible that people might be "bright in school but stupid in interpersonal relations" (Crockett, 1965, p. 55). Readers who possess academic intelligence, but lack the necessary "social intelligence," for reading will never be discovered by teachers who measure competence by how well readers remember literal facts about a text. Correspondingly, readers who never learn to bring their social competencies to literary texts will lack a fundamental prerequisite for a complete understanding of and response to literature.

We might speculate on what motivates readers to use what they know about people in their reading, and whether the social construal process is the same in literature and life. My research is beginning to show that while the two processes probably operate out of a similar knowledge base, there are often more incentives for people to engage in sophisticated inferences about others in the social world than there are in the text world. In real life, we are most interested in understanding people who affect us in some significant way, and who can teach us something about ourselves. Unfortunately, reading is often presented in a way that is neither personally significant nor enlightening to readers. In the words of one high school reader, "I see [my friends] every day. ... I live my life with them ... and a character in a book is ... it's not like they're sitting next to you, talking to you everyday, you know?" (Hynds, 1989, pp. 50–51).

In my studies, readers did not always bring personal constructs to literature, because their teachers did not reinforce notions of reading as a way of understanding people in the social world. Perhaps because of their classroom experiences, some readers did not seem to know how to make attributions about literary characters, because such attributions were never made a part of their response repertoire. Still other readers failed to analyze texts that they perceived as class assignments rather than personally meaningful experiences.

Until now, studies of social cognition in literary response have highlighted the "cognitive" rather than the "social." In a study of college students' character attributions and responses to a short story (Hynds, 1987), I found that complexity in readers' interpersonal construct repertoires related to "text-invoked" responses (e.g., inferences about characters) but not "reader-invoked" responses (e.g., personal evaluation or engagement). Although studies such as these broaden our understanding of what social-cognitive factors contribute to an understanding of characters and their motives, it is probable that readers must also be able to empathize and identify with characters (Poulet, 1980). Perhaps because of the strong influence of cognitivist models of competence, such empathic and identification processes have not been sufficiently explored for their role in reading and literary response. Presumably, readers must do more than simply *understand* texts. They must in some way encounter texts as similar to or explicative of "real life." Thus, "social competence" involves not only understanding, but also identification with others, as a part of the "reciprocal process" of personal, textual, and social understanding that Rosenblatt describes.

We must then redefine our notions of "good reading" to include not only intellectual ability but social competence as well. Beyond this, we must consider how students are asked to demonstrate such competence in schools, and how their failure to do this affects their views of themselves as readers, as well as the likelihood that they will become competent readers and ultimately literate citizens.

Pragmatics: Social Influences in the Classroom World

Unfortunately, teachers' preferred modes of assessment and teaching often have more to do with how they were taught or what is most easily testable than with any theoretically motivated notions of what constitutes a "complete reading." Often what gets tested and taught in classrooms is not competence in any objective sense, but a reader's pragmatic understanding of how to demonstrate competence in a way that is consistent with a teacher's implicit assumptions about "good reading." These implicit assumptions play a part in the stances and attitudes that young readers develop toward texts. Consider, for instance, the implicit and explicit messages that teachers send to students when they measure competence by objective tests, essay tests, response journals, or performance in class discussions. Consider also how seldom students are ever allowed to read a class-assigned book without responding at all, or how seldom they are allowed to read books of their own choosing.

Many of the students I have surveyed felt that texts were selected for what they might *teach* rather than for students' personal enjoyment. These high school students said that if they could, they would tell their teachers:

> To try to choose some very light books or stories to complement the heavy, long, serious, drawn out readings we always do.
>
> Find more interesting stories.
>
> Not to study old plays like Shakespeare.
>
> Have students read more interesting and challenging books, especially science fiction.
>
> I would like to read good stories that I can "get into." Then I would be more willing to write an essay on it and my essay would probably be better. I *don't* consider all of Shakespeare's works that good, and I would rather read a book that has more contemporary applications (i.e., *1984*, or other esteemed works — I'll compromise) than *Hamlet*. I would like to concentrate on philosophical questions raised by the story rather than simply rehashing the story in class to make sure everyone understood it.

Thus, through a complex social construal process, students learn what teachers will and will not accept. Because some readers can so easily masquerade reading skills as reading interests, some of them may graduate from formal schooling and then never pick up a book. In this case, no amount of training in "literacy skills" can make them literate. Thus, the final, and perhaps most important, element in the literacy system is the reader's will.

Volition: Reading in the Real World

George Kelly (1955) tells us that in the social world we are motivated to understand others because we want to predict and control their behaviors. It is impossible, Kelly says, to place human beings in laboratories and study them because they are studying *us* at the same time, inferring what *we* are looking for, and adjusting their behaviors accordingly.

In the past, we have studied motivational aspects of reading by measuring readers' attitudes and attribution processes against outcome variables such as reading interest or achievement. Such studies have contributed greatly to our understanding of those factors other than cognitive ones that influence reading behaviors and abilities. However, such research subtly reinforces the view of readers as inert organisms, subject to the constant push and pull of motives, drives, and needs. On the contrary, readers are always operating out of their own particular social-construal processes, including their beliefs about themselves as readers, and their views of the value placed on reading by significant people such as teachers, parents, and peers.

Readers develop the will to read through participation in supportive communities of readers. This motivation to read encourages them to seek out and master the necessary competencies and skills. On the other hand, when reading is viewed as a means to an end (grades, academic success), when readers are not given personal choices in reading materials or response modes, and when they do not envision themselves as members of a literate community, they generally do not develop literate behaviors. Unfortunately, some readers I talked with appeared to read in spite of, not because of, their experiences in English classes. Alan Purves and his associates (1981) note the importance of strong school-home relations when they say "Schools do make a difference, particularly when these schools support (either positively or negatively) the home" (p. 107).

Thus, readers become literate not simply by learning literacy skills, but by participating in an elaborate socially construed system. As they develop notions of themselves as readers through participation in reading communities, they develop both intellectual and social competence for bringing what they know about life into the text. The degree to which they "bring life to literature and literature to life" (Hynds, 1989) is related to the likelihood that they will continue to read beyond their years of formal schooling.

CHANGING THE METAPHOR

If we envision reading as a complex system of social forces, many questions arise for teachers of reading and literature. First, we might ask ourselves how we define and measure reading competence. Do we stress intellectual processes to the exclusion of social or personal understandings? Which messages do our preferred modes of teaching and evaluation give to our students about the way they ought to read? How often do we misconstrue our students' failures to guess what is in our heads as "incompetence?" What are our responsibilities, not only to develop literacy skills, but to develop literate behaviors, which lead to a lifetime of reading? How do we create, and ask parents to create, a social climate for reading, so that students are encouraged to read in school and at home?

Researchers should begin to redefine notions of reading competence to include social as well as cognitive competence. This social competence would include social-cognitive abilities necessary for comprehending characters' acts, as well as affective/identification abilities. We might explore the attributes that underlie social competence, and how those attributes might be measured (e.g., indices of differentiation, abstractness, integration of the interpersonal construct system, role-taking measures). Finally, we might investigate the contextual influences that play a part in development of social competence, as well as the motivational factors that relate to the likelihood that readers will utilize this competence in their personal and classroom reading.

Jane Tompkins (1980) contrasts the modern view of literature as a source of meaning with the ancient view of literature as a "force exerted on the world" (p. 225). In the past, theory, research, and pedagogy in reading and response to literature have envisioned the text as a document to be decoded and deciphered, rather than a powerful influence on human thought and behavior. In bringing unique experiences and world visions to literary texts, readers both transform and are transformed by their literary experiences. Discovering the competencies and the social influences that make reading a powerful force in the intellectual and personal lives of all readers is perhaps the first step toward developing and maintaining a literate society.

PART III

READING, RESPONSE, AND PEDAGOGY

CHAPTER 11

IN CONVERSATION
Theory and Instruction

Evelyn Hanssen, Jerome C. Harste, & Kathy G. Short

Given current instructional practices, students from elementary school through college barely scratch the surface of understanding what it means to be literate. Some may protest, arguing that we are doing a better job of teaching reading now than at any point in our history. And, in fact, elementary school children can sound out words better than ever before; and more middle, high school, and college students can answer simple questions about what they have read (National Assessment of Educational Progress, 1980). But these conclusions represent old values in which the transmission of information was the goal. What we currently know about literacy calls for a new set of values for reading instruction, a set of values in which the goals involve interacting with texts in dynamic and critical ways. Current constructs from literary theory challenge the assumptions underlying the way reading is currently being taught and offer a potential for educators to rethink what they are doing. This chapter examines these constructs and tells three stories of how we have used them at the elementary, secondary, and college level to rethink the what, the how, and the why of reading instruction.

What we currently see being taught in classrooms — regardless of grade level — is a standard body of texts, primarily narrative, preselected for use by someone other than the teacher or the students. At the elementary level, basal publishers select what literature will be read.

At the secondary and college levels, publishing houses and editors of anthologies do the selecting. As we travel across the country, we see a disappointing sameness to what students are reading. Students and teachers tend to approach these texts in habitual and uninspired ways.

As we look at *how* instruction occurs, again we see a great deal of similarity across grade levels. Teachers frame the discourse and do most of the talking. The elementary teacher introduces skills, sets the framework for the reading, and checks comprehension (Goodman, Shannon, Freeman, & Murphy, 1988). The secondary and college teacher explicates the meaning of the text and highlights major literary elements within different types of literature (Goodlad, 1984). In both cases, the teachers' role is one of transmission, as they attempt to model and make explicit the strategies, constructs, and experiences students need in order to do a correct reading.

The *why* of this kind of instruction has to do with what teachers believe it means to be literate (Harste & Burke, 1977). Dominant instructional practices reflect the belief that mastery of basic skills in reading at the elementary level and techniques of literary explication at the secondary and postsecondary levels are painful but necessary steps to gaining the correct meaning from a text. Being literate is implicitly defined as being able to extract this correct meaning and talk about it in terms of traditional literary categories.

We will argue that to be truly literate, reading must be seen as a tool and toy for learning. In a real sense, reading is a way of out-growing our current selves. Rather than asking students to deal with texts in prescribed ways, we would like to see students responding to texts in terms of how they, both as readers and as persons, are different as a result of having read.

We believe that if students are to see reading as a vehicle for lifelong learning, then *how* we teach is just as important as *what* we teach. In a good reading or literature program, *how* and *what* we teach are orchestrated so that no one is in doubt as to *why*.

Several constructs from literary theory—dialogue, storying, inter-textuality, and interpretive community—have helped us clarify the what, how, and why of teaching reading. In the sections that follow, we will discuss these constructs and how we have used them to improve reading instruction at elementary, secondary, and college levels.

DIALOGUE

Mikhail Bakhtin, a Marxist scholar, argues that learning has its roots in social interaction or dialogue. It is through social interaction that signs are created, and these signs become the basis for all learning. What Bakhtin is calling a sign is anything that carries meaning — an object, sound, word, gesture, shape, or virtually anything that has significance for us. He contends that something becomes a sign only because two people see it as carrying meaning between them. From the time we are born, social interactions allow us to distinguish among all the sensory data in the environment and discover what is meaningful and how it is meaningful (Bakhtin, 1973).

Bakhtin goes on to argue that the meanings created in interaction are internalized in the form of thought. These internalized interactions are used in subsequent interactions, both inner and outer dialogues (Bakhtin, 1973; Vygotsky, 1978). For example, if we sit down with our colleagues to talk about the thinking concerning Bakhtin, we will be creating meaning in our conversation. We will make connections that we would not have otherwise made. But each of us will understand what is being said in terms of the meanings we already have. The meanings in our head have come from other conversations that we have experienced. After we have parted and we think about our conversation, we will be engaging in a kind of inner dialogue between the meanings created in our conversation and those coming out of other conversations we have experienced. New ideas are created through this inner dialogue in much the same way they were created in our conversation.

So, according to Bakhtin, learning has its roots in a social dialectic or dialogue. Learning is "a response to signs with signs" that were created in interaction (Bakhtin, 1973, p. 11). Even the seemingly private act of reading rests on the signs and meanings created in previous social interactions and inner dialogues, as it is those existing signs we use to "answer" the signs on the page and make sense of them.

We believe that this notion of learning as a dialogic process has direct curricular implications. It points to the need for students to engage continually in the exchange of ideas, to be involved in dialogues of different kinds. They need to talk to each other, and to us as teachers, and they need to exchange ideas through writing. These dialogues are not simply motivational or reinforcing, they provide the foundation of learning. In the process of this exchange, the students are continually creating and testing their ideas.

STORYING

Both dialogue and storying provide metaphors for processes in which we engage in developing signs or meaning from our experiences and constructing our worldviews. The concept of storying highlights the process we engage in as we search for ways to give structure and meaning to our experiences and share our experiences with others.

In storying, we search for and create connections among the signs and dialogues we have experienced. Rosen (1984) says that from the endless stream of experiences in which we are constantly involved, we select, organize, and bring meaning to our experiences through storying. We invent beginnings and endings to create a meaningful sequence that we can then share with others. We cannot transfer the stories of others into our own worldviews. We must each construct our own stories by connecting our current experiences with our past experiences.

As we read texts, we search for unity, both within the evolving text and between the evolving text and our past texts. These past texts are ones that we previously constructed to make sense of our world. Tensions are created as we search for unity — propelling learning forward. As we search, we discover both suspected and unsuspected connections between current evolving texts and past texts, and this results in a new understanding both of those texts and of our general constructions of reality.

Perceiving and inventing a story is not enough. According to Rosen (1984), the story "must be verbalized, it must be told" (p. 14). In telling the story to others — expressing our understanding in some form — we not only bring the story to life, but we also make new connections and create new meanings. Vygotsky (1962) explains what happens psychologically in the telling of stories. Beginning with the concept of dialogue, he argues that when we internalize the dialogues we experience, we do so in a condensed form. Since we know the subject of the interaction and the context in which it took place, we need only to remember the connectives or the predicates in order to hold onto the meaning. So there is a kind of stripping down process that occurs when dialogues are internalized in thought. Just the opposite occurs when we tell stories, and move from inner to outer dialogue. In the telling of stories, we are trying to make connections clear for others, and in the process, we are forced to make them clear for ourselves.

The notion of storying has clear curricular implications. Students need to create their own stories, their own explanations of the world. In traditional school settings, teachers have tended to expect students to replicate the teachers' stories, rather than to draw from all the experiences they have had in relation to a topic and create a coherent story of their own. As students deal with a topic, they need to become aware of the connections they currently are making and the ones that they are not able to make. The stories that students tell help them to recognize and value what they know, and at the same time their stories become the focus for continued discussion and learning.

INTERTEXTUALITY

Whenever a story is shared, that text becomes a source of further dialogue and storying by both the writer and the reader. They use what they have gained from this story as they approach new texts, and these new texts will allow them to reconsider old stories (de Beaugrande, 1980; Short, 1986). But this is not merely a linguistic phenomenon. As we approach graphic art, for example, we create a story about that work: the subject, the colors, the form, the style, and the artist. We take this story to our next encounter with a work of art, attending to both similarities and differences—connections and disjunctions. In this process, we have gained a richer understanding of graphic art. We have created a bigger story in the sense that it is more encompassing, and it is a better story in the sense that it involves more complex intertextual ties. The connections allow us to link things together and help us to see new relationships. The disjunctions, the things that don't fit, force us to go back and reconsider our stories. This can lead to fundamental changes in our thinking.

The process of intertextuality takes place in a myriad of ways. One type of intertextual tying—tying across the different texts we encounter—relates to what we read. This involves both form and content. As we approach texts that deal with a particular topic, we search for ties to other texts, other stories, other dialogues relevant to that topic—ties that form both connections and disjunctions between texts. We also attend to features of form such as word choice, sentence structure, elements of transcription, voice, style, and genre as we look across texts. So, for example, when young children encounter "once-upon-a-time" stories and make connections among these stories, they construct the genre of the fairy tale and equate it to story. As these children get older and read contemporary novels, they will experience disjunction, since many of the features of story that they recognize will be violated. And if they ever read this discussion, they will experience further disjunction between the way "story" is being used here, as a unit of meaning, and the more common use of the term.

Intertextual tying also occurs in terms of how we read, the strategies we use as we approach different texts. Strategies that are useful in one reading experience are carried as potential strategies to other experiences. The student who discovers the value of skimming in the context of reading textbooks, for example, may also find it useful in approaching other materials. But that same student may experience disjunction when the strategies of gathering information used in textbook reading are not helpful in the reading of literature. This forces the student to examine existing strategies and possibly develop new ones.

Yet another type of intertextual tying relates to why we read—

the functions that texts serve. For example, the purpose of reading mystery stories is generally to figure out "who dun it." But when graduate students in a seminar on language theory were asked to read *The Name of the Rose,* a mystery novel written by a famous semiotician, the participants assumed that there must be some link to language theory and to semiotics, since that was their purpose for being in the class. This affected the kinds of connections that they made in the course of reading and the nature of the story that they constructed. Few of the participants read it in the way they would have read other mysteries (Harste, 1986). A similar kind of disjunction occurred when a first-grade student received a letter from her pen pal in another school. The letter contained a list of apparently unrelated words. (They seemed to be a list of words that the child knew how to spell). Since she was in a classroom where notes or letters always contained a real message, this student expected this letter to contain a message as well. When she could not construct one, she began searching for some way to make sense of it. Others in her class suggested that the pen pal may have written her favorite words. Working under this hypothesis, the child was able to respond to the letter (Short, 1986).

Through intertextual tying, we are able to consider each of our experiences in terms of other experiences we have had and in this way transform our understanding of them. The concept of inter-textuality has clear curricular implications. It points to the limitations of setting up curricula in a linear fashion, with one experience building on the next. This limits the potential for intertextual tying. Instead, we need to set up a web of experiences related to the topic of study so that students can draw from a number of different experiences in trying to create their own understanding. If students can draw upon a rich set of curricular experiences related to a topic, they are more able to see the relevant threads running through these experiences, and they are able to create a more varied and complex understanding of the topic.

INTERPRETIVE COMMUNITIES

When a group of people dialogue with one another and read each others' texts, shared meanings develop among them and they become part of an interpretive community (Fish, 1980). These meanings that they share affect their subsequent interactions and, over time, lead to the development of a thought style, a common approach to viewing the world (Fleck, 1979). We can recognize these common thought styles in different types of interpretive communities—the family, the church, social groups, and academic departments. The social interactions we have within these groups promote a similar view of the world by not only generating thought but also by constraining it. What we talk about within an interpretive community affects how we think, and how we think affects what we are able to talk about.

Fortunately, none of us is a member of a single interpretive community or uses a single thought style. We are part of many interpretive communities with our families, our friends, our colleagues—in fact, every time we enter into a conversation, an interpretive community is formed. As we move from one interpretive community to another, we bring with us those meanings that were developed in other communities. In this way, each member of the interpretive community contributes both on the basis of shared meanings within the common thought style and on the basis of unique perspectives that the individual brings from interactions in other interpretive communities. This movement between interpretive communities is generative in that it leads us to identify both connections and disjunctions in thought styles among different communities. Rather than a simple accumulation of experiences, this process is a dialectical or dialogic one in which a person leaves each encounter within an interpretive community changed, with new interpretive strategies and new potentials for interacting in dynamic ways during subsequent encounters within different communities. (See Bodgan's discussion of dialectic in this volume, Chapter 7).

An example of the diversity of perspectives within different interpretive communities and the generative potential in moving between them can be found by exploring the views of reading coming out of the literary community and the language-education community (as this volume attempts to do). Within the literary community, much of the discussion about reading is of a highly philosophical nature, dealing with issues of how texts signify meaning to readers. In many of these discussions, readers become an abstract construct—such as the implied reader, the ideal reader, or the narratee (Iser, 1974; Culler, 1975; Genette, 1980). Texts are generally talked about in specific terms, with frequent references made to particular works of literature—poetry, novels, and short stories.

Within the language-education community, a very different view seems to prevail. Reading tends to be talked about in more mechanistic terms with issues of signification rarely addressed. When research is reported, texts become virtually anonymous, as "passages" of narration or exposition are presented to readers. (Poetry is rarely dealt with.) Understanding becomes defined in terms of fixed responses to a set of questions. But the discourse in this community is not based on abstract notions of readers. Real readers are used to gather information concerning actual reading experiences (see *Reading Research Quarterly, Journal of Reading Behavior, Reading Psychology*).

These two interpretive communities — the literary community and the language-education community — have much to offer one another. But the generative potential comes from more than a kind of complementariness. It is the tensions between these perspectives that lead members of each community to consider a wider range of issues and to produce a dialogue in which reading comes to be viewed in broader and more sophisticated terms.

There are clear curricular implications of viewing the classroom as an interpretive community. One of these is that members of the community are assumed to have something to contribute, a unique perspective or insight to offer from the other interpretive communities of which they are members. Another is that classrooms are structured in such a way as to facilitate the sharing of these insights and to allow the students to pursue a line of inquiry that emerges out of the sharing. In this case, each member of the community is seen as vital because, without that person, a perspective would be missing and the dialogue would be impoverished. This is in direct opposition to classrooms in which only the teacher's absence is of real consequence, where only the teacher's perspectives and insights are crucial.

Dialogue, storying, intertextuality, and interpretive community are constructs that help us conceive of what it means to be literate. They also suggest some of the features of a classroom context that would support this kind of literacy. Classrooms need to become places where people exchange ideas, where people construct their own meanings in conjunction and disjunction with the meanings of others, and where the particular strengths of the individual are recognized and valued by the group.

KATHY SHORT'S STORY

In May, during the last several weeks of school when most teachers and students were trying to wait out the end of the year, several of us decided to try out a new curricular strategy. We were interested in what would happen if students read and discussed text sets (sets of related books) in their literature-circle discussion groups.

Throughout the school year, I had been working with Gloria Kaufmann and her third-grade students, and Kaylene Yoder and her sixth-grade students in exploring the use of literature circles. These literature circles had previously consisted of small groups of students with mixed ability who had chosen to read the same piece of literature and who had then met to explore their interpretations of that literature. We decided that instead of having students read the same book, we would try having each group read different books that were related in some way. We put together a variety of sets of books for each classroom that built upon the interests and needs of the students. In Kaylene's room, we offered the students the choice of text sets from among Cinderella variants, books about war and peace, books by Chris Van Allsburg, books by Betsy Byars, books about Japanese culture, books about Native Americans, and books about dragons. The text sets on Japan and Native Americans included poetry, fiction, folk tales, and information books. In Gloria's room, the students read text sets of Magic Pot variants, books by Eric Carle, information books by Anne McGovern, books from different genres about pigs, and books that had won the Caldecott Medal (the award given by the American Library Association for the best picture book in a given year). The sets ranged in size from five books to thirty books.

Students in each room signed up for the set of books they wanted to read and discuss. They were each asked to read one or two books from their set, meet with their group to share what they had read with each other, make comparisons across texts, and then present their text sets to the class.

As we observed and participated in the group over a two-week period, we were excited by the range of issues the students discussed, the variety of strategies that the groups developed for dealing with the text sets, and the creative ways in which they presented their sets to the class.

Some groups used the strategy we had suggested, with everyone reading one or two books and then coming together to compare. They varied, however, in how they went about making these comparisons. In the Betsy Byars group, for example, each student read a different book by Byars. They first described their books to each other and then made a list of the things they could compare across their books. This list included characters, the problems they faced, the enemies of the main characters, the types of ending, the ways in which their books were adventures, and how their books dealt with everyday life situations. They made this list at the end of their first discussion and then used it over the next three days to direct their discussions as they talked about each of these comparisons in detail.

Other groups, such as the Anne McGovern group, also made a list of topics to compare, but then chose only a few topics from the list to focus on during their discussion. They found that many of McGovern's books dealt with danger, so they spent a long period of time talking about danger and what makes a situation dangerous. They also became interested in talking about how writing information books is different from writing fiction.

Instead of making a list of things to compare, the group who read books in the pig set each read one or two books and then wrote questions they had about these books in their literature logs. These questions became the focus of their exploration over the next several days. Although some of the questions in their logs were specific to the book or books each had read, the questions they ended up discussing were broad questions that went across their books. These questions included: "What are pigs like? How are pigs alike and different from people? Why do authors use pigs instead of people in their books? Why don't the other pigs like runts? Why do authors choose runt pigs to write about? Why do authors often use make-believe pigs rather than real pigs?" These questions allowed each of them to share from the individual titles they had read as well as to search across their books for connections and generalizations.

Sometimes a group focused the entire discussion on a certain issue or theme rather than exploring a range of comparisons. The group that read books by Eric Carle noted during their first discussion that his books are enjoyed by people of all ages. They spent the next several days trying to decide what it was about his books that appealed to so many people. They particularly focused on the ways in which his books provided information and yet were gamelike, with the flaps and folds.

Although the previous groups involved each member of the group reading only one or two books and then sharing and comparing these books, other groups chose to have each member read most of the books in their set. The Japan group, for example, divided their books into subsets according to the genres of poetry, folk tales, and other. Each day, the group members would work with one of the subsets. They would each read one or two books from these subsets and then meet and compare the books.

The group that read Cinderella variants started out with each person reading a different variant. But after the first discussion, the group members began reading other books in the set. By the end of the week, everyone had read most or all the variants. This group often physically sorted the books into piles, depending on the comparison they were making. At the end of each discussion, they decided on what they wanted to compare the next day, and then they made entries in their literature logs about this comparison. They began their discussions by sharing from their logs. They compared settings, the magic persons or things, the stepmothers and stepsisters, the way the Cinderellas were portrayed and illustrated, the places where the Cinderellas met their princes, and the illustrating techniques.

The War and Peace group decided to read and focus on one book at a time and gradually work their way through the set. All group members read the same book and then discussed this book in depth, rather than making comparisons across books. In their discussions, they particularly focused on how the illustrations portrayed the characters' responses to war. During their last discussion, they compared how the different books portrayed war and peace. This set of books had a dramatic effect on how the group members viewed the impact of war on peoples' lives.

The Caldecott group had a more specific purpose for comparing their books. They each read two or three books that had won the Caldecott Medal and then compared their books, trying to figure out the criteria for these books receiving the award. They spent several days sorting the books into various categories and ended up developing five lists of categories under which they listed more specific criteria. These categories included illustrations, characters, writing, how problems are solved, and how the book relates to other books. They then looked at the most recent Caldecott winner and runner-up books to see which book they thought should have won the award according to their own criteria. Based on their analysis, the group decided that they disagreed with the Caldecott committee and that one of the runner-up books should have received the medal.

Throughout these discussions, our roles varied from group to group. Some groups proceeded on their own, and we only occasionally checked with them to find out what they were discussing. There were other groups that we joined for varying lengths of time to facilitate discussion and group dynamics, functioning as participants in these discussions, not as discussion leaders. The differing strategies that the groups used for discussing their text sets evolved from the group and were not directed by the teacher.

At the end of the discussion, each group brainstormed a list of ideas for how they could present their text set to the class and then decided on one idea. Their presentations reflected the kinds of topics they had explored together. The Magic Pot group put on a play of their own Magic Pot variant. The Pig group brought in a live baby pig and made bookmarks with information on pigs for the class. The Eric Carle group interviewed kindergarten, first-grade, third-grade, and sixth-grade classes as well as several adults about why they liked Eric Carle and then put on a radio show in which they reported on these interviews. The Caldecott group made a learning center where other students could sort the Caldecott books according to the criteria the group had generated. The Anne McGovern group made sandwich boards, which they used to advertise the McGovern books. The girls in the Cinderella group each dressed up like one of the Cinderellas and gave a Readers' Theater presentation that they had written themselves. The narrator attempted to tell the Cinderella story but was constantly interrupted as each character attempted to insert her version of how the story "really" happened. The Japan group served tea and read favorite haiku poems while showing nature slides. The War and Peace group put on a skit about the difference between play war and real war. The Byars group wrote advice column letters about their character's problems. The Native American group sent messages in sign language to the class. The Van Allsburg group created a house mural, and the Dragon group created posters comparing dragons to dinosaurs.

In each group, the students developed their own strategies for productively reading, discussing, and comparing their set of books. Although all groups started by describing their books to each other, they then continued their discussions in a variety of ways. Because we chose to give students broad directions for these discussion groups, they were able to develop their own group strategies for making these discussions productive.

The use of text sets in literature circles highlighted the process of intertextuality. This instructional activity created a new awareness for readers of the importance of searching for connections and patterns across books, and helped them develop strategies for making this search more productive and wide ranging. Text sets helped students see learning as a process of making intertextual ties.

As students read the books in the sets, they created their own stories around those texts. These understandings changed as they shared their stories with others and as they searched for connections among the different texts they created. Text sets encouraged students to create stories using a wide variety of connections with the different pieces of literature and with their own experiences.

The dialogue surrounding the text sets supported the process of intertextuality. Students engaged in dialogue with others who had read different books, so they were able to explore connections and disjunctions between the books they read and the ones they did not read. They engaged in dialogue with others who read the same books, so they were able to see the ties between their interpretations and those of other students. Through this sharing, new connections were made and new insights were gained.

The use of text sets also encouraged the development of an interpretive community in which everyone was seen as contributing valuable information to the discussion. The presentations promoted this sense of community as well, in that it led the students to reflect on which insights had been gained within the group that would be interesting and valuable to share with those outside the group. The presentations allowed for more connections to be made and for the process of storying to continue. Thus, we see how dialogue can support storying and intertextuality, and how all three are supported by an emerging sense of interpretive community.

EVELYN HANSSEN'S STORY

I worked for a year as a coteacher/researcher with Carol Porter in an eighth-grade English class. The curriculum we developed was organized around units focusing on genres such as legends, historical fiction, mystery, fantasy, biography, and science fiction, and it highlighted particular authors within that genre. Some of the authors were Cynthia Voigt, Ray Bradbury, C. S. Lewis, Arthur Conan Doyle, Elizabeth George Speare, and Madeleine L'Engle. Within each unit, the students chose what they wanted to read—whether they wanted to sample from various authors within a genre or read several works by one author. The students also chose what they wanted to write—either something connected to their reading or something coming out of other experiences.

In a unit on realistic fiction, the work of Robert Cormier was highlighted. Some of the students started by reading *I Am the Cheese*, a book structured so that it alternates between the narration of events on a bicycle trip and a transcript of taped conversations between the characters T and A. As the students began reading, they felt there were many more things they didn't understand than those they did. They seemed to feel that the book raised many questions and provided few answers. This was very different from the kinds of fiction they had read in the past, narratives that followed traditional story structure (Stein & Glenn, 1979). They found it both frustrating and compelling. They brought their questions and their frustrations to literature circles, where the issues that they raised were discussed. Through their reading and discussion, they came to see that they would have to figure out this story rather than simply wait for the plot to unfold. They began to approach the text as a puzzle, continually uncovering more pieces. In their discussions, they tried to put the pieces together by dealing with such issues as the relationships between the taped conversation and the narrative: whether the events actually occurred or were some type of hallucination, and what the connection was between past and present in the novel. There was a sense of accomplishment in the final discussion, as the puzzle had been solved. One boy in the group announced as I came into the room in the middle of class (having been out talking to a visitor), "We figured this whole book out and you weren't here to hear it." Fortunately, the group was willing to share the understanding its members had constructed. They had figured out why the book started and ended the same way, and they were able to fit the other pieces into place as well. One of the girls talked to me later about how this book had forced her to think, about how many connections she had to construct consciously in order for the story to make sense. This gave her a sense of confidence so that she said, "Now I can read anything."

When the *I Am the Cheese* group finished, a number of the students wanted to read another book that provided this same kind of challenge. They went on to read *The Bumblebee Flies Anyway* or *After the First Death* by Cormier. Some looked to other authors that also used a nontraditional story structure, such as Paul Zindel's *The Pigman*. But other students from the group wanted, instead, to read *The Chocolate War*, another book by Cormier, which a different group had read, and which they became interested in after hearing their classmates talk about it.

The Chocolate War is set in a Catholic boys school where a gang called the "Vigils" is in control. Archie is the assigner and thinks up various schemes that the Vigils force other students to carry out. Brother Leon, the acting headmaster of the school, has put a great deal of the school's money into the annual chocolate sale and is, therefore, forced to elicit the help of the Vigils in selling an unusually large amount of chocolate. The Vigils provide the muscle behind a spirited sales campaign, in which each student is called upon to give his "all" for the school. The number of chocolate sales for each individual is announced daily, but when the roll is called, Jerry Renault, a freshman, refuses to sell the chocolates. No one knows this is an assignment from the Vigils, that he has been singled out as the one person who will not sell. After ten days of refusing to sell and facing persecution from the entire school, the Vigils give Jerry the assignment to begin selling the chocolate. When he continues to refuse, he faces not only the persecution of the school and Brother Leon, but also the wrath of the Vigils. In the end, he is brutally beaten in a fight arranged by Archie, for which the entire student body serves as an audience while Brother Leon watches from afar.

The Chocolate War group had their first literature circle after they had read the first few chapters. Shawn had trouble with the abrupt way the first chapter started, "They murdered him." He was accustomed to the beginning of a book setting the scene, not using a figure of speech to create a tense opening. Both he and Deanna were not clear as to who the Vigils were, and they wondered about what "Body, man" meant. Tracey offered an extended explanation of the sacrament of Communion, and explained that the "body" was the Eucharist. This led to our discussing other religious allusions in the chapters we had read. We also talked about the characters. Tracey thought names like Goober were pretty strange, even though it was a nickname for

Goubert. Chris argued that lots of high school kids had nicknames, and Deanna shared the story behind one of hers. Deanna brought up the idea of role reversal when she thought it was "weird" that Brother Leon was forced to ask Archie and the Vigils for help with the candy sale. It seemed as if Archie was the one with the power and "Brother Leon was on the bottom."

This kind of small group discussion or literature circle was a major curricular structure in our class. The group functioned by involving the students in choosing the book they wanted to read from among several books. The group decided how far they would read before each meeting. We asked that, as the students read, they periodically write responses, generally after each chapter. We, as teachers, were also members of a group and wrote responses that were dealt with in the same way as those of the students. The responses might involve raising questions about things that were unclear, commenting on characters, raising objections to things that did not seem credible, identifying particular techniques that the writer used, or reacting in any other way. These written comments became the focus of discussion in the literature circles. In the course of the discussion, new issues emerged, and the conversation took on a life of its own.

As *The Chocolate War* group continued to meet a couple of times a week over a three-week period, they explored a wide range of issues. Some dealt with what we typically think of as text-based or comprehension questions. Others dealt with more interpretive issues. But the comprehension questions did not necessarily precede our dealing with the interpretive ones, as is often assumed. Each became part of the other as questions about particular characters or events led to the discussion of their significance, and issues of interpretation led to the clarification of particular events. Although specific sets of issues are being identified here, the actual discussions flowed freely among various topics.

One set of issues dealt with the structure of the book and other stylistic features. Shawn commented on the way the first chapter began, but we soon came to discover that most of the chapters had this kind of abrupt, provocative opening. We began flipping through the book and reading the first line of each chapter. This clearly fascinated the students, as they began experimenting with this kind of opening in their own writing. Deanna and a number of the students expressed their irritation about the way the book skipped around, dealing with one set of characters in one chapter and a whole new set in the next. They found this confusing. My alluding to a similar kind of jumping around that takes place on television soap operas gave the students something to hook onto as they tried to understand what was happening. Sean commented that he liked the fact that the chapters were short in the book. Dan had noticed, however, that after a particularly short chapter, the next chapter was somewhat longer.

Another set of issues related to clarification. Shawn was continually getting the characters confused and raised questions that allowed all of us to make sure we had the characters straight. Dan didn't understand why Brother Leon was so worried about the chocolate sale; Tim was able to explain that. Tracey could not figure out how there could be fifty boxes of chocolate left at the end of the sale when everyone except Jerry either met or passed their quota. We searched the text for the answer. Although we knew that the numbers had been tampered with, we were never quite able to figure out how that could be explained.

Other issues focused on character motivation. Shawn's raising a simple question concerning whether or not Jerry was one of the Vigils led to our talking about why Jerry was refusing to sell the candy, and this led Sean to comment that he thought it might be because Jerry wanted to become part of the Vigils. Tim disagreed with this interpretation and raised the issue of whether Jerry was "that kind" of person. Dan wanted to know why Goober (Jerry's only friend in the school) quit the football team. Several students thought he felt bad the assignment that he did, under orders from the Vigils, had caused a teacher to have a nervous breakdown. Dan could not figure out why anyone would feel bad about that. Other questions came up about Brother Leon, such as why he and the other priests did not break up the Vigils, what Brother Leon was trying to accomplish by humiliating students in class, how he and the other priests felt about Archie, and why Brother Leon did not stop the fight at the end of the book. Sean jokingly said he liked Brother Leon, but most of the students found Leon's viciousness inexcusable and agreed with Chris when she said, "I think he should quit the brotherhood."

Yet another set of issues dealt with the symbols and allusions in the book. Symbols related to the Bible and specifically to the Roman Catholic church were questions for many of the students, and these were often answered by a number of Catholics in the group who were coincidentally going through confirmation instruction at the time. Dan drew our attention to the illustration on the cover of one of the editions of the book. When the book was turned sideways, the goal posts in the picture looked like crucifixes, and it appeared that Jerry was hanging from one. Sean raised the issue of what a poster in Jerry's locker meant; it was a nature scene and the caption read, "Dare I disturb the universe?" — That question was central to the entire novel.

A fifth set of issues involved the participants exploring their own experiences in relationship to the book. We discussed whether we would have completed the assignments given by the Vigils had we been in that situation and what we would have done if we had been Jerry. The students contrasted their principal and previous teachers with Brother Leon and some of the teachers in the book. In considering the assignments that the Vigils handed out, we talked about pranks with which we had been involved. Sean shared his brother's reaction to the book, based on Sean's retelling. His brother thought a book about gangs selling chocolates was "pretty stupid." Other students talked about their parents' reactions and their own feelings about this rather controversial book.

In the final discussion group, I set the framework. I asked the students to come to the group with a freewrite on what they thought this book was really about. We came together and each read what we had written and discussed the various themes that the students had generated. But underlying the discussion was a kind of impatience arising from the feeling that some of the ambiguities would be cleared up in the sequel, *Beyond the Chocolate War*. The students were all anxious to read the sequel, so the process of discussion and exploration continued.

Discussion groups were a central feature of the classroom, reflecting a belief that dialogue is at the heart of learning. The students had extended opportunities to talk to one another in order to learn to articulate their own thinking and to respond to the thinking of others.

The dialogue allowed for the development of a strong sense of community in which students were free to talk about things they didn't understand and to share relevant experiences from other communities. Shawn was free to tell all of us that he had the characters confused and to get our help in straightening them out. Tracey and Dan were able to share what they were learning in their confirmation classes and enrich our discussion of the novel.

The dialogue provided the source for the creation of rich intertextual ties. All of the participants were able to make connections among the different perspectives that each person brought to the discussion. They had the opportunity to consider questions that they had never thought of asking and to consider others' answers to their questions. They had their perspectives supported and challenged as they continued to build richer understandings.

The creation and sharing of stories with others in the class came to be seen as the primary order of business. Within the units of study, individual students made decisions about the kind of storying they wanted to engage in, as they decided what direction their reading would take and what topics they would explore in their writing. The audience for their sharing were other members of the interpretive community, and not primarily the teacher as evaluator (Barnes, 1975). This sharing of stories promoted further dialogue, and learning continued.

JERRY HARSTE'S STORY

In a course I offered in the summer of 1987 at Indiana University called *Process Reading/Process Writing: The Teacher as Author, Researcher, Learner, and Curricular Informant*, the participants were immersed in authorship. The class began with my announcing, "This course is neither a curriculum nor methods course. While these issues will be addressed, the heart of the course is best thought of as a Readers' and Writers' Guild. The three reading/writing experiences that have been planned are designed to extend as well as challenge each of you to read and write in new areas of competency." I went on to explain that the course would center on response and developing lively and succinct prose though reading, writing, and responding to peers. I told students that curricular implications of class experiences could be written about in walking journals (a public forum for reaction and response that circulated among the students), but they would not be openly discussed until the last days of the course, at which time I would also make metastatements on curriculum and methods. My thinking was that teachers all too often learn to talk about, and even apply, concepts to their classrooms without having first experienced them. I wanted students to use reading and writing to learn and, on the basis of their own experience, to rethink curriculum.

To this end, I organized the course around three experiences. The first culminated in writing a personal essay. On the first day of class, I read aloud a piece of children's literature, *The Adventure of Charlie and His Wheat-Straw Hat: A Memorat* (Hiser, 1986). This story was based on the life experiences of a midwestern author and was crafted so as to lend insight into our culture. I invited students to write their own personal narrative, encouraging them to write a family story and to select one that would give the reader a glimpse of what their cultural heritage was like. I followed this invitation by reading the first chapter of *Sarah, Plain and Tall* (MacLachlan, 1987), a seventy-page Newbery Medal book that tells the story of mail-order brides and their impact on the lives of two children growing up during the 1860s in America. After reading the first chapter, I paired up the class members and gave each a copy of the book. I told them to work their way through this book by reading a chapter and discussing with each other what interested them in the book. After they were finished, I suggested they brainstorm family stories they might write about. That evening they were to draft their family story, but only after they had telephoned one other family member involved in their story, so that they could bounce off their interpretation of the event with another knowledgeable person.

The next day they shared their drafts with their partners, revised them that evening, brought them back for editing the third day, corrected and formatted them the fourth evening, and turned them in for publication by the end of the week. The class publication entitled *Finding Our Roots* was a huge success. On Tuesday of the next week, we talked as a group about our stories—what we liked and didn't like about our first efforts.

The second strand of the course had really begun before the first one was complete. This strand culminated in the writing of a professional essay. To get it started, I chose three new, small books by authors from the United States (Goodman, 1986), England (Hall, 1987), and Australia (Cambourne & Turbill, 1987) on process reading and process writing. Each of these books is somewhat controversial in that each represents an individual author's attempt to summarize and interpret what process reading or writing professionally signifies. I asked students to pick a fight with these authors and to keep a log of "things that did not click or feel right" as they were reading. These notes or anomalies were to be the focus of discussion when the group met to discuss the book. Since I had purchased six copies of each of the books, there were six people in each group. Students read a book, discussed it the next day, selected a new book to read, discussed it the next day, and in this fashion worked their way through the readings. By the end of the experience, they were to have identified an issue and drafted a professional essay. This essay went back to the group, was revised, edited, and finally published and celebrated.

Whereas the personal narrative strand involved pairs of students working together and the professional essay strand groups of six students, the third strand—journalism—was less structured. Students could select whomever they wished to bounce ideas off of and share their progress and frustrations with. I acted as a resource, helping students find materials to read on Indiana stonecutters, stained glass, ballet—whatever; helping out-of-town students find artists to interview; and helping still others arrange transportation for a face-to-face interview (my only requirement) with whomever they selected to study. The intent of this project was to find out how persons whose dominant mode of operating was something other than language "came to know." This project, freely adapted from Vera John-Steiner's book, *Notebooks of the Mind* (1986), was to result in a newspaper piece or exposé on the artist for the local newspaper.

John McInerney, a first-grade teacher from Indianapolis, wrote and published a moving story entitled "Papa Doesn't Speak English" about his embarrassment and pride in being brought up Italian. He also wrote a professional essay on the insecurities of teachers wanting to move from product-centered to process-centered classroom called "Are We There Yet?" likening the journey into "whole language" to a trip in a '64 Ford Mustang convertible with "Hydro-matic" suspension. John used this trip metaphor throughout his piece. I loved his ending: "Sure, I stop for hitchhikers; I need people to talk to and they just might know the area pretty well. Sure, I follow other people's taillights; sometimes it's the only way to make it out of a fog. And, sure, there's times I just want this trip to end, but. . . Then I remember I'm driving a '64 Ford Mustang convertible with Hydro-matic suspension and I realize that getting there isn't half the fun; it's all of it!" (McInerney, 1987). His third piece was a newspaper byline article in which he interviewed a local boy who made good. John knew Dan Wetherbee as an altar boy. He is now a famous sound editor with the Cannon Film Group and has such credits as the movie *Back to the Future* to his name.

Jody Copenhaver, a first-grade teacher from California, also wrote and published three pieces. Her narrative, "As I Like It," told the story of growing up German and how she had helped her parents become "American." Later in life, she had the opportunity to travel and appreciate her heritage. When she returned home, she wanted to tap her cultural heritage only to find that her parents had learned the early lessons "too well." Her professional essay focused on her new understanding of theory as a result of having had the opportunity to "live the curriculum" in the summer course. Her journalistic piece was a newspaper article in which she reported on how actress Jane Marrow came to play the lead role in the production of *Noises Off*, a hit British comedy playing at the Brown Country Summer Theater. Jody's piece included a photograph of the artist being interviewed on the steps of the Fine Arts Museum on Indiana University's campus.

Susan James, a study skills teacher at a small college in Missouri, wrote a personal narrative about growing up in a rural community and how at 40, they gave their father a long desired bicycle. She also wrote a professional essay on how secondary school teachers might move toward a process curriculum, and a newspaper article, "The Heart of an Artist," about an Indiana stonemason.

"Bumper Crop," the personal narrative I wrote, tried to capture the influence of my midwestern mother on my life. Like Canadian author Alice Munro (*The Moons of Jupiter*, 1974), I tried to write the piece so that readers could see their rather mundane, religious, and generally good-sized aunts and uncles as stabilizing forces and influences on our society. In my professional essay, I tried to address what I saw as the anti-intellectualism embodied in what a colleague said to me at a recent convention, "Oh, I see you whole language types are having another revival meeting." For my newspaper article, I interviewed a very talented bricklayer.

I could go on. Suffice it to say that over the course of the summer, we explored how reading and writing might be integrated, came to see ourselves as authors, and learned to know and understand what it means to support our own and others' language learning. Testimonials given on the last day of class led me to believe that in each instance this experience would profoundly affect how these teachers taught their own classes when they returned to them. With their new knowledge about process reading and writing, they simply could not continue as they had previously done in the name of "teaching reading and writing."

During the last two days of the course, students took the walking-journal entries they had written and read them in an attempt to draw a semantic map of all the connections they had made between this course and their own teaching. Afterwards, groups of students got together to look for patterns across entries, share insights, and think about the implications of what they had found for instruction more generally. The final class session ran over its allotted time by two hours. During this period, students talked about what the experience meant to them and how they saw it affecting their instruction. Each of us was fascinated and found this sharing session extremely generative. No one wanted to stop. In fact, a group of students found the experience so supportive that they fashioned a study group on its design that met monthly and has continued to do so since the course ended.

Storying was a central construct in the conception of this course, and this was reflected in the focus on students' reading and writing personal and professional stories to share with one another. The sense of authorship was strong and the celebration of authorship was enthusiastic to the point of extending beyond the class. Stories like John McInerney's comparison of his development as a teacher with a trip in a convertible came to be widely read by people outside the class, and other publications were also enthusiastically shared with outsiders. The stories served to further stimulate the process of storying both inside and outside the class.

The actual reading and writing experiences were intended to support the process of intertextual tying. The students read sets of professionally published stories, such as the family stories, and discussed connections and disjunctions among them. They then wrote their own family story, making connections with those they had read as well as the others that were being written in the class. In the process of making these connections, the students were expanding their understanding.

Both the storying and the making of connections took place within a context of rich dialogue. Whether students were reading or writing, there were continual opportunities for dialogue. The reading of *Sarah, Plain and Tall* was done in pairs to allow the readers to talk to each other as they moved through the text. Drafts of writing were brought to a partner or a small group so that they could be discussed and different perspectives brought to bear, allowing each of the participants to enrich the reading and writing experiences of the others.

A strong sense of community developed within the class. The dialogue and the sharing of stories resulted in a shared commitment to the process of storying and to supporting each other in that process. The participants came to value their membership in the Readers' and Writers' Guild, some continuing to meet after the class was over and others sharing, with people outside the class, the impact of this experience on their writing and their teaching.

CONCLUSION

We began this chapter by characterizing conventional instruction in reading, the old view of literacy. What our three classroom language stories show is that, by applying what we currently know from literary theory and other fields, we can do much to have students experience a new view of literacy.

In each instance, we invited students to dialogue with text and with each other in terms of their own experiences. Whether it was the third graders making their own judgments about Caldecott books, eighth graders commenting on characters in a novel, or college students reading and writing family stories, they were all asked to utilize their personal experiences.

In each instance, we invited students to create their own stories by making a wide range of connection or intertextual ties. We saw sixth graders examining connections and disjunctions among Cinderella variants and then creating their own variant. We saw eighth graders dealing with elements of style that represented departures from those to which they were accustomed, and then using some of those elements in their own writing. And we saw college students making connections between professional articles and their own professional lives as they wrote their own professional essays.

In each instance, an interpretive community developed. A group of sixth graders dealing with war and peace came to a new understanding about the meaning of war and felt a need to share that with others. Within discussion groups, eighth-grade students felt free to share their knowledge and experience in coming to understand complex and controversial novels. And they, in turn, shared their understanding with family and friends as they talked about these books outside class. A group of college students experienced the feeling of being part of a supportive guild and enthusiastically shared with others both what they had written and what they had experienced.

Within these three classrooms, the what, how, and why of reading instruction was orchestrated to demonstrate what we believe it means to be literate. What was read was no longer a limited, standard set of texts. Instead, a wide range of materials was used, offering choices to both teachers and students. How reading was taught no longer reflected the notion that specific skills needed to be transferred from the teacher to the students. Instead, reading became a social event in which students supported each other in seeing connections and disjunctions. The goal was not to learn to employ specific skills, but rather to become strategic in approaching text and to come to value risk taking. The why of reading instruction was no longer to produce a correct reading, but to learn to use reading as a way to outgrow ourselves. The value of a reading was now the degree to which it caused the readers to rethink what they thought they knew — and grow beyond it.

This chapter represents our "reading" of this literature and three attempts to improve reading instruction given that reading. We invite others to interrogate this literature and dialogue with us.

CHAPTER 12

A LITERARY-RESPONSE PERSPECTIVE ON TEACHING READING COMPREHENSION

Patrick Dias

Reading and Literary Reading

Over the past two decades, reading in schools and colleges has become increasingly the concern of specialists in reading, a specialty somewhat removed from the concerns of "English" (or language arts) teachers with literary reading. Although such a separation of English teacher from reading teacher is a fact of life in many institutions, it remains as surprising a separation as that of English teacher from writing teacher would be. I am not gainsaying arguments for the specialist knowledge that is necessary to help pupils develop as readers and as writers; I am concerned rather that reading has drifted far too much away from a concern with literary reading—the reading and enjoyment of literature, a body of reading that in everyday living nourishes and develops the practice of reading and readers. Thus, for instance, the index to the authoritative first edition of the *Handbook of Reading Research* (Pearson, 1984) contains no references to literary reading, be it reading poetry, fiction, or drama. References to "story" appear only under "story content," "story grammar," and "story preview." There is one reference to literary analysis and that pertains to a one-page discussion of an insight from "literary analysis" concerning the locus of meaning: not in the text, not in the reader, "but in their

283

interaction" (Bloome & Green, 1984, p. 401). Even the chapter on understanding figurative language, rather than being an exception to the rule, is in substance and emphasis, symptomatic of the neglect of literary reading. The question it addresses, for instance, is "whether figurative language is an important source of comprehension failure (particularly, but not exclusively, for the beginning reader), and if so, whether such failures have to do with reading or reading-related skills, with extratextual factors, or with both" (Ortony, 1985, p. 453). If we look at another representative work in reading, the third edition of Singer and Ruddell's *Theoretical Models and Processes of Reading* (1985), we realize that this frequently cited work is similarly lacking in references to the reading of literature.

There are several explanations of why reading theory, research, and practice have not addressed themselves in any significant way to the study of literary reading. Such study may have been perceived primarily or even exclusively as the domain of literary criticism. Again, reading has developed as a field concerned primarily with helping individuals develop as *readers*, with beginning readers and their difficulties, and with "basic" processes in reading such as the processing of letters, words, and sentences and the ascribing of sound and meaning to words. Such inquiry has led directly to a concern with discovering those aspects of text that facilitate comprehension and those that inhibit reading and understanding. Thus, reading levels and readability formulas focus on text features, the readily observable and describeable aspects of text independent of what is known about readers and how they actually process texts. Meaning is seen as located primarily in the text.

I do not intend to disparage the work of reading researchers and theorists by ascribing a narrow or a wrong-minded focus to their endeavors. I wish to point out, rather, that literature has been largely excluded from their consideration. As an aside, I should also mention that the field of literary theory has until recently remained largely oblivious to reading theory and research.

There have been several recent developments that point toward an accommodation between insights derived from reading and those derived from literary theory; however, as I hope to show, such accommodation is problematic in several respects. In what follows, I argue that current reading theory and research tend to promote practices that are at odds with the attitudes and practices that are likely to promote literary reading. Moreover, some reading researchers tend to approach literary texts from a methodological perspective that is largely at odds with the nature of literary reading. In other words, literary text is often approached as though it were not much different from nonliterary text. I go on then to consider how current understandings of literary reading can inform reading theory, research, and practice in important ways.

APPLYING READING RESEARCH TO LITERARY READING: SOME PROBLEMS

While it is desireable that the findings of reading research should inform our understanding of literary reading, there are some problems that bring into question the general applicability of reading research to literary reading. Because most findings of reading research are based in the reading of nonliterary text, the relevance of such findings to literary reading cannot but be in question, and some caution must be exercised in determining how and to what extent such findings can apply to literary reading. I wish to identify three major problems that arise largely from the methodologies and contexts that prevail in much reading research.

Problem 1: Most Reading Research Occurs in Contrived Situations

Reading theory and practice have largely operated with models of reading derived from research conducted in situations that do not resemble contexts within which literature is normally read (Dillon, 1980). Story-recall experiments, for instance, are far removed from situations in which subjects actually read and respond to stories. To read in order to recall or in order to answer questions is to alter the act of reading in a fundamental way. What is even more unnatural is that a reader is expected to recall the story or answer questions for someone, the experimenter, who is already quite familiar with the story. Most reading studies have dealt with initial and usually one-time encounters with short, nonliterary texts rather than with comprehension and response as they develop in time and over several readings.

Moreover, the texts used in many laboratory-type studies of reading are often "artificial" materials especially written for the experiment, texts which Vipond and Hunt (1987) have labeled "textoids." Using actual literary texts in reading research, it seems, might complicate rather than illuminate searches for understanding of reading development and reading difficulties. Studies that are even marginally related to literary reading, such as the comprehension of metaphor, buy empirical validity by setting contexts outside the reading of whole texts and authentic literary texts. Ortony (1985), for instance, argues that "it may sometimes be necessary to construct 'artificial' materials so that the characteristics of the materials are known, rather than use naturalistic materials where it is much less likely that they will be" (p. 159). Such an argument does not recognize that "real" texts and "real" reading situations are so fundamentally different from laboratory texts and laboratory situations that we might not even speak of them as being on the same continuum, even if poles apart. Yet findings from such research continue to direct the reading and teaching of literature in schools.

Problem 2: Generalizing from Nonliterary to Literary Reading

The second problem lies in the tendency to generalize findings related to the comprehension of nonliterary texts to the reading and comprehension of literature. There persists a general emphasis in reading studies on developing instructional procedures and materials so that reading and comprehension are "guided" rather than allowed to occur via direct and unmediated encounters with "natural" texts. One such emphasis is apparent in the attempt to make texts comprehensible by adapting them to appropriate "levels" of reading ability; but there is some doubt that comprehension actually improves with the adapted text or that readers feel more positive about the adapted texts (Bradley, Ames, & Mitchell, 1985). There are other practices that spring from a similar concern for total comprehension, practices that involve, for instance, previewing the concepts and words that are to be encountered in the text or ensuring that readers bring relevant "prior knowledge" to the coming encounter (Smith-Burke, 1982; Tierney & Pearson, 1985; Vaughan, 1982). In my view, such procedures—previews, study guides, and the like—interfere in vital ways with the processes of literary reading. Although they direct reading to meet teacher-determined objectives and are often quite effective for dealing with unfamiliar text in social studies or science, they are not necessarily compatible with, and quite likely subvert, the reader's own strategies for making sense of literary text. They are likely to cultivate a passive, receptive attitude to text at the expense of an active effort after meaning.

The tendency to direct toward predetermined meaning is related to a fundamental propensity in reading research and practice to proceed as though meaning resides largely in the text. Teaching strategies, therefore, focus on making such meaning available to the reader, even though there has been a growing recognition of extratextual factors involved in reading comprehension. (For instance, the knowledge and expectations readers bring to texts determine to a large extent how they understand the text.) From artificial-intelligence studies, reading has appropriated notions of schemata, frames, and scripts to provide central importance to the reader's role in the making of meaning. A current and persuasive description of the reading process is offered by proponents of the "interactive reading process model," a view of reading that, while rejecting reading as a set of discrete subskills, proposes a process involving "a complex set of interactions between a reader and a text to derive meaning" (Ruddell & Speaker, 1985, p. 751). The components that *interact* are usually cited as the reader's expectations and knowledge (both world knowledge and procedural knowledge), the reader's situation, and the text itself. Despite such recognitions, recognitions that are entirely compatible with the major notions of reader-response theory, there remains a reluctance to give the reader full rein. The literary text remains largely the possession of the teacher, who might guide readers toward its one "true meaning." In this sense, reading theory and research still operate within the framework of a literary critical view (the "New Criticism") that prevailed from the mid-1930s into the 1960s and saw the "poem" as contained entirely within the text and not subject to the variables of reader and situation. It is just such variables that much reading research has sought to minimize; this has created, as I argued before, experimental situations incompatible with the act of reading literature.

Reading theory has moved considerably away from a notion of reading as information processing—for example, the serial, linear model proposed by LaBerge and Samuels (1974) or the model of reading as a process involving the interaction of a set of independent knowledge sources and "a message center" that allows these sources to interact (Rumelhart, 1979). However, for a reader-response theorist such as Louise Rosenblatt, even the notion of reading as an interactive process is far too mechanistic. "Interaction" suggests that the components of such a process are viewed as acting separately and distinctly on each other rather than as aspects of a total situation, a transaction (1985b, p. 105). Like Rosenblatt, I see reading as dynamic; the text is not a static entity; it represents, rather, possibilities of meaning—what Iser has called potential meaning, meaning that is activated by readers (Iser, 1978). The several aspects of the reading process that enter into a transaction are interdependent, changing, and being changed in the process.

To take a transactional view of reading is to allow greater play for the effects of situation, the readers' personal contexts, their purposes, as well as to assert that meaning is not permanently embedded solely in the text, or the situation, or the reader, but rather is a transactional product of all three aspects of the act of reading. It is also to remind ourselves that even if some texts are far more explicit in the potential meanings they invite, there is always sufficient ambiguity to adduce reader intention and situation as an aid to understanding. Reading theory certainly needs to consider the implications of Rosenblatt's transactional model of literary reading for reading theory in general. Particularly useful in this respect is Rosenblatt's (1978) distinction between "efferent" or non-aesthetic reading and "aesthetic" reading.

> In non-aesthetic reading, the reader's attention is focused on what will remain as the residue *after* the reading—the information to be acquired, the logical solution to a problem, the actions to be carried out.... As the reader responds to the printed words or symbols, his attention is directed outward, so to speak, toward concepts to be retained, ideas to be tested, actions to be performed after the reading.
>
> To designate this type of reading, in which the primary concern of the reader is with what he will carry away from the reading, I have chosen the term "efferent," derived from the Latin, "effere," "to carry away."
>
> In aesthetic reading, in contrast, the reader's primary concern is with what happens *during* the actual reading event.... *In aesthetic reading, the reader's attention is centred directly on what he is living through during his relationship with that particular text* (pp. 23–25, Rosenblatt's emphases).

I adduce Rosenblatt's distinction between aesthetic and efferent reading primarily to argue that reading research and practice often reduce the reading of literature to obtaining a product: facts, information, answers. "School reading," both literary and nonliterary, invites, on the whole, an efferent stance on the part of the reader. Rosenblatt contends that the individual act of literary reading is not necessarily entirely aesthetic or efferent but, at any one time, falls somewhere on a continuum between the two poles, depending on the reader's expectations and whatever happens to be the focus of attention. Rosenblatt's distinction draws attention to the fact that the reader's stance determines whether a reading is literary or not. One cannot simply enforce a literary reading; thus reading teachers need to be continually aware that the stances their pupils bring to literary texts are determined considerably by the contexts they (the teachers) create for reading in general.

Problem 3: Reading Theory and Instructional Applications

I have argued thus far that reading research has generated findings that are not necessarily applicable to literary reading and are often incompatible with it. Such findings lead to instructional practices that cultivate attitudes and strategies more likely to inhibit understanding and enjoyment of literature than to promote it. I shall describe two sorts of instructional practice that in their current formulations are at odds with promoting literary reading: (1) guiding reading to promote reading comprehension, and (2) practices related to developing independent readers of literature.

Guiding Reading to Promote Reading Comprehension. Within the traditional lesson intended to develop comprehension skills, the teacher often previews the reading and highlights difficult words. During the reading, the teacher usually provides pupils with a list of questions to think about and answer as they read. After the reading, the teacher generally has the pupils reflect on the reading by relating ideas one to another. While not all or precisely these activities occur in all reading lessons, they provide a representative profile, a representativeness borne out by the NAEP report, *Who Reads Best?* (Applebee, Langer, & Mullis, 1988) and by Tierney and Cunningham's survey of research in reading comprehension (1984). They claim that such activities not only aid comprehension, but also help teachers assess pupils' comprehension and provide incentive for further reading and inquiry. It is assumed that over time the reader will internalize the strategies implicit in such procedures and no longer have to depend on such direction. Although such procedures may work well with expository texts, I believe they are fundamentally at odds with the ways we ought to approach literature.

In the first place, such activities place control of the reading largely in the hands of the teacher. Most of the questions suggested for such activities in numerous handbooks on teaching reading comprehension imply there are set, correct answers that have been predetermined within a narrow range of meaning by the teacher or the author of the textbook. These questions suggest not only that meaning resides primarily or entirely in the text, but also that pupils should anticipate the kinds of questions generally asked by the teacher and read accordingly. To read to answer someone else's questions is not to read to appropriate the text for oneself. Such an approach inevitably relegates literary reading to the category of school-based activities, dependent on instruction and teacher monitoring to validate it. In such contexts, pupils cannot but read with a "question-answering" schema in mind, a schema derived from past experiences with teachers' questioning procedures, a schema that includes consideration of the subtle verbal and nonverbal cues that signal approval and disapproval. Such an approach is inappropriate for the reading of literature, for the reading of texts for their own sake, for reading to discover and consider one's own questions.

In other words, this sort of approach to literary reading invites, in Rosenblatt's terms, "efferent" readings. Pupils, already primed by questions, read to take something away from the text. Outside most school contexts, we read literature for the pleasure of reading alone. With a story voluntarily read, for instance, we define our own intentions and are not accountable to anyone else. It is our story to make of it what we will. We may enter into discussion and accept someone else's version of the "facts" of the story as somehow accurate; but our understanding of what those facts *mean* is not open so much to dispute as it is to negotiation. Such negotiation may involve merely exchanging responses to that story so that we recall, confirm, and modify our own responses in the light of what we have heard.

Even where researchers' intentions are to help pupils develop and use independently generic questions about a short story (e.g. Singer & Donlan, 1982), such an endeavor in literary-critical terms is primarily structuralist in orientation—a concern to discover and teach how texts have the meanings they do (Culler, 1975). The structuralist enterprise has in fact been overtaken by poststructuralist literary theory, especially reader-response theory, which posits a notion of literary meaning far more dynamic than structuralist procedures allow. In light of reader-response theory, reading theory and research ought to consider and promote reading practices that assign far more responsibility to readers for the meanings they make. Such reconsideration may well begin by moving teachers out of the central, directive role they often occupy in teaching reading comprehension, so that they attend more to the reader-text transaction.

Practices Related to Developing Independent Readers of Literature. The general goal in reading instruction, to develop independent readers, extends to the reading of literature as well. Unfortunately, when the approach to literary reading stresses instruction and guided learning, it tends to subvert the reader's role in the making of meaning. The concern to instruct inevitably leads to identifying the skills and content that somehow must be imparted. The reader's experience—what the reader brings to the text and how the reader experiences the work—is effectively devalued; it must somehow mesh with instruction that covers skills and content. There are two major difficulties with such an approach to teaching literary reading. First, the teacher assumes the central directing role. Because the teacher projects a belief in specific skills and a definite content that must be taught, student readers must eventually defer to the expert reader's experience and understanding of the literary work. Such a situation is more likely to cultivate dependence than to encourage autonomy in reading.

Second, the content of literary reading is viewed in the traditional terms of plot, character, setting, point of view, formal structures, figurative language, and the like. Direct and explicit instruction on such features is considered a basic prerequisite for an adequate understanding of the work and toward the development of independent reading. I believe, on the other hand, that plot, character, and setting, for instance, are continually constructed and modified as readers proceed through the text and from one reading of that text to another. Readers, through their various experiences and understandings of human behavior, construct and reformulate that complex set of ever-shifting relationships we too often reify and label *the* plot and *the* character. Rickword (1933) provides an early formulation of such an argument:

> ... the form of a novel only exists as a balance of response on the part of the reader. Hence schematic plot is a construction of the reader's that corresponds to an aspect of that response and stands in merely diagrammatic relation to the source. Only as precipitates from the memory are plot or character tangible; yet only in solution have either any emotive valency (p. 33).

I do not believe that children need to be taught to delineate plot and character; connecting events and attributing characteristics to human actions are a staple of their daily living, even though such perceptions founder in inexperience, misinformation, and misjudgment. The best teacher is experience, a variety of reading experiences with opportunities to talk with other readers about those experiences in order to make sense of them. Such a sense of the reader's central role is hardly new. Wolfgang Iser (1978) reminds us that already in the eighteenth century, Laurence Sterne was writing, in *Tristram Shandy*:

> ... no author, who understands the just boundaries of decorum and good-breeding, would presume to think all: The truest respect which you can pay to the reader's understanding, is to halve this matter amicably, and leave him something to imagine, in his turn, as well as yourself. For my own part, I am entirely paying him compliments of this kind, and do all that lies in my power to keep his imagination as busy as my own (p. 104).

It is unfortunate that young readers are not "complimented" enough by being allowed to assume a larger role in the making of meaning.

There are reading theorists and practitioners who advocate not the teaching of content and of skills so much as introducing readers to appropriate and productive procedures toward developing independence in literary reading. I discuss in what follows three articles from recent issues of the *Journal of Reading* that take such a stance; I wish to argue that even in this seeming move away from teacher domination of learning, there are fundamental misunderstandings of the nature of literary reading.

Moore and Moore, in "Reading Literature Independently" (1987), are concerned to demonstrate how independence in literary reading can be developed. They seek to train students' ability to ask the right questions about a text by providing them with a set of generic questions that will help them "interact independently with the contents of a passage" (p. 598). They suggest that teachers provide "psychological frameworks" (p. 599) that might help students interpret the actions of characters.

The goal of such procedures is to allow for independent interpretation within a clear structure. After students have sufficiently exercised such questioning strategies, the assumption is that they will be more likely to operate independently as discerning readers of literature. Eventually they will have acquired a routine. Somehow, reading literature is seen as applying a set of templates that will allow readers to define how the text operates. Implicit also in the procedure is the suggestion that readers practice on short passages before they proceed to whole texts. This emphasis on instruction in the ways and means of reading is clearly evident in statements such as ". . . teachers could demonstrate how they would go about deciding the most important sentence in a passage and then have students employ the same procedure" (p. 599).

Despite the concern in the title and throughout the article to develop independent readers of literature, the procedure operates from a set of premises that is inconsistent with the act of reading literature. The goals of "literature instruction" (p. 596) are classified under three headings: skills (skills for understanding and processing structures of passages, specific literary analysis skills), content (message, writer's ideas about the world, student's ideas about the selection, insights about life generated by literature), and experiences (the experience of living through the text). All these represent traditional goals for the teaching of literature and are offered uncritically. My point is that reading specialists who address literary reading need to keep pace with current developments in reader-response theory and literature teaching and to reconsider some of the practices they advocate in the light of such developments. Thus, when Moore and Moore advocate that students be offered generic questions so that they can learn "to interact independently with the contents of a passage" (p. 598), they offer as models such questions as "At what level of moral reasoning are the characters functioning?" (p. 599) and "What adjective best describes each character?" with a list of thirty-six adjectives to choose from (pp. 598–599). Such questions not only place severe constraints on readers' responses, they also represent a misdirecting of the aims of literary reading. The act of reading literature is reduced to one of finding answers to questions that are not one's own—even if they are eventually appropriated by the reader. Such practices, to use Michael Polanyi's terms (1958), tend to bring to "focal awareness" procedures (if this is what good readers of literature actually do) that should operate "subsidiarily" and "tacitly" if they are to produce meaning.

In another article in the *Journal of Reading*, Baumann and Ballard (1987) argue for a "two step model for promoting independence in comprehension." The example they provide is revealing because of the reductiveness implicit in the approach. Short stories have parts: a setting, a problem and goal, and a series of events that lead to an ending or conclusion. These elements help outline a "story map" (p. 609) so that pupils can understand the "critical elements of plot" (p. 609). Such an approach, like the notion of "character" advanced in the Moore and Moore article, reifies plot as existing apart from the reader's experience of the story. After modeling by the teacher (a process of reflecting aloud) and a procedure in which the teacher "guides, corrects, and monitors their work as they proceed through the story" (p. 610), students are given full responsibility for constructing the story map. Thus, the teacher has already projected the notion that there is *one* such map; their "independent" responsibility is to find it.

Chase and Hynd in "Reader Response: An Alternative Way to Teach Students to Think about Text" (1987) take a much fuller account of recent developments in reader-response theory in developing their approach to reading literary and nonliterary texts. They use small-group discussion to encourage sharing of ideas and information. However, when they provide an example of their procedure ("a reader-response technique with 5 steps and 2 tiers," p. 532), it becomes evident that the procedures are far more teacher-directed than they have made out. Students complete an "Anticipation-Reaction Guide" (p. 534), that is a checklist intended to access their own opinions. Appropriate activities are set out as well during the actual reading and following the reading. I find such suggestions overly directive in dealing with what seem to be relatively unproblematic texts. The readers are not as free to respond as the authors suggest; the focus is too much on completing preset tasks and exercises based on what they have read. That the authors recommend using the procedure with both literary and nonliterary texts seems to indicate that their focus is more on reading and comprehension than it is on response.

RESEARCHING READING AND RESEARCHING LITERARY READING

I have argued above that approaches to reading research are not necessarily compatible with the aims and processes of literary reading, and that this incompatibility brings into question the applicability of such research to literary reading. I wish to argue as well that some research on literary reading, however well intentioned and "rigorous," is just as much constrained by a narrow view of what literary reading is. One such study is particularly illustrative in this respect. Hillocks and Ludlow ("A Taxonomy of Skills in Reading and Interpreting Fiction," 1984) attempt to define a taxonomy of skills required in reading and interpreting fiction and to prescribe a set of questions that will help identify these skills. Seven question types are described and classified under two headings: literal questions, whose answers appear directly in the text, and inferential questions, whose answers do not appear directly in the text but can be inferred from information in the text. At the literal level, we have three types of questions: "basic stated information," "key detail," and "stated relationship" (pp. 9–10). At the inferential level of comprehension, we have four types of questions: "simple implied relationship," "complex implied relationship," "author's generalization," and "structural generalization" (pp. 10–13). The argument of the study is that these questions (and skills) are "hierarchical and taxonomically related to each other" (p. 22); so that "ability to respond to any level above type 1 subsumes ability to respond at the lower levels" (p. 14). This hypothesis is said to be borne out by the results of the study.

I do not wish to argue with the statistical procedures used to validate such findings; I question instead some of the major premises of this study, premises that are not atypical of the many reading studies that posit and seek to defend a view of reading ability as the sum of sets and subsets of reading skills. For me, the bolder premise of the study is an assumption that a failure to answer a question at one level (locate key details, for instance) predicts a failure to answer questions at the next higher level (locate stated relationship). My own experience is that readers are more likely to locate key details if they have arrived at some notion, even tentative, of the larger meaning that frames the text (Dias, 1987). And they have not *necessarily* arrived at that larger meaning by an explicit attention to "key details." As the reader, prospectively and retrospectively, begins to make sense of the text, some details more than others begin to assert themselves as central. The model of reading implicit in this study describes a rather passive reader who proceeds "bottom-up," in orderly fashion, from one substratum of meaning making to another. (See Holmes & Singer, 1966.)

Just as plausible an explanation for the results of this study may be that unless readers generate a working hypothesis, an explanation that will accommodate, however tentatively, the meanings that are called up as they proceed through the text, they are likely to fail at the lower levels of Hillocks and Ludlow's taxonomy as well. In other words, misinterpretations of or a failure to notice key details may occur from a failure to comprehend a particular word or phrase or from a failure to have a controlling grasp on the discourse as a whole. It is also likely that a particular hypothesis generated by the reader to account for the emerging details of the text may cause the reader to misinterpret or ignore certain key details. We are speaking, in other words, of a process in which there is a constant interplay between the whole and its parts: the larger contexts that a text suggests are themselves modified cumulatively by each new sentence that is read, and in turn help determine how the next sentence must be read.

I am positing, then, a view of literary reading in which the whole is greater than the sum of its parts, in which the reader's attitudes, experiences, and expectations determine the kind of selective attention given a whole variety of features a literary text offers and the meanings it affords. One reader's key detail may be another reader's superfluous or unrelated cue. Such studies are not inconsequential, for Hillocks and Ludlow (1984) go on to recommend that teachers "determine at what level students can work comfortably in interpreting literature in general and . . . guide them in dealing with the next higher levels. Working at two or more levels above student competence is likely to result in failure to comprehend and hostility towards literature" (p. 23). My contention is that hostility toward literature may arise precisely from such a structured view of the reading process, a view that limits readers by denying them the right to the very strategies (the higher-order strategies) that help them unlock meaning. Moreover, such a view works from a premise that meaning is largely resident in text, and that the reader's role is to draw from the information and key details the relationships, structures, and generalizations that are implicitly present in the text. Such a view of reading represents for those who look to reading theory for guidance in literary reading a bias that undermines the role of the reader and undervalues ambiguity (that a literary text affords several possibilities of meaning) and evolving meaning, and denies, to borrow from Barthes (1975), "The Pleasure of the Text" or its *jouissance* (Miller, 1975, p. vi). Unfortunately, such studies cater to a strong need among practitioners for evidence of sequence and development in literary reading, evidence that will point the way to programs of study. Thus, one attempt to translate the findings of research into effective classroom practice (Kahn, Walter, & Johannessen, 1984) cites the Hillocks and Ludlow study as one that helps "us identify some of the complex skills involved in interpreting fiction and has other important implications for designing instruction to help students master these skills" (p. 6). When we look at the approach suggested for teaching "The Chosen," a poem by Dorothy Parker (p. 43), we find that such an application involves providing, in order, seven questions, one at each level of the taxonomy. The stated aim of the activity is to "give students practice in interpreting authors' generalizations in literary works that are more subtle and sophisticated than fables" (p. 42). Apart from applying a taxonomy developed for the study of fiction to the reading of poetry (there is nothing in Hillocks and Ludlow's study to warrant such an application), the exercise suggests that the "author's generalization" is available in the text to be inferred by the reader. Thus, question 7 asks: "State the comment or generalization the poem makes about love or love relationships. Give specific evidence from the poem to support your conclusion" (p. 43). In question 7 and in some of the preceding questions, the definite article "the" suggests that there are specific answers available in the text of the poem. The message is clear: poetic meaning (at its highest level now equated with "poet's generalization") is resident in the text, and following a particular sequence of questioning will unlock that meaning.

READING AND LITERARY READING: AN ACCOMMODATION

My major concern in this chapter has been to demonstrate how some aspects of reading research, theory, and practice are generally incompatible with the aims and processes of literary reading. I now go on to suggest some lines of inquiry and action that might help bring about an accommodation between reading and literary reading.

Reading as Transaction

Reading theory and practice need to take fuller account of the notion of reading as a transactive rather than interactive process. Such a move might begin in speaking about reading in ways that enforce the notion that meaning does not remain fixed and resident in the text but is recreated in each new encounter with the text. What is recreated is dependent on the reader's background knowledge and attitude, and the context within which the reading occurs. No act of reading proceeds in predetermined set ways. At different times in a reading, readers may attend more closely to some features in the text than to others, a sentence here or there, or they may dwell on an experience evoked by the text or recalled by some chance association. Some readers may pay heed to the writer's stated intentions; others may be directed by the demands of their own agendas. Readers may differ also in their reliance on prior knowledge as opposed to depending primarily on the text. Each reading is in effect a unique rewriting of the text.

In much current discussion of reading processes, one sees implicit acceptance of such notions; yet these notions are not consistently held. A recent article, for instance, reviewing studies concerned with how readers comprehend important information in text, speaks of readers *extracting* important information from text, as though such information is a static entity in the text and its importance already predetermined (Williams, 1986). Frank Smith (1985) argues that we need to change the metaphor that frames our view of written language. He wishes to reject the conduit metaphor, the notion of language communication as transmission of information, the view of language "solely as the means by which information is shunted from one person to another" (p. 195). Those who write about reading need to speak in terms that are more attentive to the dynamic nature of that process.

Shifts in Approaches to Reading Instruction

To speak about reading as transaction is also to consider necessary shifts in the ways in which reading instruction proceeds. It is primarily the transmission model of reading, the notion that text is basically informative, that has ensured that reading-comprehension instruction must focus primarily on helping readers receive what is transmitted. The mechanical metaphor, strengthened by artificial-intelligence notions of the brain as information processor, must be shed. Terry Beers (1987) makes an interesting case for such a revision, suggesting a design metaphor: "Readers are no longer machines processing independent texts but designers of texts built from the raw material of the environment and guided by the dynamic conceptual schemata appropriate to their shifting goals" (p. 375).

Readers' roles in the making of meaning should not only be acknowledged, but also be more fully exercised. Teachers need to shed their roles as expert interpreters and become interested listeners of the interpretations of others. Comprehension should not be taught in isolation and as an end in itself; rather, it needs to be exercised as a means toward other ends, where strategies and the degree of understanding necessary are determined by the reader's focus and intention and not by seemingly arbitrary preset questions. Much more reading and discussion of reading should occur within small groups and in the pursuit of ends the groups have appropriated for themselves.

Such small-group work is particularly important where literary reading is concerned. It is within the security of a small group that pupils will be more willing to risk offering their personal interpretations. It is in small groups that they will learn to recognize the several possibilities of meaning that are made apparent by the reports of several readers. It is there that they will perceive the relevance of their lived experience to their reading. They might learn also to live with ambiguity and not seek "the one true meaning" that has so long been the prerogative of the teacher. Small-group work also helps considerably in making literary works as accessible and familiar as last night's TV episode. As teachers assign more responsibility to small groups for the making of meaning, they need, as well, to eliminate those instructional activities that proceed as though reading and understanding occur in sequences that move from literal comprehension to inferred meaning and from cognition to aesthetic appreciation. In literary reading, if readers are trusted to read for themselves, they will often have "sensed" meaning before they have made out the literal meaning of the text.

Aesthetic and Efferent Reading

I have said earlier that one cannot enforce an aesthetic reading. Because such a reading is determined largely by the reader's stance, teachers need to reconsider the contexts within which pupils are expected to read literary texts. Quite clearly, readings followed by weekly or daily quizzes do not invite an aesthetic stance. One might keep in mind what Susanne Langer has said concerning poetry and art in general:

> The entire qualification one must have for understanding art is responsiveness. . . . Since it [responsiveness] is intuitive, it cannot be taught; but the free exercise of artistic intuition often depends on clearing the mind of intellectual prejudices and false conceptions that inhibit people's natural responsiveness. If, for instance, a reader of poetry believes that he does not "understand" a poem unless he can paraphrase it in prose, and that the poet's true or false opinions are what make the poem good or bad, he will read it as a piece of discourse, and his perception of poetic form and poetic feeling are likely to be frustrated (1953, p. 396).

Langer describes attitudes and expectations toward literary reading that are not far removed from those engendered by the kinds of reading practices I cited earlier. It is, in Rosenblatt's terms, the "lived-through experience of the text," the "evoking" of the "poem" (p. 48), that is not allowed for and acknowledged in most classroom contexts. If such teaching must be undone, if those readers are to be freed from those "prejudices and false conceptions," they need to discover that an attitude of responsiveness, an aesthetic stance, is the first step in the direction of realizing a poem. It is my experience that such an attitude is best cultivated apart from any direct instruction and most conveniently within a small group discussion setting (Dias and Hayhoe, 1988).

Literary Reading as a Means
Toward Developing Readers

It may appear that I have been pressing for a clear division between reading and literary reading in order that practices developed for reading do not promote attitudes and stances that are incompatible with literary reading. I do not really wish to advocate such a division; I believe, instead, that reading capabilities would be enhanced considerably if literary texts supplanted the vast arsenal of texts that are now used to teach reading. In my research on response to poetry, I have obtained considerable evidence that reveals that the process of reading poetry calls forth a wide variety of strategies for making sense, strategies that are just as applicable to the reading of nonliterary texts as they are to the reading of literature. (Dias, 1987). I heard recently from one school district that has implemented a small-group procedure I have designed for developing independent readers of poetry. Their report not only supports my claims for the procedure, but also suggests that a class of reluctant readers using the procedure has shown considerable gains in its ability to read and make sense of discursive text.

I am arguing, therefore, that the increased use of literary texts (without the directive assistance that so much cultivates dependence in readers) will benefit both literary and nonliterary reading. Reading research will also gain from replacing artificial texts with real texts, and from a reconsideration of the situations within which texts are read. Other than naturalistic observation, a consideration of contexts should certainly include a study of how readers' stances affect reading. Above all, teachers need to come to value the affective and experiential aspects of reading as powerful keys to understanding literary texts (see Spiro, 1982). My emphasis throughout this chapter on the holistic and the experiential, and my insistence on nondirective teaching and assigning fuller authority to readers for the meanings they make, is not intended to merely complement or even counter-balance the mechanical, piecemeal, taxonomic approaches that now so dominate reading. I would suggest that complementarity is an elusive goal and that literary reading as understood by current developments in reader-response theory and research could provide not just the material but also the principles for major revisions of reading programs.

CHAPTER 13

WAYS OF TEACHING
LITERATURE

James Moffett

Like literary criticism, the teaching of literature varies according to whether one emphasizes the author, the reader, or the text. This is not surprising since these three parts or parties represent nothing less than the basic communication triangle formed by the first, second, and third persons (*I, you,* and *it*). So the fact that the criticism and teaching of literature seem parallel may owe no more to university influences, although these have often been very strong, than to the nature of discourse itself, which is characterized by interplay among a speaker, an audience, and a subject. Schools of thought in both criticism and education keep shifting focus from the meaning the author deliberately or unconsciously gives a work, to the meaning the reader awarely or unawarely takes away from the work, to the meaning the text may have independently of either author or reader by virtue of constants in certain structural relationships in language and symbols.

But literature differs, we feel, from other written discourse, though it may never be defined except in reference to a particular society. Poems, plays, and fiction — mythic, figurative writing — usually constitute what our society deems literature, but we often include in it certain essays, autobiography, and history — nonfiction — that are artful enough and profound enough to hold up across time, whereas we exclude some verse, plays, and fiction that we regard as ephemeral entertainment of no great creative value. So we seem to define literature partly by genre, partly by sheer quality. It is as if we expect literature to correspond to mythic and figurative writing but acknowledge that genre is no guarantee of creative discourse, which may crop up in other forms. Anything good enough may qualify as literature. *Moby-Dick* defies discursive classification. Thomas Carlyle's *The French Revolution* became a literary classic because of its ornate style and dramatic narrative rhetoric, which made it more than history (or less).

For school purposes, definition need not pose a serious problem anyway, since it seems best not to distinguish strictly between response to literature and response to other texts. All kinds of reading entail matters of comprehension and appreciation, and the distinguishing of one kind of text from another ought to remain an issue across various reading experiences, not seem to be settled in advance, precisely because the definition of literature is relative. That is, the *nature* of the text in hand should be something students think about all the time along with the *subject* of the text. Deciding what is literature is too basic a process to exempt students from. Why does one author pursue a certain subject in fiction and another the same subject in nonfiction? Or can we really say the subject is then the same? Why do the language and structure of some texts seem to have a life and purpose of their own somewhat independent of the subject? When is the interplay of author, audience, and subject not just communication but, well, *play*, aesthetic sport?

If literature existed only to be comprehended, we could regard "response to literature" as merely a subclass of "reading comprehension," since literature is only one kind of reading matter. But literature exists not only to be understood but to be undergone. So actually for literature the case is the reverse: reading comprehension is a subclass of response to literature. Meaning is only part of the story. Serious fiction, plays, and poetry, or certain essays and true stories, are meant to act on our whole being—to astonish, decondition, purge, exhilarate, or dismay us, for example. Some Ancient Mariner collars or charms us and puts us through an experience that makes us feel some of the same things real experience might. It is to these effects that the term "rhetoric" applies, to this acting on others through words.

If we want to call this experience that literature puts us through part of its meaning, that's all right so long as we acknowledge that this meaning of meaning goes far beyond common school notions of "reading comprehension," which can be tested by paraphrasing or by citing passages in the text for proof. The meaning of a literary experience cannot be "objectively" tested because it is not a merely semantic matter unless we apply "semantic," as Susanne Langer does, to all the arts. The cumulative and holistic effect of a great literary work is, significantly, nonverbal, like that of music, dance, painting, and the other "semantics." This is so partly because much of the meaning has the same experiential impact on us as in the other arts, but partly also because even the meanings in the ordinary sense can be so numerous, overlaid, and interwoven that their totality becomes *ineffable*, unutterable, as critics have said of *King Lear* and *Moby-Dick*.

By contrast, school efforts to teach and test "reading comprehension" constantly betray the assumption that texts have but one meaning and that anyone reading correctly will discover that meaning. Most current literary theory would vehemently denounce this. It is no doubt part of the very definition of literature that it means on several levels at once, intended or not, and that different readers will come away with different meanings, many or most of which may jibe perfectly well with each other. So the schools' conventional pedagogy for "reading comprehension" actually conflicts in part with the purposes of literature, for which the concept is ill-suited but which the concept of "response to literature" should include.

As I enumerate various ways of teaching literature that may be used in school—but too often are not—I will try to assess them as I go and at the same time suggest connections between pedagogy and criticism but without referring to literary schools by names. What is important are some principles and perceptions common to both.

Ways of teaching literature actually involve, besides reading, the other language arts—listening, speaking, writing, and, let's add, acting. In fact, one might proceed by grouping literature methods according to which language art predominates. But since actual classroom activities often combine them—or should—it may be more practical to start with some key questions of teaching method and then go to particular activities.

The first question I raise is often bypassed because the answer is assumed. How is the text chosen? By whom and what for? Whether an adoption committee, a department head, a group of teachers, a single teacher, a group of students, or an individual student chooses will make considerable difference in which teaching methods are possible. A basal reader series or high school literature series contains its own method—often in the form of a prep talk before reading and detailed questions afterwards. It is through these series that most American youngsters have become acquainted with literature. The comprehension quiz dominates commercial literacy programs that lead into literature programs and establishes a read-to-test mentality that begins with indifferent passages written just for the program and continues into the anthologies of literature by famous authors.

These programs or series are most often chosen by adoption

committees at the school, district, or state level, fairly political levels where rank-and-file teachers may not be well represented. In high schools, decisions are usually made in the English department, more or less autocratically or democratically, but choices may have to be made from a narrow range decided above. At both elementary and secondary levels, the critical choice of whether to buy a textbook series or sets of trade paperbacks or individual copies of trade books rarely falls to classroom teachers. Purchasing policies can rule in or out different teaching methods.

Let's look a moment at the most common school purchases, hard-cover textbook anthology series. Prepackaged literature curricula lock in a certain sequence of reading and a certain organization based on genres or themes or general social history or on periods, figures, schools, and influences. Here is where a prevailing theory of literature may exert great influence on the presentation of literature—and hence where structuralism or contextualism, for example, might skew the pedagogy, since it's not very feasible to build into such a package a variety of approaches, and since a personal-response or deconstructionist approach, say, does not lend itself well to predetermined organization. Actually, what filters down into textbooks, as with linguistics, is usually some concepts that are familiar and simplistic, that don't count on teachers knowing much about literary theory and can be easily formated.

Thematic organization preinterprets the texts, we note, besides tending toward moralism and truism. Chronological organization may teach history more than literature. Genre provides the most neutral and useful organization, since it can teach literary forms simply by giving examples of each while leaving subject matter wide open and sampling any number of periods, styles, and authors. Even literature arranged by types, however, leaves methods more open if the books are straight anthologies containing no directions, questions, or other pedagogical paraphernalia. Clean compilations organized by types of writing are the only sort of school books I have ever published. The less textbooks of literature differ from trade books, the better for teaching purposes. Selections may be arranged so as to bring out relationships among the types of writing, but the order of printing does not have to be the order of reading.

Because commercial publishers center on state and district adoption agencies, which are very political, they favor conventional thematic and chronological organizations and sanitize subject matter by anticipating censors' objections. Selections may be didactic and moralistic or include too many old chestnuts that parents can recognize and that teachers are used to teaching. Most literature courses in high school are nationalistic—American or British—or internationalistic—

World—and so have the mission of "covering" a corpus produced in a certain time span. Although this mission may actually leave open the means or methods, as I believe is the case in most schools, and may well not spell out which texts shall represent the various periods to be covered, once a course is embodied in textbooks, choices vanish. Buying curriculum in a package is asking for trouble. Though putting together reading materials locally, in a school or department, may be less convenient and can also be narrow, this approach avoids at least the severe strictures of corporate practices, which put, after all, other considerations ahead of education.

Text-by-text selection opens up more teaching possibilities, because texts are not locked in a certain way and interlarded with editor-written directions or interpretations embodying a particular approach. Moreover, when a group of faculty or an individual teacher puts together a syllabus, he, she, or they must think much more about their choices. Why this and not that? In what reading order? This makes teachers deal with some of the issues literary theorists take on, such as the nature and value of literature and what happens when authors write and readers respond. What experiences can or should students have with literature? And selecting texts while thinking about teaching methods then raises the issue of whether or when students should select texts.

The ultimate flexibility in choice occurs when students themselves are let in on just such deliberations by being permitted to make decisions about what they are to read, at first perhaps in small groups and then individually. Individualized reading enjoys more support in elementary school, where the chief issue is making readers out of students, than in secondary, where literature is singled out and made a sort of content subject like social studies and biology. This shift from student-centered to subject-centered characterizes the whole transition from grade school to high school and accompanies the fragmentation of the school day into specialized subjects, teachers, and locations. But if we are to aim for a complete array of ways to teach literature, we must consider individualized reading as possible in the later grades, when "literature" succeeds "reading." Individualized reading can be introduced into the more difficult situation of secondary school by preceding it with independent reading by small groups. The fact is that too many valuable teaching methods have not penetrated schools very much because they require that students play at least some role some of the time in choosing texts (which will then very often have to be in trade books).

Discussion of methods must consider not only who produces the texts and who chooses them, but also who, finally, interprets them. Just as texts may be chosen by groups of adults, individual teachers, groups of students, individual students, or some combination of these, texts may be interpreted for students by a community or individual teacher or by students themselves, alone or together. Indeed, many ways of teaching literature vary essentially according to who is interpreting and in what circumstances.

This preamble has been necessary to make sure that neither the choice of texts, the chooser of texts, nor the interpreter of texts is taken for granted. This openness makes available a full repertory of classroom dynamics that best utilizes the human resources on hand. Now let's look at the methods themselves.

PARTNERS TAKE TURNS SIGHT-READING ALOUD TO EACH OTHER, DISCUSSING THE TEXT ALONG THE WAY

At worst, such "reading groups" have been misused to let the teacher hear and coach individuals — to the boredom of peer listeners and to the mortification of the unaccomplished reader. For such checking and coaching, it is far better to run one-to-one sessions while the rest of the class is working in other sorts of small groups. At best, group reading can be a fine social way to read a text together, help each other, and check one's own understanding. Not now obliged to coach in this group session, the teacher can leave the group alone part of the time and sit in occasionally to role-model a good participant — take a turn reading aloud and take part in discussion without leading it.

The main point is that partners do collectively what individuals might do alone some time. They read the text while giving oral interpretation and personal responses in the form of spontaneous questions and commentary. Members are encouraged to read aloud as they imagine some person might speak the words but not to regard this as performing. Anyone may remark on the text while reading or while someone else is reading. These remarks may be about what the text makes them think or feel or remember, what they think is going to happen next, or what they don't understand.

Conversing while reading not only gives a text a social setting, but helps individuals pay attention to their inner responses when they are reading silently alone. This method externalizes and dramatizes the usually unnoticed stream of responses that goes on in us as we read. Pooling understanding spreads it, and hearing others' responses to a text stimulates one to think more about it.

This is a basic method that prepares for many of the other methods to follow here. How well it works depends, as with the others, on how involved students become with the text. Better if partners choose it or work out a choice with the teacher.

PARTNERS PERFORM A TEXT AFTER REHEARSING IT

This method may grow directly out of the preceding, combining as it does voicing and discussing of a text. While the goal is some kind of prepared performance, this activity should not be regarded as a specialty called drama, but as a staple process for experiencing *any* text. The point is not to perform only scripts, but to regard all texts as scripts, not to mount a few time-consuming spectacles, but to make possible many more commonplace enactments of texts. A group selects a text they already know or scouts and sifts for a text. Then members work up a rehearsed reading and render it, text in hand; or, more rarely, they memorize and stage a text. A group may perform live or record for others to witness later.

This method may begin like the first, as turn-taking sight-reading interspersed with discussion, the way professional actors run through a script before rehearsals. Discussion deals with anything from punctuation and factual references in the text to tone of voice and overall point or purpose. The effort to work out a just rendering forces participants to analyze and interpret the text as a self-contained creation, but this effort may also make performers feel they need to learn more about the context of the work. Some of the best textual discussion possible in school occurs in preparation for performing, because the practical goal and social means ground it, direct it, and motivate it.

Specific techniques have been developed for public theater and schools that students may be introduced to. In Story Theater, some participants mime actions while others read narration and others read lines of characters. Chamber Theater is a way of dramatizing any narrative by placing the narrator on stage amid the characters. Readers' Theater favors voice over action so that actors may hold scripts and concentrate on evocation through language. All three in fact dispense with stage trappings, permit rehearsed reading without memorization, and consider any kind of text as potentially performable. (For further treatment of these and related activities, see *Student-Centered Language Arts and Reading: A Handbook for Teachers*, James Moffett and Betty Jane Wagner (1983). The performing of texts works best when accompanied by related activities such as improvisation and the writing or adapting of texts to be performed.

Performing poems may well be the best way to study them.

Consider what is involved, for example, in deciding with partners how a poem is to be voiced, that is, lines or parts of lines assigned to single or choral voices and the whole orchestrated. Interpreters understand that a new voice may be used to represent any shift of time, tone, point of view, and so on, not just a changing of "characters." I have had adult students compile a collection of old and modern poems, discuss and rehearse readings with partners, and submit a final audiotape of the anthology.

A side effect of this method is that it results, precisely, in performances that others can witness live or on audio or video recordings. The effect can be a stunning knowledge explosion as whole classes become acquainted with works that some students have not read but that others have. Such dissemination alone would justify letting students work in small groups and choose different texts. This method also increases exponentially students' sophistication about textual interpretation and technical virtuosity in the literary arts. Performers study a text with both unusual involvement and detachment, because they have to enter farther in and stand farther back, draw more on personal response and yet objectify it so that their audience can understand what they have understood.

STUDENTS LISTEN TO AND WATCH PERFORMANCES OF TEXTS

A major way of experiencing and understanding texts is to witness both professional and amateur renderings. For a school program of independent reading that I once directed (*Interaction*, 1973), I persuaded the publisher to get some professional performers to audiotape some selections so that students could follow the text with their eyes while listening. This not only enables weaker readers to gain access to texts they are mature enough for but not able to read alone, but also brings out for good readers some depths and resonances of works of other eras that they might not otherwise attune to. I used to do some Shakespeare plays with excellent prep school students by just playing records or films of them and giving them a chance from time to time to comment or question between scenes. Sometimes they had read the text or were following it for the first time; sometimes they never saw the text. Professional actors make many footnotes unnecessary by rendering through voice and body much meaning that students could miss reading alone.

A literature classroom should allow for students to know the same text in different ways and different texts in different ways. But viewing and listening should always include interludes for spontaneous questioning and exchanging of responses. Performances can be powerful stimuli to accustom students to discussing texts. When performances of the same text contrast with each other and with one's own imagining of the text, students can see how widely interpretations vary. Performing oneself, and witnessing the performances of classmates, helps considerably to assess and appreciate professional performing, including commitment to an interpretation.

STUDENTS WRITE AN EXTENSION
OF THE ORIGINAL WORK

A fine way to enter further into a literary work is to make up scenes that were not in the original but that are consistent with it—a conversation referred to in a play but relegated to offstage, or an incident that could have happened given what a novelist, say, has already established about a character or theme. Parody is a form of extending a work that one has read. Students might agree to stop at a certain point in a short story or poem and write their own ending before knowing the author's. Or they might cast the text into another medium—adapt a memoir for stage or film, illustrate a poem or short story, rewrite a folk tale as a ballad (or vice versa), and so on. Many Readers' Theater scripts have been created by editing and splicing together excerpts from diaries and letters, transcripts, memoirs, documents, and all sorts of other texts so as to make a statement or connect disparate things thematically in a kind of collage. Sometimes the scriptmakers, usually the performers, too, write further text as introduction and continuity.

Any sort of extension might be written collectively by a small group as well as individually. That is, partners compose together one story, play, essay, or whatever by pooling ideas and taking turns scribing the ideas as they are contributed around the table. Composing and revising alternate in the same session. This process can naturally elicit perceptive discussion of texts as partners recall, interpret, and extrapolate the text together.

This is a more intuitive approach than writing *about* a text, though, like performance, it *entails* analysis. Such activities induce the perceptions one needs in order to have something worthwhile to say about literature and at the same time help make the perceptions explicit enough to verbalize. Imagining an extension to a text, however, allows the reader to parlay responses further along the same level of phenomena that the author created in. It is a way of identifying with and collaborating with the author.

MEMBERS OF A SMALL GROUP DISCUSS A TEXT WITHOUT THE TEACHER

Choosing or accepting a text they really want to read makes an enormous difference here. This method assumes that the group members are capable of reading a text at home alone and are interested in sharing their responses to it without having an immediate practical aim such as performing or extending, although those activities and reading aloud together will prepare for it. After choosing what they want to read, partners agree on a time to meet to discuss it. To facilitate discussion, they understand that they are to jot down questions that arise as they read and note down any other ideas or feelings or memories that the text stimulates. The teacher can role-model this when sitting in sometimes by giving personal responses as a fellow reader not as a senior person trying to make points about the text. In this way, the teacher can help students heed and value their spontaneous responses as a basis for sharing reading experience.

Questions can be about things students didn't understand or about matters they simply want to hear their partners discuss and give opinions on. A group might then want to ask the teacher what he or she thinks, or seek factual information about the author and context of the reading selection. Without the teacher leading or testing their comprehension, group members can freely admit any puzzlement or incomprehension instead of having an investment in hiding them, which ends by hiding uncertainties from oneself.

Such sharing validates subjectivity on the one hand, but also gives learners a chance to match it with others' subjectivity and so find out what is private and what is public. Comparing responses with peers is the best way to discover how differently individuals can interpret the same text. This difference cannot be shrugged off as a generation gap or a peculiarity of English teachers. Contrast is the great teacher, and peers are the perfect ones to do this sort of cross-teaching. Adult leadership in this case would spoil the process. The interplay of personal responses brings out consensus where it exists and the universality of some feelings and experiences. It directs attention to specific features of a text as partners explain the feelings or interpretations these gave rise to.

STUDENTS TAKE NOTES OF THEIR RESPONSES WHILE READING ALONE

This method consists of keeping a reading journal by jotting down as notes for oneself all kinds of responses to the text — memories, observations, feelings, associations. Such a journal leaves an ongoing record of reading experience that students often enjoy rereading later and sharing in various ways, one of which is to make reading recommendations to classmates if they've been reading different texts. An excellent activity for its own sake when students have acquired at least the beginning of the habit of reading silently, this will also provide rich material for the small-group discussion just described or for performing, extending, and otherwise dealing with texts. It can serve well whether students are reading the same text or going separate ways.

Students can discuss with the teacher and each other how best to capture responses in notes without breaking involvement with the text. Actually, consciousness of responses can increase involvement. Reading can strongly stimulate the mental life, but students are so habituated to anticipating oral or written tests after reading that they ignore their own responses in order to concentrate on what they think they will be asked. Constant comprehension quizzing engages students' minds more with authority than with the text. This backfires because when asked to interpret or play literary critic for themselves, students then have little to work with; the personal insights and connections that would make for interesting criticism have been repressed beyond access. Ongoing reading notes raise responses to awareness, fix them for later retrieval, and establish a habit to counteract the amnesia caused by incessant comprehension testing.

With teachers themselves, I have tried an interesting variation on the journal that actually might be a good way for students to prepare for keeping one. I photocopied a number of poems, essays, and stories that I thought they would find stimulating, leaving an unusually wide margin around the text on each page in which they could note down their responses to specific passages. This annotation could include underlining, circling, arrowing, linking, and any other graphic way of indicating reactions besides verbal notes. In the case of my class, a composition course, all these annotations became fodder for their own writing, with the understanding that they did not have to write about the text as such but about ideas prompted by the text (another kind of extending). They chose one text at a time, by the way, from the dozens I gave them to pick among.

Students need not annotate a text for composition purposes only, but also for the same reasons they would keep reading journals. Some experience annotating special wide-margin copies will no doubt help to keep responses specific and anchored to particular items in a text. This is an especially useful method for poems. (In an undergraduate course I was fortunate enough to take with Archibald MacLeish, he had us keep notes on our responses to every poem we read in the full-year course, and he read these notes and responded to many of them.)

Reading responses don't just pertain to reading. They constitute an invaluable part of a student's mental life and can be used not only to enhance comprehension and appreciation of texts but to fuel thinking, talking, and writing on the many subjects to which reading experience contributes.

THE TEACHER LEADS DISCUSSION OF A TEXT BY QUESTIONING STUDENTS AND PARLAYING THE RESPONSES

This method presupposes that a whole class or some subgroup of it has read a text in common (or heard or seen it performed). The size of the group makes considerable difference, since the larger it is, the less each individual can participate and the less each can influence the direction of discussion and maintain interest in it. Teacher-led discussions can serve to establish models for thoughtful interaction, but the more the activity centers on the teacher, the more difficulty will students have eventually learning to discuss on their own. This is a method that teachers do very differently. Results vary from very positive to very negative.

I used to enter my secondary-school classroom armed with a list of what I thought were penetrating questions that would lead students to the heart of the story or poem or play. My students, who were very bright, seldom let me finish the list, because their answers pulled us in directions I had not foreseen or advanced prematurely by another route to my climactic questions. I had to adjust my list so much that I finally took to just playing to their responses as the best way to further their understanding of the text. Teachers who lead discussions of literature usually want to monitor comprehension or provoke thinking beyond what occurred during silent reading. But if they prepare questions to which they feel they know the answers, students try to guess what they have in mind and don't think for themselves. They bypass their native responses, which are what needs to be worked with if they are to develop. They look to the teacher for the definitive interpretation and learn that literature has right answers.

One possibility is for the teacher not to prepare a list of questions but to ask a few open-ended questions or simply ask for responses to some event or character or passage in the work. This sets up the chief learning activity, which is the parlaying of initial responses into a rich interaction of ideas and points of view: both the teacher and the students ask follow-up questions in response to responses. This refines thought and feeling and sensitizes participants to the *totality* of cues in a text. Connections thicken.

As teacher, I would play my own opinions into the discussion only to the extent that I felt this would not short-circuit students' thinking or close down discussion. If my students had acquired a lot of experience with the activities described before, they would probably be able to consider my personal observations as just so many more stimuli for their own thinking without feeling they had to hew to a party line. But this is a delicate issue, and teachers used to an authoritarian role or simply prone to asserting their own views may easily deceive themselves about what is beneficial for students.

If students feel free to ask questions of the teacher, on the other hand, the teacher's expertise might be drawn upon in valuable ways. They might, for example, feel that more biographical or historical background would add interest or understanding to the text. Or they might feel puzzled about something in a text that discussion has not resolved and want to know if the teacher can satisfy their curiosity.

THE TEACHER LECTURES TO STUDENTS ABOUT A LITERARY WORK

In the wrong hands, this method could be fatal to the independence of student thought, especially if it were the only or nearly only method used. But let's consider the possibilities even though the method has been much abused. Let's assume, first, that it's only one of several or many methods in the teacher's repertory and so is not a routine activity forcing out the others described here. Suppose also that students have had the previous benefit of those activities described before that foster peer learning and independent judgment.

Some lectures situating a literary work in the life of the author and his or her society and literary traditions might be welcome and valuable if students are truly interested in the work. Courses surveying American or British or world literature may make such lectures even necessary to the extent that such courses are predicated on cultural continuities or on structural connections between works of different periods and cultures. The use of lectures to present more or less factual context need not risk preinterpreting the texts themselves, though that can easily happen, or at any rate can give a historical or technical emphasis to literature that students may believe to be what they should cleave to.

A more serious danger arises when lectures consist of direct interpretation through close textual analysis. Such explanations can easily cause students to leave meaning to the teacher and just memorize the given interpretation until the test is over. But even an *explication de texte* by the teacher can actually help develop independent interpretation if done only occasionally as a sample of how close textual attention can enhance understanding and enjoyment. For such exemplary performances, the teacher would do well to choose a text students themselves are not working on and make the lecture a good show — do an expert job on it and ask nothing from students about it then or later. Make it a gift. Such a lecture becomes strictly a learning aid, a demonstration of possibilities. To increase its value, however, the lecturer might allow students to ask questions about anything in the text or the analysis of it.

Seeing what an expert can see in a text may well increase what a student can see the next time she or he reads. An astute analysis by the teacher may show specifically and memorably just how diction in a poem or point of view in a short story or juxtaposition of scenes in a play can convey meaning. A very few such performances scattered over the genres could considerably enrich student responses and sharpen comprehension. A teacher might also use such lectures to illustrate various basic literary critical approaches — emphasizing in turn, for example, social-political context, textual independence, archetypal structure, deconstruction, and so on, without necessarily naming the approaches or introducing special terms. Occasionally applying such approaches to the same text would especially contrast them and could help remind students that no single interpretation, no matter how brilliant, exhausts a text or rules out other lines of perception.

Finally, students themselves may work up their own interpretation of some literary work and present it to the class, in some cases supplying as well some background information of a biographical or social nature. The text could be one familiar to the class or one the student lecturer presents in some way as an opening.

STUDENTS WRITE ESSAYS ABOUT LITERARY WORKS OF THEIR CHOICE

The preceding activity can prepare for this one and might sometimes constitute an oral draft for it, especially if classmates and the teacher discuss the lecture afterwards. Because writing literary criticism is difficult and requires unusual motivation, it may be especially important that students choose the works they want to write essays about even if they're only choosing from a required reading list. It would be much better if they chose a work not assigned in the course, one that means something to them personally.

One way to ease into formal essays on literature is to write first about personal meaning, perhaps by making connections between the experiences of characters in a novel or play and some experiences of oneself or people one knows and observes. Reviews provide familiar examples of an excellent sort of literary criticism that also bridges from personal essay about one's reading to formal analysis. By way of assessing a performance or text for a consumer audience, students can write reviews on the models of those in periodicals. These often include background information, story summary, analysis of technique, comparison with other works on the same theme or in the same mode, and appraisal of the work leading to a recommendation.

At some point, many students might really want to take a literary work that attracts them strongly and do an all-out interpretation of it, replete, where pertinent, with close textual analysis, social background, and comparison with other works. This gives young people a chance to share their perceptions and show others what this work means to them. But even the very advanced prep schoolers I taught did not like to write frequently about books. Using literary critical writing as a way of testing literature does a disservice to both literature and composition. Essays on literature should come only after much experience with the other activities described earlier here and should be done only occasionally, not routinely. Ideally, they would be expressions of strong and honest interaction between a book and a student after discussion, performing, extending, and other more implicit ways of studying literature have had plenty of opportunity to develop students' literary sensibility and ground it in independent judgment.

STUDENTS WRITE IN THE LITERARY FORMS THEY READ IN

This is a long-range method—hardly less than a total curricular approach. It means that in addition to writing extensions of literature and writing about literature, youngsters write literature itself, at least in the sense of practicing fiction, plays, poetry, autobiography, and personal essay. Without setting up a mechanical correspondence, teachers can arrange for students to read and write in a certain form at about the same time. To write in traditional forms like fables, parables, limericks, and haiku, one indeed must read some examples first. But this is really necessary for all kinds of writing, not perhaps to get a definition of the form, which may be very common, like the short story, but to discover the possibilities of it and how professionals make use of it. We needn't get into strict "model writing." The point is to immerse oneself in reading of the sort one is trying to write— investigative journalism, memoir, poetry, how-to, or whatever.

All the professionals do this. One reads more perceptively and writes with a better grasp of techniques in that form. Students who have made up dialogue understand better what Shakespeare and Ibsen are trying to do in a certain scene or concatenation of scenes. Just as writers must role-play readers to compose well, readers must role-play writers to comprehend well. Many artful things a playwright, novelist, or poet does are wasted on readers too passive to notice what these literary craftsmen are doing. This loss affects not only comprehension, but the impact and import of a work. Writing in the forms one reads obviates a lot of formal analysis that would otherwise be necessary to call most students' attention to textual dynamics that should be affecting their responses. Along with most of the other methods set forth here, this one affords an alternative to the vivisections and postmortems on texts that have turned so many youngsters against the study of literature. Their instincts rightly tell them that literature is not written so much for cerebration as for celebration. (Thinking, yes, but in the mythic, figurative mode.) Because this last method can apply to a whole course or curriculum, as a principle for relating reading and writing, it may in the long run attune students more than any other single method to what is happening in a piece of literature.

Students need to experience eventually all the modes of discourse and all the literary types and become sophisticated about what forms in fact exist and how they relate to each other. Literature is better understood in the context of other discourse — nonfiction, scientific, utilitarian.

To conclude this summary of methods of teaching literature, let me make a few observations on the relation between this pedagogy and literary criticism. Is it necessary to teach theories of literature and introduce the concepts of various literary critical schools? Well, to do justice to the numerous movements of today would require a course in itself. Can we justify taking time for it away from literary works themselves? To limit students to one literary school of thought is arbitrary. No teacher has a right to bias students' education, especially since directions of thought in literary theory really amount to fundamental philosophical, even metaphysical, positions.

My experience has been, moreover, that youngsters will pick up the jargon and approaches of a literary theory and feel modish but substitute those borrowed terms and concepts for their own responses, which can remain undeveloped beneath the glamorous patina. The brighter the student, the more serious this problem may become. Students will learn more if they have to cast about for their own terms and concepts for what they perceive. Even old, apparently innocuous academic descriptions like plot, character, and theme usually prove more of a liability than an asset by stereotyping thinking if taken too seriously.

Insight into literature will be better served if students unwittingly recapitulate literary theories through their native efforts to engage with works in the variety of ways outlined here. These methods shift emphasis around from text to context to subjective response just as competing literary schools do. If the theories asserted in the various literary movements are worth their salt, students will recapitulate them in some form as they work with literature from the varied stances entailed in these ten methods, which do not derive from any particular theories but accommodate all.

Now, although a teacher may, when participating in discussions with students, feed in ideas from these theories so that they are all eventually absorbed into the classroom culture, it is unnecessary to teach them systematically, replete with rubrics and respective terminologies. But it does follow that the best literature teachers would benefit from knowing something about the various schools of literary criticism, which, if nothing else, at least show us all the ways in which literature can be thought about. This eclecticism should very much help a teacher lead these ten methods, which foster pluralistic, multidimensional responses to literature, in keeping with the holophrastic nature of literature itself, whereby a single set of words speaks simultaneously on several levels at once.

Theorists differ in emphasis on the writer's processes, the internal integrity of an artistic text, or the reader's responses. Some feature the meaning the author intended, some the self-contained meaning of the text as a thing in itself, some the archetypal meaning that works remote in time and space share because of certain universal structures they share, some the meaning that individual readers find for themselves, some the skewed meaning that the culture surrounding the work has imbued it with, and some the unconscious meaning that constitutes a secret text within a text—or an infinite regress of such texts. All these meanings can be present in a single literary work. So most texts offer opportunities to come onto all these meanings or viewpoints if the teaching methods themselves rotate students among all of the discursive stances generated by the wheeling trinity of persons.

CHAPTER 14

READING AS DISCURSIVE PRACTICE
The Politics and History of Reading
Robert Morgan

No "theory," no "practice," no "theoretical practice" can intervene effectively in this field if it does not stress the frame, the invisible limit of (between) the interiority of meaning . . . [and] all the empiricisms of the extrinsic. . . .

Jacques Derrida
Le Parergon

STORIES OF READING

There are two common twentieth-century stories of reading. The first stresses the reader. Its plot centers on a reader who enters an unknown text like Huck Finn lighting out for the territory: pure individuality divorced from social circumstances in search of self-definition. Eventually, and with luck, this reader-hero retrieves from the wilderness of

---

This chapter is dedicated to Philip Corrigan, inspired teacher and generous friend, who has constantly supported and challenged my work over the past five years.

words either a distilled "message," an apprehension of "total form," or a phallic "point." In current pedagogical versions of this fable, the reward for this feat is invariably described as "self-realization," "personal growth," or "self-understanding," that is, the message is somehow always about the reader's own self.

Reader-response criticism is a variation on this narrative, since underlying its approach is an epistemology that stresses human subjectivity as the condition of knowledge of texts. Catherine Greenfield (1983) puts it this way: "Readings pursued within different epistemologies . . . yield different ontological figures as the conditions of the texts whose origins these readings purportedly trace" (p. 132). Reader-response approaches, in other words, find in texts what they invest in the first place—the figure of a timeless human subject. The cataclysmic shift during the second half of this century of literary meaning from authoritative texts and master readers (i.e., teachers) to individual student readers, and the widespread proclamation of readers' rights have, in reality, done very little to displace reading from an economy of possessive individualism. As Jane Tompkins (1980) points out, the belief that literary activity chiefly consists in individuals unearthing or producing "meaning" is still the "only game in town." Yet the triumph of the psychologized and isolated reader might better be seen as a form of alienation parading as a positive value. It is merely, she suggests, the debased version of aesthetic literacy after its historical severance from more integral relations and vital connections to civic life (pp. 218–225). In this regard, it is revealing that reader-response approaches rarely raise to visibility the authority relations and political values within which literary texts are circulated and consumed in schooling. Rather, classroom approaches concentrate on the interaction between isolated *text* and individual *reader*, rarely going behind this dyad to problematize either of the privileged terms, to question, for example, what makes a particular set of books visible as "literary" and subject to a pedagogical construction as classroom "texts" in the first place. Literary reading within schooling, then, has largely remained within the Arnoldian settlement of literature as a "culture of the feelings," a mode of pedagogy originally conceived of as an explicit and indirect—but by now an unconscious—form of cultural politics (see Baldick, 1983).

The second story of reading shifts the focus to the text and the operations of language. Its plot is one in which the reader peers Buddhistlike into a text and discerns there "all the world's stories" rolled into one (Barthes, 1974, p. 3). Yet, gazing deeper, the reader discovers that to read is not to exist at all; rather it is to endlessly become. "Reading" here is but another name for forgetting, a continual bloodletting of ego. For Roland Barthes (1975), reading is interesting precisely because "it wounds" (p. 38).

To read is a labour of language. To read is to find meanings, and to find meanings is to name them; but these names are swept towards other names ... I name, I unname, I rename: so the text passes: it is a nomination in the course of becoming, a tireless approximation, a metonymic labor. ... Yet reading does not consist in stopping the chain of systems, in establishing a truth, a legality of the text. ... [Rather] I pass, I intersect, I articulate, I release, I do not count. Forgetting meanings is not ... an unfortunate defect in performance ...: it is precisely because I forget that I read (Barthes, 1974, p. 11).

Or, in Margaret Atwood's gothic formulation (1983), readers only experience "the full horror of the journey into the page" when they discover that what appeared to be an inviting narcissus pool in which they caught a glimpse of a familiar face ("their own but better") is in fact a bottomless pit. This realization always comes too late, at the very moment when language "closes over their heads without a sound, without a seam. ..." In the end, Atwood's page is not so much "a pool" for our reflection "but a skin," and it is the reader "who [is] blank and innocent, not the page" (pp. 44–45).

This is the poststructuralist account of reading, a version that writes the obituary not only of the sovereign reader (Barthes's shift above from an active, naming reader to one dis-counted and dis-composed by the reading process), but of reader-response approaches as well. It does so because it shifts our attention from psychologized readers and individual acts of interpretation to the public systems of coherence that underlie any activity of interpretation, i.e., to language and institutions (see Freund, 1987, pp. 77–89). The same system of practices (linguistic, pedagogical) that constitutes a particular book as a "literary text," and places it before me, also extends to and energizes the act of reading, making me a "reader" of a particular kind.

There is a problem with both these models of reading that my parody of them was intended to highlight. In the reader-response story, the reader's experience and meanings are the privileged objects of inquiry, whereas in the poststructuralist version, the analytic focus shifts to the narrowly textual and formalistic operations of language. The dichotomy in such positions is characterized in my opening quotation by Jacques Derrida as a choice between meanings found within the covers of a given literary work, on the one hand, or meanings originating from the extratextual and pragmatic frameworks of reading, on the other. While the poststructuralist position tends to concentrate on "the formal properties of texts at the expense of the varying social and ideological relations of reading through which the consumptions of those texts is organized" (Bennett & Woollacott, 1987, p. 6), reader-response approaches, apparently attuned to the prag-matic considerations and responses of real readers, still leave un-theorized conceptions of "text," "reader," and the discursive nature of reading. Similarly, David Morely (1986) has complained that "questions of interpretation and questions of use" (p. 13) have been treated separately in cultural analysis up until now. In this chapter, an attempt is made, therefore, not only to question the validity of these traditional approaches to reading, but also to suggest an alternative framework that transcends such binary oppositions and the subject-object disjunction that they preserve.

THE IMPLICATIONS OF FOUCAULT'S CONCEPT OF DISCOURSE FOR A THEORY OF READING

My own approach to reading depends upon the Foucaultian concept of "discourse" as an institutionally orchestrated set of statements[1] (see Foucault, 1981; Macdonell, 1986). By "discourse" Foucault does not simply mean just speech or writing; rather he points to the totality of socially constructed relations in any society, both linguistic and nonlinguistic. Social actions, words, and objects, even supposedly innocent "natural facts," are never encountered bearing their significance stamped on the surface. Instead, they acquire their meaning from their location within constantly shifting but historically determinate relationships; it is this systematic set of social relations that confers significance, which is referenced by the term "discourse."

Since such relationships are always constituted within the context of human activity, it is perhaps more useful to employ the concept of "discursive practice." Any discursive practice, according to Foucault, consists of three elements: "the delimitation of a field of objects, the definition of a legitimate perspective for the agent of knowledge, and the fixing of norms for the elaboration of concepts and theories" (1977, p. 199). These three interdependent aspects, then—a social actor with a particular orientation, a field of objects or partitioning of the material and conceptual world, and a normative and regulated set of interchanges between these two—characterize any discursive formation and embody the power relations of a society. Because the social world at any given moment is made up of a number of discursive regimes (many of which not only reinforce, but also actively compete with and contradict each other), "no discursive totality is absolutely self-contained . . . there will always be an outside which distorts it and prevents it from fully constituting itself . . ." (Laclau & Mouffe, 1987, p. 89). All these conceptions, including the basic instability and precariousness of discursive regimes, can be applied to the act of reading.

I would note first, however, that the concept of a discursive formation is incompatible with the reading paradigms touched on before. In particular, Foucault's approach breaks with a conception in which language "represents" either a prediscursive reality or "expresses" thoughts and feelings separable from the material processes of signification (Foucault, 1978; Morgan, 1987b). It also distances itself from the cognitive basis of most pedagogical accounts, which hierarchize acts of reading as more or less "correct," "mature," "insightful," etc. Moreover, in drawing attention to the contingent and socially constructed character of reading practices, a discursive approach underlines the historicity of reading (see Ross, 1987; Darnton, 1987), that is, it grasps reading as a constantly changing form of cultural production.

The analysis of the texts of popular culture by Tony Bennett and Janet Woollacott (1987) serves as a model of what a historically informed discursive approach to reading might look like. Significantly, they begin by rejecting the customary division between "intratextual" and "extratextual" accounts of reading, turning their attention instead to the historically variant "reading formations in which [books are] constituted as objects-to-be read" (p. 64). By a "reading formation," they mean

> those specific determinations which bear in upon, mould and con-figure the relations between texts and readers in determinant conditions of reading. ... [Thus] the text that is read, according to such a conception, is an always-already culturally activated object just as, and for the same reasons, the reader is ... [a] culturally activated subject. The encounter between them is always culturally and ideologically and ... inter-textually organized in such a way that their separation as subject and object is called into question (p. 64).

The relations that hold between texts and readers, therefore, are never pristine encounters, but are subject to definite forms of social organization and mediation "by the discursive and inter-textual determinations which, operating on both, structure the encounter so as to produce ... texts and readers as the mutual supports of one another" (p. 249). If we follow a discursive approach to its conclusion, they suggest, we find that "there is no fixed boundary between the extratextual and the intra-textual," nor any inherently literary text, only "[d]ifferent reading formations ... [that] produce their own texts, their own readers, and thier own contexts, not to mention ... their own authors" as functions of a particular discourse (p. 263).

Crucial to the production of a text's meaning, they argue, is the role played by "textual shifters," that is, those collateral texts that are brought to bear upon a text at a given historical juncture, causing it to be read and relayed within a specific cluster of interests (pp. 235–249). In the case of the texts of James Bond, for example, they demonstrate how the transformations of this mythic figure were effected in his disparate representation in a host of parallel texts: films and film reviews, literary criticism, the star constructions of Sean Connery and Roger Moore, interviews, forms of publicity, and the like. Kept alive between these various textual incarnations, Bond functioned as a key cultural signifier by means of which a whole "series of ideological adjustments and readjustments [were] proposed, and, in part, effected" in the relations between East and West, in the imagery of English nationhood, and finally in male constructions of sexuality and gender (p. 278). Textual shifters, therefore, operate

> alongside the other components of the reading formation . . . to organize *the relations between texts and readers.* They do not act solely upon the reader to produce different readings of "the same text" but also act upon the text, shifting its very signifying potential so that it is no longer what it once was because, in terms of its cultural location, it is no longer where it once was (p. 248, emphasis in original).

There was, in short, no primary, essential, stable novelistic James Bond, since the same text varied enormously "through time and from one context of reception to another" as it was "constituted as a text-to-be-read as a result of its insertion within differently organized social and ideological relations of reading" (p. 248). They conclude that it is necessary, therefore, to abandon the fiction that "texts, in themselves, constitute the place where the business of culture is conducted" (p. 59); rather they must be seen as sites across and between which various struggles for meaning are conducted, struggles that are always discursively articulated.

This conception is especially pertinent to education since textual shifters in the form of state-sponsored "guidelines," other books on an English course, the biographies of authors, always draw a given text into a particular ideological orbit, making it speak to and through one group of cultural concerns. As such, they constitute a subtle means of reorganizing the preferred reading relations of schooling, priming a book for one kind of reception (e.g., literal, moralistic, patriotic) against other possible uses of the same text. The implication of Bennett and Woollacott's work for a politically conscious and critical pedagogy of reading is the need to attend to the "inherently relational nature" (p. 265) of reading practices, the fact that officially endorsed protocols always exist in tension with other, competing, yet unstated methods of producing meaning. Despite the advance their contribution represents in formulating a politics of reading, their major weakness is a failure to adequately theorize the institutional matrix within which the practices of reading are first formed and take much of their subsequent shape.

TECHNOLOGIES OF READING

Here we can turn to the work of Ian Hunter (1982). Like Bennett and Woollacott, Hunter is concerned to displace the authority of texts and readers in favor of Foucault's conception of discourse; he too has no time for such questions as "What makes the good reader?" since reading is located within a discursive regime that constitutes both text as an object of knowledge and the reader as consumer or activator of those texts. His particular interest, however, has been to foreground the *pedagogical protocols* that constitute the reading experience, the operations we carry out, the rules we follow under the label "reading" within an institutional context. For Hunter, readers are produced by their insertion within a particular "discursive technology" embodied within schooling by mandatory exercises, homework questions, apparently open-ended whole-class discussions, regular examinations—in short, all the practical pedagogic surfaces that characterize a discourse at the ground level. In a brilliant analysis of an ee cummings poem, he demonstrates how, not only its meaning, but its very status as literature is constituted and varies according to the reading technology employed (Hunter, 1982, pp. 80–91). To speak of "meanings" simply found or felt is a fiction for Hunter and tells us something about a powerful myth that pervades English teaching—the idea that our methods merely facilitate natural "identifications" and "intuitive" responses. Instead, he makes visible the reading regimes of schooling, protocols too frequently passed over or effaced altogether in the rush for the meanings behind the words. In contrast to this claim of ideological innocence, Hunter points to the productivity of our methods—the fact that "we harvest what we sow," though we fool ourselves otherwise—by concentrating on the practical classroom activities that constitute both reader and text and that attempt to determine their interaction. Part of his message is the need to turn to history, to attend to the specific historical trainings imbricated in any contemporary act of reading within an institutional setting.

To exemplify this, Hunter (1983) describes the gradual formation of a set of practices of reading that emerged in late nineteenth-century schooling and resulted in a "new reading for character."

Here, "character" was not so much a property that texts possessed or dramatized but the orchestration of a set of psychological and moral discourses systematized within schooling such as "character sketches," biographical studies of an author, or written responses to illustrate personal identification with a particular character. These procedures did not simply reflect or release a subjective essence lodged somewhere within literary texts; rather, the discursive system centered upon the study and appreciation of "character" represented the implementation of an educational policy—a mandatory discourse mobilized by the state to promote character as an element in a new regime of moral training for the urban, industrial middle class. Hunter concludes that this new reading for literary character was

> in fact a practice of writing, for to speak of reading here is to speak of a definite set of techniques and operations performed upon the text. What we have to come to terms with is that to read a character in the late nineteenth century ... means to go through a series of practical operations and to employ a definite set of techniques ... by which readers construct the characters' point of view as part of the technique of identification (1983, pp. 231–232).

Our modern valorization of the reading for "individual response" coincides with this long historical development of forms of pedagogy centered upon subjectivity. By the early twentieth century, English studies did not consist of a primarily negative or repressive operation, but rather fostered certain pleasures and capacities in students. Foucault has described this strategy as "subjectification," that is, the "way a human being turns him or herself into a subject" by participating in the discourses and practical routines made available within an institution and in which individuals take an "active" part (Foucault in Rabinow, 1984, p. 11). Crucial to this self-formation process was a "self-examination" phase in which reading, and reflective writing upon that reading, played a primary role (pp. 342–343). The bridge between the political and the personal realm is often built within education through just such pleasurable routines "for setting up and developing relationships with the self, for self-reflection, self-knowledge, self-examination, for the decipherment of the self by oneself ... " (Foucault, 1986, p. 29). Such techniques enable a "government by individualization" to the extent that students adopt reading technologies that, while promoting subjective response, are functional to, and recontained within, totalizing structures (Foucault, 1982, p. 781). As I suggested earlier, to a great extent the personal-response model is complicit with this position, ironically fostering within state institutions ideas of a free, contemplative, and modern subjectivity fully compatible with the ideology of possessive individualism.

But there is another side to this issue, which Foucault's caveat alerts us to as midwives of individuation.

> For a long time ordinary individuality—the everyday individuality of everybody—remained below the threshold of description. To be looked at, observed, described in detail, followed from day to day by an uninterrupted writing was a privilege. . . . The disciplinary methods reversed this relation, lowered the threshold of describable individuality and made of this description a means of control and a method of domination. . . . The turning of real lives into writing is no longer a procedure of heroization; it functions as a procedure of objectification and subjection. . . . [It] clearly indicates the appearance of a new modality of power in which each individual receives his own individuality, and in which he is linked by his status to the features, the measurements, the gaps, the "marks" that "*characterize*" . . . (1979, pp. 191–192, emphasis added).

Reading has increasingly become part of this loop with the growing emphasis on techniques of personal engagement exemplified by student journals, reading logs, personal letters to teacher or author, all in concert with an insistent focus on the study of literary "characters," in other words, all those devices that weld the reader to an individuality. In contrast, a discursive approach would construe reading as neither a matter of unique "personal response," nor as the apprehension of objective textual forms and meanings in a flash of insight into the nature of "the text itself" (see Eagleton, 1984). Instead, it would reconceptualize both these orientations as results, particular reader-recognition effects produced by the repetition of certain rules and practices educationally empowered and reinforced (Hunter, 1982).

In Catherine Greenfield's phrase, "to read is to operate with the hypothesis of a reader" (1983, p. 67). Part of the task for a discursive pedagogy, then, would be to raise to visibility such hypotheses; it would, in short, introduce the scandal of theory into the classroom. It is there already, of course, in the tacit protocols for reading and interpretation, only it is unacknowledged, masking as the natural, obvious ways of doing literary business. There is a need, therefore, to talk *explicitly* with students about what a person is required to do within the culture of schooling at any given moment to become a "reader"—that is, *a reader with a difference*. If to speak of "reading" is always to tell a particular historical, institutional, and social story about what counts as reading, perhaps the place to begin with students is by cataloguing the dominant discursive trainings they have been exposed to, assessing the payoffs and limitations of each technology. It will also be important to foreground questions of value and political power for a discursive approach to reading, questions that become more insistent if we turn to the pedagogical history of reading.

HISTORIES OF READING

There are two levels at which we need accounts of reading. The first and more internal one focuses on the way any technique of reading is nested within a larger literary-pedagogical discursive formation, which itself embodies an ensemble of norms, practices, and institutional conditions. These relationships are particularly relevant to a discursive understanding of reading. It is important to consider, for instance, John Frow's argument (1986) that the boundaries of every literary-pedagogical system are always "policed, rigourously or tolerantly, by a constantly normalizing scrutiny designed to maintain [their] integrity" (p. 84). Yet, in spite of vigorous attempts to maintain this integrity, what counts as reading always shifts in concert with the changing nature of institutional arrangements and the dominant social discourses of a period. My own investigations of the historical development of English studies in Ontario (Morgan, 1987a) provides a number of examples of how dominant conceptions of school literary reading altered over the past century: from the etymologically correct reading, to the elocutionary reading intended for public display, from genteel notions of a tasteful reading to reinforce public morality, to readings premised upon the recovery of an authorial spirit or intention, and from these in turn to formalist versions of apprehending "aesthetic form" or "the text-in-itself." Each of these was operationalized by complementary pedagogical routines: word derivation, memorization, elocutionary training, supplementary reading, critical exegesis, etc.; each shift in turn testified to the precariousness and relativity of institutional reading practices as well as their relationship to popular forms of reading.

This is due, in part, to the fact that reading regimes are always multiple and contradictory: any official version of reading achieves its appearance of unity and stability by its location within an institution that is itself "systematized as a unity" (Frow, 1986, p. 84). The reality is that English teaching at any given moment is criss-crossed by opposing traditions and competing interest groups, each attempting to define official reading policy. Musgrove has made the productive suggestion that we need to think of school subjects like English as "social systems sustained by communications networks, material endowments and ideologies . . . as communities of people competing and collaborating with one another, defining and defending their boundaries" (in Goodson, 1981, p. 163). The belief that there is a consensus for any educational reading paradigm becomes problematic once we examine the historical record; this illusion can usefully be replaced with an approach that stresses the idea of dominant, subordinate, residual, and emergent forms of reading all in contention at any given moment. Any unity is, therefore, more of a politically convenient myth, an attempt to impose "a centralizing unity" on the part of an institution, rather than an "achieved fact" (Frow, 1986, p. 178). What binds a pedagogical-reading formation together is not some basic insight into the interrelations of language, mind, and truth, but rather "the normative authority" of the state that arbitrates between such positions, while being itself subject to continuous historical redefinition.

But there is another aspect of this instability of reading relations that needs to be underlined since it is all too frequently passed over in discussions of reading. The development of English studies in Ontario, not unlike its formation in other parts of the world (Batsleer, 1985; Mathieson, 1975; Morgan, 1989), suggests that its disciplinary boundaries are always, in Samuel Weber's phrase, "ambivalent demarcations" (1987, p. 148), that is, constructed in dialogue *with* and *against* popular forms of reading beyond the schoolroom. This is the second type of reading history we require—one focused on school reading as a dividing practice that separated some forms of decipherment and interpretation from others. Early versions of English studies in this sense both absorbed and depended upon a "range of naturalized and idealized concepts available in [the wider] culture," concepts by means of which a society sustains and justifies its existence (Nelson, 1986, p. 4), and, simultaneously, asserted its difference from popular culture. For example, on the one hand, the reading technologies of late nineteenth-century Ontario schooling embedded a range of cultural prejudices regarding race, class, and gender, as illustrated by the selections in officially authorized reading materials. On the other hand, early advocates of English studies continuously stressed that part of its value derived from its opposition to popular reading. School reading thus excluded certain texts as worthy of serious consideration, for example, the writings of women, the working-class, and "minority" cultures, as well as the most popular genres of the period—novels in particular.

Nor was this simply a question of content, but it extended to the forms and methods of reading. To quote the title of an 1872 Ontario *Journal of Education* article, "School Reading Is Not Reading" (Morton, 1872, p. 167). Educational journals of this period repeatedly asserted that school reading, reading "correctly," "reading in the right direction" (Blaisdell, 1883, p. 30), or being a "good reader" (Hart, 1882, p. 45), meant deciphering the text in a way that was fundamentally distinct from everyday reading and the perusal of popular fiction. Reading was to be seen as a form of power, "power to govern ourselves and to influence others; power to gain and spread happiness. Reading is but an instrument; education is to teach its best use" ("Current Thought" *The Canada School Journal*, 1887, p. 39). It was no longer sufficient, then, to simply inculcate the skill of alphabetic decoding in a period following an unprecedented explosion in methods of printing and book distribution (Altick, 1957; Parker, 1985). Or perhaps it was politically unsafe since at one extreme, the Minister of Education for the province, Adam Crooks, could be almost antireading: "Do not force your child to spend time in reading, but look to it that all his or her reading time be properly filled. . . . [B]eware of the silent force, that having once gained entrance, may split the purity and peace of your home" (Crooks, 1876, p. 63). Similarly, the last of twelve rules listed in an anonymous 1853 article on reading in this same journal declared, "dare to be ignorant of many things . . . forsake popular paths." In this writer's opinion, any reading scheme should "be a system of repulsion no less than of attraction" (*Journal of Education*, 1853, pp. 138–139). The implication is clear: since reading matter was now available for the middle and working classes on a scale undreamed of few decades earlier, yet "dangerous publications do not betray their character at a glance," often "wear[ing] the mask of graceful information, and even . . . piety" (Crooks, 1876, p. 63), it became necessary to develop and widely inculcate techniques for moral reading.

THE SPACE OF THE COMMENTARY

It is useful to reconsider from this perspective the role played by the numerous educational literary "primers," prefaces, introductions, annotations, and appendices published during the early years of English studies — what could be called "the space of the commentary." There were several stages in the development and function of these publications. Initially, "doing English" consisted solely of learning details from the biography of "great authors," memorizing titles of their works, and knowing the political events of their "epoch," so that authorized "Histories of Literature" occupied center stage in their own right. The disproportion between what we now characterize as criticism and literature was very lopsided by contemporary standards. For example, in William Francis Collier's *A History of English Literature: In a Series of Biographical Sketches* (1862), ten pages are devoted to Shakespeare, but only one-and-a-half feature his writing. There was no "literary text" in our sense, but rather, as Fredric Jameson (1981) has pointed out, the "wedge of the concept of a 'text'" was itself a product of this period (pp. 296–297). After a short interval in which literary histories were seen as complementary, and then later as secondary, to actual "literary works," they were discontinued altogether. Or, more accurately, they were shunted to the back of the book, becoming the "frame" or "context" of literary reading so that elements of the discourses of political epoch, authorial biography, and canonic evaluation were absorbed by footnote and preface. Finally, with the publication of "teacher's companions," official pedagogical "Manual[s] of Literature" (addressed to the teacher alone), and the establishment of specialist programs in English pedagogy, there was a consolidation and segregation of framing discourses. Ironically, the effect of specialist programs was to inoculate English teachers with a set of invariant, taken-for-granted rules and practices of reading at the outset of their careers. If, as the Russian linguist V. N. Volosinov (1973) has observed, understanding is always "an act of reference between the sign apprehended and other already known sign[s] . . . a response to a sign with signs" (p. 4) by socially motivated agents, then the act of reading, seen as the bringing to bear of one discourse (moral-pedagogical) upon another (textual), became increasingly mysterious as the theory-laden interaction it was, so far as students were concerned.

In Bennett and Woollacott's terms (1987), we can comprehend these publications as textual shifters. As such they were neither merely restrictions upon, nor neutral protocols for, reading, but were, instead, a means of securing a "correct" cultural alignment of a text. Thus, initially any reading was articulated by means of etymological, authorial, and epochal contextualizations. In this sense, school regimes of reading were forms of *cultural production*, ways of fashioning a "legitimate" significance for a text by making it hospitable to a particular range of themes and concepts. Advertised in school journals as innocent translations of meaning, devices to assist teacher and student toward an "intelligent and intelligible" understanding of a specific work, discursive apparatuses like the annotated school Reader created the "literary text" in an important sense. The space of the commentary, therefore, was neither an "extra," supplementary text, nor extraneous to the literary text per se, but was, instead, foundational.

Producing and policing the boundaries of literature, annotated texts directed attention to some relationships within language over others, cumulatively effecting the "facilitation of certain modes of thinking [about texts] and [the] correlative suppression and displacement of others" (Musselwhite, 1978, p. 208). Endlessly repetitive, school editions reflected an obsessive concern on the part of educators with a correctly disposed discourse. Commentaries thus acted in a corrective, preemptive way, establishing a "controlled institutionalisation of literacy and literature as non-political practices" (p. 209).

Like the notes, literary primers, and sample examination questions scattered throughout educational journals, these commentaries had a dual function. Their first and more local operation was to close off contradictions encountered in any reading by setting up a distinction between "surface" and "inner" meaning. Elaborate procedures for etymological tracing, parsing, and translating figurative language eventually yielded initiate readers a consistent "authorial" and "authorized" meaning located beyond the printed page, but which education could nevertheless excavate. As a writer in the *Ontario Teacher* put it in 1873, this "hidden meaning" behind the "ordinary meaning" of a passage was unlocked by fostering "a careful habit of reading . . . in the pupil, and this cannot be effected without frequent questioning by the teacher" ("G. D. P.", 1873, pp. 114–115).

This need for techniques that produced a correctly disposed and moral reading, however, can only be understood if we look beyond educational forms of reading. In particular, the institutionalization of reading practices with "taste" at their center can be seen as part of a war on popular forms of reading in which English studies engaged from its inception. In 1867, for example, the official historian of the Ontario Education Department, John George Hodgins, noted that, although there were almost no volumes of fiction in the books made available to school libraries, there was a persistent "demand" for such works (p. 306). He cites with approval an inspector's comment "that this taste, if rightly directed" (i.e., "standard novels of fine tone") could have "a refining and elevating influence" on our youth (p. 307). The initial strategy to exclude was therefore now to be tempered by selective incorporation and the restructuring of the ways of reading—methods that remained central to English studies well into the twentieth century embodied, for instance, in the "supplementary reading" program initiated in 1891 in Ontario. At the turn of the century, teachers were officially advised that since reading is "conducive to the formation of character," it was of paramount importance to

> fill the child's mind with a love for choice literature, and so to train his mind that in after years he can discriminate between the good and the bad and reject what is worthless. . . . It should be the aim of the teacher to have every pupil carry away with him the reading habit as the most precious gift of the school system. Children who form a taste for good literature are reasonably safe both intellectually and morally. . . . The love of fiction becomes with many people a mental disease. Many read scarcely any other books than novels. . . . Novel reading should be regulated. Too much time should not be given to fiction, and the novels should be of a high order. The ephemeral works of fiction that are flowing in torrents from the

printing press should receive little attention. It is folly to take up one's time reading many present-day novels, while the masterpieces are ignored (Education Department of Ontario, 1902, pp. 4–6).

This document indicates that the state was in no doubt about the nature of the literary war in which it was engaged: "by a judicious selection of books for a library and for supplementary reading, the 'dime novel' will cease to be such an obstacle as heretofore in the development of character among school children" (p. 5).

This assessment of the conflict between popular and pedagogical reading was widely shared by teachers and administrators. Public school teacher Alice Freeman concluded her speech before the Toronto Teachers' Association with the observation that "If any pupil of ours should in future years lay down some spicy sensational novel, or leave the sheets of some violently illustrated periodical uncut, because of some dim remembrance of a warning note, sounded in old school days, the knowledge should make us more satisfied with our work than had he obtained all the honours that the Universities could bestow" (1886, p. 206). Likewise J. E. Wells, the editor of the Ontario *Educational Journal* in 1887, counseled an "improved" aesthetic reading so that "under such a method, intelligently followed, nine out of ten of the active minds which are under the teacher's training in the schools could be led to such an enjoyment of good writing and thinking as would in a few years go far to drive the dime novel and sensational weekly from the book-stalls, and replace them with cheap editions of the English classics ..." (Wells, 1887, p. 236). This concern of educators to reach out and shape reading practices beyond the schoolroom even extended to a consideration of "the feasibility of establishing a Paper suitable to the requirements of the Pupils of the Common Schools" that "would tend to displace from its present position the mischievous literature of the present day" (*Annual Report and Proceedings of the OEA*, 1870, reprinted in Hodgins, 1911, pp. 149–150).

The conflict between an ethical and a "cheap," "contraband" literature is also evident in the hope, expressed by the official textbook editor for the Department of Education, D. J. Goggin (1883), "to form in children a taste for good reading, to create in them an appetite which craves only literary food" by making them "as early as possible familiar with the best English classics ..." (pp. 432–433). The underlying principle that should guide reading practices, according to Goggin, is that "there is no safeguard against a bad taste equal to the creation of a good taste" (p. 433). Specifically, this meant organizing classroom reading quite literally under the sign of the author. He recommends, for example, that teachers restrict study to a few literary giants each year, supplementing their works with the planting of trees "in honour of a favourite author," public recitations of their work, the hanging of authorial portraits in the classroom, "telling stories about his school-days, his home, his family," even holding "authorial birthday cele-brations." More than simply valorizing a limited number of male writers, such methods constructed the figures of authors as the source of value in any reading along the line of Old Testament prophets.

Authorized metatexts, commentaries, and directives about reading served therefore as the means of regulating the transformations and modifications students were to perform upon signification, not only in school but, just as importantly, beyond it. They organized a limited "textual" space and a specific cultural network into which a book should be inserted, delimiting what could and could not be said about it within a "literary" discourse, and, therefore, what other kinds of texts and wider social discourses one could connect any reading with. In effect, texts were rewritten by the pedagogical frameworks of reading so that their social affiliations were truncated: in Edward Said's sense, "appreciated and venerated" as monuments, they came to "define the limits of what [was] acceptable, appropriate, and legit-imate so far as culture [was] concerned" (1983, p. 21).

In this respect, Catherine Greenfield has shown how the reading practices of the late nineteenth century established the basic par-ameters of subsequent interpretation up to the present. By activating and coordinating the main discursive regularities of the bourgeoisie — "subjectivity" and "experience" — she maintains that the literary text was "neutraliz[ed] and naturaliz[ed] ... effectively deny[ing] its unavoidable implication in the always contested domain of power-knowledge relations; in other words the fundamental politicality of the text [was] denied" (Greenfield, 1983, p. 138). This was ac-complished by displacing a prior reading technology whose conditions of intelligibility were transcendental (spirit, truth, and sacred text) for a secular one that unified the text at the level of "reader, author and [literary] character" and that have since become the "self-evident unities ... activated in recent and current school curricula as the expected and repeated way of reading" (pp. 136–137).

Foucault has argued that every discursive practice involves not only a positive group of conceptual choices and pragmatic forms, but equally, a policed and regulated set of exclusions. The exclusionary dynamic of any discursive economy, its dialogue with what presses in upon it from the outside, is rarely theorized within a discipline, but dwells instead in the shadow of its more positive self-definitions. In contrast, a discursive approach relates pedagogically constructed readings to those wider "reading formations circulating outside the academy, through which popular reading is organized" (Bennett,

1983, p. 218). Both kinds of accounts of reading that I have touched on—the first focused on the internal curricular changes in the reading regimes within a discipline, and the second on its dialectic with societal forms—are inextricable in the final analysis. This is to reaffirm once again, though at another level, Bennett's refusal of the distinction between a "text's intra-textual and its extra-textual determinations," since "text and context are never separable from one another in the way this either/or construction suggests" (1984, pp. 121–122).

CONCLUSION

My preoccupation has been on the need for those currently working within English studies to thematize the conditions of their institutional life. The fact is that most forms of reading and interpreting in which our students engage are institutional ones—but which they are encouraged to see as natural ways of proceeding. Instead, I have argued that by looking at the history of reading regimes within schooling, we can see them as variable and powerful techniques of cultural production. Moreover, the relationship of educational reading practices to other popular forms of reading needs to be acknowledged. This is to assert that any schooled reading practice is a form of social relations with consequences for cultural life in general. It is also to shift the ground from curricular, psychological, or epistemological accounts of reading to a politics of reading. More precisely, it is to recover and rewrite, where possible, the insights of the former approaches within this larger social perspective. If we grasp reading within a political-discursive framework, making "discourse responsible for reality and not merely a reflection of it, then," as Jane Tompkins (1980) remarks, "whose discourse prevails makes all the difference" (p. xxv).

A further benefit of the historical-discursive perspective I am advocating is its displacement of traditional categories long taken for granted, such as text, author, engagement, detachment, and a stable empirical reader. These are seen instead as functions of specific forms of reading work: "Both writer and reader [become] categories of a particular literary system and of particular regimes within it, and only as such are they amenable to theorization" (Frow, 1986, pp. 185–186). Nor is a curricular history of reading of merely antiquarian interest. Ian Hunter's "reading for character" (1983) is very much on the ascendant, with current English documents at all levels focusing on literary "characters" as though they were "integrated beings, a wholeness about which permanent conclusions can be reached" (Neel, 1985, p. 201). Such documents continue to police the boundaries between primary and secondary sources, between "text" and "context."

Yet as Jasper Neel remarks about a commonly taught Shakespearean play

> Where does the text begin? Where does it end? And what does it include? For the modern reader it is almost impossible to find a copy without an Introduction, extensive glosses, and a set of equivocations about the editorial process. . . . plays come encapsulated—front and back, top and bottom, left and right—with other texts. For the experienced reader these encapsulations have become part of the text. . . . There is probably no living reader whose experience with Lear has not included several layers of encapsulation (p. 196–197).

This is equally true, however, for initiate student readers who encounter any text with preselected intertext, the entire curriculum refracted through the reading discourses circulated by state handbooks. An archaeology of reading practices along the lines I am recommending, then, has important implications for the present.

Whereas the privileged object within cultural life during the nineteenth century was the printed word, the dominant cultural form of the twentieth is indicated by the term "media." As Fredric Jameson reminds us, this word brings together three "distinct signals: that of an artistic mode or specific form of aesthetic production; that of a specific technology . . .; [and] that, finally, of a social institution" (1987, p. 199). The need to conceptualize the media in this way has challenged us in turn to rethink language and the literary text within this threefold articulation: that is, that any cultural object or practice is best understood by triangulating the relations and simultaneous pulls of aesthetic, material, and institutional dimensions. Up until now it is the last two aspects of reading practice that have been the most neglected.

NOTE

1. For a fuller discussion of the concept of discourse than is appropriate here, see Foucault (1978, pp. 48–78; 1981, pp. 7–26) and Macdonell (1986).

WORKS CITED

Adams, M. J., & Collins, A. (1985). A schema-theoretic view of reading. In H. Singer & R. B. Ruddell (Eds.), *Theoretical models and processes of reading* (3rd Edition). Newark, DE: International Reading Association.

Aiken, S. H. (1986). Women and the question of canonicity. *College English, 48*, 288–301.

Alcorn, M., & Bracher, M. (1985). Literature, psychoanalysis, and the re-formation of the self: A new direction for reader response theory. *Papers of the Modern Language Association, 100*, 342–354.

Altick, R. (1957). *The English common reader: A social history of the mass reading public, 1800–1900*. Chicago: University of Chicago Press.

Anderson, R. C. (1985). Role of readers' schema in comprehension, learning, and memory. In H. Singer & R. B. Ruddell (Eds.), *Theoretical models and processes of reading* (3rd Edition). Newark, DE: International Reading Association.

Anderson, R. C., & Pearson, P. D. (1984). A schema-theoretic view of the basic processes in reading comprehension. In P. D. Pearson (Ed.), *Handbook of reading research*. New York: Longman.

Anderson, R. C., & Pitchert, J. W. (1978). Recall of previously unrecallable information following a shift in perspective. *Journal of Verbal Learning and Verbal Behavior, 12*, 1–12.

Anderson, R. C., Reynolds, R., Shallert, D., & Goetz, E. (1977). Frameworks for comprehending discourse. *American Educational Research Journal, 14*, 367–381.

Anderson, R. C., Spiro, R. J., & Anderson, M. C. (1978). Schemata as scaffolding for the representation of information in connected discourse. *American Educational Research Journal, 15*, 433–440.

Anonymous. (1853). Suggestions for the proper choice and reading of books. *Journal of Education for Upper Canada, 6*, 138–139.

Anonymous. (1887). Current thought. *The Canada School Journal, 12*, 39.

Apple, M. (1979). *Ideology and curriculum*. London: Routledge & Kegan Paul.

Applebee, A. N. (1974). *Tradition and reform in the teaching of English*. Urbana, IL: National Council of Teachers of English.

—— (1976). Children's construal of stories and related genres as measured with repertory grid techniques. *Research in the Teaching of English, 10*, 226–238.

—— (1978). *The child's concept of story: Ages two to seventeen.* Chicago: University of Chicago Press.

Applebee, A. N., Langer, J. A., & Mullis, I. (1988). *Who reads best? Factors related to reading achievement in grades 3, 7, and 11.* Princeton: Educational Testing Service.

Arac, J., Godzich, W., & Martin, W. (Eds.). (1983). *The Yale critics: Deconstruction in America.* Minneapolis: University of Minnesota Press.

Aristotle. (1967). On the art of poetry. In T. S. Dorsch (Ed. and Trans.), *Aristotle, Horace, Longinus: Classical literary criticism.* Harmondsworth: Penguin.

Armbruster, B., Anderson, T., & Ostertag, J. (1987). Does text structure/summarization instruction facilitate learning from expository text? *Reading Research Quarterly, 22*, 331–346.

Athey, I. G. (1976). Reading research in the affective domain. In H. Singer & R. B. Ruddell (Eds.), *Theoretical models and processes of reading* (2nd ed.). Newark, DE: International Reading Association.

Atkins, A. (1967). Robert Bolt: Self, shadow, and the theatre of recognition. *Modern Drama, 10*(2), 182–188.

Atwood, M. (1983). The page. In *Murder in the dark.* Toronto: Coach House.

Ausebel, D. (1963). *The psychology of meaningful verbal learning.* New York: Grune & Stratton.

Austin, J. (1962). *How to do things with words.* Cambridge, MA: Harvard University Press.

Baker, L., & Brown, A. L. (1984). Metacognitive skills and reading. In P. D. Pearson (Ed.), *Handbook of reading research.* New York: Longman.

Bakhtin, M. (1973). *Marxism and the philosophy of language.* New York: Seminar Press.

—— (1981). *The dialogic imagination: Four essays* (trans. by C. Emerson & M. Holquist). Austin: University of Texas Press.

Baker, L., & Brown, A. L. (1984). Metacognitive skills and reading. In P. D. Pearson (Ed.), *The handbook of reading research.* New York: Longman.

Baldick, C. (1983). *The social mission of English criticism, 1848–1932.* Oxford: Clarendon.

Barnes, D. (1975). *From communication to curriculum.* New York: Penguin.

Barthes, R. (1970). *S/Z: Essais.* Paris: Seuil.

—— (1975). *S/Z* (R. Miller, Trans.). New York: Hill and Wang. (Original work published 1970.)

—— (1975). *The pleasure of the text* (R. Miller, Trans.). New York: Hill and Wang. (Original work published 1973.)

————— (1977). *Image, music, text.* (S. Heath Ed. and Trans.). London: Fontana Paperbacks.

Bartholomae, D. (1985). Inventing the university. In M. Rose (Ed.), *When a writer can't write.* New York: Guilford Press.

Bartky, S. L. (1979). Toward a phenomenology of feminist consciousness. In S. Bishop & M. Weinzweig. (Eds.), *Philosophy and women.* Belmont, CA: Wadsworth.

Bartlett, F. (1932). *Remembering: A study in experimental and social psychology.* Cambridge, MA: Harvard University Press.

Batsleer, J., Davies, T., O'Rourke, R., & Weedon, C. (1985). *Rewriting English.* London: Methuen.

Baum, G. (1979). *The social imperative.* New York: Paulist Press.

Baumann, J. F., & Ballard, P. Q. (1987). A two step model for promoting independence in comprehension. *Journal of Reading, 30,* 608–612.

Beach, R. W. (1972). The literary response process of college students while reading and discussing three poems (Doctoral dissertation, University of Illinois). *Dissertation Abstracts International, 34,* 656A.

————— (1985). Discourse conventions and researching response to literary dialogue. In C. R. Cooper (Ed.), *Researching response to literature and the teaching of literature.* Norwood, NJ: Ablex.

————— (1987). Differences in autobiographical narratives of English teachers, college freshmen, and seventh graders. *College Composition and Communication, 38,* 56–69.

Beach, R. W., & Brunetti, G. (1976). Differences between high school and university students in their conceptions of literary characters. *Research in the Teaching of English, 10,* 259–268.

Beach, R. W., & Wendler, L. (1987). Developmental differences in response to a short story. *Research in the Teaching of English, 21,* 286–297.

Beale, W. H. (1987). *A pragmatic theory of rhetoric.* Carbondale: Southern Illinois University Press.

Beers, T. (1987). Commentary: Schema-theoretic models of reading: Humanizing the machine. *Reading Research Quarterly, 22,* 369–377.

Belenky, M. F., Clenchy, B., Goldberger, N. R., & Tarule, J. M. (1986). *Women's ways of knowing: The development of self, voice, and mind.* New York: Basic Books.

Belsey, C. (1980). *Critical practice.* London: Methuen.

Benjamin, J. (1986). A desire of one's own: Psychoanalytic feminism and intersubjective space. In T. de Lauretis (Ed.), *Feminist studies/critical studies.* Bloomington, IN: Indiana University Press.

Bennett, T. (1983). Text, readers, reading formations. *Literature and History, 9*(2), 214–227.

————— (1984). The text in question. *Southern Review, 17*(2), 118–125.

Bennett, T., & Woollacott, J. (1987). *J. Bond and beyond: The political career of a popular hero.* New York: Methuen.

Bereiter, C., & Scardamalia, M. (1984). Learning about writing from reading. *Written Communication, 1,* 163–188.

—— (1987). *The psychology of written composition.* Hillsdale, NJ: Erlbaum.

Bernstein, J. M. (1984). *The philosophy of the novel: Lukacs, Marxism, and the dialectics of form.* Minneapolis: University of Minnesota Press.

Blachowicz, C. L. Z. (1983). A commentary on Johnson, Toms-Bronowski, and Buss's critique of Davis's study: Fundamental factors of comprehension in reading. In L. M. Gentile, M. L. Kamil, & J. S. Blanchard (Eds.), *Reading research revisited.* Columbus, OH: Charles E. Merrill.

Blaisdell, A. F. (1883). Reading in the right direction. *The Canada School Journal, 8,* 30–32.

Bleich, D. (1975). *Readings and feelings: An introduction to subjective criticism.* Urbana: National Council of Teachers of English.

—— (1978). *Subjective criticism.* Baltimore: Johns Hopkins University Press.

—— (1980). Epistemological assumptions in the study of response. In J. P. Tompkins (Ed.), *Reader-response criticism: From formalism to post-structuralism.* Baltimore: Johns Hopkins University Press.

—— (1986). Intersubjective reading. *New Literary History, 27,* 401–421.

Bloom, B. S. (1976). *Human characteristics and school learning.* New York: McGraw-Hill.

Bloom, H. (1975). *A map of misreading.* New York: Oxford University Press.

—— (1982). *Agon: Towards a theory of revisionism.* Oxford: Oxford University Press.

Bloome, D. (1986). Building literacy and the classroom community. *Theory Into Practice, 24,* 71–76.

Bloome, D., & Green, J. (1984). Directions in the sociolinguistic study of reading. In P. D. Pearson (Ed.)., *Handbook of reading research.* New York: Longman.

Bogdan, D. (1978). Case study, grade 13. Integrated literature and values course. *Values and literary criticism. Appendix 5, The Moral Education Project (Year 5): Curriculum and Pedagogy for Reflective Values Education Final Report 1976–77,* Principal Investigator, Clive Beck (Ontario Institute for Studies in Education); reprinted (1980) as Appendix C in *Instruction and delight: Northrop Frye and the educational value of literature.* Unpublished doctoral dissertation, University of Toronto.

—— (1981). Let them eat cake. *English Journal, 70*(1), 33–40.

—— (1982a). Is it relevant and does it work? Reconsidering literature taught as rhetoric. *Journal of Aesthetic Education, 16*(4), 27–29.

—— (1982b). Northrop Frye and the defence of literature. *English Studies in Canada, 8*(2), 203–214.

———— (1984). Pygmalion as pedagogue: Subjectivist bias in the teaching of literature. *English Education, 16*(2), 67–75.

———— (1985a). Literary criticism in the classroom. In K. B. Whale & T. J. Gambell (Eds.), *From seed to harvest: Looking at literature*. Ottawa: Canadian Council of Teachers of English.

———— (1985b). The justification question: Why literature? *English Education, 17*(4), 238–248.

———— (1986a). Literary respone as dialectic: Modes and levels of engagement and detachment. *Cuardernos de filosofia inglesa, 2,* 42–62.

———— (1986b). Virtual and actual forms of literary response. *Journal of Aesthetic Education, 20*(2), 51–57.

———— (1987a). Feminist criticism and total form in literary experience. *Resources for Feminist Research/Documentation sur la Récherche Feministe: Women and Philosophy/Femmes et philosophie, 16*(3), 20–23.

———— (1987b). Literature, values, and truth: Why we could lose the censorship debate. *English Quarterly, 20,* 273–284.

———— (1987c). A taxonomy of responses and respondents to literature. *Paideusis: Journal of the Canadian Philosophy of Education Society, 1*(1), 13–32.

———— (1988). A case study of the selection/censorship problem and the educational value of literature. *Journal of Education, 170*(2), 39–57.

———— (1989a). From stubborn structure to double mirror: The evolution of Northrop Frye's theory of reader response before and in *The Great Code. Journal of Aesthetic Education,* Summer, 1989 *23*(2), 1–12.

———— (1989b). Judy and her sisters: Censorship and the poetics of need. *Proceedings of the forty-fourth annual meeting of the Philosophy of Education Society.* Normal, IL: Philosophy of Education Society, 66–77.

Bolt, R. (1960/1963). *A man for all seasons: A play of Sir Thomas More.* Scarborough, ON: Bellhaven House.

Booth, W. C. (1961). *The rhetoric of fiction.* Chicago: University of Chicago Press.

Bracewell, R. J., Scardamalia, M., & Bereiter, C. (1978). The development of audience in writing. ERIC Document Service, Document No. ED 154 433.

Bradley, J. M., Ames, W. S., & Mitchell, J. N. (1985). The effects of text adaptation on rater appeal and difficulty. *Reading Psychology, 5,* 185–191.

Brancato, R. (1985). Fourth of July. In D. Gallo (Ed.), *Sixteen.* New York: Dell.

Bransford, J. D., & Franks, J. J. (1973). The abstraction of linguistic ideas: A review. *Cognition: International Journal of Cognitive Psychology, 1,* 211–249.

Bransford, J. D. & Johnson, M. K. (1972). Contextual prerequisites for understanding. *Journal of Verbal Learning and Verbal Behavior, 11,* 717–726.

Brewer, W. F., & Nakamura, G. V. (in press). The nature and functions of schemas. In R. S. Wyer & T. K. Srull (Eds.), *Handbook of social cognition.* Hillsdale, NJ: Erlbaum.

Britton, J. (1984). Viewpoints: The distinction between participant and spectator role language in research and practice. *Research in the Teaching of English, 18,* 320–331.

Brook-Rose, C. (1980). The readerhood of man. In S. R. Suleiman & I. Crosman (Eds.), *The reader in the text: Essays on audience and interpretation.* Princeton: Princeton University Press.

Brooks, C. (1947). *The well wrought urn: Studies in the structure of poetry.* New York: Harcourt, Brace & World.

Brooks, P. (1984). *Reading for the plot: Design and intention in narrative.* New York: Knopf.

Brown, C. L., & Olson, K. (Eds.). (1978). *Feminist criticism: Essays on theory poetry and prose.* Metuchen, NJ: Scarecrow Press.

Bruce, B. (1984). A new point of view on children's stories. In R. C. Anderson, J. Osborn & R. J. Tierney (Eds.), *Learning to read in American schools: Basal readers and content texts.* Hillsdale, NJ: Erlbaum.

——— (1980). Plans and social actions. In R. J. Spiro, B. C. Bruce, & W. F. Brewer (Eds.), *Theoretical issues in reading comprehension.* Hillsdale, NJ: Erlbaum.

Bruce, D. (1985). The how and why of ecological memory. *Journal of Experimental Psychology: General, 114*(1), 78–90.

Bruffee, K. (1984). Collaborative learning and "The Conversation of Mankind". *College English, 46,* 635–652.

Bruner, J. (1986). *Actual minds, possible worlds.* Cambridge, MA: Harvard University Press.

Burke, K. (1969). *A rhetoric of motives.* Berkeley: University of California Press.

Cady, S., Ronan, M., & Taussig, H. (1986). *Sophia: The future of feminist spirituality.* San Francisco: Harper & Row.

Calkins, L. (1983). *Lessons from a child.* Portsmouth, NH: Heinemann.

Cambourne, B. (1976–1977). Getting to Goodman: An analysis of the Goodman model of reading with some suggestions for evaluation. *Reading Research Quarterly, 12,* 605–636.

Cambourne, B., & Turbill, J. (1987). *Coping with chaos.* Roselle, Australia: Primary English Teaching Association.

Carey, R., Harste, J., & Smith, P. (1981). Contextual constraints and discourse processes: A replication study. *Reading Research Quarterly, 16,* 201–212.

Cattell, J. M. (1886). The time it takes to see and name objects. *Mind, 11,* 63–65.

Censorship cries heard as province changes textbooks. *The Globe and Mail,* July 1, 1989.

Chall, J. S. (1983). *Learning to read: The great debate.* New York: McGraw-Hill.

Chase, N. D., & Hynd, C. R. (1987). Reader response: An alternative way to teach students to think about text. *Journal of Reading, 30,* 530–540.

Chomsky, N. (1957). *Syntactic structures.* The Hague: Mouton.

———— (1959). Review of *Verbal Behavior,* by B. F. Skinner. *Language, 35*(1), 26–58.

Clark, H. H., & Haviland, S. E (1977). Comprehension and the given-new contract. In R. O. Freedle (Ed.), *Discourse production and comprehension.* Norwood, NJ: Ablex.

Clark, L. (1976). The rights of women: The theory and practice of the ideology of male supremacy. In W. R. Shea & J. King-Farlow (Eds.), *Contemporary issues in political philosophy.* New York: Science History.

Collier, W. F. (1862). *A history of English literature: In a series of biographical sketches.* London: T. Nelson.

Collins, A., Brown, J. B., & Larkin, K. M. (1980). Inference in text understanding: Perspectives from cognitive psychology, linguistics, artificial intelligence, and education. In R. J. Spiro, B. Bruce, & W. Brewer (Eds.), *Theoretical issues in reading comprehension.* Hillsdale, NJ: Erlbaum.

Collins, J. (1981). Differential treatment in reading instruction. In J. Cook-Gumperz, J. Gumperz, & H. Simons (Eds.), *Home-school ethnography project* (final report of the National Institute of Education). Washington, DC: U.S. Department of Education.

Commager, H. S. (1962). Forward. In *McGuffey's sixth eclectic reader, 1879 edition* (facsimile reprint). Toronto: New American Library of Canada.

Connors, R. J., Ede, L. S., & Lunsford, A. A. (1984). The revival of rhetoric in America. In R. J. Connors, L. S. Ede, & A. A. Lunsford (Eds.), *Essays on classical rhetoric and modern discourse.* Carbondale, IL: Southern Illinois University Press.

Cook-Gumperz, J., Gumperz, J., & Simons, H. (1981). *Home-school ethnography project* (final report of the National Institute of Education). Washington, DC: U.S. Department of Education.

Cooper, M. (1986). The ecology of writing. *College English, 48,* 364–375.

Cormier, R. (1974). *The chocolate war.* New York: Dell.

———— (1977). *I am the cheese.* New York: Dell.

———— (1979). *After the first death.* New York: Avon Books.

———— (1983). *The bumblebee flies anyway.* New York: Dell.

———— (1985). In the heat. In D. Gallo (Ed.), *Sixteen.* New York: Dell.

Crane, R. S. (Ed.). (1952a). *Critics and criticism, ancient and modern.* Chicago: University of Chicago Press.

———— (1952b). Introduction. In R. S. Crane (Ed.), *Critics and criticism, ancient and modern.* Chicago: University of Chigaco Press.

———— (1967). Ernest Hemingway: "The Killers." In *Idea of the humanities and other essays critical and historical.* Chicago: University of Chicago Press.

Crockett, W. H. (1965). Cognitive complexity and impression formation. In B. Maher (Ed.), *Progress in experimental personality research* (Vol. 2). New York: Academic Press.

Crooks, A. (1876). What to read. *The Journal of Education for Ontario, 29,* 63.

Crowhurst, M., & Piche, G. L. (1979). Audience and mode of discourse effects on syntactic complexity in writing at two grade levels. *Research in the Teaching of English, 13,* 101–109.

Culler, J. (1975). *Structuralist poetics: Structuralism, linguistics and the study of literature.* Ithaca, NY: Cornell University Press.

——— (1981). *The pursuit of signs: Semiotics, literature, deconstruction.* Ithaca: Cornell University Press.

——— (1982). *On deconstruction: Theory and criticism after structuralism.* Ithaca, NY: Cornell University Press.

——— (1983). *Barthes.* Glasgow: Collins.

——— (1986). The future of criticism. In C. Koelb & V. Lokke (Eds.), *The current in criticism: Essays on the present and future of literary theory.* West Lafayette, IN: Purdue University Press.

Culp, M. (1977). Case studies of the influence of literature on the attitudes, values and behavior of adolescents. *Research in the Teaching of English, 11,* 245–253.

——— (1985). Literature's influence on young adult attitudes, values, and behavior, 1975 and 1984. *English Journal, 74*(8), 31–35.

Dahl, S. (1981). Oral language and its relationship to success in reading. In V. Froese & S. B. Straw (Eds.), *Research in the language arts: Language and schooling.* Baltimore: University Park Press.

Darnton, R. (1987). Towards a history of reading. *Princeton Alumni Weekly, 87,* 19–32.

Davis, F. B. (1944). Fundamental factors of comprehension in reading. *Psychometrika, 9*(3), 185–197. (Reprinted in L. M. Gentile, M. L. Kamil, & J. S. Blanchard [Eds.], *Reading research revisited.* Columbus, OH: Charles E. Merrill.)

——— (1968). Research in comprehension in reading. *Reading Research Quarterly, 3,* 499–544.

——— (1972). Psychometric research on comprehension in reading. *Reading Research Quarterly, 7,* 628–678.

de Beaugrande, R. (1980). *Text, discourse, and process: Toward a multidisciplinary science of texts.* Norwood, NJ: Ablex.

de Lauretis, T. (1984). *Alice doesn't: Feminism, semiotics, cinema.* Bloomington, IN: Indiana University Press.

——— (1986). *Feminist studies/critical studies.* Bloomington, IN: Indiana University Press.

———— (1987). *Technologies of gender: Essays on theory, film and fiction.* Bloomington and Indianapolis, IN: University of Indiana Press.

de Man, P. (1969). The rhetoric of temporality. In C. Singleton (Ed.), *Interpretation: Theory and practice.* Baltimore: Johns Hopkins University Press.

———— (1971/1983). *Blindness and insight: [Essays in the rhetoric of contemporary criticism.]* In W. Godzich (Ed.), *Theory and history of literature* (Vol. 7). Minneapolis: University of Minnesota Press.

DeGeorge, R., & DeGeorge, F. (Eds.). (1972). *The structuralists: From Marx to Levi-Strauss.* New York: Anchor Books.

Derrida, J. (1977). *Of grammatology* (Gayatri Chakravorty Spivak, Trans.). Baltimore: Johns Hopkins University Press. (Original work published 1967.)

———— (1981). *Dissemination* (B. Johnson, Trans.). Chicago: University of Chicago Press. (Original work published 1972.)

———— (1987). *The truth in painting* (trans. by Geoff Bennington and Ian McLeod). Chicago: University of Chicago Press.

DeStefano, J., Pepinsky, H., & Sanders, T. (1982). Discourse rules for literacy learning in a first grade classroom. In L. C. Wilkinson (Ed.), *Communication in the classroom.* New York: Academic Press.

Diamond, A., & Edwards, L. R. (Eds.). (1977). *The authority of experience: Essays in feminist criticism.* Amherst, MA: University of Massachusetts Press.

Dias, P. (1987). *Making sense of poetry: Patterns in the process.* Ottawa: Canadian Council of Teachers of English.

Dias, P., & Hayhoe, M. (1988). *Developing response to poetry.* Milton Keynes, England: Open University Press.

Dillon, G. (1980). Discourse processing and the nature of literary narrative. *Poetics, 9,* 163–180.

———— (1985). Styles of reading. *Poetics Today, 3,* 77–88.

Dixon, J. (1966). *Growth through English.* Reading, England: National Association for the Teaching of English.

———— (1967). *Growth through English: A report based on the Dartmouth Seminar, 1966.* Reading, England: National Association for the Teaching of English.

Dorfman, M. (April, 1985). *A model for understanding the points of stories: Evidence from adult and child readers.* Paper presented at the Seventh Annual Conference of the Cognitive Science Society, Irvine, CA.

———— (1988). A model for understanding the points of stories. Paper presented at the annual meeting of the American Educational Research Association, New Orleans.

Dowling, W. (1987). Teaching eighteenth-century literature in the Pockockian moment (or, Flimnap on the tightrope, Kramnick to the rescue). *College English, 49,* 523–532.

Durkin, D. (1983). *Teaching them to read* (4th edition). Boston: Allyn & Bacon.

Dyson, A. H. (1984). Learning to write/learning to do school: Emergent writers' interpretations of school literacy tasks. *Research in the Teaching of English, 18,* 233−264.

Eagleton, T. (1976). *Marxism and literary criticism.* London: Methuen.

———— (1983) *Literary theory: An introduction.* Oxford: Basil Blackwell.

———— (1984). The "text in itself." *Southern Review, 17,* 115−118.

Eakin, P. J. (1985). *Fictions in autobiography: Studies in the art of self-invention.* Princeton: Princeton University Press.

Ecker, G. (Ed.). (1985). *Feminist aesthetics.* (H. Anderson, Trans.). London: Women's Press.

Eco, U. (1976). *A theory of semiotics.* Bloomington: Indiana University Press.

———— (1979). *The role of the reader: Explorations in the semiotics of texts.* Bloomington, IN: Indiana University Press.

———— (1984). *Semiotics and the philosophy of language.* Bloomington: Indiana University Press.

Edinger, E. F. (1987). *The Christian archetype: A Jungian commentary on the life of Christ.* Toronto: Inner City Books.

Education Department of Ontario. (1902). *Catalogue of books recommended for public school libraries by the Education Department of Ontario.* Toronto: L. K. Cameron.

Eliot, T. S. (1920). *The sacred wood: Essays on poetry and criticism.* London: Methuen.

———— (1932). *Selected essays 1917−1932.* New York: Harcourt Brace.

———— (1975). The metaphysical poets. In F. Kermode (Ed.), *Selected prose of T. S. Eliot.* London: Faber and Faber.

Elson, R. M. (1964). *Guardians of tradition: American schoolbooks of the nineteenth century.* Lincoln: University of Nebraska Press.

Empson, W. (1947). *Seven types of ambiguity.* London: Chatto and Windus.

Entwisle, D. R. (1979). The child's social environment and learning to read. In *Reading research: Advances in theory and practice* (Vol. 1). New York: Academic Press.

Ermarth, E. D. (1983a). Fictional consensus and female casualties. In C. Heilbrun & M. Higonnet (Eds.), *The representation of women in fiction: Selected papers from the English Institute.* Baltimore: Johns Hopkins University Press.

———— (1983b). *Realism and consensus in the English novel.* Princeton: Princeton University Press.

Fekete, J. (1977/1978). *The critical twilight: Explorations in the ideology of Anglo-American literary theory from Eliot to McLuhan.* London: Routledge & Kegan Paul.

Feldman, E. B., & Woods, D. (1981). Art criticism and reading. *The Journal of Aesthetic Education, 15,* 75−95.

Fetterley, J. (1978). *The resisting reader: A feminist approach to American fiction.* Bloomington, IN: Indiana University Press.

Fillmore, C. (1974). Future of semantics. In C. Fillmore, G. Lackoff, & R. Lackoff (Eds.), *Berkeley studies in syntax and semantics.* Berkeley: University of California Press.

Fischer, M. (1985). *Does deconstruction make any difference? Poststructuralism and the defence of poetry in modern criticism.* Bloomington, IN: Indiana University Press.

Fish, S. (1970). Literature in the reader: Affective stylistics. *New Literary History, 2,* 123−162.

——— (1976). Interpreting the variorum. *Critical Inquiry, 2,* 465−485.

——— (1980). Interpreting the variorium. In J. Tompkins (Ed.), *Reader-response criticism: From formalism to post-structuralism.* Baltimore: Johns Hopkins University Press.

——— (1980). *Is there a text in this class? The authority of interpretative communities.* Cambridge, MA: Harvard University Press.

Fleck, L. (1979). *Genesis and development of a scientific fact.* Chicago: University of Chicago Press.

Flower, L., & Hayes, J. R. (1980). The cognition of discovery: Defining a rhetorical problem. *College Composition and Communication, 31,* 21−32.

Foucault, M. (1977). History and systems of thought. In D. Bouchard (Ed.), *Language, counter-memory, practice.* Ithaca, NY: Cornell University Press.

——— (1978). Politics and the study of discourse. *Ideology and Consciousness, 3,* 7−26.

——— (1979). *Discipline and punish* (A. Sheridan, Trans.). New York: Vintage.

——— (1981). The order of discourse. In R. Young (Ed.), *Untying the text.* London: Routledge & Kegan Paul.

——— (1982). The subject and power. *Critical Inquiry, 8,* 777−795.

——— (1986). *The use of pleasure* (R. Hurley, Trans.). New York: Vintage.

——— (1988). *Politics, philosophy, culture: Interviews and other writing, 1977−1984* (trans. by Alan Sheridan and others; edited with an introduction by Lawrence D. Dritzman). New York: Routledge.

Frederiksen, C. H. (1975). Representing logic and semantic structure of knowledge acquired from discourse. *Cognitive Psychology, 7,* 371−458.

——— (1977). Semantic processing units in understanding text. In R. O. Freedle (Ed.), *Discourse production and comprehension.* Norwood, NJ: Ablex.

Freeman, A. (1886). Hints on teaching literature to junior pupils. *The Canada Educational Monthly, 8,* 199−206.

Freire, P. (1969). *Education for critical consciousness.* New York: Continuum.

Freund, E. (1987). *The return of the reader.* London: Methuen.

Freundlich, P. (1987, December). Gazing into Bergdorf's window: Reflections on the higher shopping. *Harper's,* 73−76.

Frow, J. (1986). *Marxism and literary history*. Cambridge, MA: Harvard University Press.

Frye, N. (1957). *Anatomy of criticism: Four essays*. Princeton: Princeton University Press.

—— (1963a). *T. S. Eliot*. Edinburgh: Oliver and Boyd.

—— (1963b). *The well-tempered critic*. Bloomington, IN: Indiana University Press.

—— (1963c). *The educated imagination*. Toronto: CBC Publications.

—— (1963d). *Fables of identity: Studies in poetic mythology*. New York: Harcourt, Brace, Jovanovich.

—— (1965). *A natural perspective: The development of Shakespearean comedy and romance*. New York: Harcourt, Brace & World.

—— (1966). Reflections in a mirror. In M. Kriegar (Ed.), *Northrop Frye in modern criticism*. New York: Columbia University Press.

—— (1967). *The modern century*. (The Whidden Lectures). Toronto: Oxford University Press.

—— (1970). *The stubborn structure: Essays on criticism and society*. Ithaca, NY: Cornell University Press.

—— (1971/1973). *The critical path: An essay on the social context of literary criticism*. Bloomington, IN: University of Indiana Press.

—— (1972). *On teaching literature*. New York: Harcourt, Brace, Jovanovich.

—— (1976). *The secular scripture: A study of the structure of romance*. Cambridge, MA: Harvard University Press.

—— (1980). *Creation and recreation*. Toronto: University of Toronto Press.

—— (1981). The beginning of the word. *Indirections*, 6(1), 4–14.

—— (1982). *The great code: The Bible and literature*. Toronto: Academic Press.

—— (1983). *The myth of deliverance: Reflections on Shakespeare's problem comedies*. Toronto: University of Toronto Press.

—— (1985). *The dialectic of belief and vision*. Address presented at the School of Continuing Studies, University of Toronto.

—— (1988). *On education*. Markham, ON: Fitzhenry & Whiteside.

G. D. P. (1873). Reading lessons. *Ontario Teacher*. 1, 114–115.

Gadamer, H. (1976). *Philosophical hermeneutics*. Berkeley: University of California.

Galda, L. (1982). Assuming the spectator stance: An examination of the responses of three young readers. *Research in the Teaching of English, 16*, 1–20.

Galloway, P. (1980). *What's wrong with high school English? ... It's sexist, un-Canadian, outdated*. Toronto: Ontario Institute for Studies in Education.

Gambell, T. (1986). Response to literature. *English Quarterly, 19*(2), 83–176.

Gardner, H. (1974). *The quest for mind: Piaget, Lévi-Strauss, and the structuralist movement.* New York: Knopf.

Genette, G. (1966). *Figures.* Paris: Editions du Seuil.

———— (1980). *Narrative discourse: An essay in method* (trans. by Jane Lewin). Ithaca, NY: Cornell University Press.

Gere, A. R. (1986). Teaching writing: The major theories. In A. R. Petrosky & D. Bartholomae (Eds.), *The teaching of writing: Eighty-fifth yearbook of the National Society for the Study of Education, Part II.* Chicago: National Society for the Study of Education.

Gibson, E. J., & Levin, H. (1975). *The psychology of reading.* Cambridge, MA: The MIT Press.

Gibson, W. (1980). Authors, speakers, readers, and mock readers. In J. P. Tompkins (Ed.), *Reader-response criticism: From formalism to post-structuralism.* Baltimore: Johns Hopkins University Press.

Gilbert, P. (1987). Post reader-response: The deconstructive critique. In B. Corcoran & E. Evans (Eds.), *Readers, texts, teachers.* Portsmouth, NH: Boynton/Cook.

Gleason, J. B. (Ed.). (1985). *The development of language.* Columbus: Merrill.

Godzich, W. (1983). Introduction: Caution! Reader at work! In P. de Man (Ed.), *Blindness and insight: Essays in the rhetoric of contemporary criticism* (2nd edition, revised) (Theory and History of Literature, Volume 7). Minneapolis: University of Minnesota Press.

Goggin, D. J. (1883). Literature in schools. *The Canada Educational Monthly, 5,* 432–37.

Golden J. M., & Guthrie, J. T. (1986). Convergence and divergence in reader response to literature. *Reading Research Quarterly, 21,* 408–421.

Gombrich, E. (1960). *Art and illusion: A study in the psychology of pictorial representation.* New York: Pantheon.

Goodheart, E. (1984). *The skeptic disposition in contemporary criticism.* Princeton: Princeton University Press.

Goodlad, M. I. (1984). *A place called school: Prospects for the future.* New York: McGraw-Hill.

Goodman, K. S. (1967). Reading: A psycholinguistic guessing game. *Journal of the Reading Specialist, 4,* 126–135.

———— (1969). Analysis of oral reading miscues: Applied psycholinguistics. *Reading Research Quarterly, 5,* 9–30.

———— (1970). Behind the eye: What happens in reading. In K. S. Goodman & O. S. Niles (Eds.), *Reading process and program.* Urbana, IL: National Council of Teachers of English.

———— (1971). Decoding: From code to what? *Journal of Reading, 14,* 455–462, 498.

———— (1982a). *Language and literacy: The selected writings of Kenneth S. Goodman:*

Volume 1: Process, theory, research (F. V. Gollasch, Ed.). Boston: Routledge & Kegan Paul.

———— (1982b). *Language and literacy: The selected writings of Kenneth S. Goodman Volume 2: Reading, language, and the classroom teacher.* (F. V. Gollasch, Ed.). Boston: Routledge & Kegan Paul.

———— (1985). Unity in reading. In H. Singer & R. B. Ruddell (Eds.), *Theoretical models and processes of reading* (3rd ed.). Newark, DE: International Reading Association.

———— (1986). *What's whole in whole language?* Portsmouth, NH: Heinemann.

Goodman, K. S., Shannon, P., Freeman, Y. S., & Murphy, S. (1988). *Report card on basal readers.* Katonah, NY: Richard C. Owen.

Goodman, Y. M., & Burke, C. L. (1972). *Reading miscue inventory: Procedures for diagnosis and evaluation.* New York: Macmillan.

Goodson, I. (1981). Becoming an academic subject: Patterns of explanation and evolution. *British Journal of Sociology of Education, 2,* 163–180.

Göttner-Abendroth, H. (1985). Nine principles of a matriarchal aesthetic. In G. Ecker (Ed.), *Feminist aesthetics.* London: Women's Press.

Gough, P. B. (1972). One second of reading. In J. F. Kavanagh & I. G. Mattingly (Eds.), *Language by ear and by eye.* Cambridge, MA: MIT Press.

Graesser, A. (1981). *Prose comprehension beyond the word.* New York: Springer Verlag.

Graves, D., & Hansen, J. (1984). The author's chair. In J. Jenson (Ed.), *Composing and comprehending.* Urbana, IL: National Conference on Research in English and the ERIC Clearinghouse for Communication and Reading Skills.

Gray, W. S. (1984). *Reading: A research retrospective, 1881–1941* (reprinted from *The encyclopedia of educational research,* New York: Macmillan; edited by J. T. Guthrie). Newark, DE: International Reading Association.

Green, J. (1977). Pedagogical style differences as related to comprehension performances: Grades one through three (Doctoral dissertation, University of California, Berkeley). *Dissertation Abstracts International, 39,* 02A.

Greene, M. (1986). Toward possibility: Expanding the range of literacy. *English Education, 18,* 231–243.

Greenfield, C. (1983). On readers, readerships and reading practices. *Southern Review, 16*(1), 121–142.

Grice, J. (1975). Logic and conversation. In P. Cole & J. L. Morgan (Eds.), *Syntax and semantics: Vol. 3. Speech acts.* New York: Academic Press.

Guerin, W. L., Labor, E. G., Morgan, L., & Willingham, J. R. (1979). *A handbook of critical approaches to literature* (2nd Edition). New York: Harper.

Guthrie, L. F., & Hall, W. S. (1984). Ethnographic approaches to reading research. In P. D. Pearson (Ed.), *Handbook of reading research*. New York: Longman.

Hall, N. (1987). *The emergence of literacy*. Kent, England: Hodder & Stoughton.

Hanslick, E. (1986). *On the musically beautiful: A contribution toward the revision of the aesthetics of music* (G. Payzant, Trans. and Ed.). Indianapolis: Hackett.

Harding, D. W. (1967). Considered experience: The invitation of the novel. *English Education, 1*(2), 12.

Harker, J. W. (1987). Literary theory and the reading process. *Written Communication, 4*, 235–252.

——— (1988/1989). Information processing and the reading of literary texts. *New Literary History, 20*, [465]–481.

Harste, J. C. (1986, December). *Good readers as informants: What it means to be strategic.* Paper presented at the Annual Meeting of the National Reading Conference, San Antonio.

Harste, J. C., & Burke, C. (1977). A new hypothesis for reading teacher research: Both the teaching and learning of reading are theoretically based. In P. D. Pearson (Ed.), *Theory, research and practice* (Twenty-sixth yearbook of the National Reading Conference). Clemson, SC: National Reading Conference.

Harste, J. C., Woodward, V. A., & Burke, C. L. (1984). *Language stories and literacy lessons.* Portsmouth, NH: Heinemann.

Hart, J. (1888). Be a good reader. *The Canada School Journal, 7*, 45.

Hassan, I. (1987). Making sense: The trials of postmodern discourse. *New Literary History, 18*, 437–459.

Hawkes, T. (1977). *Structuralism and semiotics.* Berkeley, CA: University of California Press.

Heap, J. L. (1980). What counts as reading: Limits to certainty in assessment. *Curriculum Inquiry, 10*, 265–292.

——— (1982). Understanding classroom events: A critique of Durkin, with an alternative. *Journal of Reading Behavior, 14*, 391–411.

Heath, S. B. (1982a). Protean shapes in literacy events: Ever-shifting oral and literature traditions. In D. Tannen (Ed.), *Spoken and written language: Exploring orality and literacy.* Norwood, NJ: Ablex.

——— (1982b). Questioning at home and at school: A comparative study. In G. Spindler (Ed.), *The ethnography of schooling.* New York: Holt, Rinehart & Winston.

——— (1985). Being literate in America: A sociohistorical perspective. In J. N. Niles & R. Lalik (Eds.), *Issues in literacy: A research perspective.* Rochester, NY: National Reading Conference.

Heidegger, M. (1971). *What are poets for? Poetry, language, thought* (A. Hofstadter, Trans.). New York: Harper & Row.

Hickman, J. (1980). Children's response to literature: What happens in the classroom. *Language Arts, 57,* 524–529.

——— (1981). A new perspective on response to literature: Research in an elementary school setting. *Research in the Teaching of English, 15,* 343–354.

Hillocks, G. (1980). Toward a hierarchy of skills in the comprehension of literature. *English Journal, 69,* 54–59.

——— (1986). *Research on written composition: New directions for teaching.* Urbana, IL: National Conference on Research in English and the ERIC Clearinghouse on Reading and Communication Skills.

Hillocks, G., & Ludlow, L. H. (1984). A taxonomy of skills in reading and interpreting fiction. *American Educational Research Journal, 21,* 7–24.

Hirsch, E. D. (1987). *Cultural literacy: What every American needs to know.* Boston: Houghton Mifflin.

Hiser, B. T. (1986). *The adventure of Charlie and his wheat-straw hat: A memorat* (illustrated by Mary Szilagyi). New York: Dodd, Mead.

Hodgins, J. G. (1867). The public school libraries of Upper Canada. *HEP & D, 31,* 306–308.

——— (1911). *Documentary history of education in Upper Canada 1791–1876* (Vol. 22). Toronto: King's Printer.

Hoetker, J. (1982). A theory of talking about theories of reading. *College English, 44,* 175–181.

Hoffman, M. S. (Ed.). (1987). *The world almanac and book of facts 1988.* New York: Pharos.

Hofstadter, A. (1971). Introduction. In A. Hofstadter (Ed. and Trans.), *Poetry, language, thought* (By M. Heidegger). New York: Harper.

Holland, N. H. (1968). *The dynamics of literary response.* New York: Norton.

——— (1973). A letter to Leonard. *Hartford Studies in Literature, 5,* 9–30.

——— (1973). *Poems in persons.* New York: Norton.

——— (1975). *Five readers reading.* New York: Norton.

——— (1980). Unity identity text self. In J. Tompkins (Ed.), *Reader-response criticism: From formalism to post-structuralism.* Baltimore: Johns Hopkins University Press.

——— (1985). *I.* New Haven: Yale University Press.

Holmes, J. A. (1953). *The substrata-factor theory of reading.* Berkeley: California Book.

Holmes, J. A., & Singer, H. (1966). *Speed and power of reading in high school* (U.S. Department of Health, Education, and Welfare, Cooperative Research Monograph No. 14). Washington, DC: U.S. Government Printing Office.

Holub, R. C. (1984). *Reception theory: A critical introduction.* London: Methuen.

Hopkins, C. J. (1981). Evaluating children's oral language. In V. Froese &

S. B. Straw (Eds.), *Research in the language arts: Language and schooling*. Baltimore: University Park Press.

Huey, E. B. (1908/1968). *The psychology and pedagogy of reading*. New York: Macmillan. (Reprinted Cambridge, MA: The MIT Press.)

Hunt, C. L., Jr. (1957). Can we measure specific factors associated with reading comprehension? *Journal of Educational Research, 57,* 161–171.

Hunt, R. A. (1987, December). *From the study to the lab to the easy chair: Theory-driven hypotheses in the study of literary reading*. Position Paper, First International Congress for the Empirical Study of Literature, Siegen, West Germany. (Forthcoming in *Poetics*.)

Hunt, R. A., & Vipond, D. (1986). Evaluations in literary reading. *TEXT, 6*(1), 53–71.

——— (1987). Aesthetic reading: Some strategies for research. *English Quarterly, 20,* 178–183.

Hunter, I. (1982). The concept of context and the problem of reading. *Southern Review, 15*(1), 80–91.

——— (1983). Reading character. *Southern Review, 16*(2), 226–243.

Hyman, S. E. (1947). *The armed vision: A study in the methods of modern literary criticism*. New York: Random House.

Hynds, S. (1985). Interpersonal cognitive complexity and the literary response processes of adolescent readers. *Research in the Teaching of English, 19,* 386–404.

——— (1987). *Social cognition, literary response, and character attribution processes among young adult readers*. Manuscript submitted for publication.

——— (1988, May). *Bringing life to literature and literature to life: Social constructs and contexts of four adolescent readers*. Paper presented at the meeting of the International Reading Association, Toronto.

——— (1989). Bringing life to literature and literature to life: Social constructs and contexts of four adolescent readers. *Research in the Teaching of English, 23*(1), 30–61.

Iran-Nejad, A. (1987). The schema: A long term memory structure or a transient functional pattern. In R. J. Tierney, P. Anders, & J. Mitchell, (Eds.), *Understanding readers' understanding: Theory and Practice*. Hillsdale, NJ: Erlbaum.

Iser, W. (1972). The reading process: A phenomenological approach. *New Literary History, 3,* 279–300.

——— (1974). *The implied reader: Patterns of communication in prose fiction from Bunyan to Beckett*. Baltimore: Johns Hopkins University Press.

——— (1978). *The act of reading: A theory of aesthetic response*. Baltimore: Johns Hopkins University Press.

——— (1980). Texts and readers. *Discourse Processes, 3,* 327–343.

Jaeger, W. (1943). *Paideia: The ideals of Greek culture*. (Trans. Gilbert Highet:

Volume 1: Archaic Greece: The mind of Athens. Volume 2: In Search of the Divine Centre). New York: Oxford University Press.

Jameson, F. (1971). *Marxism and form: Twentieth-century dialectical theories of literature*. Princeton: Princeton University Press.

——— (1981). *The political unconscious: Narrative as a socially symbolic act*. Ithaca, NY: Cornell University Press.

——— (1987). Reading without interpretation: Post-modernism and the video-text. In N. Fabb, D. Attridge, A. Durant, & C. MacCabe (Eds.), *The linguistics of writing*. New York: Methuen.

Jauss H. R. (1982). *Aesthetic experience and literary hermeneutics* (Trans. by Michael Shaw.) Minneapolis: University of Minnesota Press.

Jefferson, A., & Robey, D. (Eds.). (1982). *Modern literary theory: A comparative introduction*. London: Batsford.

Jensen, J. M. (Ed.). (1984). *Composing and comprehending*. Urbana, IL: National Conference on Research on English and the ERIC Clearinghouse for Communication and Reading Skills.

John-Steiner, V. (1986). *Notebooks of the mind*. Albuquerque: University of New Mexico Press.

Johnson, D. D., Toms-Bronowski, S., & Buss, R. R. (1983). A critique of Frederick B. Davis's study: Fundamental factors of comprehension in reading. In L. M. Gentile, M. L. Kamil, & J. S. Blanchard (Eds.), *Reading research revisited*. Columbus, OH: Charles E. Merrill.

Johnson, N. (1986). Origin and artifact: Classical rhetoric in modern composition texts. *English Quarterly, 19*, 207–216.

Johnson, R. A. (1983). *We: Understanding the psychology of romantic love*. San Francisco: Harper & Row.

Jordan, J. E. (Ed.). (1965). *A defense of poetry: The four ages of poetry: Shelley and Peacock* (The Library of Liberal Arts). New York: Bobbs-Merrill.

Jose, P. E., & Brewer, W. R. (1984). Development of story liking: Character identification, suspense, and outcome resolution. *Development Psychology, 20*, 911–924.

——— (1988). Liking of plan-based stories: The role of goal importance and goal attainment difficulty. *Discourse processes, 11*, 261–273.

Just, M. A., & Carpenter, P. A. (1980/1985). A theory of reading: From eye fixations to comprehension. *Psychological Review, 87*, 329–354. (Reprinted In H. Singer & R. B. Rudell [Eds.], *Theoretical models and processes of reading* [3rd ed.]. Newark, DE: International Reading Association.)

Kahn, E. A., Walter, C. C., & Johannessen, L. R. (1984). *Writing about literature*. Urbana, IL: National Council of Teachers of English.

Kaivola, K. (1987). Becoming woman: Identification and desire in *The Sound and the Fury. Reader, 17*, 29–43.

Kamil, M. L. (1984). Current traditions of reading research. In P. D. Pearson (Ed.), *Handbook of reading research*. New York: Longman.

Kamuf, P. (1986). Floating authorship [Review of *Against theory: Literary studies and the new pragmatism*]. *Diacritics, 16,* 3–13.

Kaplan, C. (Ed.). (1975). *Criticism: The major statements.* New York: St. Martin's Press.

Kelly, G. (1955). *The psychology of personal constructs.* New York: Norton.

Kintsch, W. (1974). *The representation of meaning in memory.* Hillsdale, NJ: Erlbaum.

Kintsch, W., & van Dijk, T. A. (1978). Toward a model of text comprehension and production. *Psychological Review, 85,* 363–394.

Knapp, S., & Michaels, W. B. (1982). Against interpretation. *Critical Inquiry, 8,* 723–742.

Koelb, C., & Lokke, V. (Eds.). (1987). *The current in criticism: Essays on the present and future of literary theory.* West Lafayette, IN: Purdue University Press.

Kolodny, A. (1985). Dancing through the minefield: Some observations on the theory, practice, and politics of a feminist literary criticism. In E. Showalter (Ed.), *The new feminist criticism: Essays on women, literature, and theory.* New York: Pantheon.

Kroll, J. (1986). William Hurt and "The Kiss of the Spiderwoman." *Esquire, 106*(4), 105–111.

Kuhn, T. (1970). *The structure of scientific revolutions.* Chicago: University of Chicago Press.

LaBerge, D., & Samuels, S. J. (1974). Toward a theory of automatic information processing in reading. *Cognitive Psychology, 6,* 293–323.

Labov, W. (1972). *Language in the inner city: Studies in the black English vernacular.* Philadelphia: University of Pennsylvania Press.

Laclau, E., & Mouffe, C. (1987). Post-Marxism without apologies. *New Left Review, 166,* 79–106.

Langer, S. K. (1953). *Feeling and form.* New York: Scribners.

Lavery, R. H., & Straw, S. B. (1986, May). *Responding to theme in short story: An investigation of students' responses.* Paper presented at the Fourth International Conference of the International Federation of Teachers of English, Ottawa, Ontario, Canada.

LaZansky, J. (1988, April). *The themes children generate in response to stories.* Paper presented at the annual meeting of the American Educational Research Association, New Orleans, LA.

Leitch, V. (1983). *Deconstructive criticism: An advanced introduction.* New York: Columbia University Press.

Lentricchia, F. (1980). *After the new criticism.* Chicago: University of Chicago Press.

Lester, N. (1982). A system for analyzing characters' values in literary texts. *Research in the Teaching of English, 16,* 321–338.

Lipking, L. (1983/1984). Aristotle's sister: A poetics of abandonment. In R. von Hallberg (Ed.), *Canons*. Chicago: University of Chicago Press.

Lokke, V. (1987). Introduction: Taxonomies are never innocent. In C. Koelb & V. Lokke, (Eds.), *The current in criticism: Essays on the present and future of literary theory*. West Lafayette, IN: Purdue University Press.

Longinus. (1967). On the sublime. In T. S. Dorsch (Ed. and Trans.), *Aristotle, Horace, Longinus: Classical literary criticism*. Harmondsworth: Penguin.

Lukacs, G. (1971). *The theory of the novel* (trans. by Anna Bostock). London: Merlin Press.

Lucking, R. (1977). A study of the effects of hierarchically ordered questioning techniques on adolescents' responses to short stories. *Research in the Teaching of English, 10,* 203−225.

Macdonell, D. (1986). *Theories of discourse*. Oxford: Basil Blackwell.

MacLachlan, P. (1987). *Sarah, plain and tall*. New York: Harper.

Mailloux, S. (1982). *Interpretive conventions: The reader in the study of American fiction*. Ithaca, NY: Cornell University Press.

Mandler, J. M. (1978). A code in the node: The use of story schema in retrieval. *Discourse Processes, 1,* 14−35.

Mandler, J. M., & Johnson, N. S. (1977). Remembrance of things parsed: Story structure and recall. *Cognitive Psychology, 9,* 111−151.

Markman, E. M. (1981). Comprehension monitoring. In W. P. Dickson (Ed.), *Children's oral communication skills*. New York: Academic Press.

Marlow, D. R. (1983). How directed discussions and nondirected discussions affect tenth grade students' responses to four selected short stories (Doctoral dissertation, University of Georgia). *Dissertation Abstracts International, 44,* 08A.

Marshall, J. (1987). The effects of writing on students' understanding of literary texts. *Research in the Teaching of English, 21,* 30−63.

Martin, J. R. (1985). *Reclaiming a conversation: The ideal of the educated woman*. New Haven: Yale University Press.

Maslow, A. H. (1954). *Motivation and personality*. New York: Harper.

────── (1970). *Motivation and personality* (2nd ed.). New York: Harper & Row.

Mathieson, M. (1975). *The preachers of culture: A study of English and its teachers*. London: Allen & Unwin.

McCormick, K. (1985). Introduction. *Reader, 14,* [1]−4.

McDermott, R. (1976). Kids make sense: An ethnographic account of the interactional management of success and failure in one first grade classroom (Doctoral dissertation, Stanford University). *Dissertation Abstracts International, 38,* 03A.

McInerney, J. (1987). Are we there yet? In J. Harste (Ed.), *Essays in literacy* (mimeographed). Bloomington, IN: Indiana University, Language Education Department.

McKellar, P. (1957). *Imagination and thinking*. London: Cohen & West.

Meyer, J. F. (1975). *The organization of prose and its effects on memory*. Amsterdam: North-Holland.

Michaels, S. (1981). Sharing time: Children's narrative styles and differential access to literacy. *Language in Society, 10*, 423–442.

Miller, B. E. (1980). *Teaching the art of literature*. Urbana, IL: National Council of Teachers of English.

Miller, G. A. (1962). Some psychological studies of grammar. *American Psychologist, 17*, 748–762.

——— (1964). The psycholinguists. *Encounter, 23*(1), 29–37.

Miller, R. (1975). A note on the text. In R. Barthes, *The pleasure of text* (trans. by R. Miller). New York: Hill and Wang.

Mills, P. J. (1987). *Woman, nature and psyche*. New Haven: Yale University Press.

Mitchell, K. (1981). *Sinclair Ross: A reader's guide*. Regina, SK: Cotean.

Mitchell, W. J. T. (Ed.). (1986). *Against theory: Literary studies and the new pragmatism*. Chicago: University of Chicago Press.

Moffett, J. (1968). *Teaching the universe of discourse*. Boston: Houghton-Mifflin.

——— (1973). *Interaction: A student-centered language arts and reading program, K–12* (Out of print). Boston: Houghton-Mifflin.

——— (1988a). *Storm in the mountains: A case study of censorship, conflict, and consciousness*. Carbondale, IL: Southern Illinois University Press.

——— (1988b). *Coming on center: Essays in English education* (2nd ed.). Portsmouth, NH: Boynton/Cook.

Moffett, J., & Wagner, B. J. (1983). *Student-centered language arts and reading, K–13: A handbook for teachers* (3rd edition). Boston: Houghton-Mifflin.

Moi, T. (1985). *Sexual/textual politics: Feminist literary theory*. London: Methuen.

Moore, D. W., & Moore, S. A. (1987). Reading literature independently. *Journal of Reading, 30*, 596–600.

Morely, D. (1986). *Family television*. London: Commedia.

Morgan, R. (1987a). *English studies as cultural production in Ontario, 1860–1920*. Unpublished doctoral dissertation, University of Toronto, Toronto.

——— (1987b). Three dreams of language. *College English, 49*, 449–458.

——— (1989). The Englishness of English teaching. In I. Goodson & P. Medway (Eds.), *Bringing English to order*. Philadelphia: Falmer Press.

Morton, E. (1872). School reading is not reading. *Journal of Education for Ontario, 25*, 167.

Mosenthal, P. B. (1987a). Meaning in the storage-and-conduit metaphor of reading. *The Reading Teacher, 41*, 340–342.

——— (1987b). Metaphors for reading in an information age. *The Reading Teacher, 41*, 82–84.

Mosenthal, P., & Davidson-Mosenthal, R. (1982). Individual differences in children's use of new and old information during reading lessons. *Elementary School Journal, 83*, 24–34.

Mosenthal, P., & Na, T. (1980). Quality of text recall as a function of children's classroom competence. *Journal of Experimental Child Psychology, 30*, 1–21.

Munro, A. (1974). *The moons of Jupiter.* New York: Knopf.

Murdoch, I. (1977). *The fire and the sun: Why Plato banished the artists.* Oxford: Oxford University Press.

Musselwhite, D. (1978). The novel as narcotic. In F. Barker (Ed.), *1848: The sociology of literature.* Colchester: University of Essex.

National Assessment of Educational Progress. (1980). Denver: National Assessment of Educational Progress.

Neel, J. (1985). Plot, character, or theme? Lear and the teacher. In C. Atkins & M. L. Johnson (Eds.), *Writing and reading differently.* Lawrence, KS: University Press of Kansas.

Neisser, U. (1982). *Memory observed: Remembering in natural contexts.* San Francisco: Freeman.

Nelson, C. (1986). Against English: Theory and the limits of the discipline. *ADE Bulletin, 85*, 1–6.

Newkirk, T. (1984). Looking for trouble: A way to unmask our readings. *College English, 46*, 756–766.

———— (1986). *Only Connect: Uniting Reading and Writing.* Portsmouth, NH: Boynton/Cook.

Norris, C. (1982). *Deconstruction: Theory and practice.* London: Methuen.

Nussbaum, M. (1985). Finely aware and richly responsible? Moral attention and the moral task of literature. *The Journal of Philosophy, 82*, 516–529.

Nye, R. B. & Grabo, N. S. (Eds.). (1965). *American thought and writing* (Volume 1: The Colonial Period). Boston: Houghton Mifflin.

Nystrand, M. (1987). *The structure of written communication.* New York: Academic Press.

O'Keefe, D. J., & Sypher, H. E. (1981). Cognitive complexity measures and the relationship of cognitive complexity to communication. *Human Communication Research, 8*, 72–92.

Olsen, S. H. (1978). *The structure of literary understanding.* Cambridge: Cambridge University Press.

Orr, R. P. (1981). *The meaning of transcendence: A Heideggerian reflection.* (The American Academy of Religion Dissertation Series no. 35.) Chico, CA: Scholars Press.

Ortony, A. (1985). Theoretical and methodological issues in the empirical study of metaphor. In C. R. Cooper (Ed.), *Researching response to literature and the teaching of literature: Points of departure.* Norwood, NJ: Ablex.

Page, A. (1983). Children's story comprehension as a result of story telling and story dramatization: A study of the child as spectator and participant (Doctoral dissertation, University of Massachusetts). *Dissertation Abstracts International, 44,* 04.

Parker, G. (1985). *The beginnings of the book trade in Canada.* Toronto: University of Toronto Press.

Pearson, P. D. (Ed.). (1984). *Handbook of reading research.* New York: Longman.

Pearson, P. D., & Johnson, D. D. (1984). *Teaching reading comprehension* (2nd edition). New York: Holt, Rinehart and Winston.

Pearson, P. D., & Tierney, R. J. (1984). On becoming a thoughtful reader: Learning to read like a writer. In A. Purves and O. Niles (Eds.), *Becoming readers in a complex society: Eighty-third yearbook of the National Society for the Study of Education.* Chicago: University of Chicago Press.

Pereleman, L. (1986). The context of classroom writing. *College English, 48,* 471–479.

Perrine, L. (1963). *Sound and sense: An introduction to poetry.* New York: Harcourt.

Peters, W. H., & Blues, A. G. (1978). Teacher intellectual disposition as it relates to student openness in written response to literature. *Research in the Teaching of English, 12,* 127–136.

Petrosky, A. (1982). From story to essay: Reading and writing. *College Composition and Communication, 33,* 19–36.

Pettit, P. (1975). *The concept of structuralism: A critical analysis.* Dublin: Gill and Macmillan.

Pitchert, J. W., & Anderson, R. C. (1977). Taking different perspectives on a story. *Journal of Educational Psychology, 69,* 309–315.

Plato. (1961/1980). Symposium and Republic. In E. Hamilton and H. Cairns (Eds. and Trans.), *Plato: The collected dialogues.* Princeton: Princeton University Press.

Plato. (1973). Phaedrus. In W. Hamilton (Ed. and Trans.), *Phaedrus and the seventh and eighth letters.* Harmondsworth: Penguin.

Polanyi, M. (1958). *Personal knowledge: Towards a post-critical philosophy.* London: Routledge & Kegan Paul.

Poulet, G. (1980). Criticism and the experience of interiority. In J. P. Tompkins (Ed.), *Reader-response criticism: From formalism to post-structuralism.* Baltimore: Johns Hopkins University Press.

Pratt, L. (1976). *A speech-act theory of literary discourse.* Bloomington, IN: University of Indiana Press.

Propp, V. (1928/1968). *Morphology of the folktale* (2nd ed.). Austin: University of Texas Press.

Purkey, W. W. (1970). *Self concept and school achievement.* Englewood Cliffs, NJ: Prentice-Hall.

Purves, A. C. (1980). Putting readers in their places: Some alternatives to cloning Stanley Fish. *College English, 42,* 228–236.

—— (1986, February). *Cultural literacy and research in response to literature.* Paper presented at the annual meeting of the National Council of Teachers of English Assembly on Research Conference, Chicago.

Purves, A. C., Harnisch, D. L., Quirk, D. L., & Bauer, B. (1981). *Reading and literature: American achievement in international perspective.* Urbana, IL: National Council of Teachers of English.

Purves, A. C., with Rippere, V. (1968). *Elements of writing about a literary work: A study of response to literature.* Urbana, IL: National Council of Teachers of English.

Rabinow, P. (Ed.). (1984). *The Foucault reader.* New York: Pantheon Books.

Radway, J. (1984). *Reading the romance.* Chapel Hill, NC: University of North Carolina Press.

Ransom, J. C. (1941). *The new criticism.* Norfolk, CT: New Directions.

Reddy, M. (1979). The conflict metaphor—A case of frame conflict in our language about language. In A. Ortony (Ed.), *Metaphor and thought.* Cambridge: Cambridge University Press.

Resnick, L. B., & Robinson, B. H. (1979). Motivational aspects of the literacy problem. In J. B. Carroll (Ed.), *Toward a literate society.* New York: McGraw-Hill.

Reynolds, R. E., & Anderson, R. C. (1982). Influence of questions on the allocation of attention during reading. *Journal of Educational Psychology, 74,* 623–632.

Reynolds, R. E., Taylor, M. A., Steffenson, M. A., Shirey, L. L., & Anderson, R. C. (1981). *Cultural schemata and reading comprehension* (Technical report No. 201). Urbana: University of Illinois, Center for the Study of Reading.

Richards, I. A. (1925). *Principles of literary criticism.* New York: Harcourt, Brace & World.

—— (1926). *Practical criticism: A study of literary judgment.* London: Paul Trench Trubner.

—— (1929). *Practical criticism.* New York: Harcourt, Brace & World.

Rickword, C. H. (1933). A note on fiction. In F. R. Leavis (Ed.), *Towards standards of criticism.* London: Wishart. (Reprinted 1976.)

Riffaterre, M. (1984). *Semiotics of poetry* (Midland edition). Bloomington: Indiana University Press.

Robinson, J. C. (1987). *Radical literary education: A classroom experiment with Wordsworth's Ode.* Madison, WI: University of Wisconsin Press.

Roen, D. H., & Willey, R. J. (1988). The effects of audience awareness on drafting and revising. *Research in the Teaching of English, 33,* 75–88.

Rogers, T. (1988). *Students as literary critics.* (Doctoral dissertation, University of Illinois at Urbana). *Dissertation Abstracts International, 49,* 2569A.

Rogers-Zegarra, N., & Singer, H. (1985). Anglo and Chicano comprehension of ethnic stories. In H. Singer & R. B. Ruddell (Eds.), *Theoretical models and processes of reading* (3rd Edition). Newark, DE: International Reading Association.

Rorty, R. (1982). Introduction: Pragmatism and philosophy. In *Consequences of pragmatism (Essays: 1972–1980)*. Minneapolis: University of Minnesota Press.

Rosen, H. (1984). *Stories and meanings*. Sheffield, England: National Association for the Teaching of English.

——— (1986). The importance of story. *Language Arts, 63*, 226–237.

Rosenblatt, L. M. (1938). *Literature as exploration*. New York: Appleton-Century.

——— (1978). *The reader, the text, the poem: The transactional theory of the literary work*. Carbondale, IL: Southern Illinois University Press.

——— (1985a). *Literature as exploration* (3rd ed.). New York: Modern Language Association.

——— (1985b). Viewpoints: Transaction versus interaction: A terminological rescue operation. *Research in the Teaching of English, 19*, 96–107.

Ross, C. (1987). Metaphors of reading. *The Journal of Literary History, 32*, 19–24.

Ross, M., & Stevens, J. (Eds.). (1967). *In search of ourselves*. Toronto: Dent.

Ross, S. (1971). The painted door. In A. Lucas (Ed.), *Great Canadian short stories*. New York: Dell.

Roudiez, L. S. (Ed. and Trans.). (1980). Introduction. In J. Kristeva, *Desire in language: A semiotic approach to literature and art*. New York: Columbia University Press.

Rubin, S., & Gardner, H. (1985). Once upon a time: The development of sensitivity to story structure. In C. R. Cooper (Ed.), *Researching response to literature and the teaching of literature*. Norwood, NJ: Ablex.

Ruddell, R. B., & Speaker, R. (1985). The interactive reading process: A model. In H. Singer & R. B. Ruddell (Eds.), *Theoretical models and processes of reading* (3rd ed.). Newark, DE: International Reading Association.

Rumelhart, D. E. (1977). Toward an interactive model of reading. In S. Dornic (Ed.), *Attention and performance* (Vol. 6). Hillsdale, NJ: Erlbaum.

Rumelhart, D. E., & Ortony, A. (1977). The representation of meaning in memory. In R. C. Anderson, R. J. Spiro, & W. E. Montague (Eds.), *Schooling and the acquisition of knowledge*. Hillsdale, NJ: Erlbaum.

Ryan, M. (1982). *Marxism and deconstruction: A critical articulation*. Baltimore: Johns Hopkins University Press.

Sadowski, M. (1983). An exploratory study of the relationships between reported imagery and the comprehension and recall of a story. *Reading Research Quarterly, 19*, 110–123.

Said, E. (1983). *The world, the text, the critic*. Cambridge, MA: Harvard University Press.

———— (1985). *Beginnings: Intention and method*. New York: Columbia University Press.

Salvatori, M. (1985). The dialogical nature of basic reading and writing. In D. Bartholomae & A. Petrosky (Eds.), *Facts, artifacts & counterfacts*. Portsmouth, NH: Boynton/Cook.

Samuels, S. J. (1985). Word recognition. In H. Singer & R. B. Ruddell (Eds.), *Theoretical models and processes of reading* (3rd Edition). Newark, DE: International Reading Association.

Samuels, S. J., & Kamil, M. L. (1984). Models of the reading process. In P. D. Pearson (Ed.), *Handbook of reading research*. New York: Longman.

Scardamalia, M., & Bereiter, M. (1985). Development of dialectical processes in composition. In D. R. Olson, N. Torrence, & A. Hildyard (Eds.), *Literacy, language, and learning: The nature and consequence of reading and writing*. Cambridge: Cambridge University Press.

Schank, R. C., & Abelson, R. P. (1977). *Scripts, plans, goals, and understanding: An inquiry into human knowledge structures*. Hillsdale, NJ: Erlbaum.

Schmidt, S. J. (1982). *Foundation of the empirical science of literature*. Hamburg: Buske.

———— (1989). *Die emergenz des literatursystems im 18. jahrhundert*. MS, Siegen: Institut fur Empirische Literatur- und Medienforschung.

Scholes, R. (1979). *Fabulation and metafiction*. Urbana, IL: University of Illinois Press.

———— (1985). *Textual power: Literary theory and the teaching of English*. New Haven: Yale University Press.

Schön, D. (1979). Generative metaphor: A perspective on problem-setting in social policy. In A. Ortony (Ed.), *Metaphor and thought*. Cambridge: Cambridge University Press.

Schweickart, P. P. (1986). Reading ourselves: Toward a feminist theory of reading. In E. A. Flynn & P. P. Schweickart (Eds.), *Gender and reading: Essays on readers, texts, and contexts*. Baltimore: Johns Hopkins University Press.

Scollon, R., & Scollon, S. (1981). *Narrative, literacy, and face in interethnic communication*. Norwood, NJ: Ablex.

———— (1982). Cooking it up and boiling it down: Athabascan story retellings. In D. Tannen (Ed.), *Coherence in spoken and written language: Exploring orality and literacy*. Norwood, NJ: Ablex.

Searle, J. (1969). *Speech acts*. New York: Cambridge University Press.

Shank, R. (1982). *Dynamic memory*. Cambridge: Cambridge University Press.

Shank, R. C., & Abelson, R. P. (1977). *Scripts, plans, goals and understanding: An inquiry into human knowledge structures*. Hillsdale, NJ: Erlbaum.

Shannon, P. (1983). The use of commercial reading materials in American elementary schools. *Reading Research Quarterly, 19*, 68–85.

Shantz, C. (1983). Social cognition. In F. Flavell & E. Markman (Eds.), *Cognitive development* (In D. E. Mussen [Ed.], *Handbook of child psychology, Volume III*). New York: John Wiley & Sons.

Shedd, P. (1976). *The relationship between attitude of the reader toward someone's changing role and response to literature which illuminates women's role.* Washington, DC: National Institute of Education. (ERIC Document Reproduction Service No. ED 142 956.)

Short, K. (1986). *Literacy as a collaborative experience.* Unpublished doctoral dissertation, Indiana University, Bloomington.

Showalter, E. (Ed.). (1985). *The new feminist criticism: Essays on women, literature, and theory.* New York: Pantheon.

Sidney, P. (1966). *A defence of poetry* (J. A. Van Dorsten, Ed. and Trans.). London: Oxford University Press.

Singer, H. (1960). *Conceptual ability in the substrata-factor theory of reading.* Unpublished doctoral dissertation, University of California at Berkeley.

———— (1962). Substrata-factor theory of reading: Theoretical design for teaching reading. In J. A. Figerel (Ed.), *Challenge and experiment in reading.* New York: Scholastic.

———— (1964). Substrata-factor patterns accompanying development in power of reading, elementary through college levels. In E. Thurston & L. Hafner (Eds.), *The philosophical and sociological bases of education: Fourteenth yearbook of the National Reading Conference.* Marquette, WI: National Reading Conference.

———— (1965). A developmental model for speed of reading in grades three through six. *Reading Research Quarterly, 1,* 29–49.

———— (1983). A critique of Jack Holmes's study: The substrata-factor theory of reading and its history and conceptual relationship to interaction theory. In L. M. Gentile, M. L. Kamil, & J. S. Blanchard (Eds.), *Reading research revisited.* Columbus, OH: Charles E. Merrill.

———— (1985). The substrata-factor theory of reading. In H. Singer & R. B. Ruddell (Eds.), *Theoretical models and processes of reading* (3rd ed.). Newark, DE: International Reading Association.

Singer, H., & Donlan, D. (1982). Problem-solving schema with question generation for comprehension of complex short stories. *Reading Research Quarterly, 17,* 166–186.

Singer, H., & Ruddell, R. B. (Eds.). (1985). *Theoretical models and processes of reading* (3rd edition). Newark, DE: International Reading Association.

Skelton, R. (1978). *Poetic truth.* London: Heinemann.

Slatoff, W. (1970). *With respect to readers: Dimensions of literary response.* Ithaca, NY: Cornell University Press.

Smith, F. (1971). *Understanding reading.* New York: Holt, Rinehart, & Winston.

———— (1984). Learning to read like a writer. In J. Jensen (Ed.), *Composing and comprehending*. Urbana, IL: National Conference on Research in English and the ERIC Clearinghouse on Reading and Communication Skills.

———— (1985). A metaphor for literacy: Creating worlds or shunting information. In D. R. Olson, N. Torrance, & A. Hildyard (Eds.), *Literacy, language, and learning: The nature and consequences of reading and writing*. Cambridge: Cambridge University Press.

Smith, J. H., & Parks, E. W. (Eds.). (1951). *The great critics* (3rd edition). New York: W. W. Norton

Smith-Burke, M. T. (1982). Extending concepts through language activities. In J. A. Langer and M. T. Smith-Burke (Eds.), *Reader meets author: Bridging the gap*. Newark, DE: International Reading Association.

Snow, C. P. (1959). *The two cultures and the scientific revolution*. Cambridge: Cambridge University Press.

Spearritt, D. (1972). Identification of subskills of reading comprehension by maximum likelihood factor analysis. *Reading Research Quarterly, 8,* 92–111.

Spender, D. (1980). *Man made language*. London: Routledge & Kegan Paul.

Spiro, R. J. (1980). Constructive aspects of prose comprehension and recall. In R. J. Spiro, B. C. Bruce, & W. F. Brewer (Eds.), *Theoretical issues in reading comprehension*. Hillsdale, NJ: Erlbaum.

———— (1982). Long-term comprehension: Schema-based versus experiential and evaluative understanding. *Poetics, 11,* 77–86.

Spivey, N. (1984). *Discourse synthesis: Constructing texts in reading and writing*. Newark, DE: International Reading Association.

Squire, J. R. (1964). *The responses of adolescents while reading four short stories*. Urbana, IL: National Council of Teachers of English.

Stanislavski, K. (1936). *An actor prepares* (E. R. Hapgood, Trans.). New York: Theatre Arts Books.

Stanovich, K. E. (1980). Toward an interactive-compensatory model of individual differences in reading fluency. *Reading Research Quarterly, 16,* 32–71.

Steedman, C. (1986). *Landscape for a good woman: A story of two lives*. New Brunswick, NJ: Rutgers University Press.

Steffenson, M. S., Joag-Dev, C., & Anderson, R. C. (1979). A cross-cultural perspective on reading comprehension. *Reading Research Quarterly, 15,* 10–29.

Stein, N. L. (1979). How children understand stories: A developmental analysis. In L. Katz (Ed.), *Current topics in early childhood education* (Vol. 2). Norwood, NJ: Ablex.

Stein, N. L., & Glenn, C. G. (1979). An analysis of story comprehension in elementary school children. In R. O. Freedle (Ed.), *New directions in discourse processing*. Norwood, NJ: Ablex.

Stein, N. L., & Nezworski, T. (1978). *The effects of organization and instructional set on story memory* (Technical Report No. 68). Urbana, IL: University of Illinois Center for the Study of Reading.

Stein, V. (1987). *Elaboration: Using what you know* (Report No. 6). Pittsburgh: Carnegie Mellon University, Center for the Study of Writing.

Steiner, G. (1974). *Nostalgia for the absolute: The Massey lectures.* Toronto: CBC Publications.

Stevens, W. (1959). *Poems.* New York: Vintage.

Stierle, K. (1980). The reading of fictional texts. In S. R. Suleiman & I. Crosman (Eds.), *The reader in the text: Essay on audience and interpretation.* Princeton: Princeton University Press.

Stone, L. (1989). Towards a transformational theory of teaching. *Philosophy of Education, 1988: Proceedings of the Forty-fourth Annual Meeting of the Philosophy of Education Society, San Diego.* Normal, IL: Philosophy of Educational Society.

Straw, S. B. (1986). *The collaborative interpretation of poetry.* Paper presented at the meeting of the National Council of Teachers of English, San Antonio, Texas.

—— (1989). Collaborative learning and response to theme in poetry. *Reading-Canada-Lecture, 7,* 191–200.

—— (1990). Reading and responding to literature: Transactionalizing instruction. In S. Hynds & D. Rubin (Eds.), *Perspective on talk and learning.* Urbana, IL: National Council of Teachers of English.

Suleiman, S. R. (1980). Introduction: Varieties of audience-oriented criticism. In S. R. Suleiman & I. Crosman (Eds.), *The reader in the text: Essays on audience and interpretation.* Princeton: Princeton University Press.

Suleiman, S. R., & Crosman, I. (Eds.). (1980). *The reader in the text: Essays on audience and interpretation.* Princeton: Princeton University Press.

Sullivan, E. (1987). Critical pedagogy and television. In David W. Livingston (Ed.), *Critical pedagogy and cultural power.* Toronto: Garamond Press.

Sutherland, R. (1971). The Calvinist/Jansenist pantomime. *Second image: Comparative studies in Quebec/Canadian literature.* Toronto: Newpress.

Svennson, C. (1985). *The construction of poetic meaning: A cultural-developmental study of symbolic and non-symbolic strategies in the interpretation of contemporary poetry.* Västervik, Sweden: Liber Forlag.

Thomson, J. (1987). *Understanding teenagers' reading: Reading processes and the teaching of literature.* Melbourne: Methuen Australia.

Thorndike, E. L. (1917). Reading as reasoning: A study of mistakes in paragraph reading. *Journal of Educational Psychology, 8,* 323–332.

Thurstone, L. L. (1946). Notes on a reanalysis of Davis's reading tests. *Psychometrika, 11*(3), 185–188.

Tierney, R. J. (1987). Voices, images, experiences and perspectives: Transaction between readers, writers and the world of the text. *Proceedings of the 13th*

Australian Reading Association Annual Conference. Grosford: Ashton-Scholastic.

Tierney, R. J., & Cunningham, J. W. (1984). Research on teaching reading comprehension. In P. D. Pearson (Ed.), *Handbook of reading research.* New York: Longman.

Tierney, R. J., & LaZansky, J. (1980). The rights and responsibilities of readers and writers. *Language Arts, 57,* 606–613.

Tierney, R. J., LaZansky, J., Raphael, T., & Cohen, P. (1987). Authors' intention and readers' interpretations. In R. J. Tierney, P. L. Anders, & J. Mitchell (Eds.), *Understanding readers' understanding.* Hillsdale, NJ: Erlbaum.

Tierney, R. J., & McGinley, W. (1987). *Exploring reading and writing as ways of knowing. Proceedings of the 13th Australian Reading Association Annual Conference.* Grosford: Ashton-Scholastic.

Tierney, R. J., & Pearson, P. D. (1984). Toward a composing model of reading. In J. Jensen (Ed.), *Composing and comprehending.* Urbana, IL: National Conference on Research in English and the ERIC Clearinghouse on Reading and Communication Skilk.

——— (1985). Learning to learn from text: A framework for improving classroom practice. In H. Singer & R. B. Ruddell (Eds.), *Theoretical models and processes of reading* (3rd ed.). Newark, DE: International Reading Association.

Tolkien, J. R. R. (1964). On fairy stories. In *Tree and leaf.* London: Allen & Unwin.

Tompkins, J. P. (1980). *Reader-response criticism: From formalism to post-structuralism.* Baltimore: Johns Hopkins University Press.

Trimble, C. (1984). *The relationships among fairy tales, ego development, grade level, and sex* (Doctoral dissertation, University of Alabama). *Dissertation Abstracts International, 46,* 04A.

Updike, J. (1966). A & P. In J. Moffett & K. McElheny (Eds.), *Points of view.* New York: New American Library.

Valéry, P. (1972). The idea of art. In H. Osborne (Ed.), *Aesthetics.* London: Oxford University Press.

van Dijk, T. A. (1972). *Some aspects of text grammars.* The Hague: Mouton.

van Dijk, T. A., & Kintsch, W. (1983). *Strategies of discourse comprehension.* New York: Academic Press.

VanDeWeghe, R. (1987). Making and remaking meaning: Developing literary responses through purposeful, informal writing. *English Quarterly, 20,* 38–51.

Vaughan, J. L., Jr. (1982). Instructural strategies. In A. Berger & H. Allan Robinson (Eds.), *Secondary school reading.* Urbana, IL: National Council of Teachers of English.

Venezky, R. L. (1984). The history of reading research. In P. D. Pearson (Ed.), *Handbook of reading research.* New York: Longman.

Vipond, D., & Hunt, R. A. (1984). Point-driven understanding: Pragmatic and cognitive dimensions of literary reading. *Poetics, 13,* 261–277.

——— (1987). Shunting information or making contact? Assumptions for research on aesthetic reading. *English Quarterly, 20,* 131–136.

——— (1989). Literary processing and response as transaction: Evidence for the contribution of readers, text, and situations. In D. Meutsch & R. Viehoff (Eds.), *Comprehension of literary discourse: Results and problems of interdisciplinary approaches.* Berlin: deGruyter.

Vipond, D., Hunt, R. A., Jewett, J., & Reither, J. A. (in press). Making sense of reading. In R. Beach & S. Hynds (Eds.), *Becoming readers and writers during adolescence and adulthood.* Norwood, NJ: Ablex.

Vipond, D., Hunt, R. A., & Wheeler, L. C. (1987). Social reading and literary engagement. *Reading Research and Instruction, 26,* 151–161.

Volosinov, V. N. (1973). *Marxism and the philosophy of language.* New York: Seminar Press.

Vygotsky, L. (1962). *Thought and language.* Cambridge, MA: The MIT Press.

——— (1978). *Mind in society.* Cambridge, MA: Harvard University Press.

Waller, G. G. (1985). Working within the paradigm shift: Poststructuralism and the college curriculum. *ADE Bulletin, 81,* 6–12.

Wattenburg, W. W., & Clifford, C. (1964). Relation of self-concepts to beginning achievement in reading. *Child Development, 35,* 461–467.

Weaver, C. (1985). Parallels between new paradigms in science and in reading and literary theories: An essay review. *Research in the Teaching of English, 19,* 298–316.

Weber, S. (1987). *Institution and interpretation.* Minneapolis: University of Minnesota Press.

Weedon, C. (1987). *Feminist practice & poststructuralist theory.* Oxford: Blackwell.

Wellek, R., & Warren, A. (1949). *Theory of literature.* London: Jonathan Cape.

Wells, J. E. (1887). Can English literature be taught? *The Educational Journal, 1,* 236–237.

Westerhoff, J. H. III. (1978). *McGuffey and his readers: Piety, morality, and education in nineteenth century America.* Nashville, TN: Abingdon.

Whitney, P. (1987). Psychological theories of elaborative inferences: Implications for schema-theoretic views of comprehension. *Reading Research Quarterly, 22,* 299–310.

Widdowson, P. (Ed.). (1982). *Re-reading English.* New York: Methuen.

Willet, J. (1959). *The theatre of Bertolt Brecht.* New York: Wiley.

Williams, J. P. (1986). Extracting important information from text. In J. A. Niles & R. V. Lalik (Eds.), *Solving problems in literacy: Learners, teachers, and researchers: Thirty-fifth yearbook of the National Reading Conference.* Rochester, NY: National Reading Conference.

Wilson, J. R. (1966). *Responses of college freshmen to three novels.* Urbana, IL: National Council of Teachers of English.

Wimsatt, W. K. (Ed.). (1954). *The verbal icon: Studies in the meaning of poetry.* Lexington, KY: University of Kentucky Press.

Wimsatt, W. K., & Beardsley, M. C. (1946a/1954). The affective fallacy. In W. K. Wimsatt (Ed.), *The verbal icon: Studies in the meaning of poetry.* Louisville: University of Kentucky Press.

——— (1946b/1954). The intentional fallacy. In W. K. Wimsatt (Ed.), *The verbal icon: Studies in the meaning of poetry.* Louisville: University of Kentucky Press.

Winograd, T. (1976). A framework for understanding discourse. In M. A. Just & P. A. Carpenter (Eds.), *Cognitive processes in comprehension.* Hillsdale, NJ: Erlbaum.

Wittgenstein, L. *Lectures & conversations on aesthetics, psychology, and religious belief.* C. Barrett (Ed.). Berkeley: University of California Press. (Delivered, 1938).

Wittrock, M. C. (1984). Writing and the teaching of reading. In J. M. Jensen (Ed.), *Composing and comprehending.* Urbana, IL: National Conference on Research on English and the ERIC Clearinghouse for Communication and Reading Skills.

Woodman, M. (1985). *The pregnant virgin: A process of psychological transformation.* Toronto: Inner City Books.

Young, C. (1987). Readers, texts, teachers. In B. Corcoran & E. Evans (Eds.), *Readers, texts, teachers.* Upper Montclair, NJ: Boynton/Cook.

Zaharias, J. A. (1986). The effects of genre and tone on undergraduate students' preferred patterns of response to two short stories and two poems. *Research in the Teaching of English, 20,* 56–68.

Zindel, P. (1968). *The pigman.* New York: Dell.

NAME INDEX

SUBJECT INDEX